Cybernetic Revolutionaries

Cybernetic Revolutionaries

Technology and Politics in Allende's Chile

Eden Medina

The MIT Press
Cambridge, Massachusetts
London, England

First MIT Press paperback edition, 2014

For information about special quantity discounts, please email special_sales@mitpress.mit.edu

This book was set in Stone Sans and Stone Serif by Graphic Composition, Inc., Bogart, Georgia. Printed and bound in the United States of America.

Library of Congress Cataloging-in-Publication Data

Medina, Eden, 1976–
Cybernetic revolutionaries : technology and politics in Allende's Chile / Eden Medina.
   p.   cm
Includes bibliographical references and index.
ISBN 978-0-262-01649-0 (hardcover : alk. paper) — 978-0-262-52596-1 (pb.)
1. Chile—Economic conditions—1970–1973—Case studies. 2. Chile—Economic conditions—1970–1973—Case studies. 3. Government business enterprises—Computer networks—Chile. 4. Government ownership—Chile. 5. Cybernetics—Political aspects—Chile. I. Title.
JL2631.M43   2011
303.48'33098309047—dc22

                                                                2011010109

10   9

To Cristian

Contents

Preface

I like to think that I came upon the history of Project Cybersyn, the 1970s Chilean computer network for economic management, because I was looking in the right place, and because it was a place that few in the history of technology had visited. I was a doctoral student at MIT, and I wanted to learn more about the history of computing in Latin America, the region of my birth. MIT has some of the best holdings in the country on the history of computing, but it soon became clear that material on Latin American computing was rather sparse. While I was digging in the stacks, bits and pieces of the story of Project Cybersyn caught my attention.

There wasn't much there—two paragraphs and a footnote in one book. The book described the project using such phrases as "cybernetic policy," "decentralized computer scheme," and "telex network operating in real-time," and linked it to a British cybernetician I had never heard of, Stafford Beer. This system was built in Chile and brought together "in one project, political leaders, trade unionists, and technicians."[1] Perhaps because I was reading about this curious cybernetic project while standing in one of the institutional birthplaces of cybernetics, the project took on special significance. Or maybe the story struck a chord because it so clearly brought together the social, political, and technological aspects of computing and did so in a Latin American setting. Whatever the reason, I was hooked and felt compelled to learn more about this curious system. Over the next ten years, the two paragraphs and a footnote that I had stumbled across evolved into this book on the history of Project Cybersyn.

The book began as an attempt to understand how countries outside the geographic, economic, and political centers of the world used computers. I was particularly interested in how Latin American experiences with computer technology differed from the well-known computer histories set in the United States, a difference I address in the pages that follow.[2] The absence of Latin America specifically, and other areas of the global south more generally, is also apparent in the history of technology, although it seems that this is slowly beginning to change.[3] But as I was writing this book, it gradually became clear that what I was writing was an empirical study of the complex relationship of technology and politics and the story of how a government used technology in innovative ways to advance the goals of its political project.

However, it was not just any political project. In 1970 Chile began an ambitious effort to bring about socialist change through peaceful, democratic means. It built on the reform efforts of the previous Chilean president, the Christian Democrat Eduardo Frei Montalva (1964–1970), who had tried to lessen social and economic inequality in Chile through increased foreign investment, import substitution industrialization, agrarian reform, and greater government ownership of Chile's copper mines. When the Socialist Salvador Allende became Chile's president in November 1970, he accelerated many of these changes and made them more profound. For example, he called for the government to bring the most important national industries under state control and developed policies to redistribute national wealth. He also stressed that socialist change would occur within the bounds of Chile's existing democratic institutions.

Nor was Project Cybersyn just any technological system. It was conceived as a real-time control system capable of collecting economic data throughout the nation, transmitting it to the government, and combining it in ways that could assist government decision-making. This was at a time when the U.S. ARPANET, the predecessor of the Internet, was still in its infancy, and the most technologically advanced nations of the developed world were trying to build large-scale real-time control systems. In fact, the Soviet Union had already tried and failed to build a national computer system for managing a planned economy. By 1970 Chile had approximately fifty computers installed in the government and the private sector, most of which were out of date, whereas approximately 48,000 general-purpose computers were installed in the United States at the time.[4] However, those involved in Project Cybersyn believed that cybernetics, the interdisciplinary postwar science of communication and control, would allow them to create a cutting-edge system that used Chile's existing technological resources. This book seeks to explain how technology and politics came together in a Latin American context during a moment of structural change and why those involved in the creation of Project Cybersyn looked to computer and communications technologies as central to the making of such changes.

To tell this story I have relied upon a diverse range of source materials, including design drawings, newspaper articles, photographs, computer printouts, folksong lyrics, government publications, archived correspondence, and technical reports that I amassed from repositories in the United States, Britain, and Chile. I have made extensive use of the documents housed at the Stafford Beer Collection at Liverpool John Moores University in England, which holds sixteen boxes of papers relating to Beer's work in Chile. This history also benefited from the personal archives of project participants Gui Bonsiepe, Roberto Cañete, Raúl Espejo, and Stafford Beer. How these documents survived is a story in its own right, and it shows that those involved with the project viewed it as a special accomplishment. I present part of that story in the pages that follow.

In addition, I used documents from a number of Chilean government agencies (including the State Development Corporation, the State Technology Institute, and the now-defunct National Computer Corporation); the library of the United Nations Economic Commission on Latin America in Santiago; the archives of the Catholic University of Chile; and the institutional holdings of IBM Chile. The rich holdings of the National Library in Santiago and the libraries at the University of Chile, the Catholic University of Chile, and the University of Santiago allowed me to supplement these primary sources with press accounts, other archived materials, and relevant secondary sources. A full list of consulted repositories appears in the bibliography.

I conducted more than fifty interviews in Chile, Argentina, Mexico, the United States, Canada, England, Portugal, and Germany between 2001 and 2010. Interview subjects included Cybersyn project participants, high-ranking members of the Allende and Frei governments, early members of the Chilean computer community, managers in Chilean factories, and members of the international cybernetics community, among others. Some interviews lasted thirty minutes, while others spanned two days. Some took place by means of extended e-mail correspondence. Unless otherwise noted, I have translated to English all the passages excerpted from Spanish-language interviews and written sources. Only a small number of the people interviewed for this project actually appear in the book, but all the conversations I had shaped my interpretation of this history.

I had difficulty locating workers who remembered Project Cybersyn because, as I explain later, so few factory workers were involved in the project. Nor did the project dovetail with the simultaneous worker participation efforts that were taking place on the shop floor of Chile's factories. However, I did talk to a number of workers at the National Labor Federation and at the Chilean factory MADECO, which formed part of Project Cybersyn. I also advertised in a popular leftist newspaper that I was looking for workers who remembered the project. Not a single worker responded to this advertisement, although it did put me in touch with several government technologists who remembered working on Cybersyn. That the project is remembered by technologists, not factory workers, is historically significant, as I discuss.

Therefore, this is not a history from below in a traditional sense. However, it also would be inaccurate to say that this is a history told from above. Scientists, engineers, designers, and technologists are the main protagonists of this story and, while many of them worked for the Chilean government, they were not politicians, nor were they, with one exception, members of the government elite. This book shares a goal with more traditional histories from below in that it aims to add new voices and experiences, previously absent, to the historical literature.

All source materials, including oral histories, have their ingrained subjectivity and must be read with a critical eye. The reader should bear in mind that, in some cases, the memories presented in the pages that follow have been shaped by the post-coup experiences of the interviewees, and some participants used the interview process as a way to revisit and come to terms with one of the most contentious periods of the Chilean past. Project Cybersyn also received substantial media attention while I was conducting this research, in part because my research was becoming public as the thirty-year anniversary of Allende's death approached. Although I do not believe any of my subsequent interviewees were less than frank, I do believe that press coverage of Project Cybersyn influenced some of my later interviews, either by making people more willing to meet with me or by making them more aware of their public image. Thus, the memories that people related to me cannot be viewed as objective accounts of what happened but, when juxtaposed with one another, can represent a confluence of many histories, a diffraction of voices, some overlapping, some not.[5] These oral narratives have enriched the telling of this history, and material taken from my transcripts is documented as such. In general, I place greater weight on archival documents than on personal testimonies. This book began as an attempt to learn more about computing in Latin America, but it ended up being about much more. While I did not stick to my original research question of trying to understand how nations outside the political and economic centers of the world use computers, my hope is that the history presented in this book will illustrate the value of asking such questions.

Acknowledgments

In 1971, the British cybernetician Stafford Beer traveled to Santiago, Chile, for the first time to explore how cybernetics and technology could be used to further a project for structural and political change. The experience changed his life. Thirty years later I followed Beer's footsteps to Chile, hoping to learn more about how cybernetics, computation, and politics came together in Chilean history. My journey, like Beer's, also proved transformative. It resulted not only in this book but also in numerous friendships, intellectual ties, institutional connections, and extended family. It is now a pleasure to look back and thank those who made this book possible.

Like Project Cybersyn, this book represents the collective effort of many dedicated individuals. Peter Winn and David Mindell offered critical guidance throughout the research and writing process and read multiple drafts of this work. This book has profited from their expertise and generosity. In addition, the following individuals read early excerpts of this manuscript and provided comments: Lessie Jo Frazier, Emily Maguire, Lucy Suchman, Slava Gerovitch, David Hakken, Selma Šabanović, Kalpana Shankar, Tom Gieryn, Erik Stolterman, Deborah Cohen, David Hounshell, Ronald Kline, Thomas Misa, Matt Francisco, Heather Wiltse, Ben Peters, and the anonymous reviewers from the MIT Press.

This work would not have been possible without support from the National Science Foundation in the form of Scholar's Award #0724104 and Dissertation Improvement Award #0322278. The School of Informatics and Computing at Indiana University, Bloomington, provided an interdisciplinary environment that introduced me to new bodies of literature and shaped my thinking during the writing process. I thank Bobby Schnabel, Michael Dunn, Marty Siegel, and Filippo Menzcer for supporting this work at different moments with school resources. The Center for Latin American and Caribbean Studies, the Office of the Vice Provost for Research, and the Office of the Vice President for International Affairs at Indiana University also deserve mention for supporting this project at critical moments, as do the Charles Babbage Institute, the Social Science Research Council, and the American Council for Learned Societies. I was fortunate to receive intellectual and financial support from the MIT Program in

Science, Technology, and Society and the Dibner Institute for the History of Science and Technology. Individuals at both institutions shaped the intellectual development of this work, and its author, in ways too numerous to list.

The following individuals also deserve special mention (in alphabetical order): Mariella Arredondo, Bill Aspray, Eric Carbajal, Claude Clegg, Michele Dompke, Karla Fernández, Bernard Geoghegan, Dennis Groth, Hugh Gusterson, Doug Haynes, Stephen Kovats, Bruno Latour, Allenna Leonard, Marta Maldonado, Constantin Malik, Francisca Mancilla, Mara Margolis, Marco Medina, Mauricio Medina, Pedro Medina, Rosa Moscoso, Jennifer Nicholson, Catalina Ossa, Hugo Palmerola, Angel Parra, Alejandra Perez, Andrew Pickering, Cecilia Riveros, Enrique Rivera, Luis Rocha, Alfio Saitta, María José Schneuer, Daniela Torres, Peter Weibel, and David Whittaker. Alfredo Rehren arranged for me to have a visiting position in the Political Science Department at the Pontificia Universidad Católica de Chile. Raúl O'Ryan and Pablo Sierra similarly arranged for me to have a visiting position in the Industrial Engineering Department of the Universidad de Chile and generously provided an Internet connection and office space. Cristian Medina drew the map of Chile that appears in this book. This book has further profited from the editing talents of Polly Kummel, the indexing talents of Janet Perlman, and the attentions of Marguerite Avery, Matthew Abbate, Erin Hasley, Susan Clark, Katie Persons, Paula Woolley, and the staff at the MIT Press. Early research for this book appeared in my article "Designing Freedom, Regulating a Nation: Socialist Cybernetics in Allende's Chile," *Journal of Latin American Studies* 38, no. 3 (2006): 571–606. I thank Cambridge University Press for allowing the republication of excerpts from that earlier text.

To the individuals who generously opened their homes, trusted me to document their experiences, or took a risk by giving me access to their web of connections, I thank you. It is difficult to do justice to the lifetimes of accomplishment that now reside on my interview tapes and computer hard drive; I hope this text is worthy of the confidence these individuals have shown its author. Raúl Espejo, Gui Bonsiepe, Roberto Cañete, Italo Bozzi, Allenna Leonard, and the late Stafford Beer provided primary source documents and photos from their personal archives that enriched my telling of this history.

Finally, this book would not have been written were it not for the support of my family. My parents, Mary Ann and Robert Miller, have provided a lifetime of encouragement and unconditional love. Their supportive words—and babysitting services—made it possible for me to bring this project to a conclusion. My son, Gael, entered my life in the midst of the research and writing process. I thank him for lightening my day with dimpled smiles and easy laughter and for sharing his mother with this book, a rival sibling.

I dedicate this book to my husband, Cristian, for teaching me to love his homeland and for making it possible for me to write one small part of its history.

Abbreviations

CEREN	Center for Studies on National Reality
CORFO	State Development Corporation
CONICYT	National Commission for Science and Technology Research
ECOM	National Computer Corporation
EMCO	National Computer Service Center
ENTEL	National Telecommunications Enterprise
INTEC	State Technology Institute
MAPU	Movement for Popular United Action
ODEPLAN	National Planning Ministry
OR	Operations Research
PDC	Christian Democratic Party
UP	Popular Unity

Prologue

One day this will make quite a story.
—Stafford Beer, 3 August 1972

On 30 December 1972, Chilean president Salvador Allende visited a futuristic operations room that seemed more like a set for a Stanley Kubrick film than a command center for a South American government in the midst of economic war.

The hexagonal room reflected the aesthetic of 1970s modernity. In it, seven white fiberglass swivel chairs with orange cushions sat atop a brown carpet. Wood paneling covered the walls. On one wall a series of screens displayed economic data from the nation's factories. A simple control mechanism consisting of ten buttons on the armrest of each chair allowed occupants to bring up different charts, graphs, and photographs of Chilean industrial production and display them on the screens. On another wall a display with flashing red lights indicated current economic emergencies in need of attention; the faster the flashes, the more dire the situation. A third wall displayed an illuminated color image of a five-tiered cybernetic model based on the human nervous system. This abstract model, seemingly out of place in a space for emergency decision making, was there to remind occupants of the cybernetic ideas that had guided the construction of the control room. Cybernetics, the postwar science of communication and control, looked for commonalities in biological, mechanical, and social systems. The room formed part of a larger system designed to help the economy adapt quickly to changes in the national environment.

The operations room was created to help Allende implement his vision of socialist change. Its creators had expected that high-ranking members of the government would use the room to make rapid decisions based on current data and a macroscopic view of national economic activity. Eventually, the technologists hoped, the government would construct similar rooms in each government ministry and the presidential palace.

The president sat in one of the futuristic orange-and-white swivel chairs and pushed the buttons on the armrest. He expected the data displayed on the screens would

Figure P.1
The Cybersyn operations room. Image used with permission from Gui Bonsiepe.

change and that he would see how using such a room could help him manage an economy in crisis. Two months earlier a national strike had threatened to end his presidency. In less than ten months he would be overthrown in a violent military coup that would end Chilean democracy and his life. But at this moment the president was still struggling to stay in power.

Allende probably was hoping to see a new form of socialist modernity that could help his government survive. But the heat of the South American summer had raised the temperature of the electronics in the room beyond their tolerance. Once activated, the projectors promptly brought up economic graphs and charts, but they were not the graphs and charts that had been requested. The president told his engineers to keep working, and they did, until the end. Both the operations room and the Chilean road to socialism were utopian dreams of a new form of governance. But neither materialized in the way its designers imagined.

Introduction: Political and Technological Visions

In Chile, I know that I am making the maximum effort towards the devolution of power. The government made their revolution about it; I find it good cybernetics.
—Stafford Beer, February 1973

This book tells the history of two intersecting utopian visions, one political and one technological. The first was an attempt to implement socialist change peacefully and through existing democratic institutions. The second was an attempt to build a computer system for real-time economic control more than twenty years before the Internet became a feature of everyday life. Like all utopias, these visions were beautiful yet elusive. However, studying them brings to light how a South American government tried to take control of its destiny at the height of the cold war and how that same government made computer technology part of a political project for structural transformation. This book uses the confluence of these two utopian visions to address a central question in the history of technology: What is the relationship of technology and politics?

Cybernetics, the interdisciplinary postwar science of communication and control, plays a role in both utopian projects and links them together. Cybernetic ideas shaped the design of this ambitious computer system; they also shaped how the people who built it viewed processes of political change. However, this book is not concerned only with machines and ideas. At its core this is a study about a group of people who tried to create a new political and technological reality in the early 1970s, one that broke from the strategic ambitions of both the United States and Soviet Union.

The setting is Chile, the narrow sliver of the South American continent bordered by the Andean cordillera on one side and the Pacific Ocean on the other (figure I.1). In 1970 Chilean voters opted to pursue a democratic road to socialist change under the guidance of Salvador Allende Gossens. Chile's turn toward socialism came after a more moderate Christian Democratic reform failed to reach its goals in the 1960s.[1]

As Chile's first democratically elected Socialist president, Allende proposed a political third way, something different from the politics and ideology of either superpower.

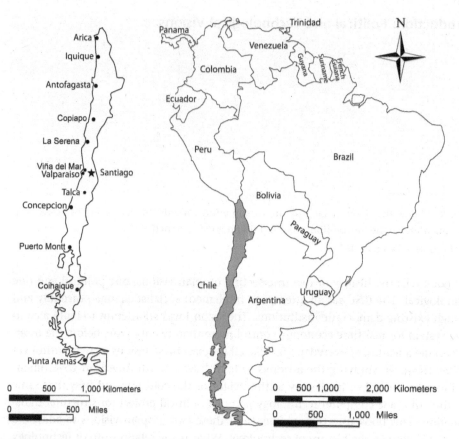

Figure I.1
Map of Chile.

Allende wanted to make Chile a socialist nation, but he also wanted change to occur peacefully and in a way that respected the nation's existing democratic processes and institutions. Moving property ownership from foreign multinationals and the Chilean oligarchy to the state, redistributing income, and creating mechanisms for worker participation were among the top priorities of the Allende government.[2] Among the democratic institutions that Allende wished to preserve were respect for election results, individual freedoms (such as the freedom of thought, speech, press, and assembly), and the rule of law. His commitment to socialist change through constitutional means set Chile's socialism apart from that of Cuba or the Soviet Union. His platform became known as the "Chilean road to socialism."

Chile was an exceptional nation within Latin America. From 1932 to 1973 Chile boasted the longest period of uninterrupted democratic rule in Latin America.[3]

Allende's outward commitment to peaceful socialist change and the free expression of ideas stood in sharp contrast to the political situation in neighboring countries such as Argentina and Brazil. In 1970 these two nations had repressive military governments that had seized control, ostensibly to stop the threat of communism. Chile was also a battleground in the global cold war and a focus of U.S. attention. From 1962 to 1969 Chile received more than a billion dollars in U.S. aid, more than any other nation in Latin America, as part of the Alliance for Progress.[4] The United States believed such levels of aid would help raise living standards for Chileans and thus stop members of the poor and working classes from turning to communism.

The United States responded to Allende's election by adopting a "non-overt course" to prevent Chile from turning socialist. This included funding government opposition parties and opposition-owned media outlets and sabotaging the Chilean economy. For example, the United States established an invisible financial blockade and significantly reduced its aid to Chile. It also used its substantial influence to cut international and bilateral aid and private bank credit to Chile, prevented Allende from renegotiating the national debt he had inherited from his predecessor, and decreased the value of U.S. exports to Chile.[5] Allende's commitment to changing Chile's long-standing social and economic structures also met with strong opposition from members of Chile's privileged classes. Nevertheless, Chile's long and solid commitment to its democratic institutions led Chileans and onlookers from around the world to wonder whether Allende and his government might succeed in pioneering a new political model.

This political experiment set the stage for an ambitious technological experiment. Bringing Chile's most important industries under state control challenged the management capabilities of the Allende government.[6] The rapid pace of nationalization added to these challenges, as did the number of employees in the state-run enterprises, which was growing in concert with Allende's efforts to lower unemployment. Moreover, the government lacked sufficient numbers of qualified people to run the newly nationalized industries, and production was hindered by shortages of spare parts and raw materials. A small team of people in the Chilean government believed such problems could be addressed through the use of computer and communications technology, and set out to create a new system for industrial management in collaboration with a group of British technologists.

From 1971 to 1973 the transnational team worked on the creation of this new technological system, which they called Project Cybersyn in English or Proyecto Synco in Spanish. The system they envisioned pushed the boundaries of what was possible in the early 1970s and addressed difficult engineering problems such as real-time control, modeling the behavior of dynamic systems, and computer networking. More impressive, the team tackled these problems using Chile's limited technological resources and in the process proposed solutions that were different from those explored by other, more industrialized nations. The system they proposed used new communications channels to transmit current production data to the government from the state-run factories. These data were fed into statistical software programs designed to predict future factory performance and thus to enable the Chilean government to identify and head off crises before they came to pass. The system included a computerized economic simulator, which would give government policy makers an opportunity to test their economic ideas before implementation. Finally, the proposed system called for the creation of a futuristic operations room where members of the government could convene, quickly grasp the state of the economy, and make rapid decisions informed by recent data.

Some members of the team even speculated that this technical system could be engineered in ways that would change Chilean social relationships and bring them in line with the goals of Chilean socialism. For example, some saw the system as presenting ways to increase worker participation in factory management. The statistical software evaluated factory performance using a model of production processes. Team members argued that workers should participate in the creation of these models and thus in the design of this technology and in economic management at the national level. In a little over a year the team built a prototype of the system and hoped that, once complete, it would help the government stay in power and improve the state of the Chilean economy.

In this book I study the intersection of these political and technological visions and the efforts made by historical actors to bring them into being. I use these intersections to understand the interplay of technology and politics in history. The book draws from important early work in the history and sociology of technology that has shown that technologies are the product not only of technical work but also of social negotiations.[7] However, this book does not seek to uncover the hidden politics of a technological project by breaking down a dichotomy of the social and the technical. Instead, I take the absence of such a dichotomy as my starting point. Politics touched almost every aspect of Chilean life during the Allende period, including science and engineering activities and the design and use of technologies such as Project Cybersyn. Politics also colored how outsiders reacted to Project Cybersyn in Chile and abroad. Politics are thus an explicit, not hidden, part of this history of technology.

In addition, this book is not centrally concerned with the question of whether technologies are neutral.[8] As earlier work in the history, sociology, and philosophy of technology has shown, technologies are not value-neutral but rather are a product of the historical contexts in which they are made.[9] As a case study, Project Cybersyn provides a clear example of how particular political and economic contexts support the creation of particular technologies.

This book is an attempt to understand (1) how governments have envisioned using computer and communications technology to bring about structural change in society; (2) the ways technologists have tried to embed political values in the design of technical systems; (3) the challenges associated with such efforts; and (4) how studying technology can enhance our understanding of a historical moment. I use the term *political values* to refer to the particular concepts, ideas, and principles that are central to a political project, such as democracy, participation, liberty, and state control. I use the term *technologist* throughout the book to refer to white-collar professionals with technical expertise, such as cyberneticians, engineers, computer scientists, operations research scientists, statisticians, and, at times, industrial designers. I decided against using the more familiar word *technocrat* because of its pejorative connotation during Allende's presidency, when it was frequently used to refer to those who believed that technology and the empowerment of technical experts were more important than political change. The term *technocrat* is also associated with the Pinochet dictatorship, when experts in fields such as engineering, economics, or finance used it to signal their belief that they were apolitical and that they wanted to use their knowledge to advance the Chilean nation. Neither definition is an appropriate description of the technical experts involved in this history.[10]

This book addresses these questions by studying a historical moment when government technologists, administrators, politicians, and members of the general public were engaged in an explicit discussion of the relationships between technology and politics and how technologies could be designed or used to enact or embody a political goal. This book therefore builds on the pathbreaking work of historians such as Gabrielle Hecht, Paul Edwards, and Ken Alder who have used similar historical moments to show how goals of nationalism, command and control, and technocratic revolution led to the creation of particular technologies and, conversely, how technologies framed these goals, shaped power configurations, and became instrumental in political strategies.[11] Like these scholars, I use history to show the ways that technology and politics are deeply intertwined and mutually constitutive; however, I do so in a context outside of the United States or Europe.

I also push this observation further to show how technology can complicate our readings, and thus our understanding, of politics. Phrases such as "political goal" or "political project" suggest that a consensus exists about what needs to be achieved and how to achieve it. Yet reality is not so neat. Disagreements, inconsistencies, and controversies pervaded the Chilean road to socialism, and this plurality of views made it difficult, if not impossible, to create a technology that embodied a political ideal. There were many views on how to make Chile socialist within the governing coalition, within each member party, and among communities of technologists. Here I use the history of a technical system, Project Cybersyn, to illustrate the diversity of opinions present in Chile's socialist experiment and to show how technologists, government officials, factory managers, and workers struggled to define a course of action. I use the history of a technical system to open this black box of politics, just as I use politics to open this black box of technology.

There are other reasons why it is extremely difficult to make a technology embody political values, even when governments expend substantial human, financial, and technological resources on the effort. Central to this discussion is the idea of sociotechnical engineering, my term for the designing of a technology, and the social and organizational relationships that surround it, to uphold a configuration of power congruent with the aims of a political project.[12] Through sociotechnical engineering practices, Chilean and British technologists tried to make Project Cybersyn implement and uphold principles of Chilean democratic socialism. For example, the system included mechanisms to preserve individual liberty within a context of greater state control. Some Cybersyn technologists also tried to use Project Cybersyn as a vehicle for increasing worker participation in economic management and proposed having workers collaborate with Chilean operations research scientists. I argue that, for the system to support values such as worker participation or decentralized control, Cybersyn needed to implement and maintain the social, organizational, and technical relationships specified by its designers. Yet the reverse was also true: changing these social, organizational, and technical relationships could cause the system to produce configurations of political power, including totalitarianism, that were very different from Chilean democratic socialism.

Finally, this book demonstrates that studying the development of technology can help scholars understand historical and political processes. Studying Project Cybersyn reveals the limitations of the Chilean revolution; the ongoing tension between the revolution from above and the revolution from below; the legacy of class prejudice, gender bias, and systematized bureaucracy; and the underlying assumptions about modernity that privileged foreign expertise and technology, even within the context of socialist revolution and increased nationalism. Technologies are historical texts. When we read them, we are able to read history.[13]

Chilean Cybernetics

Cybernetics plays a central role in this book. It is impossible to give a universal definition of this term, since members of the field have defined cybernetics in many ways over the years. However, the MIT mathematician Norbert Wiener, one of the originators of the field, offers one of the most-cited definitions. In 1948 he described cybernetics as the study of "control and communication in the animal and the machine."[14] Cybernetics often mixed metaphors from engineering and biology to describe the behavior of complex systems ranging from the electromechanical operation of a computer to the function of the human brain. Some members of the cybernetics community viewed cybernetics as a universal language for the scientific study of machines, organisms, and organizations. In the late 1940s and early 1950s, these insights and appeals to universality resonated with a number of distinguished researchers from fields as diverse as physiology, psychology, anthropology, mathematics, and electrical engineering. Cybernetic thinking influenced subsequent work in information theory, computing, cognitive science, engineering, biology, and the social sciences. Cybernetics also spread outside academia and entered areas such as industrial management, the area explored in greatest depth here.

This book is in conversation with the growing literature on the history of cybernetics. It adds another national experience to this already rich area of scholarship, which includes studies of cybernetics in the United States, the Soviet Union, Britain, East Germany, China, and France.[15] In the context of these other national cybernetic histories, the Chilean experience provides evidence for the validity of the "disunity of cybernetics" thesis put forth by historian Ronald Kline. In contrast to earlier studies of cybernetics, which emphasized how members of the U.S. cybernetics community tried to build a universal science, Kline argues that cybernetics assumed a variety of forms depending on its national, historical, and disciplinary context.[16] This book builds on Kline's work by showing how Chile's political, economic, and historical context shaped the Chilean experience with cybernetics and set it apart from the experiences of other nations.

It also demonstrates that the history of cybernetics is more than a collection of different national experiences; it is a transnational story. Histories of science and technology often involve transnational collaborations and the movement of scientific ideas and technological artifacts from one national context to another. However, such movements are especially visible when we look at science and technology in areas of the global south where legacies of colonialism and economic dependency make the movement of scientific ideas and technological artifacts more pronounced and thus more visible. However, this book challenges simple models of technological diffusion that frame science and technology as flowing from north to south. Scientific ideas and technologies originate in many different places and travel in multiple directions, including from south to north.

The history of Chilean science and technology in the twentieth century is highly transnational, and so is its history of cybernetics. Chile was connected to the international cybernetics community almost from the outset. The archive of Norbert Wiener's papers, housed at the Massachusetts Institute of Technology, contains a 1949 letter that Wiener received from Chile a mere three months after the first printing of his book *Cybernetics*, the book widely credited for bringing the new interdisciplinary science to the attention of the public. The letter came from a Chilean named Raimundo Toledo Toledo, who asked the famed MIT mathematician for advice about a simple calculating machine Toledo was building. Toledo had learned of Wiener's work from an article in *Time* magazine, and he asked Wiener to send him a copy of *Cybernetics*.[17] As this correspondence shows, Chileans had learned of U.S. work on cybernetics from U.S. publications and were connecting with leading members of the U.S. cybernetics community, engaging with cybernetic ideas, and trying to build their own computing machinery as early as 1949. That Chile's involvement in the history of cybernetics dates almost to the origin of the field suggests that the history of cybernetics played out over a far wider geography than the existing literature has thus far recognized and that these international stories are necessarily intertwined with one another.

This book tells the story of another transnational cybernetics connection, primarily between Chile and Britain. This connection is a good example of the historical contingency of technological development. Project Cybersyn was made possible because of a very specific confluence of ideas and people, as well as technological and political moments. In Chile in the early 1970s, national efforts to foment political change converged with the ideas of the British cybernetician Stafford Beer and the efforts the Chilean government had already made to increase its technological capabilities, especially in the area of computing. As this book shows, Chile's specific historical, political, and technological circumstances allowed the Allende government to use computers and apply cybernetic ideas in ways that were not, and arguably could not be, replicated in wealthier nations.

Readers should be aware that several central characters and events in this story are highly controversial. Allende, for example, is a polarizing figure in Latin American history. He has been depicted as a martyr because he assumed the Chilean presidency with a dream of social justice and was deposed in a violent coup that brutally ended the Chilean road to socialism and resulted in his death. Yet Allende has also been portrayed as a villain who destroyed the Chilean economy and brought on widespread consumer shortages. Other interpretations have portrayed the former president as a conflicted and contradictory figure who loved women and bourgeois luxuries even as his political dream called for the creation of a more just society. Allende's presidency exacerbated political and class divisions already present in Chilean society, and members of these different groups experienced the Allende period, and the Pinochet dictatorship that followed, in different ways. The scars from these memories have yet to heal completely and continue to shape interpretations and understandings of Allende's presidency.

In recent years Project Cybersyn has also been the subject of radically different kinds of interpretations.[18] Chilean artists have variously portrayed the project as part of a socialist utopia, the result of Beer's drinking too much whiskey, and evidence that technical prowess is a part of Chilean culture.[19] A science fiction book published in 2008 cast the project as a tool for totalitarian control and evidence that socialist success has a dark side, whereas recent postings on Chilean technology blogs show that some Chileans view the system as an inspiration.[20] Yet several Chilean computer pioneers interviewed for this book believed that Project Cybersyn did not warrant historical attention because it never reached completion. However, as this book demonstrates, there is historical value in studying innovative technological systems, even if they are never fully realized.

Stafford Beer, the British cybernetician whose ideas were central to Cybersyn's design, was also no stranger to controversy. Beer's admirers view his intelligence, breadth of knowledge, and willingness to think in unconventional ways as signs of misunderstood genius. On the other hand, his detractors paint a picture of a self-promoter who made grandiose claims that were not backed by his actual accomplishments.[21]

Even cybernetics, the interdisciplinary study of communication and control, is the subject of conflicting interpretations. It is well documented that some of the top scientific minds of the postwar era were drawn to the field and its promise of universality, and that cybernetic ideas on feedback, control, systems analysis, and information transmission shaped work in a number of fields. For example, cybernetic thinking influenced the trajectory of operations research, computer engineering, control engineering, complex systems, psychology, and neuroscience.

Yet few scientists today identify themselves as cyberneticians first and foremost. Why this is the case is outside the scope of the book and, moreover, has been studied in depth by historians such as Kline.[22] Popular misunderstandings of cybernetics have led members of the scientific community to view the term with disdain, and cybernetics is not part of the lexicon used by government funding agencies. Even in the 1950s, arguably the heyday of the field, members of the scientific community viewed it as shallow because of its interdisciplinary reach, criticized it for lacking quantitative rigor, and claimed its methodology consisted of little more than making analogies. It did not help that in the popular imagination cybernetics was often linked to science fiction or fads such as Dianetics, the theory on the relationship of mind and body developed by L. Ron Hubbard in 1950.

In 1959 Beer wrote that "the new science [cybernetics] is often open to derision, and is not yet academically respectable." But Beer was optimistic and added, "Not very long ago, however, atom-splitting was derided; yet more recently space travel was not respectable."[23] He hoped that the scientific profile of cybernetics might improve as people recognized the value of this science of control. In 2010 the American Society for Cybernetics had only eighty-two members.[24] Although cybernetics continues to be an active field, it has not attained the widespread influence that Beer, and other members of the cybernetics community, had imagined.

Presenting a balanced picture of these people, technologies, and ideas, all while capturing the nuances of the period that brought them together, has constituted a central challenge in writing this book. The resulting text forms part of an ongoing conversation about defining cybernetics, the Allende government, Project Cybersyn, and the work of Stafford Beer and understanding their collective significance.[25] At the same time, the varied and often contradictory readings of these ideas, people, technologies, and historical moments are what make it possible to study the complicated and highly nuanced relationships of technology and politics that I explore in this book.

Structure

This book has six chapters that unfold chronologically and illuminate different facets of the relationship of technology and politics. Chapter 1 explores why a member of the Chilean government would decide to apply ideas from Stafford Beer's writings on management cybernetics to the regulation of the Chilean economy. I argue that this connection between cybernetics and Chilean socialism came about, in part, because Beer and Popular Unity, as Allende's governing coalition was called, were exploring similar concepts, albeit in the different domains of science and politics. For example, both were interested in developing ways to maintain system stability while facilitating structural change and striking a balance between autonomy and cohesion. In addition, the chapter explains some of the core concepts in Beer's work that later shaped the design of Project Cybersyn.

Chapter 2 describes the Popular Unity economic program and the challenges the government faced at the end of Allende's first year in office. It explains why a cybernetic approach to management would seem to address these challenges and thus why it would appeal to someone involved in leading Allende's nationalization program. I discuss how members of the Chilean government viewed computer and communications technology as a way to implement the structural changes associated with the Popular Unity platform. Moreover, I delineate how the design of this system differed from contemporaneous efforts to use computers for communication and control, yet was still representative of the Popular Unity stance on science and technology. By following how Chile's innovative political experiment with democratic socialism led to the creation of this innovative computer system, the chapter argues that political innovation can spur technological innovation.

Chapters 3 and 4 explore the ways that political goals, contexts, and ideologies shape the design of technological systems. Both chapters document how the Chilean ideas on democratic socialism influenced the design of Project Cybersyn and its goal of helping to raise production levels while creating a broadly participative, decentralizing, and antibureaucratic form of economic management. Both chapters also examine how technologists, British and Chilean, tried to embed political values in the design of this technology. In chapter 3, I also trace how Chile's limited technological resources, made worse by the U.S.-led economic blockade, forced Cybersyn technologists to engineer a new approach to computer networking that differed from the approaches used by other nations.

Chapter 4 documents how Cybersyn technologists attempted to embed political values not only in the design of the technology but also in the social and organizational relationships of its construction and use. I use these attempts at sociotechnical engineering to show that these historical actors held a limited view of revolution. In particular, preexisting ideas about gender, class, and engineering practice constrained how Cybersyn technologists imagined political transformation as well as technological possibility.

Chapter 5 demonstrates that technology can shape the path of political history by making certain actions possible. In a moment of crisis—namely, a massive strike begun by Chilean truck drivers that threatened to end the Allende government—the communication network created for Project Cybersyn was used to connect the vertical command of the national government to the horizontal activities that were taking place on the shop floor of Chilean factories. This communications network gave the government access to current information on national activities that it used in its decision making. It then used the network to transmit its directives quickly and reliably the length of country. These abilities helped the government withstand and survive a crisis that is commonly viewed as a watershed moment in the Allende government. Chapter 5 is therefore the most important chapter in this book from the perspective of Chilean history. This chapter also documents the diverging views within the project team on how Project Cybersyn should be used to advance the Chilean road to socialism, and thus shows how historical readings of technology can make visible the complexities internal to a political project.

Chapter 6 analyzes how the cold war influenced the ways that journalists, members of the Chilean government, and members of the British scientific community viewed Project Cybersyn. Even though members of the project team tried to design the system to reflect and uphold the values of Chilean democratic socialism, outside observers frequently viewed Project Cybersyn as implementing a form of totalitarian control. These interpretations reflected British and Chilean fears of an all-powerful state, the ideological polarization of the cold war, and the opposition's attacks against Allende. Building on chapter 5, this chapter also traces the multiple, often conflicting views of how Cybersyn and, by extension, the Popular Unity government could best address Chile's mounting economic crises. On 11 September 1973, a military coup brought the Popular Unity government to a violent end. When the military cut short Chile's political experiment with socialism, it also ended the nation's technological experiment with cybernetic management. International geopolitics therefore can play a decisive role in technological development, regardless of the merits or shortcomings of the system under construction.

Chile was not able to implement its political dream of democratic socialism or its technological dream of real-time economic management. However, the story of Chile's attempt to create this unusual, ambitious, and in many ways futuristic technology sheds light on the ways that people have tried to use computer and communications technology to effect social, economic, and political change. It further shows how a country with limited technological resources used what resources it did have in creative ways to push the boundaries of what was considered technically feasible at the time. Finally, it demonstrates that technological innovation in the area of computing has occurred across a broader geography than is typically recognized. This broader geography of innovation cannot be viewed as a discrete collection of national stories, for it is connected by the multidirectional and transnational flows of artifacts and expertise and the far-reaching effects of international geopolitics.

1 Cybernetics and Socialism

The more I reflect on these facts, the more I perceive that the evolutionary approach to adaptation in social systems simply will not work any more. . . . It has therefore become clear to me over the years that I am advocating revolution.
—Stafford Beer, Address to the Fifth Annual Conference of the Pierre Teilhard de Chardin Association of Great Britain and Ireland, October 1970

In July 1971, the British cybernetician Stafford Beer received an unexpected letter from Chile. Its contents would dramatically change Beer's life. The writer was a young Chilean engineer named Fernando Flores, who was working for the government of newly elected Socialist president Salvador Allende. Flores wrote that he was familiar with Beer's work in management cybernetics and was "now in a position from which it is possible to implement on a national scale—at which cybernetic thinking becomes a necessity—scientific views on management and organization."[1] Flores asked Beer for advice on how to apply cybernetics to the management of the nationalized sector of the Chilean economy, which was expanding quickly because of Allende's aggressive nationalization policy.

Less than a year earlier, Allende and his leftist coalition, Popular Unity (UP), had secured the presidency and put Chile on a road toward socialist change. Allende's victory resulted from the failure of previous Chilean governments to resolve such problems as economic dependency, economic inequality, and social inequality using less drastic means. His platform made the nationalization of major industries a top priority, an effort Allende later referred to as "the first step toward the making of structural changes."[2] The nationalization effort would not only transfer foreign-owned and privately owned industries to the Chilean people, it would "abolish the pillars propping up that minority that has always condemned our country to underdevelopment," as Allende referred to the industrial monopolies controlled by a handful of Chilean families.[3] The majority of parties in the UP coalition believed that by changing Chile's economic base, they would subsequently be able to bring about institutional and ideological change within the nation's established legal framework, a facet that set Chile's path to socialism apart from that of other socialist nations, such as Cuba or the Soviet Union.[4] Flores worked for the Chilean State Development Corporation, the agency responsible for leading the nationalization effort. Although Flores was only twenty-eight when he wrote Beer, he held the third-highest position in the development agency and a leadership role in the Chilean nationalization process.

Beer found the Chilean invitation irresistible. Flores was offering him a chance to apply his ideas on management on a national level and during a moment of political transformation. Beer decided he wanted to do more than simply offer advice, and his response to Flores was understandably enthusiastic. "Believe me, I would surrender any of my retainer contracts I now have for the chance of working on this," Beer wrote. "That is because I believe your country is really going to do it."[5] Four months later, the cybernetician arrived in Chile to serve as a management consultant to the Chilean government.

This connection between a Chilean technologist working for a socialist government and a British consultant specializing in management cybernetics would lead to Project Cybersyn, an ambitious effort to create a computer system to manage the Chilean national economy in close to real time using technologies that, in most cases, were not cutting edge. Such a connection between British cybernetics and Chilean socialism was rather unusual, not only because of their geographical separation but also because they represented very specific strains of scientific or political thought. As I argue in this chapter, Beer and Flores joined forces in part because Beer and Popular Unity were exploring similar intellectual terrain in the different domains of science and politics.

Beer's writings on management cybernetics differed from the contemporaneous work taking place in the U.S. military and think tanks such as RAND that led to the development of computer systems for top-down command and control. From the 1950s onward, Beer had drawn from his understanding of the human nervous system to propose a form of management that allowed businesses to adapt quickly to a changing environment. A major theme in Beer's writings was finding a balance between centralized and decentralized control, and in particular how to ensure the stability of the entire firm without sacrificing the autonomy of its component parts.

Similarly, the Popular Unity government confronted the challenge of how to implement substantial social, political, and economic changes without sacrificing Chile's preexisting constitutional framework of democracy. A distinguishing feature of Chile's socialist process was the determination to expand the reach of the state without sacrificing the nation's existing civil liberties and democratic institutions. Both Beer and Popular Unity were thus deeply interested in ways of maintaining organizational stability in the context of change and finding a balance between autonomy and cohesion.

For Beer and the Popular Unity government, these were not simply questions of intellectual interest; they also shaped practice. Beer applied his understanding of adaptive control to improve industrial management in areas ranging from steel production to publishing. In the Chilean context, understandings of democratic socialism shaped the relationships among the executive, legislative, and judicial branches of government and influenced economic policy. These conceptual commonalities, combined with the emphasis both Beer and Popular Unity put on translating these ideas into action, led Flores to contact Beer and motivated Beer to accept Flores's consulting invitation.

Beer occupies a central role in this chapter and in this book as a whole. Some of the key ideas in his cybernetic writings before his first trip to Chile in 1971 show the correspondence between his cybernetics and Chilean socialism. Nevertheless, it is important to recognize that Beer was only one person in a highly collaborative transnational team. He may have come to Chile thinking that he would bring the ideas he formed in Britain to Latin America and apply them in a developing world context. However, readers should keep in mind that Beer's work in Chile, and with members of the Chilean government, transformed him personally, enriched his thinking on cybernetics and government, and took his work and life in new directions.

Understanding Beer's ideas at the outset of his Chilean collaboration is key to understanding the eventual design of Project Cybersyn and why its designers believed the design was consistent with the values of Chilean socialism, which I discuss in subsequent chapters. This brief analysis of management cybernetics will also make clear why Flores viewed Beer's work as potentially beneficial to the Chilean road to socialism. This chapter introduces the reader to the interdisciplinary postwar science of cybernetics and contextualizes Beer's work in the field. Most important, the chapter argues that the synergy between Beer (cybernetics) and Flores (politics) was based on a mutual understanding of core problems in the history of both areas. Specifically, how do you create a system that can maintain its organizational stability while facilitating dramatic change, and how do you safeguard the cohesion of the whole without sacrificing the autonomy of its parts?

Stafford Beer

The history of cybernetics is filled with curious characters, and Stafford Beer was not an exception. He wore a long beard for much of his life, habitually smoked cigars, and drank whiskey from a hip flask while discussing scientific ideas late into the night. He included his own poetry and drawings in his scientific publications. Later in his life he gave up many of his material possessions and lived in a small cottage in Wales lacking running water, central heating, and a telephone line.[6] Beer has been described as a "swashbuckling pirate of a man," a "cross between Orson Welles and Socrates," and a guru.[7] His writings addressed subjects as diverse as economic development, socialism, management science, terrorism, and even tantric yoga. Beer was born in 1926 and died in 2002. He was married twice, the first time to Cynthia

Hannaway (1947) and the second time to Sallie Steadman (1968), and fathered seven children.[8]

Among the cybernetics community in the 1950s and 1960s, Beer stands out as someone who built a lucrative private-sector career in the application of cybernetic concepts. By age thirty (1956), Beer was the director of the Department of Operational Research and Cybernetics for all of United Steel, the biggest steel company in Europe.[9] At United Steel, Beer managed more than seventy professionals and supervised pioneering work in computer simulation.[10]

In 1961, when he was thirty-five, Beer left United Steel to codirect the new consulting firm Science in General Management (SIGMA), where he applied cybernetic ideas and operations research (OR) techniques to problems in industry and government (figure 1.1).[11] Jonathan Rosenhead, former president of the Operational Research Society, described SIGMA as "the first substantial operational research consultancy in the UK," and it grew to more than fifty employees under Beer's leadership.[12] Beer doubled his salary while working at SIGMA and lived comfortably. He owned a Rolls Royce and a home in the stockbroker belt of Surrey, England. He named the home Firkins after a unit for measuring beer, and he furnished it with eccentricities, including a goldfish pond in the study, a sound-activated waterfall in the dining room, and walls covered with cork and fur.[13]

Figure 1.1
Stafford Beer, ca. 1961–1966, when he was employed at SIGMA. Image reproduced with permission from Constantin Malik. Original kept at Liverpool John Moores University, Learning and Information Services, Special Collections and Archives.

Beer left SIGMA after five years and accepted a position as the development director for International Publishing Corporation (IPC), then the largest publishing company in the world. There he applied management science techniques and computer technology to improve company operations and started a research and development unit that advanced printing technology as well as new forms of information and image transfer using computers. His obituary reveals that he coined the term *data highway* during this period, thirty years before high-tech pundits adopted the term *information superhighway* to describe the Internet.[14] In 1970 Beer left IPC to work as an independent consultant, and this was what he was doing when Flores contacted him.

Beer was a prolific writer, publishing ten books on cybernetics in his lifetime. In the ten years between 1961 and 1971, Beer published two books; eight book chapters; twenty-one papers, one of which appeared in the premier science journal *Nature*; and twenty-five articles for popular, business, and scientific publications.[15] Although Beer identified himself as a cybernetician, he was arguably better known for his contributions to operations research, and served as the president of the British Operational Research Society (1970–1971). His book *Decision and Control* won the 1966 Frederick W. Lanchester Prize of the Operations Research Society of America for the best English-language publication of the year in operations research and management science.

Despite his primary ties to industry rather than academia, Beer was well connected with the cybernetic elite in Europe and in the United States.[16] "My stroke of luck was that I came into this field [cybernetics] just as it was getting under way," Beer told me. His charismatic and extroverted personality most likely helped him build his professional network as well. Beer rubbed elbows with some of the leading scientific thinkers of his day, such as Warren McCulloch, Heinz von Foerster, Ross Ashby, and Claude Shannon. Beer met Norbert Wiener, the famous MIT mathematician credited for coining the term *cybernetics*, in 1960 during Beer's first trip to the United States, shortly after the publication of his first book, *Cybernetics and Management* (1959).[17] "Everyone called [Wiener] the father of cybernetics, and he very sweetly called me the father of management cybernetics," Beer said.[18] This title stayed with Beer for the rest of his life.

Beer's accomplishments are even more striking considering that he never received an undergraduate degree. At sixteen he began his studies at the University College London, where he took classes in philosophy, mathematics, psychology, neurophysiology, and statistics. His studies were cut short by mandatory military service in the British armed forces.[19] Later he received a master's degree from the University of Manchester Business School, which the university awarded so Beer would have the qualifications to teach on its faculty. In 2000, when Beer was seventy-three years old, the University of Sunderland recognized the cybernetician's published work by awarding him a doctor of science degree.

While Beer enjoyed many professional successes, he also attracted controversy. His willingness to tackle big problems and propose uncommon solutions drew devoted followers as well as vocal critics, and both sides expressed their opinions of him quite passionately. Beer's charisma and bold claims made him an admired, larger-than-life figure to some and, as he acknowledged, caused others to regard him as a charlatan.[20] One prominent member of the British operations research community opined that Beer's propensity for making grand claims and modeling complex systems in their entirety proved more off-putting than persuasive to some, as did his preference for prose over mathematics. Throughout Beer's life the same characteristics that were regarded as his greatest strengths also fueled his critics. One journalist described him as "a frighteningly articulate man."[21]

Beer's interests spanned poetry, Eastern philosophy, neuroscience, and management, but he always identified himself first as a cybernetician. When he read Wiener's book *Cybernetics* a few years after its publication in 1948, he said it "blew my mind." He realized, "This is what I'm trying to do."[22] Cybernetics, which Wiener defined as the study of "control and communication in the animal and the machine," brought together ideas from across the disciplines—mathematics, engineering, and neurophysiology, among others—and applied them toward understanding the behavior of mechanical, biological, and social systems.[23] The interdisciplinary scope of the new field appealed to Beer, and he saw how such concepts could be applied to industrial management. He created a new definition of cybernetics that better fit his work in management: for Beer, cybernetics became the "science of effective organization." While Beer drew from Wiener and other major figures in cybernetic history, his focus on management and his willingness to apply cybernetic concepts to government organizations and political change processes set him apart from other prominent members of the field.

Cybernetics

Wiener did not originate the term *cybernetics*, but he was the one who made it famous.[24] In 1947 Wiener used the term to describe a collective body of research that combined such formerly disparate topics as the mathematical theory of messages, the study of computation and automata, and the functioning of the neurosystem. Cybernetics brought these fields together to help postulate the shared characteristics of machines and organisms in the areas of communication, feedback, and control so that these behaviors could be better understood. The word *cybernetics* derived from the Greek word *kubernêtês*, or steersman, a choice that recognized the steering engines of ships as "one of the earliest and best developed forms of feedback mechanisms."[25] In ancient Greece the *kubernêtês* was a human being who directed the 170 oarsmen powering a trireme warship and told the rowers to change their activities based on the current speed and course of the craft.

Another translation of *kubernêtês* is "governor." Steam engines such as those created by James Watt in the eighteenth century used centrifugal governors to measure the speed of the engine and regulate the amount of steam that entered the engine chamber. Wiener's reference to these early regulators highlights the feedback and control aspects of cybernetics that fascinated the originators of the field. Although Wiener dates the beginning of cybernetics to around 1942, subsequent historical scholarship has linked the field to earlier work in servomechanisms, radar, telephony, and control engineering.[26]

Cybernetics has many origin stories, but all link the field to research by Wiener and MIT engineer Julian Bigelow that the U.S. government funded during World War II. The challenge was to create an antiaircraft servomechanism capable of accurately aiming weapons to shoot down an enemy aircraft. Bigelow and Wiener viewed the antiaircraft challenge as a problem of feedback, or circular causality, that included the machine as well as the human operator and his decision-making processes.[27] Their inclusion of the human operator led the pair to consult with the Mexican neurophysiologist Arturo Rosenblueth, whom Wiener had gotten to know while Rosenblueth was on the faculty of Harvard Medical School in the early 1930s. With Rosenblueth's help the group began to see the similarity between the physiological forms of feedback found in the human brain and those that were needed in the antiaircraft servomechanism. For example, the mock gun turret Wiener and Bigelow built to test their predictive fire-control apparatus would sometimes swing wildly from one side to another. Rosenblueth associated this behavior with a "purpose tremor," a neurological disorder that caused people to swing their arms from side to side when they tried to pick up an object. Although the latter stemmed from a problem in the cerebellum, the area of the brain in charge of sensory perception and motor control, and the former from a problem in circuit design, Rosenblueth, Wiener, and Bigelow came to see both as problems of feedback, or control through error correction. The study of feedback processes in machines, organisms, and social organizations became a distinguishing feature of cybernetic work and departed from the linear cause-and-effect relationships that, until then, had dominated scientific practice.

In 1948, Wiener published these and other insights in the book *Cybernetics*, which popularized the new science. It "took the postwar engineering world by storm," according to Wiener biographers Flo Conway and Jim Siegelman.[28] The insights about feedback processes in machines and organisms that were advanced by Wiener and others in the "cybernetics group" appealed to researchers in a range of disciplines, including engineering, mathematics, psychology, physiology, and the social sciences. Cybernetic practitioners tried to create a universal science by devising a universal language. This new language allowed cybernetics to make disciplinary "border crossings" and thus increase its legitimacy as a useful way of viewing the world.[29] However, the interpretative flexibility and broad applicability of cybernetic ideas also caused some in the scientific community to dismiss the field as a pseudoscience that lacked disciplinary rigor.[30]

Wiener's book had substantial influence on both sides of the Atlantic. *Cybernetics* inspired engineers to introduce feedback into industrial regulation processes. Conway and Siegelman assert that "the postwar explosion of industrial expansion, economic growth, and technological progress owed much to Wiener's work" and that cybernetics shaped research in such areas as electronics and fueled both the production and consumption of electronic goods.[31] *Cybernetics* was also one of the rare technical books to become a crossover hit with the general public; it went through five printings in the six months after its release. Wiener and his work were featured in the popular magazines *Time, Newsweek, Life,* the *New Yorker,* and *Fortune.* The connections the book drew between machines and living organisms captured the public's interest, making both cybernetics and Norbert Wiener household words.[32] In its review of *Cybernetics, Time* posited that computers might eventually learn "like monstrous and precocious children racing through grammar school" and that "wholly automatic factories are just around the corner."[33] Such statements fueled the public imagination about the future of technology and the social ramifications of the new electronic computer, which, like cybernetics, had also grown out of wartime research. The term took on a futuristic appeal.

Within the academic community, cybernetics promoted a model of scientific research that differed from the departmental structure found on most university campuses in the 1940s. From its earliest days cybernetics valued the cross-disciplinary pollination that occurred when experts from a variety of fields convened to discuss a common problem. The conferences organized by the Josiah Macy Foundation from 1946 to 1953, which laid the groundwork for the field of cybernetics, are the most notable example of such collaboration. For example, the attendance list at the first Macy conference included the anthropologist Gregory Bateson, neurophysiologist Warren McCulloch, mathematician John von Neumann, anthropologist Margaret Mead, logician Walter Pitts, Rosenblueth, Bigelow, and Wiener, among others.[34] Attendees at the Macy conferences drew inspiration from cybernetics' encouragement of the use of common metaphors to describe biological and mechanical systems and took this innovation back to their home disciplines.

In 1956 W. Ross Ashby, a British psychiatrist and Macy conference attendee, wrote that one of the greatest contributions of cybernetics was that it provided a vocabulary and a set of concepts that scientists could use to describe biological, mechanical, and social systems. Cybernetics "is likely to reveal a great number of interesting and suggestive parallelisms between machine and brain and society," Ashby predicted. "And it can provide the common language by which discoveries in one branch can readily be made use of in the others."[35] To Ashby and others, including Beer, cybernetics held promise as a universal language for science and a field with the power to illuminate new commonalities in the behavior of animate and inanimate systems.

Cybernetic approaches quickly spread outside academia and influenced U.S. government efforts to quantify the social in the 1950s and 1960s, albeit in different ways from those pursued by the Chilean government in the early 1970s. Institutions such as MIT and the defense think tank RAND applied techniques from cybernetics and operations research to managing complex social and organizational problems. At RAND these techniques were merged with fields such as game theory, probability, statistics, and econometrics to arrive at a more general theory of "systems analysis."[36] RAND systems analysts sought to quantify the world by remaking complex social and political phenomena into a series of equations whose variables could be fed to an electronic computer. Such equations formed the backbone of mathematical models that, once transformed into software code, could process these variables and be used to predict future system behavior under conditions of uncertainty.

Such computer-based systems proliferated in the U.S. defense community in the 1950s and 1960s, often with the help of scientists from RAND and MIT, and formed part of U.S. efforts for top-down command and control. The SAGE (Semi-Automatic Ground Environment) air defense system is perhaps the most frequently cited example of such a system in the literature of the history of computing. Designed to locate hostile aircraft flying in U.S. airspace, SAGE used real-time radar data to calculate the future position of an enemy aircraft. Paul Edwards, a historian of computing, credits the SAGE system as the first application of computers "to large-scale problems of real-time *control*" rather than for information and data processing.[37] Systems analysis and computer modeling also played important roles in formulating strategies used by the U.S. government during the Vietnam War. These approaches allowed the government to compile detailed quantitative maps of the political climate in different regions of Vietnam and use these data to guide U.S. wartime tactics. Secretary of Defense Robert S. McNamara championed these so-called scientific approaches and used them to create what he believed to be objective policies that emphasized cost effectiveness and centralized decision making.[38]

The U.S. civilian sector also adopted techniques from systems analysis. Fields such as geography, political science, and urban planning adopted quantitative modeling practices that drew from systems analysis, cybernetics, and operations research.[39] These quantitative approaches seemed to give policy makers a way to predict the behavior of complex systems, reduce uncertainty in policy making, improve centralized planning, and ground policy decisions in numerical data. In her study of defense intellectuals in urban planning, historian Jennifer Light notes that the Pittsburgh Department of City Planning pioneered the use of computer modeling, systems analysis, and cybernetics for urban renewal projects in the early 1960s. Pittsburgh city planners drew explicitly from the work of defense intellectuals at RAND and elsewhere and used these approaches to predict future city processes, such as determining residential patterns. In New York City, Mayor John V. Lindsay (1966–1973) used systems analysis to transform city management practices and, with RAND, created the New York City RAND Institute in 1969. Lindsay's view of the city as an information system spurred the creation of computerized data systems to increase data sharing among city departments and centralize decision making and control, although such efforts did not succeed in cutting city operating expenses nor, as Light observes, did they make life noticeably better for city residents.[40] Beer's computerized system for economic management in Chile was later compared with these contemporaneous efforts taking place in New York City.[41]

Increased levels of military funding on university campuses, and the elevated position of science and engineering after World War II, encouraged academic social scientists to adopt these quantitative approaches and raised their profile in the U.S. academy. These approaches have subsequently been criticized for oversimplifying the dynamics of social systems and for encouraging policy makers, academics, and Wall Street bankers to place too much trust in numbers. In addition, critics have pointed out that quantitative approaches encourage top-down management hierarchies that have grafted the structure and culture of the military onto the civilian agencies, businesses, and institutions of a democracy.[42]

Cybernetic ideas helped shape these quantitative systems-oriented approaches to modeling social systems. In the U.S. context, cybernetics has a clear historical link to military engineering activities and what historian Paul Edwards calls the "closed-world" discourse of command and control.[43] But that is not the entire story of cybernetics in the United States or elsewhere. In her study of metaphor in twentieth-century biology, Evelyn Fox Keller asserts that viewing "cybersciences" such as cybernetics, information theory, systems analysis, operations research, and computer science as only "extending the regime of wartime power, of command-control-communication, to the civilian domain" is oversimplistic and one-dimensional. Keller instead argues that the cybersciences also emerged as a way to embrace complexity and "in response to the increasing impracticality of conventional power regimes."[44] This is especially true in the history of British cybernetics and is highly evident in Stafford Beer's work on management cybernetics.

Management Cybernetics

British cybernetics, as practiced by Beer, differed from the U.S. approach in significant ways. In his book *The Cybernetic Brain*, Andrew Pickering distinguishes British cybernetics (as represented by the careers of Beer, Ashby, Grey Walter, Gregory Bateson, R. D. Laing, and Gordon Pask) from the better-known story of cybernetics in the United States, which is often tied to the career of Norbert Wiener and Wiener's military research at MIT during the Second World War. Pickering notes that British cybernetics was tied primarily to psychiatry, not military engineering, and focused on the brain.[45]

According to Pickering, British cyberneticians such as Beer did not view the brain as an organ that created representations of the world or knowledge. Instead, they saw it as an "embodied organ, intrinsically tied into bodily performances."[46] This "cybernetic brain" allowed the body to do things in the world and, above all, to adapt to its environment. As Pickering writes, "The cybernetic brain was not representational but *performative* . . . and its role in performance was *adaptation.*"[47] This idea of the performative brain shaped Beer's approach to complex systems and his ideas about management cybernetics.

Indeed Beer's work bears the hallmarks of British cybernetics as described by Pickering. Beer studied and worked in psychiatry, and he made frequent references to the field in his writings. He often used metaphors from neuroscience, including references to the brain and its behavior, to illustrate and support his approach to management. He embraced complexity, emphasized holism, and did not try to describe the complex systems he studied, biological or social, in their entirety. To put it another way, Beer was more interested in studying how systems behaved in the real world than in creating exact representations of how they functioned. Furthermore, he was centrally concerned with developing mechanisms to help these systems self-regulate and survive. He stressed that cybernetics and operations research should drive action, not create mathematical models of increasing complexity and exactitude.[48]

Beer's emphasis on action over mathematical precision set him apart from many of his peers in the academic operations research community who, Beer believed, privileged mathematical abstraction over problem solving.[49] It also set him apart from Wiener, who saw cybernetics as ill-suited for the study of social systems because they could not generate the long-term data sets under the constant conditions that his statistical prediction techniques required.[50]

Beer's management cybernetics cast the company as an organism struggling to survive within a changing external environment. He wrote, "The company is certainly not alive, but it has to behave very much like a living organism. It is essential to the company that it develops techniques for survival in a changing environment: it must adapt itself to its economic, commercial, social and political surroundings and learn from experience."[51] These techniques included building statistical mechanisms that showed managers how the company had reacted to earlier environmental changes so that the manager might better position the business to adapt to future fluctuations and upheavals. Cybernetic management prioritized the long-term survival of the company over the short-term goals of any one department. This attention to overall survival reinforced the importance of holistic management and of Beer's conviction that effective management functioned like the human nervous system. Most companies of his time divided their operations into departments that oversaw the company's activities in assigned areas and dealt with the problems that arose in these areas. Beer believed that this fragmented, reductionist approach could result in decisions that benefited a particular department in the short term but that moved the company toward a greater instability in the long term. Creating the kind of holistic, adaptive system that in Beer's mind functioned like the human nervous system required a different approach to the problem of control.

Adaptive Control

The idea of control is commonly associated with domination. Beer offered a different definition: he defined control as self-regulation, or the ability of a system to adapt to internal and external changes and survive. This alternative approach to control resulted in multiple misunderstandings of Beer's work, and he was repeatedly criticized for using computers to create top-down control systems that his detractors equated with authoritarianism and the loss of individual freedom. Such criticisms extended to the design of Project Cybersyn, but, as this book illustrates, they were to some extent ill-informed. To fully grasp how Beer approached the control problem requires a brief introduction to his cybernetic vocabulary.

Beer was primarily concerned with the study of "exceedingly complex systems," or "systems so involved that they are indescribable in detail."[52] He contrasted exceedingly complex systems with simple but dynamic systems such as a window catch, which has few components and interconnections, and complex systems, which have a greater number of components and connections but can be described in considerable detail (figure 1.2). Beer classified the operation of a computer or the laws of the visible universe as complex systems. Examples of exceedingly complex systems included the economy, the company, or the brain; such systems defied the limits of reductionist

Systems	Simple	Complex	Exceedingly complex
Deterministic	Window catch	Electronic digital computer	EMPTY
	Billiards	Planetary system	
	Machine-shop lay-out	Automation	
Probabilistic	Penny tossing	Stockholding	The economy
	Jellyfish movements	Conditioned reflexes	The brain
	Statistical quality control	Industrial profitability	THE COMPANY

Figure 1.2
Simple, complex, and exceedingly complex systems. Reprinted from Stafford Beer, *Cybernetics and Management*, 2nd ed. (London: English Universities Press, 1967), 18. Image reproduced with permission from Constantin Malik.

mathematical analysis. The behavior of exceedingly complex systems could not be predicted with perfect accuracy, but it could be studied probabilistically. You could have a good idea of what such a system might do, but you could never be one hundred percent certain.

In Beer's opinion, traditional science did a good job of handling simple and complex systems but fell short in its ability to describe, let alone regulate, exceedingly complex systems. Cybernetics, Beer argued, could provide tools for understanding and controlling these exceedingly complex systems and help these systems adapt to problems yet unknown. The trick was to "black-box" parts of the system without losing the key characteristics of the original.[53]

The idea of the black box originated in electrical engineering and referred to a sealed box whose contents are hidden but that can receive an electrical input and whose output the engineer can observe. By varying the input and observing the output, the engineer can discern something about the contents of the box without ever seeing its inner workings. Black-boxing parts of an exceedingly complex system preserved the behavior of the original but did not require the observer to create an exact representation of how the system worked. Beer believed that it is possible to regulate exceedingly complex systems without fully understanding their inner workings, asserting, "It is not necessary to enter the black box to understand the nature of the function it performs" or to grasp the range of the subsystem's behaviors.[54] In other words, it is more important to grasp what things do than to understand fully how they work. To regulate the behavior of such a system requires a regulator that has as much flexibility as the system it wishes to control and that can respond to and regulate all behaviors of subsystems that have been black-boxed.

Creating such a regulator is extremely difficult. Imagine, for example, an exceedingly complex system such as a national economy. It has many component parts, including factories, suppliers of energy and raw materials, and a labor force, all of which are intricately configured and mutually dependent. Each component can assume a range of states or, as Ashby puts it, "a well-defined condition or property that can be recognized if it occurs again."[55] For instance, a factory may constitute one subsystem in the example of the national economy. This factory may have a level of production output that typically falls within a certain range. However, a labor strike could bring production to a halt. Oil prices could increase and cause a significant rise in transportation costs for the factory and negatively affect a range of economic activities throughout the country. In short, the factory can assume a great number of states, only a subset of which is desired. Beer refers to the total number of possible states as the "variety" of a system. In the example given here, each factory can pass through a wide array of states. Once these and other components of the economy are connected, the overarching system (the national economy) can assume an even greater number of states, or have a higher variety.

Controlling an exceedingly complex system with high variety therefore requires a regulator that can react to and govern every one of these potential states, or, to put it another way, respond to the variety of the system. "Often one hears the optimistic demand: 'give me a simple control system; one that cannot go wrong,'" Beer writes. "The trouble with such 'simple' controls is that they have insufficient variety to cope with the variety in the environment. . . . Only variety in the control mechanism can deal successfully with variety in the system controlled."[56] This last observation—that only variety can control variety—is the essence of Ashby's Law of Requisite Variety and a fundamental principle in Beer's cybernetic work.[57]

The Law of Requisite Variety makes intuitive sense: it is impossible to truly control another unless you can respond to all attempts at subversion. This makes it extremely difficult, if not impossible, to control an exceedingly complex system if control is defined as domination. History is filled with instances of human beings' trying to exert control over nature, biology, and other human beings—efforts that have failed because of their limited variety. Many of the most powerful medicines cannot adapt to all permutations of a disease. Recent work in the sociology of science has positioned Beer's idea of control in contrast to the modernist ethos of many science and engineering endeavors, which have sought to govern ecosystems, bodily functions, and natural topographies. Despite the many successes associated with such projects, these efforts at control still have unexpected, and sometimes undesirable, results.[58]

Beer challenged the common definition of control as domination, which he viewed as authoritarian and oppressive and therefore undesirable. It was also "naïve, primitive and ridden with an almost retributive idea of causality." What people viewed as control, Beer continued, was nothing more than "a crude process of coercion," an observation that emphasized the individual agency of the entity being controlled.[59] Instead of using science to dominate the outside world, scientists should focus on identifying the equilibrium conditions among subsystems and developing regulators to help the overall system reach its natural state of stability. Beer emphasized creating lateral communication channels among the different subsystems so that the changes in one subsystem could be absorbed by changes in the others.[60] This approach, he argued, took advantage of the flexibility of each subsystem. Instead of creating a regulator to fix the behavior of each subsystem, he found ways to couple subsystems together so that they could respond to each other and adapt. Such adaptive couplings helped maintain the stability of the overall system.

Beer called the natural state of system stability *homeostasis*.[61] The term refers to the ability of a system to withstand disturbances in its external environment through its own dynamic self-regulation, such as that achieved by coupling subsystems to one another. Beer argued that reaching homeostasis is crucial to the survival of any system, whether it is mechanical, biological, or social. Control through homeostasis rather than through domination gives the system greater flexibility and facilitated adaptation,

Beer argued. He therefore proposed an alternative idea of control, which he defined as "a homeostatic machine for regulating itself."[62] In a 1969 speech before the United Nations Educational, Social, and Cultural Organization, Beer stated that the "sensible course for the manager is not to try to change the system's internal behavior . . . *but to change its structure*—so that its natural systemic behavior becomes different. All of this says that management is not so much part of the system managed as it is the system's own designer."[63] In other words, cybernetic management as described by Beer looked for ways to redesign the structure of a company or state enterprise so that it would naturally tend toward stability and the desired behavior.

In addition, cybernetic management sought to create a balance between horizontal and vertical forms of communication and control. Because changes in one subsystem could be absorbed and adapted to by changes in others (via lateral communication), each subsystem retained the ability to change its behavior, within certain limits, without threatening the overall stability of the system and could do so without direction from the vertical chain of command. To look at it another way, cybernetic management approached the control problem in a way that preserved a degree of freedom and autonomy for the parts without sacrificing the stability of the whole.

The first edition of Beer's 1959 book *Cybernetics and Management* did not make many references to computer technology, although the book's description of a cybernetic factory includes several tasks suitable for large-scale data processing, among them the generation of statistical data to predict the future behavior of the company. The second edition of the text, published eight years later in 1967, includes a postscript—"Progress to the Cybernetic Firm"—and a section dedicated to the misuse of computers in industry. (Beer often objected to how businesses and government offices used computers.)

Mainframe computer technology entered the business world during the 1950s and 1960s, primarily as a means of increasing the speed and volume of data processing. Beer argued that most applications simply automated existing procedures and operations within the company instead of taking advantage of the new capabilities offered by computer technology to envision new forms of organization and better methods of management. Applied differently, computer technology could help organize the parts of the business into a better-functioning whole and allow companies to focus on the future instead of compiling pages of data that documented past performance. Computers did not need to reinforce existing management hierarchies and procedures; instead, they could bring about structural transformation within a company and help it form new communications channels, generate and exchange information dynamically, and decrease the time required for those in the company to make an informed decision. In short, Beer believed that computer technology, used differently, could help implement cybernetic approaches to management.[64] His focus was not on creating more advanced machines but rather on using existing computer technologies to develop more advanced systems of organization.

Cybernetics and Chilean Socialism

Beer's ideas on management cybernetics resembled the Chilean approach to demo-cratic socialism. First, Allende and Popular Unity, like Beer, wanted to make structural changes and wanted them to happen quickly. However, they needed to carry out these changes in a way that did not threaten the stability of existing democratic institutions. Second, Allende and his government, Popular Unity, did not want to impose these changes on the Chilean people from above. The government wanted change to occur within a democratic framework and in a way that preserved civil liberties and respected dissenting voices. Chilean democratic socialism, like management cybernetics, thus wanted to find a balance between centralized control and individual freedom. Third, the Chilean government needed to develop ways to manage the growing national economy, and industrial management constituted one of Beer's core areas of expertise. In the next chapter I will explore how Beer's approach to industrial management ad-dressed the goals of Allende's economic program and, in particular, the government's emphasis on raising national production. For now it is sufficient to say that Beer's work in cybernetics was exploring some of the same issues as Chilean socialism, although Beer was working in the domain of science rather than politics. This common concep-tual ground motivated Flores to contact Beer. But how this connection occurred is a story of historical contingency, and it requires stepping back in time to the early 1960s.

By 1961 Beer had achieved an international reputation in Europe and the United States. Around 1962, when he was codirector of SIGMA, the director of Chile's steel industry requested SIGMA's services. Beer refused to go himself—he had never been to South America, and his hectic schedule made the lengthy transit time seem unrea-sonable—but he put together a team of English and Spanish employees to travel to Chile in his place. SIGMA's work in the Chilean steel industry had gradually expanded to include the railways. Because the amount of work was large, the SIGMA team in Chile often hired students to pick up the slack. Among them was the young Fernando Flores, who then was studying industrial engineering at the Catholic University in Santiago.

Flores was born in 1943 in the town of Talca, which is located south of the Chilean capital city of Santiago. His father was a railroad engineer, and his mother owned a small lumber company. He was a good student with a quick mind and ability for math-ematics. Although Flores did not know what he wanted to do with his life, he realized that becoming an engineer was "a big deal," and so he applied to the School of Engi-neering at the prestigious Catholic University and was accepted. In a 2003 interview he speculated that he may have been the first in his family to receive a university educa-tion.[65] Flores's discovery of cybernetics and of Beer resulted from a particular series of personal connections, work experiences, and political changes that occurred outside his formal university education. Within the university Flores studied operations research with Arnoldo Hax, the director of the school of engineering at the Catholic University (1963–1964) who later accepted a professorship at MIT's Sloan School of Management.

Because Flores was trained in operations research, SIGMA hired him to work on the contract for Chilean railways. It was then that he discovered *Cybernetics and Management*, a book he describes as "visionary." Flores graduated in 1968 with a degree in industrial engineering. After graduation he visited Hax in the United States, and someone serendipitously passed him a copy of Beer's second book, *Decision and Control*. "I found this book to be better than the others," Flores said, "more concrete, more clear, intriguing. I found that [Beer] had a great mind for these kinds of things. Different from the others, who always thought that operations research was connected with techniques. They didn't have the core, and I was looking for the core. . . . Always." Flores was drawn to the connective, philosophical foundation that cybernetics offered and that Beer articulated. Flores believed that Beer's approach to management was the best around.[66]

From 1968 to 1970 Flores served as the academic director of the engineering school at the Catholic University, although his duties gradually expanded to include activities throughout the university. The university reform movement was under way during this period, and Flores oversaw many changes in the university's engineering curriculum, including efforts to increase community involvement with university activities. Like many of his contemporaries, Flores was active in academic and political circles. In 1969 a group of young intellectuals at the Catholic University, including Flores, broke from the Christian Democratic Party and established the Movement of Popular Unitary Action (MAPU), a small political party of young intellectuals who were critical of the centrist Christian Democrats and Chilean president Eduardo Frei Montalva (1964–1970); they aligned themselves with the Communists and Socialists of the leftist Popular Unity coalition. The addition of the MAPU to Popular Unity, combined with the inability of the right and the Christian Democrats to form a winning coalition, contributed to the Socialist Allende's narrow victory in the 1970 presidential election.

As an acknowledgment of Flores's political loyalty and technical competency, the Allende government appointed Flores the general technical manager of the Corporación de Fomento de la Producción (CORFO), the State Development Corporation, which Allende charged with nationalizing Chilean industry. Flores held the third-highest position within the agency, the highest position held there by a member of the MAPU, and the management position most directly linked to the daily regulation of the nationalized factories.[67]

Flores remembered Beer's writings and thought that the ideas found in his management cybernetics overlapped with the political ideas of the Chilean road to socialism, in that Chilean democratic socialism was struggling with the question of "how to combine the autonomy of individuals with the [needs of the] community." From his perspective in CORFO, Flores felt that the government was "paying pure lip service" to this question and had "nothing concrete" that could be put into practice. Flores believed that Beer might give the government a way to turn its political ideology into practice.[68]

Flores also had the financial and political resources to bring Beer to Chile in order to apply his expertise to the Chilean economy. "When I came to CORFO," Flores said, "I found that I had the small amount of power that I needed to do something bigger." He decided to use part of that power to bring Beer to Chile. Few in Chile, outside academia, knew of cybernetics, and management cybernetics was even more obscure. Flores's decision to approach Beer was well outside mainstream thinking at the development agency. Darío Pavez, then its general manager and Flores's boss, reportedly viewed Flores's decision to recruit Beer as crazy. However, he decided to give Flores leeway because he recognized Flores's value to CORFO.[69] It also helped that Flores was a very persuasive individual despite his youth. He expressed his ideas passionately and was not afraid to ruffle feathers to get things done. He was also large physically; Beer later described the young engineer as a bear. In addition, Flores had a sharp mind and strong personality.

Flores was drawn to Beer's work because of the connection he saw between cybernetics and socialism. Flores's personality and position in the government allowed him to transform these conceptual commonalities into a real collaboration.

Beer's New Models

Flores did not know that Beer's interest in how to use cybernetics for social change had increased in the late 1960s and early 1970s, as had his commitment to improving government effectiveness by developing ways to change its structure. In 1970 alone, Beer delivered ten public lectures that he referred to as "arguments of change."[70] He later published these lectures in his fifth book, *Platform for Change* (1975).

In addition, Beer had been working on two innovative—but potentially related—models of systems organization: the Liberty Machine and the Viable System Model. The Liberty Machine (1970) was a new kind of technological system for government administration. Beer argued that such a system could be built without using cutting-edge technology and that it could help government offices minimize bureaucracy and adapt to crises. Beer spent 1971 finalizing the Viable System Model, a general model that he believed balanced centralized and decentralized forms of control in organizations. He argued that it could be applied to a range of organizations, including government. From Beer's perspective, both the Liberty Machine and the Viable System Model could be applied to address the tension between top-down and bottom-up decision making in Chilean socialism and the challenges Chile faced as a developing nation with limited technological resources. Thus, the invitation from Flores was not only a chance for Beer to apply his cybernetic ideas on a national scale but also a consulting opportunity that aligned perfectly with the cybernetician's intellectual trajectory.

The Liberty Machine

Beer presented his idea for a Liberty Machine in a 1970 keynote address to the Conference on the Environment organized by the American Society for Cybernetics in Washington, D.C. An edited version of this text later appeared in a 1971 edition of the journal *Futures* and later in *Platform for Change*. In the address Beer described government as an "elaborate and ponderous" machine that has such "immense inertia" that changing government organization seems to require "destroying the machinery of the state and going through a phase of anarchy."[71] Ineffective organization had serious long-term implications and limited government efficacy to act in the present and plan for the future.[72] Therefore, Beer argued that government institutions needed to change and that this could be accomplished without the chaos of destroying the existing state.

The Liberty Machine modeled a sociotechnical system that functioned as a disseminated network, not a hierarchy; it treated information, not authority, as the basis for action, and operated in close to real time to facilitate instant decision making and eschew bureaucratic protocols. Beer contended that this design promoted action over bureaucratic practice and prevented top-down tyranny by creating a distributed network of shared information. The Liberty Machine distributed decision making across different government offices, but it also required all subordinate offices to limit their actions so as not to threaten the survival of the overall organization, in this case, a government. The Liberty Machine thus achieved the balance between centralized control and individual freedom that had characterized Beer's earlier work.

Beer posited that such a Liberty Machine could create a government where "competent information is free to act," meaning that once government officials become aware of a problem, they could address it quickly; expert knowledge, not bureaucratic politics, would guide policy. However, Beer did not critically explore what constitutes "competent information" or how cybernetics might resolve disagreements within the scientific community or within other communities of expertise. Moreover, it is not clear how he separated bureaucracy from a system of checks and balances that might slow action but prevent abuse.

Beer envisioned that the physical Liberty Machine would consist of a series of operations rooms that received real-time information from the different systems being monitored and used computers to "distil the information content."[73] The people inside these rooms, whom Beer described as "responsible officials answerable to constitutional masters," would use this information to run simulations and generate hypotheses about future system behavior. Color television screens would be used to display data to these officials.

The image of a futuristic operations room would come to define Project Cybersyn. Beer's interest in building such rooms has an interesting etiology. Beer came of age during World War II, and the successful use of operations research techniques by the

British armed forces during the war left a lasting impression on him. In a 2001 interview, Beer said that through his work at SIGMA he "was trying to change industry and government in the same way the army, navy and air force had been changed by making mathematical models and other kinds of models" during World War II. The image of the war room that Winston Churchill used to direct and control the complexities of the British war effort also deeply impressed Beer. In his 1968 book *Management Science*, Beer argues, "The 'Battle of Britain' in World War II was successful only because it could be directed, from moment to moment, from this central control headquarters near London. This was made possible by information gathering and communication techniques unknown a few years previously."[74] In his 1970 inaugural address as the new president of the British Operational Research Society, Beer eluded to the battle encounters "spread out on a vast map in the war-time Operations Room" as a successful governing technique that had worked for Churchill and the British armed forces and that could be a cornerstone for cybernetic government. "I envision a government operations center," Beer said, "laid out on comparable lines, relating the pieces of the national problem in an integral way. Industrial managements could have this room if they wanted it; so could a new kind of Cabinet Office."[75] By 1971 Beer had concluded that governments did not necessarily need access to the most cutting-edge technologies to construct such a system. A "tool of this potency could be forged by anyone commanding adequate resources," who could then "take virtual control of affairs," Beer wrote.[76] The Liberty Machine, a distributed decision-making apparatus of operations rooms connected by real-time information-sharing channels, was a proposal waiting for a government to take a chance on its implementation.

The Viable System Model
The Viable System Model is one of the most central and enduring concepts in all of Beer's work. It was the subject of three of his ten books on cybernetics, and Beer wrote in 1984 that he had been on a quest to explain "how systems are viable" since the 1950s.[77] Beer first presented the Viable System Model in his fourth book, *Brain of the Firm* (1972), but the model was almost fully formed by the time Flores contacted him in July 1971. In *Brain of the Firm*, Beer defines a viable system as "a system that survives. It coheres; it is integral. It is homeostatically balanced both internally and externally, but has none the less [*sic*] mechanisms and opportunities to grow and to learn, to evolve and to adapt—to become more and more potent in its environment."[78] By the mid-1980s Beer had refined this definition even further to create a system that is "capable of independent existence."[79] Here I describe the Viable System Model as Beer described it in *Brain of the Firm*, supplemented with commentary from some of his later works, to enable the reader to understand the system as it was presented to the Chilean team. However, since the model evolved in Beer's subsequent work, the description presented here is not identical to the one used today.[80]

The Viable System Model offered a management structure for the regulation of exceedingly complex systems. It was based on Beer's understanding of how the human nervous system functioned, and it applied these insights more generally to the behavior of organizations such as a company, government, or factory.[81] Though Beer would later describe Allende's Chile as the "most significant and large-scale" application of the Viable System Model, it was also a testing ground for the model, which in size and scope Beer was never able to equal.[82]

In its full form the Viable System Model is complex; what follows is only a brief description of some of its general principles. Despite the model's biological origins, Beer maintained that the abstraction of the structure could be applied in numerous contexts, including the firm, the body, and the state. In keeping with Beer's emphasis on performance rather than representation, it was not a model that accurately represented what these systems were; rather, it was a model that described how these systems behaved. The Viable System Model functioned recursively: the parts of a viable system were also viable, and their behavior could be described using the Viable System Model. Beer explains: "The whole is always encapsulated in each part. . . . This is a lesson learned from biology where we find the genetic blue-print of the whole organism in every cell."[83] Thus, Beer maintained that the state, the company, the worker, and the cell all exhibit the same series of structural relationships.

The Viable System Model devised ways to promote vertical *and* lateral communication. It offered a balance between centralized and decentralized control that prevented both the tyranny of authoritarianism and the chaos of total freedom. Beer considered viable systems to be largely self-organizing. Therefore, the model sought to maximize the autonomy of its component parts so that they could organize themselves as they saw fit. At the same time, it retained channels for vertical control to maintain the stability of the whole system. These aspects of the Viable System Model shaped the design of Project Cybersyn and provide another illustration of how Beer and Popular Unity were exploring similar approaches to the problem of control.

The Viable System Model consisted of five tiers that Beer based on the human nervous system.[84] As in Beer's other work, the model black-boxed much of the system's complexity into subsystems. The model also established channels of communication that coupled these subsystems to one another. This allowed them to share information, adapt to one another and the outside world, and keep the entire system stable.

Figure 1.3 provides a biological rendering of Beer's five-tier system, but in its most basic form the Viable System Model resembles a flow chart. In his writings Beer switches freely among metaphors drawn from organizations, organisms, and machines when describing each of the system's five levels. These different metaphors helped him to communicate his ideas to his reader, emphasize the ideas' scientific origin, and stress that biological, social, and mechanical systems shared similar characteristics. Beer first

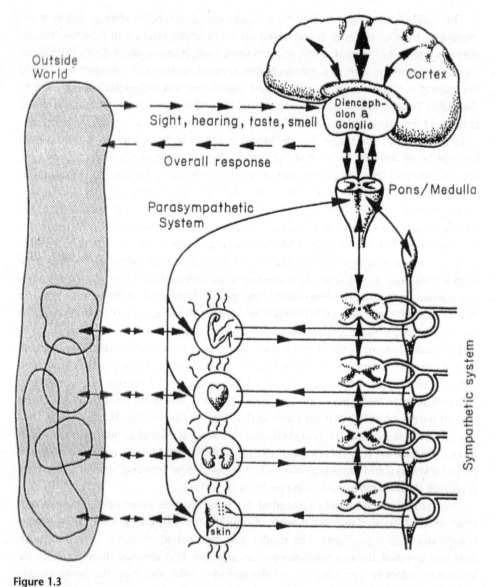

Figure 1.3
Viable System Model (biological). Reprinted from Stafford Beer, *Brain of the Firm: The Managerial Cybernetics of Organization*, 2nd ed. (New York: J. Wiley, 1981), 131. Image reproduced with permission from Constantin Malik.

described the model in its biological form, which I present here. I will later explore how Beer mapped the model onto Chilean industrial production.

Beer referred to System One of the Viable System Model as the sensory level. It consisted of the limbs and bodily organs (such as the lungs, heart, or kidneys). Because members of System One are in contact with their environment, they are able to respond to local conditions and behave in an "essentially autonomous" manner, although they are regulated to behave in ways that ensure the stability of the entire body. For example, our kidneys and heart, when working properly, automatically adjust to the surrounding conditions. Under normal conditions our breathing also happens automatically without conscious thought. Beer asserted that in most instances, our body parts are capable of regulating their own behavior. However, changes in the behavior of one organ may affect the operating environment, and thus the behavior, of other body parts.

System Two acts as a cybernetic spinal cord. It enables rapid lateral communication among the different body parts and organs so that they can coordinate their actions and adapt to one another's behavior. "Each organ of the body," writes Beer, "would be isolated on its lateral axis if it were not for the arrangement of each organ's own controller into a cohesive set of such controllers—which we have called System Two."[85] System Two also filters information from System One and passes the most important information upward to System Three. Given its name, System Two seems to be hierarchically above System One, but Beer insisted that it was not; instead, he countered, System Two should be seen as a service to System One. The Viable System Model did not impose a hierarchical form of management in a traditional sense. The dynamic communication between System One and System Two enabled a form of adaptive management that was made possible by rapid information exchange, coordinated action, and shared understanding.[86]

System Three (which Beer equated to the pons, medulla, and cerebellum of the brain) monitors the behavior of each organ (System One), as well as the organs' collective interaction, and works to keep the body functioning properly under normal conditions. In management terms, Beer later described System Three as being "responsible for the *internal* and *immediate* functions of the enterprise: its 'here-and-now,' day-to-day management."[87] Because System Three has access to the macroscopic picture of what is going on at the lower levels, it can help coordinate System One actions to maintain the overall stability of the body or the enterprise. Beer described System Three as belonging to "the vertical command axis"; it is a "transmitter of policy and special instructions," and "a receiver of information about the internal environment."[88] However, System Three does not receive data on all aspects of System One's operation, only the information deemed most important. This filtering allows System Three to grasp the totality of what is taking place without being overwhelmed by minutiae. Periodic audits of System One behavior allow System Three to make sure it is not losing important details to this filtering process.[89] System Three also filters the wealth of information it receives from the lower systems and directs only the most important information upward to System Four.

As "the biggest switch," System Four (which Beer equated to a combination of the diencephalon, basal ganglia, and the third ventricle of the brain) provides the vital link between voluntary and involuntary control.[90] It permits filtered information from System Three to flow upward and alert System Five (the cerebral cortex). It also permits System Five to send directives downward to System Three and modify behavior at the lower levels. Thus, System Four allows the lower levels to retain their autonomy under normal circumstances, but it also permits System Five to intervene in these activities if the need arises. Long-term planning also resides in System Four. It is connected to the outside world and monitors the environment, continually searching for signals that adaption or new learning must take place. In the biological version of the model, this is where the brain considers the environment external to the body and the future action the body should take. Beer lamented that many companies relied solely on System Three, day-to-day management, and did not create a proper System Four dedicated to their future development. Beer coupled System Four to System Three; just as the information from day-to-day management was necessary for future planning, long-term and medium-term plans could also affect daily management decisions. Therefore Beer did not see System Four as the boss of System Three but rather as its partner in an ongoing conversation. On a technological level, Beer envisioned System Four as an operations room akin to the rooms that formed part of his proposed Liberty Machine.

System Five is the final level of the model. Just as the cerebral cortex interconnects millions of neurons with one another, System Five does not consist of a single manager, Beer maintained. Rather, it consists of a group of managers who communicate vertically to their immediate superiors and subordinates, laterally to managers who are outside their formal hierarchy, and diagonally to managers who are several levels above their position but outside the chain of command. Beer calls this arrangement a "multinode" and argues that this redundant system of interconnectedness increases viability by eliminating errors caused by misinformation, incomplete information, or poor judgment and thereby minimizes the deleterious effects of centralization. System Five also resolves conflicts between System Three and System Four, and maintains the identity and coherence of the entire organism.

The Viable System Model draws a distinction between the bottom three levels of the system, which govern daily operations, and the upper two levels of management, which determine future development and the overall direction of the enterprise. Because the lower three levels manage day-to-day activities and filter upward only the most important information, the upper two levels are free to think about larger questions. In this sense, Beer's model tackled the idea of information overload long before the Internet required us to wade into and make sense of an expanding sea of information.

In an emergency System One (the organ or the limb) can immediately send a "cry of pain" up the vertical axis to System Three, Four, or Five. Beer called this cry of pain an "algedonic signal." Beer formed the term *algedonic* from two words, *algos*, meaning "pain," and *hedos*, meaning "pleasure." This signal alerted higher levels of management to a discrete event taking place in System One, information that might have been lost to filtering or aggregated into a more comprehensive measure of system behavior. The algedonic signal allows higher management to communicate with System One, address the problem immediately, and thus minimize the effect of the emergency on the rest of the system.

The Viable System Model included communications channels to improve the responsiveness of top-down control mechanisms. More often, however, the model struck a balance between autonomy and collective good and encouraged the different systems to communicate and dynamically adapt to one another. It proposed that self-organization, adaption, and learning were central to helping systems survive in a changing environment.

Management Cybernetics and Revolution

The tension inherent in Beer's model between individual autonomy and the welfare of the collective organism mirrors the struggle between competing ideologies found in Allende's democratic socialism. Allende's interpretation of Marx's writings emphasized the importance of respecting Chile's existing democratic processes in bringing about socialist reform, a possibility that Marx alluded to but never realized.[91] In contrast to the centralized planning found in the Soviet Union, Allende's articulation of socialism stressed a commitment to decentralized governance with worker participation in management, reinforcing his professed belief in individual freedoms. Yet he also acknowledged that in the face of political plurality the government would favor the "interest of those who made their living by their own work" and that revolution should be brought about from above with a "firm guiding hand."[92]

Both Allende and Beer emphasize the importance of individual freedoms and the need for decentralization while recognizing situations in which, as Beer describes it, "the needs of one division must be sacrificed explicitly to the needs of other divisions."[93] Thus, the collective welfare of the state or the homeostasis of the system takes priority over the mechanisms devised to ensure autonomy, freedom, and liberty. According to Beer, this conflict of values can be resolved only at the top, a belief supported by Allende's determination that the Chilean government would favor policies protecting the rights and interests of the workers, despite the legislative provisions that granted equal rights to the opposition.

Flores did not know about the Viable System Model when he contacted Beer. However, for Beer the similarity between the Viable System Model and Chilean socialism was not only professionally fortuitous, it also suggested that cybernetics could shed light on the internal dynamics of a political process and assist in its management.

In October 1970, nine months before Beer heard from Flores, the cybernetician delivered an address in London titled "This Runaway World—Can Man Gain Control?" In this lecture Beer unknowingly foretold his coming involvement with the Allende government. Commenting that government in its present form could not adequately handle the complex challenges of modern society, Beer concluded: "What is needed is structural change. Nothing else will do. . . . The more I reflect on these facts, the more I perceive that the evolutionary approach to adaptation in social systems simply will not work any more. . . . It has therefore become clear to me over the years that I am advocating revolution."[94] Beer added, "Do not let us have our revolution the hard way, whereby all that mankind has successfully built may be destroyed. We do not need to embark on the revolutionary process, with bombs and fire. But we must start with a genuinely revolutionary intention: to devise wholly new methods for handling our problems."[95] Less than one year later, Beer would be in Chile helping a government accomplish exactly this.

Connecting Cybernetics and Socialism

The history of science and technology contains multiple instances of political ideas and ideologies that have influenced the practice and content of science as well as the design and use of technology.[96] However, I am making a different argument here: I am showing the deep conceptual similarities between Beer's work in management cybernetics and Popular Unity's approach to democratic socialism. These similarities led Flores to believe that management cybernetics could help the Allende government understand and manage the political process it had set in motion.

Both Beer and Popular Unity were interested in making structural changes to existing organizations. Both were interested in finding ways to make these changes happen quickly while maintaining the stability of the overall organization. And both were interested in the problem of control but eschewed the idea of ruling with an iron fist. Instead, they wanted to find a balance between individual freedom and top-down control, a balance that preserved autonomy but recognized that maintaining the stability of a state or company may require limiting freedom or sacrificing the needs of some to the needs of others.

Such commonalities drew Flores to Beer. Beer's emphasis on action grounded in scientific rationality also appealed to the young Chilean. Timing played an important role in making this connection happen, since Flores's letter reached Beer just when he had become increasingly interested in how to make government adaptive, via the Liberty Machine, so that it could respond to changing societal needs or crisis situations. Beer's new thinking on management structures that embraced the tension between top-down and bottom-up decision making used that tension to increase the stability of the overall organization (the Viable System Model).

These similarities were not a result of fully shared political convictions. Unlike Allende, Beer was not a Marxist. However, he did describe himself as a socialist on multiple occasions and reported voting for the British Labor Party. Although Beer did not specify where he positioned himself on the spectrum of British socialism, his position was closer to Fabian socialism, a British intellectual movement that favored a peaceful reformist approach to socialism (instead of revolutionary armed conflict) and that had influenced the formation of the Labor Party.[97] Beer thus would have been sympathetic to the aims of Chilean democratic socialism, even if he was not centrally concerned with Marxist ideas such as class struggle and even though he made a comfortable living as an international management consultant. Such sympathies may have further increased Beer's willingness to assist the Allende government. However, there is nothing in Beer's early writings to suggest that his approach to adaptive control was shaped by any political ideology. While Beer did believe that cybernetics and cyberneticians had the power to create a better world through the regulation of complexity, and had a social responsibility to do so, he was not a socialist revolutionary.

Therefore, what brought Flores and Beer together was not shared politics per se but rather conceptual commonalities in specific strains of scientific and political thought that Flores recognized and Beer appreciated. These conceptual similarities drew Beer and Flores together despite their different cultural and political convictions. This connection was furthered by Beer's enthusiasm to apply cybernetic thinking and operations research techniques in the domain of politics.

The resulting collaboration of Beer and Flores would spur the design of a technological system that would reflect the distinguishing features of Chile's revolutionary process and bear the hallmarks of Beer's cybernetic work. In the process, it would change the lives of both men. This unique merger of cybernetic curiosity and political necessity would lead to one of the most ambitious applications of cybernetics in history, Project Cybersyn. This project would tackle key problems in the design of political, technological, and organizational systems and address them through the design of a political technology. Project Cybersyn would undertake the questions of how to maintain the stability of a system while facilitating change, how to ensure the cohesion of the whole without sacrificing autonomy, and how to find a balance between vertical and lateral forms of communication. This project stemmed from a conviction that Beer and Flores shared in 1971, namely, that marrying management cybernetics to Chilean socialism could further political, economic, and social change in Chile.

2 Cybernetics in the Battle for Production

I really do have the most extraordinary feelings about this situation.
—Stafford Beer, letter to Fernando Flores, 29 July 1971

Imagine receiving a request from a national government that wanted to use your ideas to help run a country and for a utopian project that you believed in. In Stafford Beer's case this opportunity eclipsed the size, scope, and complexity of his previous projects, such as those he accomplished in the steel industry and in the world of publishing. It also gave him an opportunity to flesh out and test some of his newer cybernetic ideas, including the Viable System Model and the Liberty Machine, and make his "arguments for change" more than rhetoric.[1] Beer described quite clearly the intellectual thrill produced by the Chilean invitation: "I had an orgasm," he said.[2] From the perspective of his professional development, intellectual curiosity, and personal beliefs, Chile had offered Beer a dream scenario, and it is easy to understand why the cybernetician decided to travel halfway around the world to work with the Chilean government.

Why Fernando Flores, the general technical manager of the State Development Corporation (CORFO), believed management cybernetics could help the Chilean government is a more complicated story. I provided a partial answer to this question in chapter 1 by tracing the conceptual similarities between Beer's management cybernetics and Chilean socialism. However, cybernetic management addressed a central challenge in the Popular Unity program, namely, raising production levels in Chilean industries, especially in the growing state-run sector of the national economy.

As the Chilean government began bringing the country's most important industries under state control in Allende's first year as president, and as it began to follow the path he charted for the Chilean revolution, it faced numerous challenges. Flores was clearly thinking outside the box when he decided to contact Beer in July 1971. But management cybernetics did address the multifaceted problem of industrial management that Flores was confronting. Examining this problem illuminates why someone in the trenches of the economic nationalization process would consider management cybernetics an approach worth pursuing and support building a high-risk technological system for economic management.

This part of the story begins with Allende's election. It illustrates why, from Flores's perspective, it seemed that the Popular Unity economic program could benefit from management cybernetics and shows that political innovation can lead to technological innovation.

Salvador Allende Gossens was a medical doctor whose training introduced him to the afflictions of the poor while he was still enrolled at the university.[3] He became a socialist when he was twenty-four and entered politics fighting on behalf of his cousin Marmaduke Grove, the air force commander who became Chile's first Socialist president for twelve days in 1932. After establishing a branch of the Socialist Party in his hometown of Valparaíso, Allende quickly rose through the ranks and was elected to Congress in 1937 and named minister of health in 1939. He was elected to the Senate in 1945 and subsequently ran for president in 1952, 1958, 1964, and again in 1970. Unlike many of his more radical contemporaries, Allende always favored pursuing socialist reform through existing democratic practices and consistently pushed for a leftist agenda from the Senate floor and later from the presidential palace.

Allende's election as president radically changed the path of Chilean history. His 1970 victory signaled the success of the leftist Popular Unity coalition, which brought together Socialists, Communists, and small factions of the Radical Party and the MAPU, a small party led by a tiny faction of former Christian Democrats. Allende's winning margin was slim—1.3 percent—over his closest competitor, the rightist candidate and former president Jorge Alessandri, who had defeated Allende in 1958 by a similar margin. However, Allende had won a plurality, not a majority, in a tight three-way race. Technically, Popular Unity had won the electoral support that it needed to begin implementing its forty-point program of economic and social reforms. However, the country remained sharply divided about the correct path for the nation.[4] Still, Allende had reason to feel optimistic. Two of the three candidates for the presidency had run on a platform of change. Both Allende and the Christian Democratic candidate, Radomiro Tomic, had stressed the need to accelerate the social and economic reforms begun by Allende's predecessor, Eduardo Frei Montalva (1964–1970). Between them, Allende and Tomic had won nearly two-thirds of the vote, allowing Allende to claim that a majority wanted structural change in Chile. In this context Allende believed that he could increase his base of popular support and leverage it to implement change democratically, rather than by force, using Chilean legal and political institutions. It would be a revolution with the taste of "red wine and empanadas."[5] Change would occur without sacrifice and would have a distinctively Chilean flavor.

The success of the UP in the 1970 election vaulted Chile onto the world political map and drew international attention, particularly that of the United States and Europe.[6] Although many progressives believed that Chile would pioneer a political third way between the ideological poles of the superpowers, such a possibility was both frightening and inspiring in those cold war years. U.S. government documents reveal that on the day of Allende's election, U.S. Ambassador Edward Korry sent eighteen cables from Santiago to Washington, D.C., apprising the Nixon administration of the latest poll results. According to Secretary of State Henry Kissinger, "Nixon was beside himself" because of the election returns and promised to "circumvent the bureaucracy" in the future.[7]

On the morning of 15 September 1970, eleven days after the election, Nixon held a private breakfast meeting with Kissinger, Pepsi Cola chairman Donald Kendall, Attorney General John Mitchell, and Augustín Edwards, owner of the conservative Chilean newspaper *El Mercurio* and a Pepsi Cola bottling plant. Edwards pleaded for Nixon's assistance in keeping Allende from assuming the presidency and predicted disaster for the region if he did. A report from Senator Frank Church's Select Committee on Intelligence Activities, which documented covert action in Chile from 1964 to 1973, reveals that after this meeting Nixon met with CIA Director Richard Helms and instructed the agency to prevent Allende from taking power by arranging a military coup d'etat. Nixon did not inform the State Department, Department of Defense, or the U.S. ambassador in Santiago. In addition, the Church Committee report, *Alleged Assassination Plots Involving Foreign Leaders*, asserts that Helms left the meeting with a page of handwritten notes authorizing a budget of $10 million—"more if necessary"—to prevent Allende's confirmation, as well as instructions to "make the [Chilean] economy scream."[8] These instructions evolved into Project FUBELT, a covert operation that resulted in the death of Chilean Army General René Schneider but failed to provoke a military coup or block Allende's confirmation. Nixon's instructions also set the hostile tone for U.S. policy toward Chile from 1970 to 1973, which was marked by an "invisible economic blockade" and a multitude of covert CIA initiatives designed to destabilize the Allende government and to set up its overthrow. These operations, which cost the CIA $8 million, ranged from the manipulation of the Chilean media to "direct attempts to foment a military coup."[9] Historians are still uncovering the full extent of these initiatives.

Stafford Beer arrived in Chile on Tuesday, 4 November 1971, the first anniversary of the Allende government. On that same day the president addressed the Chilean people directly from the National Stadium in Santiago and detailed what his government had achieved during the preceding year. This unorthodox move broke from the traditional presidential practice of delivering one annual state of the union address before Congress in May. Allende promised that his government would continue to communicate directly with the public. He opened by telling the crowd gathered in the national stadium, and those listening to radio and television broadcasts of their *compañero presidente*, "Chileans, people of Santiago, a year ago . . . the people said, 'We shall win,' and we did."[10]

The president listed many accomplishments during the speech; among the most important was the nationalization, intervention, or expropriation by the government of Chilean- and foreign-owned enterprises.[11] Through these actions "Chileans have recovered what belongs to them, their basic wealth which was formerly held by foreign capital. . . . Today we can speak of our copper, our coal, our iron, our nitrates, and our steel."[12] Because of these significant strides, Allende now had a pressing need in his second year to find ways to manage the new and ever growing public sector.

Allende's speech amplified the excitement that had taken hold in the capital city. Several weeks earlier Chileans had learned that one of their own, the poet Pablo Neruda, had won the Nobel Prize for literature. The Swedish academy described Neruda as one who "brings alive a continent's destiny and dreams."[13] According to Chilean newspapers of the period, Chileans of every political persuasion were proud of Neruda's prize and the international recognition it bestowed upon their country. However, given Neruda's public support for the Popular Unity government—he was Allende's ambassador to France—and his long-standing membership in the Communist Party, the prize could also be viewed as validating the Chilean path toward socialist change. This angle was not lost on Allende, who observed that, with the award, "the quality of Neruda the poet, our country with its popular government and the Communist Party of Chile are being recognized."[14] Neruda's triumph gave the parties of the Popular Unity coalition a common reason to celebrate, but like-mindedness was fleeting. As 1971 drew to a close, ideological fissures within the coalition continued to deepen. In December 1971 the Communist Party publicly criticized the government's strategy for gaining control of the national economy because it emphasized speed instead of a gradual process of economic consolidation.

Beer's visit also coincided with another significant event. On 10 November 1971, six days after Beer's arrival, Fidel Castro landed in Santiago to lend his support to Chile's revolutionary process, marking the end of Cuba's political isolation in the hemisphere. His visit intensified the hopes and fears that Chileans associated with the Cuban revolution and roused the media, especially as Castro extended his ten-day trip to more than three weeks and filled his schedule with public appearances, speeches, interviews, and headline-grabbing antics. Chilean media outlets of all political sympathies covered Castro's visit heavily. The leftist publication *Clarín* described the public reaction to Castro's visit as the "the most magnificent reception in history," a statement that illustrates the level of public attention Castro received even if it is grossly exaggerated. Others hoped that conservative, law-abiding Chileans would catch the revolutionary fever. "Chile is not a revolutionary country and you are a symbol of revolution," Chilean author Manuel Rojas observed in an editorial addressed to the Cuban leader. "You will not gain anything from visiting Chile, but it is possible that Chile will benefit from your visit. . . . You not only represent your country, you represent the Revolution, its spirit."[15] Castro's presence evoked a strong reaction from the opposition press, which published ad hominem attacks against him. His visit also prompted the first public demonstrations in opposition to the Allende government, hinting at the public demonstrations that were to come.

Given the media circus that surrounded Castro and the polarized reaction he evoked among Chileans, it is no surprise that few noticed the presence of a British cybernetician despite his memorable bearded visage. "Most of the Chilean guys went to see Fidel Castro," Flores recalled. "I went to see Stafford Beer. It was kind of a joke."[16] Despite Beer's relative anonymity, the Chilean government treated him well during his stay. Flores used his position within CORFO to secure the funds needed to cover Beer's salary and travel expenses. Beer received a daily fee of US$500 (equal to approximately $2,650 in 2009 dollars) for the ten days he spent in Santiago.[17] The government also reserved a room for Beer at the posh Hotel Carrera, located across the street from the presidential palace, and first-class airline tickets on LAN Chile, the national airline.[18]

Flores and Beer began work immediately, applying cybernetic principles to Chilean economic management. Flores had already recruited a small team to work with Beer; most were Flores's former colleagues at the Catholic University. Many, like Flores, were also members of the MAPU; all were university-trained experts in science and technology. "It was very informal at the beginning, like most things are. You look for support in your friends," Flores said.[19] The team met at the headquarters of the State Technology Institute, the government research and development center also known by its Spanish acronym, INTEC. Flores served as chairman of the institute's board, in addition to his position at CORFO, and had the power to allocate institute resources for the project and to recruit expertise. The initial group included the vice director of the institute, José Valenzuela, who was a friend of Flores and a former professor; Jorge Barrientos, a university classmate who worked at the institute in operations research; Lautaro Cárcamo from CADE, a private Chilean consulting company in business administration, which often hired graduates of the Catholic University; Raúl Espejo, an industrial engineer who met Flores at the Catholic University and subsequently became an operations research scientist at CORFO; Hernán Santa María, a respected math professor from the Catholic University; Eduardo Navarrete, who studied at the Catholic University, joined the MAPU, and then worked for the Industrial Projects Division at CORFO; Gui Bonsiepe, director of the industrial design group at the institute who had taught at the Catholic University; and Alfredo del Valle, chief of planning for CORFO's energy sector, who held an engineering degree from the Catholic University and was active in the MAPU.[20] In addition, Flores hired Roberto Cañete, a former navy officer, university-trained mechanical engineer, and U.N.-certified Spanish-English translator. Cañete served as Beer's interpreter when he was in Chile and later assumed a more technical role in addition to these duties.

Although few Chileans knew of Beer's work, many members of Flores's handpicked team were familiar with Beer's book *Decision and Control* because of its recognized importance in operations research.[21] Several members had discovered Beer's work during trips to Europe or the United States, while others had learned about the cybernetician through conversations with Flores. However, by their own account they did not know much about cybernetics and lacked formal training in the area. In his memoir of the project Beer observed that "the general terminology of cybernetics was perfectly familiar to the team" from the first meeting on.[22] Beer might have placed too much faith in the initial preparation of his Chilean colleagues, for Espejo later noted that "simply reading a book [*Decision and Control*] and having conversations [about it] does not mean [we were] a group that was well trained in the area."[23]

Perhaps Beer's overstatement illustrates the level of faith he had in the abilities of his Chilean colleagues or the intellectual prowess that his new colleagues displayed during these first meetings. Espejo recalled that Beer brought them all up to speed with a thorough explanation of his cybernetic theories, such as the Viable System Model, and his considered responses to the Chileans' questions. They clearly were enthralled by what they were learning: when Beer gave manuscript copies of his still unpublished book *Brain of the Firm* to the Chileans, they had finished reading it by the time he returned to London. This is an impressive feat, considering the length of the text, its level of technical detail, that it was written in English, and that many of the Chileans had other job duties quite apart from cybernetics.

Beer acted as both teacher and student in Chile. He presented his work in cybernetic management to Chilean scientists, engineers, and politicians and taught them its concepts. At the same time, he also needed to understand the nuances of Chilean politics and the government's plan for peaceful socialist change. Flores arranged for Beer to meet with people outside the project team who might help the cybernetician understand the transformation under way. In this context Beer met Herman Schwember, a former lecturer in the Catholic University's engineering school and a member of the MAPU.[24] When Allende became president, Schwember had left the university and was working in the national copper industry, a job he described as technical, not political. But Schwember had a keen understanding of Chilean politics, a talent that helped solidify his friendship with Flores. When Flores asked Schwember if he would like to discuss Chilean politics and economics with Beer, Schwember agreed because he "felt that it [would be] interesting to meet this famous guy."[25]

Three days after Beer arrived in Chile, Schwember and Flores went to see him at the Hotel Carrera. Schwember's first impression of the cybernetician was not entirely positive when he discovered one of Beer's hallmark eccentricities. "I remember that Stafford was very shocked because he had lost his cigars and his chocolates. And in those days it was impossible to buy those things in Chile. He had three obsessions: chocolates, cigars, and whiskey. . . . It sounded to me a bit silly," Schwember said. "Eventually, well, when I became more friendly with him . . . I discovered that in those days he was living on whiskey, chocolates, and cigars."[26] That night Schwember and

Flores discussed Chilean economics and politics with Beer, and Schwember doubled as an ad hoc translator for Flores. Although Schwember was not yet an official member of the Flores team, he also participated in conversations Beer had with Flores, Bonsiepe, and others (see figure 2.1). Later, Schwember would play an important role in applying cybernetic principles to the Chilean revolution.

Beer also met with and learned from high-ranking members of the Allende government, including Oscar Guillermo Garretón, the undersecretary of economics. Although he was only twenty-seven, Garretón was on the front line of Allende's economic nationalization process, and he had a reputation for siding with Chilean workers. Six months earlier he had directed the controversial expropriation of the Yarur Textile Mill, the first factory taken by its workers and nationalized against the explicit wishes of President Allende. Photographs of Garretón from the era show a young man with dark curly hair and a beard playing a guitar in celebration of a factory takeover or marching in solidarity with factory workers, despite his high-ranking position in the government. Garretón described Beer as "an odd gringo," but found him to be both enthusiastic and knowledgeable.[27] Beer noted only that Garretón "was much calmer than Fernando," an observation that perhaps says more about Flores. With Cañete translating, Garretón explained his impression of the complex changes under way in Chile. Beer reported spending substantial time studying Chilean history and politics before he went to

RESTAURANT CURA NÚRIN VINA DEL MAR (CHILE) 1971

Figure 2.1
Gui Bonsiepe, Stafford Beer, Herman Schwember, and Fernando Flores in Viña del Mar (1971). Image reproduced with permission from Constantin Malik.

Santiago, and this preparation no doubt helped him absorb the waves of information presented by Garretón and others during his short visit.[28]

Allende's First Year

Archived source materials do not permit a complete reconstruction of what Beer learned during this initial visit. However, his surviving notes from these meetings are quite detailed and devoid of political slogans, although they do contain discussions of Marxist theory. They also list the achievements and shortcomings of the Popular Unity economic policies, presenting a remarkably balanced view, given the polemics and the ideologically polarized state of Chilean politics.

Beer learned many details of the economic program Allende had put in place the previous year. Structuralist economics and Keynesian "pump priming" had achieved economic growth through increased purchasing power and higher employment rates. Land reform programs and the inception of government-sponsored assistance to rural workers boosted the spending power of people in the impoverished agrarian sector. Given the government's lag in publishing statistical data, it is doubtful that Beer knew the precise magnitude of these changes, but they were substantial. By November 1971, workers in Chilean factories had realized a 30 percent average increase in real wages.[29] As a result, a growing segment of the population had money to spend, thus stimulating the economy, increasing demand, raising production, and expanding the popular base of support for the UP coalition. In the Allende government's first year, the gross domestic product grew by 7.7 percent, production increased by 13.7 percent, and consumption levels rose by 11.6 percent.[30] By the end of 1971, the government had transferred all major mining firms and sixty-eight of Chile's most important industries from the private to the public sector.[31] The speed of the changes must have impressed Beer, who often criticized governments for their sluggish bureaucracy and inability to implement change.

Chile was fighting a "battle of production," meaning that it viewed raising industrial production levels as key to the success of Chilean socialism and aimed to do this by taking control of the "commanding heights" of the economy.[32] Allende's key political goal was to bring about a socialist transformation using a democratic framework. However, he knew that the economy played a central role in this process; he could not make Chile socialist unless he could also make the economy thrive.

Another vital part of the battle of production was nationalization. The government planned to purchase Chile's most important industries and bring them under the control of the state. Industries would be put in either the Social Property Area, where the state was the sole owner, or the Mixed Property Area, where the state shared ownership with private investors (see appendix 1, which discusses the state-run areas of the economy in greater detail). Allende placed both areas under the control of Flores's agency, CORFO. This agency had been formed in 1939 as part of a national program for economic recovery from the Great Depression. Its mission was to expand and develop mining, agricultural, commercial, and industrial activities; promote the national consumption of Chilean goods; increase national production levels; and introduce the practice of economic planning to improve national living standards.[33] Although it had no experience directing the most important industries in the Chilean industrial apparatus, by the end of 1971 it was responsible for more than 150 enterprises, including twelve of the twenty largest companies in Chile.[34]

To make the Social and Mixed Property Areas more manageable, CORFO divided them into four branches: consumer goods, light industry, building materials, and heavy industry. Within each branch CORFO identified a number of industrial sectors. For example, the consumer goods branch contained the food, textile, furniture, and pharmaceutical sectors; and the light industry branch contained the automotive, rubber and plastics, copper manufacturing, and electronics sectors. Sector committees oversaw the operation of the individual enterprises within their purview and the activities within the sector as a whole. At the level of the enterprise (which might have more than one factory), the government appointed one or more *interventors* (a Chilean coinage) to manage day-to-day activities in place of its previous owners and executives. Beer's notes indicate that he had a clear understanding of the structure of the State Development Corporation and the structure of the state-controlled economy by the time he returned to London.

Although the government had a defined structure for the Social and Mixed Property Areas, it had not been clear, or consistent, in articulating the process for bringing enterprises into these areas or in stating the criteria for nationalization. Even Beer used vague language to describe how the enterprises transferred to state control, and simply noted that the two hundred enterprises the government marked for nationalization would be "integrated into the state in var[ious] ways."[35] The government had legally expropriated the copper mines through congressional legislation, and hoped to purchase the remaining enterprises that made up the "commanding heights" of the economy. By December 1971 the Allende administration had bought most of the twenty-three private banks, including major foreign-owned banks such as Bank of America and First National City Bank, giving the state control of two-thirds of national bank credit. Yet many owners of Chile's most important manufacturing industries, many of them family-owned, refused to sell.[36]

Allende turned to a decree passed in 1932. Written during the Great Depression, the decree gave the executive the power to intervene in the management of an enterprise that produced goods of primary necessity if it could not maintain its production levels or if there was a labor dispute that could not be resolved. The government could create these conditions easily. The Christian Democrats accused the administration of encouraging workers aligned with the left to go on strike and stop production. Once production stopped, the government could send an interventor to the enterprise to replace its managers or executives and intervene in factory production practices by bringing the newly nationalized factory under the control of the state. In theory this intervention was temporary, but it was also indefinite. Owners retained their legal rights of ownership, but they were powerless to run their factories and, moreover, were responsible for the debts incurred by the government interventors. Popular Unity policies increased salaries, raised employment levels, and fixed prices, which made it easy for an interventor to make an enterprise not profitable, especially if the government wanted to squeeze an owner to sell. The government's strategy for acquiring industries produced conflict among the political parties. In July 1971 the Christian Democrats accused the government of abusing the 1932 decree to acquire desirable industries. They proposed an amendment that would require congressional approval for all acts of intervention and requisition. If enacted, the amendment would weaken Allende's executive power considerably.

The rapid pace of the government's nationalization program, coupled with its lack of a clear, consistent structure and delimitation, stirred the fears and insecurities of owners of small- and medium-sized Chilean businesses. It did not help that the government began to lose control of the nationalization process six months after Allende became president. Although Allende had stated that the revolution would be controlled from above, government promises of social change set in motion a revolution from below—workers took control of their factories, and peasants seized control of their lands. Fewer than 25 percent of the firms expropriated during Allende's first year had been on the government's list for incorporation into the public sector.[37]

Beer knew that management had become a central concern in the nationalization process and that the government planned to prioritize industrial management in its second year. At a fundamental level the rapid growth of the nationalized sector created an unwieldy monster that the government had no experience in regulating. The increasing number of industries under state control and the number of employees within each industry presented the government with the difficult task of managing an economy that became harder to monitor with each passing day. The newly formed sector committees had undefined roles, and we know from his notes that Beer viewed the committees as having adopted three distinct approaches. Some held more of a support role than a management role, some took a very active role in enterprise management, and others put political management above all else. Early attempts by CORFO to implement mechanisms for centralized industrial management also met with frustration. For example, the government sent forms to the nationalized enterprises requesting information about production, sales, labor, finances, and investment, but the responses were overly general and not useful. Beer blamed these unhelpful responses on the lack of direction the enterprises received from the government.[38]

Increasing worker participation in the state-run factories (co-management) constituted another challenge for the government.[39] In December 1970 the Allende government formed a joint commission with the National Labor Federation (CUT) to create a
new form of participatory management in the state-run enterprises. By June 1971 they
had produced a document known as the basic norms of participation (*normas básicas
de participación*) that outlined a new structure for worker co-management. Among other
things, the document called for the creation of administrative councils, new decision-
making bodies at the enterprise level that would consist of blue- and white-collar
workers and state representatives. Although the government supported the measures
outlined in this document, it did not make them law. As a result, sector committees
and state enterprises interpreted the document in their own way and at their own pace,
increasing the inconsistencies in state management. Power struggles between newly
elected worker representatives and union leaders, who had previously acted as the sole
representative of labor, further complicated the situation.[40]

Government interventors also created problems. Although many were competent
and dedicated to their jobs, others were severely unqualified for the positions, and
some were corrupt. In textile manufacturing, for example, the government had only
one qualified textile engineer to appoint as an interventor, yet in May 1971 alone the
government had brought twelve textile firms under state control.[41] The problem of effectively managing the new Social and Mixed Property Areas was exacerbated by the
decision to distribute appointments equally among the political parties, regardless of
the level of competency found in their respective talent pools. Even parties within the
UP coalition criticized Allende's choice of interventors: members of the Communist
Party argued that some interventors merely replaced the managers who had preceded
them, occupying similar houses and driving similar cars.[42] From the Communists' perspective, not only did these representatives fail to provide an adequate means of bringing production under the control of the people, but they also helped veil a continuing
status quo. Daily operations within the factories suffered further from the political
strife caused by interventors who saw themselves as representatives of their party. At
times workers in some enterprises refused to listen to managers who hailed from political parties different from their own; this in turn necessitated a frustrating process of
party meetings and negotiations.[43] In addition, the interventors often had extremely
difficult jobs. After the government nationalized the BIMA lumber mill, for instance,
its manager left the country and took important information about the mill's operation
with him—including the list of the mill's clients.[44] Moreover, government price freezes
almost guaranteed losses in the Social Property Area, and, unlike the owners of private
businesses, government-appointed interventors could not make up for these losses by
selling goods on the black market.

Beer most likely did not know all the difficulties facing the appointed interventors
or the full extent of the problems they caused. He did receive several briefings on the

state of Chilean economic management, and the example of the BIMA lumber mill comes directly from his notes. He also knew that many government appointments were made on the basis of patronage, and that this caused problems. Such patronage "blocks internal reform" and creates "overstability," or the inability of an organization to change, Beer noted.[45] Given the inexperience of many interventors and the size of their task, Beer encouraged the government to put some of its best managers at the level of the sector committees, not the enterprises, so that they might assist in the direction of multiple enterprises.[46]

Additional challenges originated outside Chile. Foreign investors in Chilean copper mines and telecommunications companies (for example, ITT) further complicated the situation by insisting that they be fully compensated for what the government had taken.[47] In September 1971 Anaconda Copper, Ford Motor Company, First National City Bank, Bank of America, Ralston Purina, and ITT met with U.S. Secretary of State William Rogers to discuss forming an economic blockade that would destabilize the Allende government. Although Beer and his Chilean colleagues could not have known the details of these international maneuverings, Beer's notes from his November 1971 visit show that he recognized the vital role of the U.S. government and international lending organizations in Chile's economic viability and the success of its socialist government.[48]

Beer could not address the threats posed by foreign multinationals and the U.S. government, but thinking cybernetically helped him identify ways to improve how the Chilean government managed its economy. For example, Beer identified places where the government could create new communications channels to facilitate data exchange and increase the speed of government decision making. Yet he also recognized the limitations of what he could do. Forming new government agencies or radically reorganizing existing government institutions might have brought the biggest improvements to state management capabilities, but speed was of the essence. The government did not have time to create a new regulatory agency, nor could it substantially overhaul an existing agency and rebuild it from the ground up.

Nevertheless, CORFO needed to change, and Beer and Flores both agreed that simple fixes, such as increasing the number of employees on the agency payroll, would not suffice. Flores felt the agency had to change its approach—and therefore its thinking—from one of state administration and long-term planning, which was its role during the previous administration, to one of action and daily decision making. This latter approach, Flores argued, was what the Allende government needed to implement its ambitious program of socialist change.[49] Beer also felt that CORFO needed to change its practices and worried that the "*quickest* solution" to managing the enterprises "will be imposed before any new thinking has time. Unless cyb[ernetics] can move faster."[50]

Beer and Flores imagined a dual role for cybernetic science. Cybernetic views of management, in particular the Viable System Model, could guide the organizational changes that CORFO required and prevent the implementation of quick fixes that could prove ineffective or detrimental in the long term. Cybernetic ideas about feedback and control could also shape the development of new technological systems to improve the management of the nationalized sector, from the shop floor to the offices of CORFO. Drawing from Beer's idea of a "Liberty Machine," such a system would act as a network of real-time information exchange and use mainframe computer technology. It would allow managers and government administrators to ground their decisions in current data and change their course of action quickly without being mired in government bureaucracy. Management cybernetics also offered ways to improve how the government received information from the state-run enterprises.

With these improved data flows, Flores and Beer believed that the government could increase its control over Chilean industrial activities and ultimately win the battle of production. Furthermore, management cybernetics promised to give the Chilean government economic capabilities that it lacked and sorely needed. For example, the creation of new information channels allowed the government to establish new points of management authority that could support inexperienced interventors. Improving government control over production also seemed vital, given that the government had to do more with less. Supply needed to keep up with the increased demand brought about by income redistribution programs, and it had to do so with drastically reduced levels of foreign credit and without the ability to import U.S.-made machinery and spare parts. Chile was going through a time of dramatic change. By promising to transform the economy into an adaptive and evolving organism, management cybernetics seemed to provide a way to keep Allende's economic program alive and well.

Chilean Computing in Context

During his first visit Beer learned the extent of the Chilean government's computer resources, most of which were controlled by the National Computer Corporation (ECOM). In 1971 the computer agency had access to four mainframe machines, of which three were IBM System/360 mainframes and one was a Burroughs 3500 mainframe, all of which were low- to mid-range machines.[51] Even though these machines were regarded as modern computer technology, Chile would need many more than four computers if each state-run enterprise were to have its own dedicated computer center that could then be linked to others to form a national information-sharing network.

The Chilean government did, however, have decades of experience in using computer and tabulating technology in its public administration. In the 1960s it had begun using state funds to make government workers computer-literate. There is no evidence that Beer knew of Chile's experience with computer technology; most likely he did not question how these four machines arrived in Chile or why Chile had created a national computer agency. Nonetheless, this history explains Chile's computer capabilities in the 1970s and illustrates the novelty of the computer system that Beer proposed to build.

IBM appears to have been the first company to sell tabulating machinery to the Chilean market. It began exporting such machines to Chile for government use as early as 1921.[52] IBM Chile quietly opened its first branch office in downtown Santiago, the fourth IBM office in South America, on 10 April 1929, with only two employees.[53] Both were charged with assisting the newly formed Chilean Statistics Bureau in its effort to conduct the population census for 1930 (see figure 2.2). Judging from advertisements of the period, Burroughs calculating machines, National Cash Register's cash registers, and Remington typewriters also secured a client base within Chile. Burroughs, for example, claimed in the pages of *El Mercurio* that, with forty-two years of experience, it could offer a "Burroughs machine for any business."[54] In 1929 alone, Chile imported 282 calculating machines, 786 adding machines, 390 cash registers, and 4,368 typewriters from the United States, sales totaling approximately $560,000, or $7 million in 2009 dollars.[55] IBM dominated the Chilean market for tabulating machinery until electronic computers came along; it then dominated the Chilean market for mainframe computers in the 1960s and 1970s. Therefore I will focus on the history of IBM Chile and will use it to give a brief overview of how tabulating machines, and then electronic computers, entered Chilean public administration, formed part of state regulatory practices, and motivated the Chilean government to form a national computer agency.

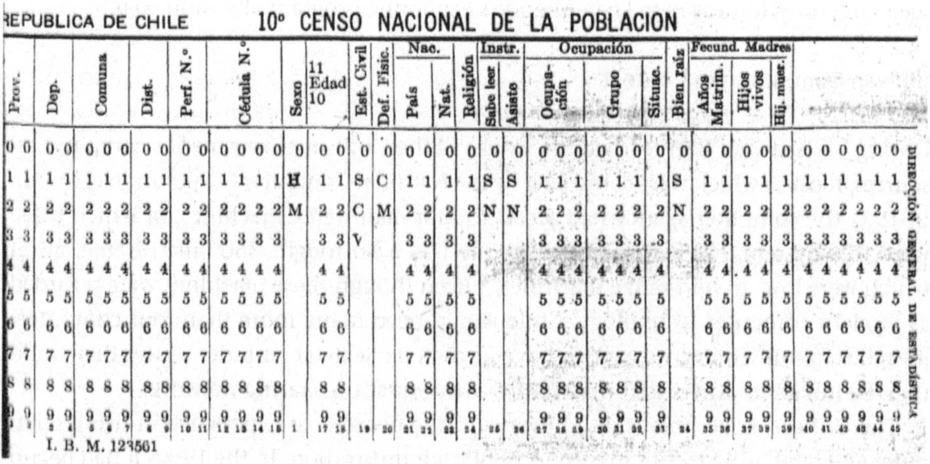

Figure 2.2
A punch card used in the 1930 Chilean population census. Image reproduced with permission from the National Statistics Institute, Santiago, Chile.

As tools for mechanized data processing, tabulating machines contributed to the massive expansion of the Chilean state that began in the 1920s and continued through 1973.[56] During the 1930s and 1940s the Chilean bureaucracy and IBM's Chilean operations expanded in lockstep, and the government remained one of Big Blue's best customers in Chile.[57] Despite an initial drop in sales in the early years of the Depression, IBM Chile continued to grow; by 1933 the number of its Chilean employees had swelled to twenty, and by 1939 seventy employees were on the payroll.[58] By 1956 IBM Chile had grown to more than one hundred employees, and it needed larger quarters. It relocated its central office in 1960 to a high-rise in downtown Santiago, where it occupied two floors. IBM now had contracts with the Chilean navy (1951), the National Petroleum Company (ENAP, which installed IBM unit record machines in Patagonia in 1957), and the Chilean Electric Company (1959). In 1962 IBM Chile started selling electronic computers, and the Customs Office, treasury, and air force all acquired IBM 1401 machines, a model that would not be available to the private sector for another year.[59] In 1963 the Chilean State Railroad Company and the Pacific Steel Company also acquired IBM 1401 machines. Appendix 2 provides a chronological overview of Chilean state expansion and the government's concurrent and increasing use of computers and tabulating machines from 1927 to 1964.

Computing under the Christian Democrats

From 1964 to 1970, Chilean politics shaped the state's adoption of computer technology, while dramatic changes in computer technology made new forms of state power possible. In 1964 Chileans gave 56 percent of the popular vote to Eduardo Frei Montalva. Also in that year, IBM released its highly successful System/360, a family of computers and peripheral equipment that IBM chair and CEO Thomas Watson Jr. called the most important in company history.[60] These developments, combined with long-standing government practices of using IBM unit record machines, helped provide the impetus for the Chilean government to form the National Computer Service Center, the predecessor of the National Computer Corporation.

Frei had won the 1964 presidential race on the platform of "revolution in liberty."[61] His victory represented a gain for the Chilean political center and for those who wanted a third way, other than capitalism or communism, of bringing about economic and social change. Frei's platform included plans to improve Chile's social conditions through increased public spending on education, housing, and health care; agrarian reform; the "Chileanization" (or state majority ownership) of the nation's copper mines; and programs to increase industrial production, foreign investment, and the use of advanced technology. These strategies were in line with the stated goals of United Nations development agencies and reform programs such as the U.S.-led Alliance for Progress.[62]

Centralized economic planning took on new levels of importance during the Frei administration, which presented Chile to the world as an ordered nation attractive to foreign investment and foreign aid. Under Frei's guidance the Chilean state grew to include new offices and agencies dedicated to centralized planning, administrative management, and data collection. During the previous administration the government had used tabulating machines for data processing and had introduced organization-and-methods techniques.[63] Applying powerful mainframe technology to state administration and management seemed a logical next step.[64]

Moreover, the Frei government had a natural disposition toward the use of mainframe technology, despite its high cost. Frei believed strongly in the promise of science and technology for advancing society and felt that the state should play an active role in support of both. These sentiments were no doubt bolstered by the substantial number of university-educated engineers, economists, and technocrats who held high positions within his party, the Christian Democracy. In 1967 Frei's government formed the National Commission for Science and Technology Research, known as CONICYT, an organization similar to the National Science Foundation in the United States, and charged it with directing Chilean science and engineering initiatives to meet national needs. The same year Frei formed the Commission for Data Processing within the Ministry of Finance to study the application of computer technology within public administration. In 1968 his government formed the State Technology Institute (INTEC), the research facility that Flores headed when Beer arrived in Santiago.

The 1960s also proved to be an important time for IBM. The company announced its new System/360 on 7 April 1964.[65] In the words of CEO Watson, the System/360 represented "a new generation—not only of computers—but of their application in business, science and government."[66] Developing the new product line was a risky move for IBM because it required a tremendous investment by the company. As *Fortune* magazine reporter Tom Wise wrote, the System/360 was "IBM's $5 billion gamble."[67] But the gamble paid off: orders for the new machines quickly outstripped what IBM could supply.

Mainframes from the 360 series quickly became sought-after commodities in Chile. IBM Chile sold its first IBM 360 mainframe to the Chilean private sector in 1966. When the University of Chile acquired an IBM 360/40 in 1967, President Frei himself attended the elaborate welcoming ceremony.[68] Because of the high price of the machine and its ability to process data around the clock, the university and the government reached an agreement whereby the mainframe would serve the research and teaching needs of the university and the data-processing needs of several government agencies, including CORFO and the National Health Service. This arrangement eased some of the demand within the Chilean public administration, but other agencies and government offices also wanted access to mainframe technology and could not afford to purchase their own machines.

On 5 September 1968, the Chilean government formally established the National Computer Service Center (EMCO) as an enterprise within the government. CORFO provided 80 percent of the computer center's initial budget, and the remaining 20 percent came from the State Telecommunications Enterprise and the State Electric Company.[69] The computer center was the culmination of Chile's gradual acquisition of computing machinery and expertise throughout the 1960s, its longer history of using punch-card tabulating machines in government, and the government's desire to centrally control the application of data-processing technologies. The computer center also represented Chile's financial limitations, for the nation could not afford to purchase a multimillion-dollar mainframe for the exclusive use of each government agency. Chilean law excused government agencies from paying tariffs, making the government one of the few early adopters of the imported technology, but even so the price of these machines and the limited availability of the foreign credit required to make their purchase possible presented a strong argument for centralizing Chilean computer resources.

On 16 January 1969, four months after the government established the National Computer Service Center, the agency celebrated the arrival of its first machine, an IBM 360/40 purchased with $2 million in French credit.[70] Frei again attended the arrival ceremony, but this time he also delivered a speech in which he linked the technology to the creation of a modern state and to "orienting, advancing, and coordinating all of its national activities"—goals that were central to his administration.[71] In 1970 the center purchased two more IBM 360 mainframes and, later, a Burroughs 3500 mainframe.

Some benefits from the new government computer service center were almost immediate. Establishing the computer center permitted the government to import more advanced, costlier technologies and gave smaller government agencies access to computers. Within six months EMCO was serving twenty-two government agencies.[72] In addition to purchasing and maintaining the government's computer machinery, the center provided advice, services, and training. According to the center's first general director, Efraín Friedmann, its initial tasks included creating a cost-effective system of computation; setting up compatible computer systems in every government agency so that the same data archive could be used in the future; and establishing an emergency training program to produce the specialists needed to carry out the first two goals.[73] The center also represented considerable gains in Chile's computing power. According to the United Nations, by 1970 Chile was home to forty-six computers, the majority in the public sector (table 2.1).[74] However, unlike the three IBM machines that EMCO had bought, most of these computers were outdated by 1970.

Chile had fewer computer resources than other nations in Latin America. In 1971 the index of Computer Industry Development Potential ranked Chile sixth out of twenty-one Latin America nations, putting it behind Argentina, Brazil, Mexico, Puerto Rico, and Venezuela. According to *Datamation*, Chile had substantially fewer machines than these other nations—Chile owned approximately 50 computers in 1970, whereas Argentina owned 445 computers, Brazil 754, Mexico 573, and Puerto Rico and Venezuela 300 each.[75] However, the National Computer Service Center, which changed its

Table 2.1
Number of Computers Installed in Chile by Year and Model

Year of installation	IBM 1401	IBM 1620	IBM 1130	IBM 360	NCR 315	NCR 200	Burroughs B-3500	PDP PDP-8	Other Models	Total
1962	3								1	4
1963	8								1	9
1964	10	2							2	14
1965	10	2							2	14
1966	13	3		1					2	19
1967	13	3	1	6	1				2	26
1968	14	3	3	8	1				3	32
1969	14	3	4	10	1				4	36
1970	14	3	8	12	1	3		1	4	46
1971	14	3	9	14	1	3	2	4	7	57

Source: United Nations, *The Application of Computer Technology for Development, Second Report of the Secretary General* (New York, 1973).

name in 1970 to the National Computer Corporation (ECOM), helped Chile centralize, and thus improve, the use of the machines it did have.[76]

The agency's computers ran short-term and long-term economic models that the National Planning Ministry used to formulate regional and national planning policies. The computers also registered Chilean imports for the Central Bank, tabulated the salaries and pensions for civil service employees, and scored the college entrance exams taken by Chilean high school students. The Ministry of Housing used the agency's services to record its expenses for paving roads and supplying drinking water. The agency's computers also helped to tally the results of the Fourth National Manufacturing Census, create a national registry of public service employees, and generate graphs that showed national electricity consumption.[77] In general the agency used its computers to perform traditional data-processing tasks for payroll, billing, inventories, pensions, payments, banking transactions, investments, and statistics. Sergio Molina, an economist who served as Frei's finance minister, credited the new computers with being "indispensable in diagnosing, analyzing, and implementing new methods and functional administrative procedures."[78]

The sheer amount of information collected and generated by the Chilean government between 1964 and 1970, coupled with its technological capabilities of rapid data processing, resulted in an extraordinary leap in the annual production of government documents and reports. The exponential increase in the number of punch cards processed annually by the Chilean treasury paralleled the rise in the number of pages it generated annually (table 2.2), as well as the greater length of the annual report that accompanied the presidential address to Congress (105 pages in 1965; 496 pages in 1967; and 1,075 pages in 1970, illustrated each year by ever more graphs and tables).[79] The Christian Democrats used computers to process large quantities of data that later appeared in graphs and charts in government reports and informed multiyear plans.

Beer proposed doing something quite different from the Christian Democrats, but he nonetheless benefited from the computer resources they had amassed and the structure they had created to manage those resources. For example, the Chilean government had attracted some of the nation's top computer talent to work at its computer corporation. Isaquino Benadof, who was running the Research and Development Department at the National Computer Corporation when Beer arrived in 1971, held a master's degree in computer science from Stanford University, one of the top programs in the United States. Benadof was one of Chile's first academically trained computer scientists. His technical abilities would later play an important role in translating Beer's ideas into working software code.

Because the state, not the private sector, owned the bulk of Chile's computer power, Beer had no trouble gaining access to the computers he needed, including the agency's most modern machines. After Allende's election, the state had centralized its control over Chile's computer resources to an even greater extent. From 1970 to 1973 the

Table 2.2
Data Processing and Documentation Output for the Chilean Treasury (1962–1969)

Year	Number of Punch Cards Processed	Number of Report Pages Produced
1962–64	540,000	231,000
1965–66	600,000	245,000
1967	2,307,000	736,000
1968	5,500,000	1,080,000
1969	5,200,000	1,200,000

Source: Sexto mensaje del Presidente de la República de Chile don Eduardo Frei Montalva al inaugurar el periodo de sesiones ordinarias del Congreso Nacional, 21 May 1970 (Santiago, Chile, 1970).

government assumed near-monopoly control over Chile's computer resources, including whether the private sector could import new machines and peripheral equipment, a change that reflected Chile's socialist transition and the heightened level of state intervention it demanded. Beer therefore needed only to secure support for his project from the National Computer Corporation; he did not have to worry about the conflicting demands or power struggles that might have ensued if he had needed to enlist various computer centers in different areas of the government.

Computers as Communication Networks

Beer imagined that his "Liberty Machine" would use computers to form real-time communication networks to permit rapid flows of information and data exchange and encourage the making of quick, informed decisions. Such a system could connect the State Development Corporation to the factory floor and help managers at both identify problems and maintain economic productivity. It would also give the government a bird's-eye view of the economy using current production data, rather than data compiled and published over the course of a year. This was a very different use of computer technology from the applications envisioned by the Christian Democrats, who in essence used mainframes as giant, expensive calculators. I will discuss the design of Beer's system in detail in chapter 3. For now it is sufficient to note that the system Beer imagined built on Chile's existing computer resources and would have been impossible without them, but it used them in ways entirely different from the ways Chile had used its computers in the past.

Building a computer network to manage the economy was not a new idea. In the late 1950s Soviet scientists and mathematicians had begun experimenting with ways to use cybernetics and computer technology to optimize national economic activity. The initial push for this application came from cyberneticians working for the Soviet military who hoped to create a centralized network of computing centers for national defense that could dedicate excess processing time to economic planning.[80] Yet Chile's first attempt to build a computer network did not involve defense funding, nor was it tied to military applications, both of which heavily shaped the early work on computer networking in the Soviet Union and the United States.

Soviet scientists had proposed building networks of "control machines" to assist economic decision making as early as 1956. By 1959 the Soviet Communist Party had given serious consideration to a proposal to automate economic management using large networks of electronic computers. In the 1960s the idea of optimizing the Soviet economy with computers became known as "economic cybernetics." Soviet mathematicians discussed constructing a technological system that would optimize production and replace the market by monitoring all labor, production, and retail activities. They detailed a complex three-tiered computer network that would use tens of thousands of local computer centers to collect "primary information." These local centers would be linked to thirty to fifty computer centers in major Soviet cities, and all the information collected at these midlevel centers would eventually flow to one central computer in Moscow dedicated to government use. In his study of Soviet cybernetics, Slava Gerovitch shows that this proposal for economic management by computer encountered significant resistance from managers, bureaucrats, and liberal economic reformers. While the first two groups feared the network would reduce their power or put them out of a job, the economic reformers worried that the network would set in stone ineffective forms of centralized economic planning and would prevent the introduction of market incentives to stimulate innovation and increase production. The proposed system also challenged the authority of the Central Statistical Administration and the State Planning Commission. With both agencies fighting to maintain their power, they could not agree on the structure or function of the network. Gerovitch notes that while this debate continued, other government agencies and enterprises built 414 independent information management systems between 1966 and 1970, no two of which were connected. In the early 1970s each government ministry built its own information management system. The different systems were not networked and were often built with incompatible hardware and software.[81] Thus the vision of a Soviet economy managed by networked computers never came to fruition.

The Soviet system was not a viable model for the Chilean government. By one estimate, the centralized design of the proposed Soviet system required monitoring fifty million variables, processing capabilities that well exceeded the capability of the four computers owned by Chile's National Computer Corporation. More importantly, the centralized design of the Soviet system ran counter to Allende's articulation of democratic socialism, a political project grounded in its respect for individual freedom and political compromise instead of government by iron fist. Beer was well aware of the Soviet approach to cybernetic management, and he viewed it with open contempt. He regarded the centralized approach as bureaucratic and overly complex, as well as vulnerable to manipulation. Factory managers and government bureaucrats could easily change the value of the data they submitted to the computer centers in order to put their management skills in a more favorable light.

A more successful example of computer networking was under way in the United States, but it was not a suitable model for the Chile project either. The U.S. Advanced Research Projects Agency (ARPA) had begun funding work on computer networking in the 1960s. It resulted in the creation of the packet-switching network known as the ARPANET, which later evolved into the Internet of today. ARPANET began operation in 1969 and connected four institutions in the western United States (the University of California–Los Angeles, the University of California–Santa Barbara, the University of Utah, and Stanford Research Institute) by the end of the year. Although it was originally envisioned as a tool that would allow institutions to share resources, its users quickly discovered that it was best used as a communication network. E-mail emerged in 1971 when users began experimenting with ways of sending electronic messages from one networked computer to another. In her study of the Internet's origins, Janet Abbate writes that e-mail "remade" the ARPANET system and caused it to be seen "not as a computer system but rather as a communication system."[82] By 1971 the ARPANET network had grown to fifteen nodes and spanned the continental United States, a significant accomplishment but still a long way from the Internet of today. Still, the 1971 version of the ARPANET network had almost four times the number of nodes that Chile could hope to build if it used all the resources held by the Chilean National Computer Corporation.

The ARPANET system was an unsuitable model for Chile for yet other reasons, not the least of which was the scarcity of mainframe computers. After Allende was elected, Burroughs opted to discontinue operations in Chile rather than risk government expropriation of its Chile office. IBM used its international scope to transfer more than eighty Chilean employees to other IBM offices throughout Latin America and Europe for the same reason. The size of IBM's Chilean operation was thus reduced to the bare minimum required to maintain existing service contracts and, the company hoped, would diminish its attractiveness to the government as a candidate for nationalization. These changes, combined with the hostile stance the U.S. government took toward Chile, prevented Chilean businesses and government offices from ordering additional mainframes from U.S. multinationals. The National Computer Corporation later began negotiations with the French computer company CII, but the CII machines were incompatible with the government's existing hardware and software systems and did not arrive while Allende was in power. Four nodes was the maximum size of the network the Chilean government could build using National Computer Corporation resources. Yet by September 1973 the nationalized sector of the economy contained more than four hundred enterprises.

Science in Context

Given the limitations of computer networking in the early 1970s, Beer's proposal to build a computer network in Chile, a country with approximately fifty computers—most of which were outdated—was extremely ambitious and not at all an obvious goal to pursue. However, from a broader perspective, building a computer system to manage the economy cybernetically did fit with the Popular Unity position on science and technology. The government would later be criticized for being antitechnology because of its growing inability to import capital machinery and spare parts and its willingness to make management appointments in Chilean industry based on patronage instead of technical qualifications. Yet, from the activity taking place in science and engineering circles during the first two years of Allende's presidency, it is clear that when the government had the resources to devote to science and engineering, it viewed laboratories and drawing boards as spaces for revolution, and believed work on national science and engineering projects would further Chile's socialist transformation.[83]

Describing the changes he saw in 1971, British journalist Nigel Hawkes wrote in *Science* magazine that "the application of science and technology are crucial to the success of the Chilean experiment."[84] These changes help to explain why Flores believed a technological innovation such as Project Cybersyn could contribute to Chilean socialism and why others in the government decided to back the ambitious cybernetic project.

The term *oriented research* had entered the Chilean lexicon during the Frei administration and took on even greater importance under Allende. It referred to the idea that Chile should use its science and engineering resources to address problems of national relevance. Later it also signified that the goals of the Chilean revolution, such as social justice and the domestic use of national resources, should guide the direction of science and engineering. Calls for orienting research emerged as part of the university reform movement of the late 1960s, which, among other things, challenged Chilean universities to strengthen the link between university activities and the need to solve national problems.[85] The practice of orienting Chilean science and technology toward national problems also fit with the economic framework of dependency theory, the new school of economic thought that was emerging from the Santiago offices of the United Nations Economic Commission on Latin America (ECLA). Dependency theory gained popularity toward the latter part of the 1960s and subsequently became an economic pillar of the leftist ideology.[86]

Dependency theorists criticized the import substitution policies that the Chilean government had first adopted during the Great Depression, when it tried to foster development through industrial growth. Unlike the import substitution model, which saw domestic industrial growth as a path toward economic development, dependency theory viewed capitalist industrialization as inadequate for ending the inequalities of the world capitalist system. U.S. foreign policy toward Latin America had maintained that all countries could become industrialized if given the right opportunities. In contrast, dependency theory cast underdevelopment as necessary for the developed world to amass its wealth. Underdevelopment was the very product of the existing global economic order. Transnational corporations based in industrialized nations, such as the United States and those in Western Europe, continued to own the means of production in the practice of the import substitution model. These corporations used their economic advantage to create local subsidiaries and thus to control the industrialization of Latin American nations and prevent them from achieving economic equality. Since every economic link behaved as a social link capable of establishing relations of domination and subordination, improving the Chilean condition required increasing national autonomy, decreasing the reliance on foreign capital, changing Chilean economic structures, and establishing Chile's economic centrality to the world market. Technology played an important role in this framework. According to dependency theorists, import substitution policies required Chileans to import foreign technologies from wealthy nations, creating a form of "technological colonialism" that forced Chileans to use technologies that suited the needs and resources of the wealthy nations while preventing alternative, local forms of knowledge and material life to flourish. Dependency theorists therefore encouraged Latin American nations such as Chile to orient their science and technology resources toward improving industry, harnessing natural resources, and educating a workforce able to address national problems.

Under Popular Unity, technologies thus became political instruments, and some high-ranking government technologists openly embraced their work as social rather than merely technical. For example, in 1971 José Valenzuela, the deputy director of the State Technology Institute, observed that "technology is not an end in itself but a means to achieve social objectives."[87] The State Technology Institute also questioned the idea of technological neutrality. "The myth of aseptic technological neutrality has been destroyed," announced an article in the institute's magazine, INTEC. "Extra-technologic decisions infiltrate techno-scientific work, although the subjective conscience does not always realize this and at times represses it." Contrary to the positivist thought that had dominated the twentieth century to date, the 1971 article observed that science and technology did not exist as "an untouchable king, undisturbed by conflicts and interests."[88] Directed national research-and-development efforts produced technologies tailored for Chilean industries which could boost their productivity while also being better suited for advancing UP social programs. By questioning the assumption that imported technologies were superior, Chilean scientists, engineers, and designers expanded the criteria for measuring technical superiority and introduced design considerations they had ignored in the past.

Funding for science and technology research and development increased from 0.39 percent of the gross domestic product to 0.49 percent in 1971 and 0.51 percent in 1972. According to the 1971 *Science* magazine article, the level of Chilean investment in research and development "[put] Chile clearly among the underdeveloped countries of the world."[89] It was far less than the 1.90 percent of gross domestic product that France spent on research and development in 1971, or the 2.48 percent of gross national product spent in the United States.[90] Moreover, in Chile much of this money was used to hire additional personnel because of the government's push to cut the unemployment rate. To cite one example, the National Commission for Science and Technology Research (CONICYT) grew from 40 employees to 280 employees during the Popular Unity years, and, rather than awarding competitive research grants, it used its budget to increase salaries.[91] State-sponsored research institutes such as the State Technology Institute saw their government funding increase significantly during this period, up by 38 percent between 1970 and 1971. Especially notable was the level of state funding for research activities at these institutes, which eventually surpassed the levels of government funding for science and technology research at the universities. Since members of the university community—including all the university presidents—openly guarded university autonomy and sought to limit state intervention in university life, including research activity, it makes sense that the government decided to invest more heavily in research institutions completely under its control.

Pursuing a technological solution for the problem of economic management conformed to the ideas of economic progress found in dependency theory, but only to a point. Through its novelty, such a computer system would help Chile assert its technological autonomy, even if it was built on a mainframe imported from a U.S. multinational under the watchful eye of a British consultant. Such a project, which would apply one of Chile's most advanced capital technologies to one of the nation's most pressing predicaments, would require significant resources, both human and technological—and it got them. Some of its money came from the State Technology Institute, whose budget continued to grow, and from CORFO, one of the best-funded government agencies in the country, given its job of directing the national economy. Flores, of course, held top management positions in both organizations, as third in the chain of command at CORFO, the development agency, and as board chair of the State Technology Institute. He was willing to use the full extent of his social and organizational network to secure the financial, material, and human resources the project required, and he secured most of these resources through informal channels. "I had a lot of power," Flores acknowledged. Even so, CORFO in particular was so immense that the project he proposed with Beer required only a small percentage of its budget.[92]

As the head of Chile's effort to use cybernetics to fight the battle of production, Fernando Flores's willingness to channel scarce technological resources, expertise, and foreign exchange reserves toward building an experimental technological system is striking, more so in a budget increasingly stressed by U.S. efforts to destabilize the Chilean economy. Yet it is understandable, especially given the specific nature of the economic problems Flores witnessed at CORFO and his personal belief that the Chilean state should emphasize action over planning and end the sluggish, bureaucratic behavior that had long characterized its public administration. Flores saw cybernetics as a way to increase government control of the state-run enterprises and to help it raise national production levels. Winning the battle of production was crucial to the success of Allende's economic program. Flores hoped technological innovation would give the government a needed edge, and therefore he decided to bring Stafford Beer to Chile. Now it was up to Beer to design a cybernetic system to maintain and, Flores hoped, to galvanize production on a national scale.

In October 1971 Minister of the Economy Pedro Vuskovic publicly acknowledged that government economic policies had dramatically reduced Chile's investments and depleted its foreign exchange reserves—its reserves had dropped from $343 million in 1970 to $32.3 million by the end of 1971. The price of copper, Chile's major export and key source of revenue, had been falling since Allende's election, making it impossible for the government to replenish its falling reserves with revenue from copper sales.

Yet at this point the Chilean government still believed it could overcome its economic challenges and win the battle of production, and in this context we can understand why Flores contacted Beer. Flores viewed the application of Beer's management cybernetics as one way to improve the management of the state-run enterprises and raise production levels. Management cybernetics also offered Flores a way to transform CORFO from a sluggish bureaucracy to an organization that was able to take action quickly and base decisions on recent economic data. Nevertheless, Flores's interest in creating a new technological system for economic management grounded in cybernetic thinking was not shared widely by his colleagues in CORFO.

Flores's decision to apply scientific ideas and expensive capital technologies, such as the mainframe computer, to the management problem was, however, consistent with the Popular Unity stance that science and technology should be used to solve national problems. Cybernetic management seemed to offer a way for Flores to transform the Chilean economy into an adaptive, evolving organism. It did so by creating new channels for communication and data sharing that allowed the government to collect recent economic data to use in its decision making. In October 1971, Flores believed that building such a technology could help make the Chilean economy thrive while advancing Allende's nationalization program. By now it was clear the Chilean revolution would not take place with empanadas and red wine. But perhaps it could be managed with cybernetics and computation.

3 Designing a Network

At last, *el pueblo.*
—Salvador Allende, November 1971

Stafford Beer, Fernando Flores, and the small Chilean team worked to exhaustion for eight solid days before Beer concluded his initial Chile trip and returned to London. At stake was the design of a computer system that would not only facilitate production in an economy in crisis but also instantiate the Chilean vision of socialist democracy. Because the technological solution they devised took into account Chile's technological and financial limitations, Beer and the Chilean team were pushed to use these resources in innovative ways. The system they proposed was grounded in the logic of Beer's cybernetic thinking and the beliefs of Chilean democratic socialism.

In this chapter I present the design Beer and the Chilean team proposed. I explain how the proposed system worked and show how the design of this system took into account the political values and political goals of the Popular Unity government as well as Chile's limited technological, financial, and human resources.

In addition, this chapter follows Beer and Flores as they started to transform their conceptual design into an engineering project that had an aggressive timeline for completion. Creating this cybernetic management system would push the boundaries of both Chilean and British expertise. Building this system quickly required a number of collaborative relationships between British and Chilean technologists, who had to tackle similar problems in parallel, often in consultation with one another. The system also drew from ideas and technologies developed in other parts of the world, specifically, the United States and the Soviet Union. It incorporated computer software and approaches to computer modeling from the United States and explicitly rejected comparable Soviet efforts to build computer systems for managing a planned economy. While the United States worried about Chile's going communist, these technological decisions are evidence that the Allende government did not intend to replicate Soviet socialism. Technologically Chile was, and tried to remain, connected to the United States, despite U.S. efforts to sever the relationship.

Technology for an Adaptive Economy

Beer prepared two reports during his November 1971 trip, one theoretical, the other a plan for action. The first report, titled "Cybernetic Notes on the Effective Organization of the State with Particular Reference to Industrial Control," mapped the Viable System Model onto the various levels of the Chilean economy, from the individual plants in the state-run enterprises to the president of the republic. This exercise allowed Beer to think cybernetically about the Social and Mixed Property Areas of the Chilean economy, where the government controlled industrial activity, and to translate this exceedingly complex system into a series of cybernetic models.

Through this cybernetic analysis Beer identified management problems in the nationalized sector and suggested solutions. For example, his report critiqued Chile's conventional planning methods, which used snapshots of the economy at discrete moments, inundated government managers with a sea of data, and managed from the top down. Instead, he proposed the idea of "roll-up," an iterative process wherein policies traveled down to the factories from the government and the needs of the factories traveled upward. He positioned management in the middle, where it formed a homeostat that coupled the needs of the lower levels with the resources allocated from above. Government officials could therefore change and adapt government policies to meet the needs of the factories, so long as such changes did not have substantial negative effects on other areas of the economy. Beer wrote, "THIS system destroys the dogmas of centralization and decentralization alike. This approach is *organic*."[1] The roll-up approach was also continual and adaptive in accordance with Beer's vision of cybernetic control. Moreover, it used cybernetics as a reference point for how the government might implement the democratic socialism that Allende proposed; it gave the state control of production but still allowed broad participation.[2]

The second report was a proposal for "Project Cyberstride," a "preliminary system of information and control for the industrial economy." It offered the first concrete articulation of a computer system the government might build to address the problem of economic management. Beer noted that the system, if built, would "demonstrate the main features of cybernetic management" and "begin to help [the government] in the task of actual decision-making by March 1972"—four short months away.[3] Project Cyberstride incorporated ideas from Beer's earlier writings, including the control room described in his essay "The Liberty Machine." The system would rely on data collected daily from state-controlled industries and would use mainframe technology to make statistical predictions about future economic behavior. The system would update these predictions daily after Chilean computer operators entered the new data arriving from the enterprises.

A communications network for real-time data exchange would form the backbone of Project Cyberstride. Connecting the State Development Corporation (CORFO) to the factory floor would create the conditions for "roll-up" management and allow the government to quickly address emergencies, such as shortages of raw materials, and adapt its policies accordingly. Up-to-date production data would also allow Chile's more experienced managers, placed at the level of the sector committees or higher, to help the less experienced interventors identify problems in their factories and change production activities in the enterprise when necessary to meet national goals. Beer envisioned that this information exchange would happen quickly, continually, and always with the goal of facilitating action. Communication, adaptation, and action were all core considerations of management cybernetics and, taken together, referenced the parallel that Beer drew between organizations and biological organisms. Both needed to adapt quickly to survive in a changing environment. Flores shared Beer's preoccupation with time; both men believed that data are wasted if they do not lead to action.[4]

In addition to the communications network and the software that would generate economic predictions, Project Cyberstride called for a computer simulation of the Chilean economy. Furthermore, members of CORFO would compile and display national production data in an operations room in a format that would be easy for government decision makers to understand. Such displays would help decision makers to visualize the state of the economy and create policies grounded in the current realities of Chilean industry.

The proposed design of Project Cyberstride took into account Chile's technical limitations. The director of the National Computer Corporation (ECOM), Raimundo Beca, offered Beer processing time on only one mainframe computer, an IBM 360/50—the top-performing mainframe machine owned by ECOM.[5] Given that the computer agency owned four mainframe computers, all in high demand, Beca's offer of one machine is understandable. But it meant Beer's team had to create a computer network that consisted of one computer.

As a solution to a seemingly impossible mandate, Beer offered a design for Project Cyberstride that consisted of a communications network attached to the single mainframe computer. To make this nontraditional network architecture work, Beer and the team needed to find a way to inexpensively transmit numerical data and text in close to real time over long distances. The solution seemed to be the telex, or teletype, machines which were connected to an existing network of telephone lines, satellites, or microwave channels. By the 1970s telex machines were widely used throughout the world and were hardly cutting-edge. Each telex machine had an identifying number, similar to a telephone number, which the user dialed to make a connection between machines. Users composed messages using the machine's keyboard, which it translated into holes punched on paper tape. The machine then read the tape and transmitted the message. Often users prepared the tape ahead of time to minimize connection costs, although the machines also permitted typed conversations between the users at each end. Once a message was received, the recipient machine printed the lines of text in a series of noisy clacks that bore a closer resemblance to an electric typewriter than a fax machine. In Chile in the early 1970s, telephones were a scarce resource and connections were unreliable. Telex machines offered an alternative way for Chileans to communicate nationally and internationally.[6] Thus Beer proposed that Project Cyberstride be built using a network of telex machines that the team could attach to the single IBM mainframe.

The system Beer proposed worked in the following way. Interventors would use the telex machines at their enterprises to send production data to the telex machine located at the National Computer Corporation. Chilean computer experts would then punch the data onto cards and feed them to the mainframe. The computer ran statistical software programs that compared the new data with those collected previously, searching for significant variations. If the program encountered such a variation, it alerted the computer operators, who would send the data over the telex network to CORFO and the interventors affected. As a result, CORFO would communicate with the interventors in order to better understand the situation and help resolve the problem, if one existed. Given the simplicity of telex technology, Beer and the Chilean team could build such a network with few technical challenges so long as they had access to the machines. And here the team hit a wall. CORFO owned only one or two teletype machines, and it did not have the funds to purchase more.

Gustavo Soto, a Chilean army major who worked for Flores at CORFO, gave the team its first break. He learned that ENTEL, the National Telecommunications Enterprise, had four hundred telex machines in storage. The Frei government had purchased them during the 1960s but never installed them. Raúl Espejo, a CORFO engineer who would later direct Project Cybersyn, the successor to Project Cyberstride, described the ENTEL storage space as "our Aladdin's Cave," laden as it was with telex riches. With this find the team could begin to build the network Beer proposed without needing to import additional telex machines right away. That had been a major concern, given Chile's dwindling foreign reserves and the invisible U.S.-led blockade.

Socialist Technology

Beyond the challenges posed by Chile's geopolitical problems and limited technological resources, Beer suggested that his design should address the issues of key importance to achieving democratic socialism in Chile. First, he wanted to create an honest, but accountable, relationship between factory managers and CORFO. Beer felt that the statistical profiles generated by the computer software would make it difficult for interventors to fake production data in the same way factory managers in the Soviet Union faked data when pressured to meet production goals. He believed Cyberstride would make anomalies obvious immediately, prompting further investigation. Cyberstride therefore offered another way for the government to distinguish Chilean socialism from that of the Soviet Union.

Second, Cyberstride, like the Viable System Model, tried to find a balance between autonomy and cohesion. For example, when the system detected a production anomaly, the National Computer Corporation would alert both CORFO and the factory intervenor. The government would then give the intervenor a limited window of time to resolve the problem on his own. The enterprises therefore maintained their autonomy to a reasonable degree. If the intervenor could not resolve the problem within this limited period, CORFO would intervene. Such intervention would limit the autonomy of the factory, but Beer reasoned it was nonetheless essential for preserving the viability of the entire economic system.

Third, the system's design reflected Allende's commitment to raising employment levels, a key part of the government program. Unlike concurrent uses of computer technology in industry, Cyberstride would use computers in a way that did not lead to unemployment. In industrial settings, computers are often linked to factory automation, which can raise productivity levels but also allow companies to downsize their workforce. Rather than automating labor or replacing management, Cyberstride would offer factory managers and CORFO a tool to help them increase factory productivity using the human and material resources available.

Work on Cyberstride would be spread across the State Development Corporation, the State Technology Institute, the National Computer Corporation, and the nationalized enterprises themselves. Completing the project required a broad range of expertise, beyond what Flores had already assembled. Beer suggested that the team should include an applied statistician, a mathematician, an operations research scientist (someone who was more interested in application than in mathematical theory), an economist, a social scientist, and a "computer man." The team also needed a director. Finding the right person "does not mean he has to be the best scientist," Beer observed; "Motivation and organizing ability are the top requirements" for this position. Most important, "none of these professionals is to despise the professional area of any other."[7] Successful interdisciplinary collaboration hinged on mutual respect and a willingness to benefit from the expertise and insights of others. But even collaboration had its limitations. In a footnote Beer made this cheeky observation: "All men (in an interdisciplinary team) are equal. (The director is of course more equal than others.)"[8] This final observation was perhaps a reference to the criticism that George Orwell—a vocal supporter of democratic socialism—had leveled against Stalinism in his classic work *Animal Farm*.

Beer proposed forming an additional team in London to write the software code. The coding would be complicated and required "OR insight as well as mathematical sophistication . . . in addition to programming skill."[9] Given the tight timeline for the project and the limited number of Chileans with the requisite expertise in all three areas, Beer felt it best to pursue other personnel options in Britain upon his return home.

In creating the proposal for Cyberstride, Beer fits the definition of a "heterogeneous engineer" proposed by the sociologist John Law—a technical expert who can move beyond the technical aspects of engineering and mobilize human as well as material resources to achieve a goal.[10] In addition to defining the technical specifications of Project Cyberstride, Beer charged himself with preparing "a presentation about this project and its implications" that would be "capable of 'selling' the whole idea of cybernetic control to [Chilean] Ministers and to Managers."[11] Having a novel and potentially useful idea was not enough. In fact, the novelty of his ideas had historically earned Beer detractors as well as supporters, and he suspected that changing Chilean government practices to conform to an untried computer system would be a difficult task, despite the desire of the government and its supporters to break with the ways of the past. The project could succeed only if Beer garnered the firm support of those at the highest levels of government and in the nationalized enterprises.

It is clear that Beer felt personally invested in the project from the outset. On a professional level Project Cyberstride gave him a unique opportunity to apply his cybernetics on a national scale and in a political context that shared conceptual similarities with management cybernetics. On a personal level he quickly formed friendships with Fernando Flores and his other Chilean colleagues, and he sympathized with the political aims of the Allende government and wanted the Chilean political experiment to succeed. Reflecting almost a decade later on how much the group had accomplished in one week and how much work it was planning to complete in the months ahead, Beer said, "It shows just how much proper preparation on all sides, the recognition of realities, monstrously hard work by all concerned, and burgeoning friendship, can do."[12] Although the cybernetician had other commitments scheduled in the coming months, he offered to devote all his available time to the project to help the team meet its March deadline.[13]

Beer and Allende

Beer presented Project Cyberstride to Oscar Guillermo Garretón, the undersecretary of economics, on 12 November 1971, and received his approval. The cybernetician then left the Ministry of Economics and crossed the street to the presidential palace, La Moneda, to secure the president's support. Although Allende had been briefed on the project ahead of time, Beer was charged with explaining the system to the president and convincing him that it warranted government support.

Accompanied only by Roberto Cañete, Beer's interpreter, Beer entered the presidential palace while the rest of his team waited anxiously at a bar across the street in the Hotel Carrera. "A cynic could declare that I was left to sink or swim," Beer later remarked. "I received this arrangement as one of the greatest gestures of confidence that I ever received; because it was open to me to say anything at all."[14]

According to Beer and Cañete, the meeting went quite well. When I interviewed Beer in 2001, he gave a detailed account of his meeting with Allende, which I have summarized in the paragraphs that follow. Thus Allende's responses come to us through the filter of Beer's memory thirty years after the meeting took place, and through Beer's account in *Brain of the Firm*, published ten years after the meeting. Still, the vividness of Beer's oral account indicates that the meeting left a lasting impression on him. Cañete confirmed Beer's account when I interviewed him in 2003.

Once Beer and Allende were sitting face to face (with Cañete in the middle, discreetly whispering translations in each man's ear), Beer began to explain his work in management cybernetics and the Viable System Model. Allende, who had trained as a pathologist, immediately grasped the biological inspiration for Beer's cybernetic model and nodded knowingly throughout. This reaction left quite an impression on the cybernetician: "I explained the whole damned plan and the whole Viable System Model in one single sitting . . . and I've never worked with anybody at the high level who understood a thing I was saying."[15] Beer knew he would have to be persuasive. He acknowledged the difficulties of achieving real-time economic control but emphasized that a system based on a firm understanding of cybernetic principles could, even with Chile's limited technological resources, accomplish technical feats deemed impossible in the developed world. Once Allende became familiar with the mechanics of Beer's model and with Project Cyberstride, the president began to reinforce the political implications of the project and insisted that the system behave in a "decentralizing, worker-participative, and anti-bureaucratic manner."[16] These words stayed with Beer and convinced him that the system needed to be more than a toolbox for technocratic management; it needed to create social relations that were consistent with the political ideals of the Allende government.

When Beer finally brought his discussion around to the top level of his systematic hierarchy, the place in the model that he had reserved for Allende himself, the president leaned back in his chair and said, "At last, *el pueblo* [the people]."[17] With this succinct utterance Allende reframed the project to reflect his ideological convictions and view of the presidential office, which often equated his political leadership with the rule of the people. This comment resonated with Beer because it upheld his belief that System Five should not consist of one person acting alone but should behave as a multinode, described in chapter 1 as a group of managers who are interconnected in complex, and often redundant, ways.[18]

"The only snaggy thing," Beer recalled, was when Allende asked, "'Are you going to use the Communist Party and all the apparatus that the Communists have developed in Moscow?'" Beer opted for a direct response: "I said, 'I'm sorry—it's all rubbish.'" Allende smiled, perhaps because he too was trying break from the Soviet model of socialism.

"I've never had an international consultant before," the president remarked. "How does it work?"

"I'm deeply respectful of your office," the cybernetician replied. "If I constantly am battering on your door, you would get very tired of me." However, "when people find out that I am working directly for you and have immediate access to you," Beer continued, "they will tend to do what I ask for." The president laughed and said, "Yes, I can see that." Beer suggested that the president allow him to lead the project with relative autonomy but added, "I won't do anything that I'm not sure of, and if I think I may not be sure, I'll come see you and ask. And then we shan't waste each other's time." This working relationship pleased the president, who, in Beer's paraphrasing, replied, "I like this. Well done." By the end of the conversation, Beer had secured Allende's blessing.

Beer returned triumphant to his team waiting at the Hotel Carrera bar. "I came back across the square, and I said, 'We're on!'" Upon hearing the news, the team "drank a lot and ate and had a heck of a time," Cañete said. The next day Beer returned to London.

The meeting between Allende and Beer is one of the best-known anecdotes of Beer's time in Chile. Here I have retold this encounter as Beer told it to me, interlaced with comments and observations from other interviews and written accounts. All accounts agree that Beer met with Allende to secure the president's permission to continue the project. However, Beer believed the meeting had an additional purpose. He suspected that Flores wanted to apply cybernetic principles more broadly in the Chilean government, beyond the management of the nationalized sector of the economy, and that the meeting would help Flores pave the way for future projects. Schwember, one of the more politically savvy members of the group, offered an alternative reading. Flores "is a man of a higher brain," Schwember said. "Very complex, sophisticated, shrewd. Sometimes devious. But very shrewd." As such, Flores recognized early on that the system had technical and political value. In Schwember's opinion, while Beer met with Allende to explain the cybernetic management system under development, the meeting also was for "Allende to realize that there was a guy, Flores, who had this power," who was a technical expert, and who was doing interesting, ambitious, and potentially valuable things for the government.[19] Most important, the meeting also sealed the working alliance between Flores and Beer and drew Allende into the project. It underlines the interdependence of technological innovation and political innovation that was taking place along the Chilean road to socialism.

Allende's second year started with setbacks in Chile's transition to socialism. On 1 December 1971, thousands of Chilean women took to the streets to protest consumer shortages and Fidel Castro's extended visit. Banging empty pots, the women marched toward La Moneda chanting slogans such as "Chile sí!—Cuba no!" and "The left has left us without food!"[20] Altercations between Allende supporters and opposition marchers, male and female, led to violence, and the police resorted to tear gas and fire hoses to subdue the crowd. Ninety-nine people were injured, ten seriously.

Allende dismissed the female marchers as wealthy women from upper-class neighborhoods who were manipulated by reactionaries rather than representing their own interests.[21] Yet Castro saw evidence of a growing counterrevolution that would challenge the model of democratic socialism articulated by Popular Unity, which in his view was fatally flawed. The day after the march he publicly denounced Chile's peaceful approach to socialist change. "All decadent social systems have defended themselves with tremendous violence throughout history," Castro said. "No social system has ever resigned itself to disappearing of its own free will. I will return to Cuba more of a revolutionary than when I came here! I will return to Cuba more of a radical than when I came here! I will return to Cuba more of an extremist than when I came here."[22] When Castro boarded the plane to return home, it was clear that he and Allende had very different views on revolutionary change and the methods to make it happen. Fundamentally, the two leaders differed in their understandings of sociopolitical systems and processes of change, a terrain that was also being explored by cybernetics and cyberneticians such as Beer.

Meanwhile Project Cyberstride was progressing smoothly. Beer used a telex machine in the London office of Chile's state copper company to maintain contact with his team in Santiago. These telexes are archived in Beer's papers at Liverpool John Moores University and permit a detailed reconstruction of how the project progressed over time. Beer also maintained written correspondence with several of his Chilean colleagues, especially Cañete, who by now was also in charge of building the telex network and was responsible for keeping Beer up to date on the project. Cañete also took it upon himself to describe Chile's changing political situation to Beer. Cañete's letters provide a valuable firsthand account of Cyberstride and the political context that shaped its creation.

On 21 December 1971, Flores sent a telex to Beer in Spanish stating that the government was sending Beer his fee of $10,000 (approximately $53,000 in 2009 dollars) to cover work from 15 November 1971 to 10 March 1972.[23] Flores estimated that the first telexes from the nationalized enterprises to the National Computer Corporation would begin in early January and said that the team hoped to have representative enterprises from four sectors—textiles, forestry, construction materials, and agroindustry—connected to the system by the time Beer returned in March.[24] In Britain, Beer also continued to work according to the ambitious timeline he and Flores had agreed upon, namely, to complete the programming for Project Cyberstride and start work on the economic simulator in less than three months.

Getting Started

The expertise that Project Cyberstride required and the time constraints under which the team was working led Beer to contract out part of the work to several British technologists in his network. Yet though the project team was transnational by necessity, the resulting collaboration was not an instance of British technologists' sharing their preformed expertise with members of the Chilean team. Building this new technological system to help manage the Chilean national economy required the British experts to think in new ways and augment their existing knowledge in areas such as statistical forecasting and computer modeling. The project gave British and Chilean technologists alike an opportunity to work on a new technological system for cybernetic management. In order to meet the tight deadlines, the Chilean and British teams had to work in parallel to code the system's software. In the case of Project Cyberstride, unidirectional models of technology transfer were both impossible and undesirable.

The Temporary Suite

In January 1972 Beer sought out his longtime friend David Kaye, who worked as a senior consultant for the firm of Arthur Andersen and Company. Beer asked whether the consulting firm would be able to design the software for Project Cyberstride and complete the programming by the ambitious March deadline. Arthur Andersen agreed to examine the situation and prepare an estimate before the end of the year.[25]

After reviewing the Cyberstride project proposal, the Andersen consultants returned with bad news. They could write the software Beer requested, but they would need twenty-three weeks to complete the task, well beyond the March deadline Beer had set. The consultants felt they could not code, test, and document the requested software in two months, especially since the Chilean government required code that was robust and bug-free.[26] They drafted a new schedule for the software project which put the delivery date in mid-June, three months behind schedule.

Beer thought the Andersen consultants could do better. He began a series of negotiations that he described as intense and time-consuming. He first asked if they could they prepare a preliminary version of the code by March and then continue the debugging process until June. The consultants refused but came up with an alternative: they could write and install a "temporary suite" by mid-March. This temporary code would accept only a limited range of input values, but it would give the Chilean team something to work with by the original deadline. Since the consultants would need to cut many corners to complete the temporary suite by the March deadline, it could not be used in the final Cyberstride system; the consultants would also need to write a separate, robust, permanent suite. To save time, the Andersen consultants suggested forming two teams, one to write the temporary suite and the other to write the permanent suite. The two teams would work in parallel, learn from one another, and thus make faster progress toward the final system.[27]

By now it was January, and Beer needed to make a hard decision to keep the project on schedule. He gave the consulting firm permission to begin work on the software coding before he received confirmation from Santiago that the Chilean government would pay the consultant's fees of £34,000—roughly $516,000 in 2009 dollars, a considerable sum. "The total cost of this composite plan adds up to pounds 34,000 which is more than I expected," Beer wrote in a January telex to Flores. "This is due to my insistence on having the temporary suite operating in March. My belief is that this is worth the extra money."[28] But Flores disagreed, and asked Beer to find a less expensive alternative. This response worried Beer, and he wondered whether he would be able to pay for the services for which he had already contracted.[29]

Beer took Flores's response back to Arthur Andersen, and after another round of negotiations the consultants put together a less expensive proposal. Andersen agreed to complete the temporary suite and design the permanent suite, but the Chilean team would perform the coding and installation of the final software. To assist in this process, three Arthur Andersen consultants would travel to Santiago: one to install the temporary suite, one to assist the Chilean programmers with coding the permanent suite, and a senior partner to sign off on the project once it was complete. Kaye agreed to fill the senior position and direct the Arthur Andersen contract. Alan Dunsmuir took charge of the day-to-day work on the temporary suite and agreed to travel to Santiago for its installation. The last consultant was not named, but he or she would work closely with the government computer expert Isaquino Benadof, who had been named the project manager for the Cyberstride software suite. This new proposal would cost the government £19,000 ($289,000 in 2009 dollars), a substantial reduction.[30]

But the new arrangement made the Arthur Andersen consultants anxious because it restricted the work they could accomplish and the payment they might receive for work completed. Moreover, they worried that the Chileans might not be able to pay for their services, given the fluctuating foreign exchange rates. For the Chilean government, the arrangement meant that the final code would not be written by Arthur Andersen and Company, and they would have to pay to write the Cyberstride software twice. It was not an ideal situation for either side, but for the Chilean government the price was right. Flores reviewed the new proposal and gave his approval.[31] Back in London, Beer must have breathed a sigh of relief.

The Cyberstride software broke new ground in cybernetic management. It was the first software written to implement Beer's Viable System Model.[32] The program also implemented a new and untried method of Bayesian statistical forecasting known as the Harrison-Stevens Approach, which first appeared in the December 1971 edition of *Operational Research Quarterly*.[33] Dunsmuir stumbled onto the method while performing a literature review for the project. He convinced Beer that the new method would recognize significant variations in the production data and predict whether these initial data points signified the beginnings of a linear trend, an exponential trend, a step function, or an anomaly that would return to normal (figure 3.1). In this way, the software was able to make predictions; it did not simply record and compile historical performance. Furthermore, when a computer operator input new production values, the software could revise its predictions on the fly.

Beer argued that the Cyberstride software would eventually permit the Chilean government to discard its traditional reporting methods—exhaustive printed reports of considerable length based on data collected monthly or yearly. He envisioned that the

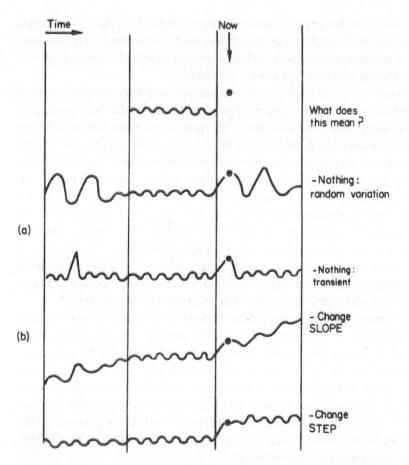

Figure 3.1
Examples of statistical change. Reprinted from Stafford Beer, "Fanfare for Effective Freedom: Cybernetic Praxis in Government," in his *Platform for Change* (New York: J. Wiley, 1975), 440. Image reproduced with permission from Constantin Malik.

continuous reporting and prediction provided by Cyberstride "would save a great deal of time, effort, *and* money," although he understood that the Chileans might wish to stick with traditional methods until the new system proved its worth. Since Cyberstride discarded all data classified as normal, Beer felt the system would not become part of a "vast bureaucratic machine," nor would it become an oppressive form of all-knowing centralized management. Instead, it would allow the government to prioritize and channel its attention toward the industries in greatest need at any given time.[34] Cyberstride instantiated a new type of socialist technology, one that did not try to put the government everywhere at once but instead helped it channel its limited resources where they were needed most.

Implementing Cyberstride also meant that mainframe computers would no longer be used exclusively for data processing; they would also be tools for adaptive management and rapid decision making. The cybernetic factory Beer had described thirteen years earlier in *Cybernetics and Management* would be one step closer to reality.

The Economic Simulator

In the Project Cyberstride report Beer alluded only briefly to building an economic simulator, yet he made significant progress on this component of the project while he was back in London. He intended the simulator to complement the Cyberstride software and act as "the government's experimental laboratory." Once complete, the simulator would allow government decision makers to plan beyond day-to-day operations and experiment with different long-term economic policies.[35] Therefore, the simulator needed to be able to reflect the frequently changing behavior of an economy in transition, an extremely difficult proposition. It would need to be able not only to accept changing input values but also to restructure how different variables related to one another and to introduce new considerations. Since all these changes happened continuously in the real world, the model would also need to handle dynamic change.

Beer decided to adopt a less common approach to modeling. At the time, many economic simulations followed an "input-output" approach and used large data sets to calculate the interdependence of different production processes. Such analyses could require several years of data collection and used fixed equations to calculate the behavior of the system. Beer condemned such methods as "deplorably static." If the "objective is to actually restructure the economy," Beer wrote, then such rigid methods were "poor tool[s] indeed."[36] Aiming for a different approach, Beer looked to the work of the famous MIT engineer Jay Forrester.

In the history of computing, Forrester is best known for his work on magnetic core memory and for directing the computer design team of the SAGE land-based air defense system.[37] However, Forrester's work shifted in the late 1950s to study problems in industrial management. He expressed a particular interest in the modeling of complex systems that changed over time, a field of inquiry he referred to as system dynamics. Forrester began this line of research by modeling industrial processes and in 1961 published his first book on the subject, aptly titled *Industrial Dynamics*. His research in this area continued to grow in scope and complexity throughout the 1960s and early 1970s, as illustrated by his publication of *Urban Dynamics* in 1969 and *World Dynamics* in 1973.[38]

Forrester favored real-world problems over academic theories. He argued that, unlike human beings, computers could study multiple, interacting feedback loops that produced nonlinear relationships. They could thus help industrial managers or policy makers identify the root causes of a problem, instead of simply treating its symptoms. Forrester's approach to modeling focused on structure rather than data. He posited that it was more important to identify the relationships among the different parameters of a complex system, and account for these relationships when building the model, than to compile comprehensive data sets for each parameter. Such an approach "follows the philosophy of the manager or political leader more than the scientist," Forrester wrote, acknowledging that managers and political leaders often had to make decisions using incomplete information.[39] However, such an approach to modeling was often criticized for lacking an empirical foundation.

Forrester encouraged policy makers to use models to identify the few parameters that, when changed, produced the results desired. Policy makers could then focus their efforts in these areas. To code his models of dynamic systems, Forrester developed the programming language DYNAMO, and Beer found this language appropriate for coding the new simulator. DYNAMO would later be used to run the models for the widely read but controversial book *Limits to Growth: A Report for the Club of Rome's Project on the Predicament of Mankind* (1972), which predicted that human demands would outstrip planetary resources within one hundred years, and helped launch the field of global computer modeling.[40] Forrester wanted his work in system dynamics to assist decision making and, according to Fernando Elichirigoity, "allow experts in different fields to see the whole."[41] It is easy to see why Forrester's work appealed to Beer and why Beer believed Chile's economic simulator should be based on system dynamics instead of input-output analyses. However, the controversy surrounding *Limits to Growth* later raised doubts about Beer's decision to use the same modeling language, DYNAMO, for the Chilean economic models. (Beer responded: "To me, that is like blaming the pornographic content of a book on the English language in which it is written.")[42]

Beer approached Ron Anderton, a systems engineer, operations research scientist, and leading British expert on DYNAMO, and asked him to begin work on the simulation project. K. A. Gilligan, a mathematical physicist, statistician, and expert modeler, also signed on to the project. Both men possessed the technical expertise the project needed and sympathized with the goals of the Chilean revolution. Anderton and Gilligan agreed to write "a rough approximation of the model" by March and charged £2,500 for its development: £1,500 for fees and £1,000 for computer time at Queen Mary College, London (a total of approximately $38,000 in 2009 dollars).[43]

Beer found qualified people to work on the simulator and the software suite in London, but he had difficulty convincing British technical experts to travel to Chile for extended periods. "The press is full of alarmist reports about Chile, and these cause concern for men with wives and children. Everyone, married or single, is concerned about financial stability—seen as a function of political stability," he wrote.[44] Yet he did locate a few potential collaborators willing to make the trip to Santiago, including Jonathan Rosenhead, then a mathematician at the London School of Economics and a founding member of the British Society for Social Responsibility in Science. Rosenhead had the political disposition, and he held an academic position with some schedule flexibility.

Moreover, he was interested in the Chilean government's application of managerial cybernetics and operations research techniques. Rosenhead would later play a role in the Cybersyn story through his involvement with the British Society for Social Responsibility in Science, although the role he played was far from the one Beer had imagined.

El Arrayán

Meanwhile, back in Chile, the team continued to make rapid progress on the project despite the hot summer sun. January is the peak of summer in Santiago. By the end of the month a heat wave had settled over the city, and residents were sweltering. The heat did not slow the small Chilean team. Work on Project Cyberstride continued at a fast clip, always moving toward the March deadline. "All over the place one can feel Fernando's driving hand," Cañete wrote to Beer about Flores. "I felt it, in the smooth operation and the quiet efficiency of the staff of very young engineers working on the project . . . specially [sic] since their job implies a good effort toward the betterment of our country." Cañete added that due to the heat, "all our political patriarchs are away from Santiago resting their tongues and I hope also their brains." Cañete felt frustrated as he watched the political parties bicker, but he drew inspiration from his relationship with Beer.[45] The cybernetician had sent copies of his books to Chile, and receiving the package affected Cañete viscerally. "It is quite difficult to put into words what I felt," Cañete wrote in response, "something like a pressure in the chest, as if the ribcage does not have enough room to contain [the] lungs and [the] heart, this is what I have defined as the feeling of contact with greatness. Meeting you was undoubtedly a key point in my life, never shall things be the same for me again."[46] Though the project was still in its initial stages, for some it had already become a life-changing event.

However, summer did not bring an end to Chile's political struggles, despite Cañete's wishes, and the Chilean political context was becoming increasingly volatile and complex. Although the government was making progress on the industrial management problem, support for Popular Unity continued to fall, and fissures deepened within the Popular Unity coalition. The coalition lost two congressional seats in the January 1972 by-elections, one to the Christian Democrats, the other to the opposition party National Liberty. Splits within the MAPU, Flores's party, and the Radical Party raised the number of parties in the Popular Unity coalition from six to eight. The addition of these new parties—the Leftist Radical Party (PIR) and the Christian Left—further complicated the administration's distribution of patronage appointments. These new parties also exacerbated political infighting and strategic maneuvering, and they sought short-term political gains at the expense of long-term changes. In this environment, satisfying the diverse members of his coalition and governing the country became increasingly difficult for Allende.

At the same time the political center, embodied most by the Christian Democrats, continued to shift toward the opposition. The Christian Democrats repeatedly challenged the administration's legal practices, especially with regard to the nationalization process, and insisted that it adhere to the letter of the law in all cases, not only when it was convenient. In addition, the Christian Democrats tried to impeach Allende's minister of the interior, who under Chilean law also served as vice president.[47] Allende managed to sidestep these charges by reshuffling his cabinet and having the interior minister swap jobs with the minister of defense. The maneuver allowed Allende to keep his cabinet intact but gave further credence to complaints that his administration twisted the law to suit its needs.

The Christian Democrats also pushed for a constitutional amendment to limit the scope and pace of nationalization. They wanted to force the government to articulate the limits of nationalization, state clearly how it planned to integrate workers into the management of the nationalized enterprises, and bring the act of nationalization under the control of Congress. This last part, if enacted, would seriously limit the power of the executive. While the Christian Democrats argued that such clarifications were essential for an orderly program, the Socialists responded by accusing them of trying to impede the revolution.

Allende worked to solidify his base. He reached out to the Christian Democrats and in January 1972 agreed to cut the number of enterprises slated for nationalization from 250 to 90. He hoped this would appease the Christian Democrats and mollify small- and medium-sized business owners who feared losing their property. If he could assuage their fears, the president felt he could gain their political support and encourage them to invest once again in their businesses.

To this end, the administration took steps to solidify the direction of the Popular Unity coalition and bolster support for Allende's economic program.[48] In February 1972 coalition members met in El Arrayán, on the outskirts of Santiago, for a series of three meetings. Although their purpose was to find common ground among the different parties, the meetings also made plain their ideological differences.

Center stage at El Arrayán was the economy. Those present wondered whether the administration should throttle back on state economic controls and give a greater role to market forces. Conversely, they considered whether the administration should maintain its approach but act more boldly by increasing state economic controls and improving economic regulation methods. By the end of the meetings, the coalition parties had agreed on the second approach, to increase the regulatory powers of the executive branch, but also decided to reach out to the Christian Democrats. The decisions made at El Arrayán implicitly supported the approach of initiatives such Project Cyberstride, which aimed to increase the regulatory powers of the government and provide new tools and methods for improving economic management.[49]

The El Arrayán consensus quickly fell apart, in part because of government efforts to bring the Christian Democrats into the coalition. Once Congress passed the Christian Democrats' constitutional amendment to limit the executive's power to nationalize Chilean industries, internal disagreements resurfaced within Popular Unity.

Allende vetoed the amendment. He still planned to seek a compromise with the Christian Democrats and thus increase the support for his government among those at the political center. However, not all members of the Popular Unity coalition, especially members of Allende's own Socialist Party, agreed with this tack. Perhaps the Socialist congressman Mario Palestro expressed his party's stance best when, in the midst of the El Arrayán meetings, he challenged the administration to "take off its white gloves of democracy and put on its boxing gloves." As Castro himself maintained, socialist transformation required revolutionaries, not gentlemen.[50] In mid-February the central committee of the Socialist Party came out against compromise with the Christian Democrats and even called the negotiations reactionary. The Christian Democrats formally withdrew their support for the administration and resumed their stance of challenging Allende's commitment to Chilean democracy.[51]

In the midst of these political negotiations the government began losing ground in its "battle of production." Economic policies to raise wages for all but the most elite sectors of the population stretched government resources. Higher wages also raised demand for consumer goods and food, bringing the first signs of real consumer shortages and providing an opening for black-market suppliers. All the while inflation continued to climb. By February 1972 the consumer price index was 34 percent higher than it had been twelve months earlier and 81.9 percent higher than it had been in December 1969.[52] The government strategy of printing money to meet its expenses further exacerbated inflation.[53] Still, Allende's advisers hoped they could produce their way out of the crisis, a goal that made Cyberstride seem all the more critical to those who were involved in building the system. Beer and the Chilean team worked with urgency to help the Allende government. However, when Beer returned to Chile in March, he found the country in even worse political and economic straits than it had been when he had left four months earlier.

March 1972

Beer traveled to Chile again on 13 March 1972, just as Penguin Press published his fourth book, *Brain of the Firm*. The new book formally presented many of the concepts and theories underlying the work in Chile, concepts that he, Flores, and the Chilean and British teams had already transformed into software code and a growing communications network.

Remarkably, the team had constructed the preliminary set of tools by the ambitious March deadline. To do so, the Chilean project team had expanded from ten to thirty-five people, many of whom worked on Cyberstride in addition to other projects.[54] Cañete was directing the construction of the telex network, and new team member Fernando Améstica was in charge of its implementation. Both men had made substantial progress in the preceding months. On 28 January 1972, Cañete had reported, "I gave the first training course to the telex operators of the textile companies including the Textile [sector] Committee."[55] These five operators had already begun sending information to the telex communications center with "good results." Cañete estimated that by the end of February, the telex network would cover one hundred industries, a goal they did not make.[56] Still, within four short months Cañete and Améstica had created a communications network that linked the various levels of Chilean economic management to the factory floor, a pace that took even Cañete by surprise. "Strange things have happened," Cañete noted. "We expected some kind of resistance to integrat[ing] the network, [but the] reality was quite the opposite, several industries who were not considered in the initial list have actually requested to be integrated to the network and now one of my immediate jobs is to assign priorities to [the] list [of industries the government had identified for expropriation]."[57] The copper mines and agriculture were noticeably absent from this network, as they did not fall under the jurisdiction of CORFO.

Alan Dunsmuir brought the completed temporary suite from London to Santiago in early March. In mid-March, the computer agency transmitted the first results from the Cyberstride program to CORFO, simulating the daily practice that would take place once the permanent suite was in place. The arrival of this message elated Beer, who sent Anderton a jubilant telex stating, "Cyberstride suite really works too. For the first time government can be poised for anticipatory action instead of attending the wake. . . . The whole thing was impossibles [sic] and we did it."[58] Beer's glee was understandable but premature. Much work remained to complete a final software suite that would truly give the government the capability for "anticipatory action." However, this first transmission served to prove a concept, a public demonstration that Cyberstride could work once the team finished building the tools.

The completion of the permanent suite still had a long way to go. Six people from the computer agency labored on the project, including Benadof, and it proved substantially more complicated than the work completed by the Andersen consultants in London.[59] For example, the permanent suite required Chilean operations research scientists to undertake studies of every nationalized enterprise and determine which production indicators the software should monitor; they also had to establish the acceptable range of values for these indicators. Institute engineers began studying enterprises in the textile, energy, and agroindustrial sectors only in mid-March.

By March 1972 Anderton had programmed an initial version of the economic simulator, which was now known as CHECO (CHilean ECOnomic simulator). Eventually, Anderton wrote, such a simulator would allow CORFO to "acquire, by stages, dynamic understanding of systems with 10–100 variables, as compared with 5-10 variables which is the limit for the unaided brain." But at this point it was still a simple program designed to teach model-building skills to the members of the CORFO staff, so they could then make the model "more elaborate, more realistic" and "finally integrated with the rest of the control operation."[60] Even in its final version, however, the model would not function as a predictive black box that gave definitive answers about future economic behavior. Rather, it offered a medium with which economists, policy makers, and model makers could experiment and, through this act of play, expand their intuition about economic behavior and the interplay of price controls, wages, production levels, demand, taxation policies, foreign exchange reserves, import and export rates, and other factors. Thus, the simulator was not meant to replace human expertise but to enhance it.

Beer noted that Alberto Martínez, the director of industrial planning at CORFO, was one of several critics who objected to CHECO because it did not represent the true complexity of the Chilean economy.[61] In response to such criticisms, the cybernetician repeated Anderton's assertion that the simulator far exceeded the capacities of the human brain. Moreover, it was designed to provide insight about the dynamics of the economy and determine which factors deserved more attention than others, instead of providing definitive answers. Anderton wrote: "Although much more complex than the mental model it augments, the model might be thought of as too simple in relation to the reality it represents. In reply, it must be said that the aim is not to make a detailed 'road map' of the economy, but to pick out as a result of experimentation on the model, those quantities which determine the dynamics of its behavior. If this cannot be done with the limits of a twentieth-order system, then further thought and understanding is needed, rather than a proliferating model."[62] This approach differed substantially from a representational approach to modeling, which sought to replicate the complex web of relationships found in the system under study.[63] Instead, it focused on understanding the behavior of this exceedingly complex system and identifying the key variables that had the greatest affect on economic performance. This emphasis on behavior, not representation, was congruent with Beer's general approach to modeling complexity.

Anderton recommended that CORFO form a small team in Santiago to refine the model. Mario Grandi became the Chilean leader for the CHECO project, and he met with Beer on 20 March to discuss its future. The next day Beer sent a telex to Anderton, saying, "Your Chilean colleagues send you thanks, deep appreciation, and warm personal regards." The Chileans especially appreciated the contributions of Queen Mary College programmer Patsy Williams, whom Beer described as "the pin-up girl of the Santiago intelligencia."[64] While work on Project Cyberstride would necessitate the creation of a collaborative, transnational work culture that would push those involved to think in new ways, it would not challenge or change gender norms of the period or the male-dominated culture of engineering work in Britain and Chile.

Project Cybersyn

Cyberstride underwent a major change during Beer's March visit. The project acquired a new name: Project Cybersyn, a synthesis of *cybernetics* and *synergy*. The new name pointed to the project's cybernetic foundations and the team's belief that the whole system—humans and machines—exceeded the sum of its parts. Cyberstride now referred exclusively to the suite of software being designed by Arthur Andersen and the National Computer Corporation to measure factory productivity.[65] As a larger umbrella, Project Cybersyn would include a committee to coordinate work on the different subprojects.[66] Cybersyn made sense as a project name in English, but it did not roll off the tongue in Spanish. The project thus acquired a separate Spanish name, SYNCO, an acronym for Sistema de Información y Control.

In addition to the three projects that had previously constituted the Cyberstride system—the telex network (Cybernet), the statistical software (Cyberstride), and the economic simulator (CHECO)—Cybersyn placed greater emphasis on a fourth component: the operations room, a realized version of the war room that Beer had proposed in his essay "The Liberty Machine." "The objective of CYBERSYN," Beer wrote, "is to draw . . . [these tools] together in an effective control center—the operations room to be installed by November 1972."[67] Beer proposed building a model of the room in London with guidance from Gui Bonsiepe, the head of the State Technology Institute's Industrial Design Group.[68]

The room later broke new ground in interface design, not because of its technical newness but because of the priority its designers gave to the human operator. "Special attention will be paid to the development of man-machine interfaces," Beer specified, focusing once again on the user and prioritizing human understanding over technological flashiness. He continued, "The Operations Room should be thought of *NOT* as a room containing interesting bits of equipment *BUT* as a control machine comprising men and artifacts in symbiotic relationship. It needs designing as a totality and as an operational entity."[69] The operations room would later emerge as the iconic image of Project Cybersyn and the symbolic heart of the project.

Project Cyberfolk

In addition to his work on Project Cybersyn, Beer had started thinking about other cybernetic applications to aid Chile's revolutionary process and, through their function, uphold the values of Chilean socialism. He expressed particular interest in the social organization of the Chilean state and ways to improve the sluggish pace of the Chilean bureaucracy. Beer was never a fan of bureaucracy, as his earlier writings made clear. The negative effects of bureaucracy were even more pronounced in Chile because the state could not accommodate and address the rapid political, economic, and social changes that were taking place. Focusing on one part of this problem, Beer asked how cybernetics might help the state respond quickly to the demands of the people.

Beer observed the government's use of media technologies, such as television and radio, and their success in getting the government's message to the Chilean people. Television viewing increased in the early 1970s, in part because of the manufacture of the low-cost IRT Antú television. According to the U.N. Economic Commission for Latin America, the annual production of television sets rose in Chile from 123,000 units in 1970 to 190,700 units in 1972, raising the number of television sets in operation to approximately 500,000. The government also used radio broadcasts to communicate with the Chilean people, although Beer did not explicitly mention this more common form of mass communication in his writings.[70] Yet these technologies did not offer a balanced form of communication: they permitted elected leaders to communicate with the people en masse, but the people could not communicate in the same way with their representatives. Beer felt this inequality "disbalances the homeostatic equilibrium" and could lead to political unrest in the form of demonstrations or violence.[71]

Thus Beer proposed building a new form of real-time communication, one that would allow the people to communicate their feelings directly to the government. He called this system Project Cyberfolk. In a handwritten report Beer describes how to build a series of "algedonic meters" capable of measuring how happy Chileans were with their government at any given time.[72] As noted in chapter 1, Beer used the word *algedonic* to describe a signal of pleasure or pain. An algedonic meter would allow the public to express its pleasure or pain, or its satisfaction or dissatisfaction with government actions.

Unlike polls or surveys, these algedonic meters would not limit or prompt answers by asking set questions. The user simply moved a pointer on a dial somewhere between total dissatisfaction and absolute happiness. This design "uses the [human] brain as a computer," Beer wrote, "structured and programmed by individuality."[73] Reminiscent of Beer's attention to autonomy and broad participation, the meter permitted users to construct their own scale of happiness and did not impose a standardized definition. Unlike many survey techniques, the meter did not require users to rationalize their level of happiness or normalize it to fit on a uniform scale. Instead, the meter recorded the user's gut feeling at a particular moment; the position of the knob on the meter would determine the voltage output on the device. Beer wrote that the meters could be installed in any location with a television set, such as in a Chilean home or in select community centers. Government officials could collect public responses easily by adding up the voltage output from the various machines and dividing the figure by the number of machines present. The meters therefore offered a representation of public satisfaction that was easy to generate, possible to update continuously, and simple to understand. Beer argued that the government could then use this information to improve public well-being (figure 3.2). However, although the meters provided a reading

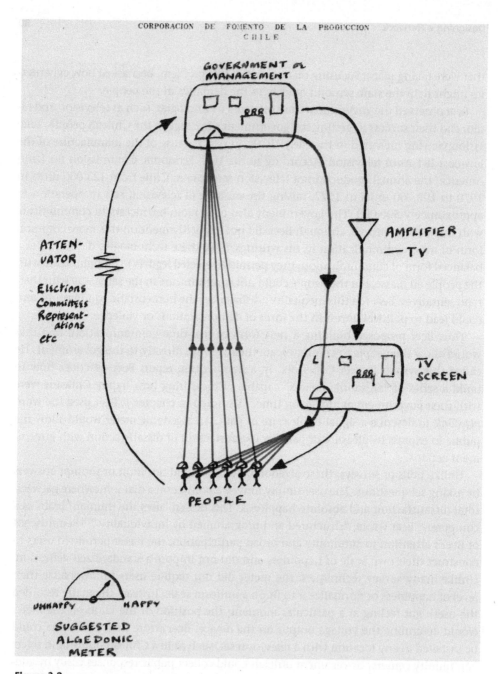

Figure 3.2

Drawing by Beer of how the algedonic meters from Project Cyberfolk could help the government and the Chilean people adapt to one another. Image reproduced with permission from Constantin Malik. Original kept at Liverpool John Moores University, Learning and Information Services, Special Collections and Archives.

of a general level of happiness or dissatisfaction, they did not show why people felt this way, nor did they provide a uniform scale of satisfaction that government officials could interpret with certainty.

Project Cyberfolk consisted of a relatively simple technological system that would function within a complex social system with the aim of improving its management. In cybernetic terms, the algedonic meters would serve as a homeostat: they would allow two complex systems, the government and its constituency, to adapt to one another and reach the stable condition of homeostasis. Beer proposed building several such meters and using them to conduct experiments on how technology could further popular participation and democracy. Flores suggested that Beer could use the meters to study worker participation within the nationalized enterprises.[74]

Despite Beer's good intentions, it is easy to imagine how a government might abuse such a device or how partisan groups might manipulate them to suit their interests. Beer foresaw these possibilities, and his writings show that he took them into consideration when designing the meters. Scholars such as Lawrence Lessig, Langdon Winner, and Batya Friedman have shown that values can be designed into technologies, meaning that they can uphold certain principles by enabling certain types of behavior and discouraging others.[75] Beer's work fits in this vein, for he added features to the meters to promote visibility and transparency rather than authoritarian control or oppression. For example, the meters were designed to make public sentiment visible but would give everyone access to the same information at the same time.[76] In a factory this continual display of worker happiness or dissatisfaction would alert workers and managers alike to when they needed to make changes. It would also provide a continual reminder of when management had ignored workers' concerns, which could then increase workers' solidarity or allow management to head off potential strikes or lengthy labor negotiations. Beer wrote that the meters could make "explicit the outcome of continuous dialogue among the workers themselves, as to their satisfaction with the conditions in general, which would otherwise remain implicit in a host of small encounters never fully articulated."[77] Thus the meters would provide a new channel of communication that functioned from the bottom up and in real time.

Moreover, Beer recognized that the meters, like the telephone voting systems already in existence at the time, brought with them the potential for political oppression. He did not write much about how the algedonic meters would preserve user anonymity if built. But he did insist that the devices be analog, not digital, which would make it more difficult to identify individual meters and, by extension, individual users. He also proposed assigning three people to a meter to add an additional layer of anonymity, although this design decision would substantially limit the number of voices the meters could represent and perhaps empower those whose voices and opinions already dominated public discussion. The meters had their shortcomings. Nevertheless, Beer's writing on Project Cyberfolk illustrates that he tried to embed the values that mattered to him in the design of these simple meters and that he viewed the project with a critical eye. Cyberfolk also shared with Cyberstride several features that consti-tute signature characteristics of Beer's cybernetics: using technology to create real-time communication channels, aiming to increase participation from the bottom up, and seeking to restructure top-down management practices. On 22 March 1972, Beer pre-sented Project Cyberfolk to members of the Center for Studies on National Reality, the leftist interdisciplinary research center known as CEREN, at the Catholic University in Santiago.[78] Beer hoped CEREN would eventually pursue sociological research relating to the meters. But the meeting also had a more immediate purpose. Beer's notes on the meeting read, "22nd March 1972 Meeting at CEREN . . . General discussion of 'Cyber-folk.' No actual use, but brings CEREN into ambit of the CORFO Team for first time."[79] In fostering this new connection, Beer recognized that networks of human beings stood at the core of any successful technological project. Again, Beer was engineering both the social and the technological environment as a way to further his cybernetic work.

Beer commissioned several prototype meters and used them in small group experi-ments. They were never implemented as the form of real-time, adaptive political com-munication that Beer imagined. However, the meters do provide another illustration of how Beer saw cybernetics, and its emphasis on real-time communication, feedback, and adaptation, as assisting the Chilean revolutionary process. More than thirty years later, television networks such as CNN would use similar devices to collect and display real-time viewer reactions to candidate responses during the 2008 U.S. presidential de-bates. But unlike Beer's meters, the CNN meters made this information available only to CNN viewers, and not to the candidates themselves. As a result, candidates could not adapt their message to the public's reaction.[80]

Implementing a Vision

More invested than ever in the Chilean experiment, Beer returned to London on 24 March 1972. He requested £7,000 ($106,000 in 2009 dollars) from the Chilean govern-ment to cover his expenses from 25 March to 6 November, the date he picked for his next trip to Chile. The amount was half his usual fee, but it was not a negligible figure, considering Chile's dwindling foreign exchange. "Please don't tell anyone!" Beer joked. "I should lose my 'international' status."[81] The cybernetician estimated he would spend seventy days on Project Cybersyn during the next seven months—a gross underesti-mate, as he would soon discover.

Beer's increasing devotion to Project Cybersyn and the success of Chilean socialism stands in contrast to how U.S. multinationals and the U.S. government were using technology to affect the Allende government. Three days before Beer left Chile, the U.S. journalist Jack Anderson made public a series of confidential ITT documents that linked the international communications giant to the anti-Allende activities coordinated by the CIA and the Nixon White House. One document described a conversation between ITT senior vice president E. J. Gerrity and the Clandestine Services Division of the CIA that took place on 29 September 1970. According to Gerrity, the CIA planned to bring Chile to the point of economic collapse by urging companies to "drag their feet in sending money, in making deliveries, in shipping spare parts, etc." and to "withdraw all technical help and not provide any technical assistance in the future."[82] We may never know the full extent of U.S. intervention in Chile during the Allende government or the entire role played by companies such as ITT, but we do know that the U.S.-led economic blockade created shortages of spare parts, caused significant problems for Chilean industries, stopped industrial machinery, and affected the production and repair of consumer goods. Chilean access to spare parts and foreign expertise continued to decline throughout 1972 and 1973. From machine parts to computer systems, technology played a key role in the battle of production.

By the end of March 1972, Beer and Flores had designed a series of technological solutions they believed would help the Chilean government improve its management of the national economy and support the Chilean transition to socialism. These tools were technologically simple, but they could help the government respond to the constantly changing behavior of exceedingly complex systems, such as the national economy or the attitudes of the Chilean people. These tools also took into account technological limitations such as having access to only one mainframe computer.

Moreover, the group designed these tools to function in ways that were consistent with Chilean views on democratic socialism. The tools would facilitate top-down management yet still included mechanisms to preserve factory autonomy and bottom-up participation. Collectively, the Cybersyn system would use computers to increase industrial production levels but not in ways that automated the labor of workers or managers. Instead, Beer, Flores, and the Chilean team envisioned a computer system to assist, rather than replace, human decision making.

To transform these ideas into reality, Beer and Flores broadened the composition of the team in Chile, began assembling transnational teams composed of Chilean and British engineers, and established an aggressive timeline for the project's completion. Beer and Flores believed this technology would help the government win the battle of production by allowing it to quickly make informed decisions about the economy. The system could create a broadly participative, decentralizing, and antibureaucratic form of management—the very traits that Allende had listed when he met with Beer in the presidential palace. Yet it was still not clear whether the team could finish creating the system it had begun or whether it could engineer the social relations that surrounded the technology with the same level of dexterity. In the coming months, the team's efforts at sociotechnical engineering would be challenged by political conflict and the effects of an economy in decline.

4 Constructing the Liberty Machine

Let us bring together all of science
before we exhaust our patience.
—Angel Parra, June 1972

Constructing Cybersyn was a complex affair. In addition to building the actual system, members of the Cybersyn team needed to create a work culture, transfer expertise and technology from Britain to Chile, and gain the support of factory managers and production engineers. The Cybersyn team viewed their work as helping the Allende government improve its control of the economy and raise production levels. Some members of the team also saw technology as a way to build Chilean socialism. Indeed, the Allende government had made technology political. In addition to Project Cybersyn, it supported the creation of low-cost consumer goods for mass consumption. It also emphasized the use of Chilean resources in national research, development, and production activities and oriented Chilean science and technology toward meeting national needs.

However, Beer argued that technology could be political in other ways. He believed that creating a technological system entailed developing a technology that could be integrated into a social and organizational context. Thus, engineering a technology also provided opportunities to engineer the social and organizational relationships that surrounded it.

Beer saw Cybersyn as a way to reengineer the relationships between white-collar technologists and blue-collar workers, workers and the state, and the state-run enterprises and the national government and to reconfigure these relationships in ways that were congruent with Chilean socialism. Sociotechnical engineering gave Cybersyn technologists a way to embed political values in the Cybersyn system. In this chapter I discuss several examples of how Cybersyn technologists tried to make Cybersyn socialist by engineering the social and organizational relationships that surrounded the system. At times, the methods and practices that Chilean technologists used to build the system contradicted the political aims of the Allende government as well as the rhetorical connection between technology and politics that Beer and others articulated. The construction of Project Cybersyn illustrates how difficult it is to build political values into a technological system.

Beer's two visits thus far had largely focused on the design of Project Cybersyn and getting the work off the ground. By April the team had decided on a design and divided the responsibilities for the different subprojects. Building the system now became the central priority of the Cybersyn team.

This chapter encompasses the six-month period from April 1972 to September 1972, when the team made the greatest progress in building the four components of Project Cybersyn: the telex network (Cybernet), the statistical software (Cyberstride), the economic simulator (CHECO), and the control room (Opsroom). Members of the Cybersyn team were still optimistic about the potential of these components for effecting revolutionary change, despite the worsening economic situation and increased political polarization.

In fact, the economy was already in dire straits. On 1 April the rightist Chilean newspaper *El Mercurio* announced: "The economic state of the country cannot be worse." The headline, though intended to strengthen anti-Allende sentiments among the Chilean people, also signaled that Chile was facing a deteriorating balance of payments; declining savings, investment, and production levels; the beginnings of consumer shortages; and inflation.[1] Meanwhile, the position of Allende's political coalition, Popular Unity, grew more precarious each day. In early April the Leftist Radical Party (PIR), a small center-leaning member of Popular Unity, broke from the coalition—a sign that Popular Unity was losing the center. In addition, Popular Unity had not won over the working class as Allende had predicted. May elections for the leadership of the National Labor Confederation, the national federation of labor unions, gave 25 percent of the vote to the Christian Democrats. Since the Christian Democratic Party had always had worker support, this in itself was not surprising; however, it was surprising that more than a year into Chile's revolutionary process Popular Unity had still failed to attract one quarter of Chilean workers to its program of socialist change.[2] Meanwhile, the deteriorating economic situation pushed growing numbers of the middle class toward the opposition. These trends suggested that Popular Unity would not be able to hold, let alone increase, its support base and called the viability of the Popular Unity program into question.

Nevertheless, at this point the political situation did not even give the Cybersyn team pause. After reporting the election results to Beer in a letter, Cañete observed that "the political situation does not alter our project because we are 'in' with the man himself [Allende] and *he* is staying, no doubt about that."[3] Cañete could not have imagined that in less than two years Allende and Chilean democracy would come to a violent, brutal end.

Creating a Culture

In April Flores asked Beer to spend more time in Chile working on Cybersyn and Cyberfolk and thinking of other ways to apply cybernetics to government. The invitation proved irresistible to the cybernetician. After a short trip to Saint Simon Island, Georgia, for an invitation-only conference on speculative technology hosted by the U.S. National Aeronautics and Space Administration, Beer canceled all but two of his other scheduled consulting jobs for the remainder of the year.[4] He estimated he would spend "total formally 20 weeks to year end" on the Chile project but noted, "As usual, it would actually be more."[5] The Chile project now accounted for the majority of Beer's income until 1973, which made him nervous. The Chilean government had not yet paid Arthur Andersen for its work on the temporary suite, and no one knew what would happen to Chilean exchange rates in light of the economic problems and the U.S. blockade. Because of this uncertainty, Beer requested "substantial advance payment" for his work.[6] He also asked for a formal letter from Allende that Beer could use to help "get out of many small commitments" while preserving his professional reputation. The president sent the letter, but it did not reach Beer until the end of May, well after he had canceled his contracts and felt some professional embarrassment.[7]

When Beer returned to Chile in mid-May, he did so not as a foreign consultant but as the official scientific director of the Cybersyn project. In the new management hierarchy that Beer had devised, Flores assumed the role of political director, and Raúl Espejo, the industrial engineer and operations research scientist who had worked with Flores at the Catholic University and then at the State Development Corporation (CORFO), became the project coordinator.

As scientific director Beer created a work culture closer to the startup culture of the 1990s than to the chain-of-command bureaucracy that flourished in the 1960s and 1970s and was characteristic of Chilean government agencies. He viewed his position as scientific director more as that of a "free agent" than a micromanager. After establishing offices at the State Technology Institute (INTEC) and the Sheraton, he informed the team that he would work at either location at his discretion and call on project team members as required. Moreover, he refused to stick to a traditional nine-to-five work schedule. Team members often found themselves working alongside the bearded cybernetician into the wee hours of the morning. This schedule enabled them to attend to other projects at their regular jobs during the day and helped create an informal camaraderie among team members that bolstered their enthusiasm for the project. On the other hand, the long hours affected the home lives of the Chileans. Isaquino Benadof noted, quite diplomatically, that the project made his marriage an "interesting experience." He quickly learned that if his wife didn't understand what he was doing and that he was "really passionate, putting [his] heart into it," she might feel abandoned or unloved. So Benadof tried to make her a member of the team by extension. "I shared with her all of the problems, all of the talking, all of the expectations," he recalled. He also introduced her to his fellow team members, including Flores and Beer. Benadof recalled that she did not much care for Flores's gruff style and even told him so to his face.[8]

As the project team grew, Beer worked increasingly with a core group of Chileans, most of whom were the directors of the different subprojects. By May 1972 the core group included Fernando Améstica, who concentrated on building the telecommunications infrastructure for the telex network; Jorge Barrientos, who was charged with defining production indicators for the textile and forestry sectors; Benadof, who directed the development of the Cyberstride permanent suite; Gui Bonsiepe, the head designer of the operations room; Roberto Cañete, who was coordinating the construction of a central telex room at CORFO; Espejo, the project coordinator; Humberto Gabella, who studied cybernetic principles to determine how they could improve the government's control of the economy; Mario Grandi, the Chilean director of the CHECO (Chilean economic) simulator; Hernán Santa María, who was in charge of data management; and Alfredo del Valle, who defined production indicators for the energy sector.

The work culture Beer created put human dynamics before solving technical problems and resulted in a team that, at least initially, had a shared vision of risk taking and cybernetic possibility that transcended political differences. When Beer interviewed Benadof for a spot on the team, he first asked Benadof how he learned new things and whether the computer scientist was interested in undertaking an adventure. Beer "felt that if he didn't have a team with the spirit to break in a new paradigm, the whole project would fail," Benadof noted. "He was more interested in the power of the person than what he knew about the [particular] problem."[9] Beer brought to Santiago a copy of the popular novel *Jonathan Livingston Seagull* by Richard Bach and wrote the names of different team members on the seagulls drawn on the cover. He charged those listed with reading the book and asked them to place an *X* by their name once they finished. The book tells the story of a seagull who struggles to do something different and breaks from the conventional behavior of the flock. Beer hoped the book would give the team a shared reference point for what they were trying to do.

Beer and Flores also began cultivating a "unique friendship" grounded in mutual respect, a shared intellectual curiosity, and a common goal. "A level of sympathy was developed," Flores recalled, despite the differences between the men: "I was a national leader, he was an international leader, and also we were of a different age."[10] While Beer imparted knowledge of cybernetics, Flores sought to educate Beer on Chilean politics, language, and South American culture. At Flores's insistence, Beer read Gabriel García Márquez's masterpiece, *One Hundred Years of Solitude*, and used it as a text for understanding the magic realism of South American life.[11] Beer thereafter referred to Flores as "Aureliano," the name of García Márquez's revolutionary who survived fourteen attempts on his life, seventy-three ambushes, and a firing squad. Flores responded in kind by calling Beer "Melquíades," the name of García Márquez's gypsy who brought news of scientific and technological innovations from the outside world to the tiny imagined Colombian town of Macondo.

Beer's new management structure for the Cybersyn team reflected the five-tier structure of the Viable System Model, another common reference point for the group. The drawing put Flores at the highest level (System Five), placed Beer in charge of future development (System Four), and gave Espejo control of day-to-day activities (System Three). System Two consisted of the directors of the different subprojects, and System One comprised the subproject teams themselves. However, like the democratic socialism of the Allende government and the design of Cybersyn itself, the management structure of the team preserved autonomy, this time among the different subprojects. In a memo to the Cybersyn team, Beer explains that he broke Cybersyn into clearly defined subprojects that small teams could address intensively. This arrangement allowed for a "meeting of the minds" within the smaller group, and because the small team did not need approval from the larger group, it could progress quickly. At the same time Beer insisted that each team keep the others informed of its progress. He arranged large brainstorming sessions that brought together the members of different subteams. In these sessions, he instructed, "sniping and bickering are OUT. Brain-storming is essentially CREATIVE. . . . At least everyone gets to know everyone else, and how their minds work. This activity is essentially FUN: fun generates friendship, and drags us all out of our personal holes-in-the-ground." Project leaders could then take ideas from the brainstorming sessions and use them to improve their part of the project, thus incorporating the suggestions of others. Beer contrasted this "fun" style of management with the more common practice of bringing all interested parties together to make project decisions. That approach, he felt, eventually led to bickering, sniping, or sleeping. It "masquerades as 'democratic,' [but] is very wasteful," he observed.[12] In addition, he required all project leaders to write a progress report at the end of each month and distribute it to the other team leaders. Beer viewed the brainstorming sessions and the written project reports as serving a function similar to the signals passed between the different organs of the body: they kept members of the team aware of activities elsewhere. They also allowed the different subteams to adapt to progress or setbacks elsewhere and helped Cybersyn maintain its viability as a coordinated project while it advanced toward completion.

Beer soon realized that he needed someone to serve as his eyes and ears in Chile when he was in England and asked the administration for an assistant. "She will *not* be a secretary," he specified but rather would assist him and help coordinate the work among the different project teams. Sonia Mordojovich joined the project as Beer's assistant shortly thereafter (figure 4.1). A recent business administration graduate of the Catholic University, Mordojovich had met Flores during an internship at CORFO.[13] She spoke fluent English, having lived a year in Pasadena, California, as part of a high school exchange program. She also understood many technical aspects of the project

Figure 4.1
Stafford Beer and Sonia Mordojovich. Image used with permission from Constantin Malik. Original kept at Liverpool John Moores University, Learning and Information Services, Special Collections and Archives.

because of her university training. Mordojovich arranged Beer's schedule, acted as an interpreter, attended meetings in Beer's absence, and became a liaison between Beer and the team when he was not in Chile.[14] These new management arrangements helped coordinate the work on the four subprojects and allowed the team to work quickly.

Beer created a work culture that emphasized friendship, risk taking, independent learning, and creativity. This culture helped the team make rapid progress in building each of the four subprojects and made those who were involved in the project feel that they were part of something special.

Technology Transfer

In April 1972 Chile hosted the Third United Nations Conference on Trade and Development (UNCTAD III), which Allende hoped would showcase the success of Chilean socialism. Allende's speech at the U.N. conference is perhaps best remembered for its attack on multinational companies and their treatment of Third World nations. However, Allende also used his time at the podium to consider how underdeveloped countries like Chile could have access to modern science and technology. He outlined two ways that Chile might increase its scientific and technological capabilities. The first was to continue policies of import-substitution industrialization and use foreign investments and imported technologies to industrialize the country—policies that historically caused unemployment and underemployment, stressed the value of consumption based on foreign models, and put foreign interests above Chilean interests. The other possibility consisted of "creating or reinforcing our own scientific and technological capabilities," by transferring knowledge from the international community and basing these capabilities "on a humanist philosophy that has man as its chief objective."[15] The Chilean cybernetic project, now entering its sixth month, fit with the latter approach. It relied on foreign expertise but consciously transferred this expertise from the foreigners—Beer; Ron Anderton, a British systems engineer and operations research scientist; and the Arthur Andersen consultants—to the Chileans who were building Cybersyn's various components. The president's insistence that Cybersyn enhance worker participation was another example of how technology could contribute to the construction of a more humane and just society that recognized the dignity of all Chilean people.

The transfer of technology and expertise from Britain to Chile played a central role in the development of the Cyberstride statistical software. So far British and Chilean software developers had written the software code for Cyberstride in parallel on opposite sides of the Atlantic. In May, Arthur Andersen sent consultant Giles Hemmings to Santiago to assist the Chilean programmers with coding the permanent suite. Hemmings stayed in Santiago from 7 to 12 May, and his observations were mixed. "The work has not progressed sufficiently far," he wrote, but "this does not mean, nor does it imply, that we expect our work or the Cyberstride System to be anything but a success."[16] Although the work was not up to the standards Hemmings expected, it was still fixable.

In the process of pointing to a number of things that required attention, Hemmings painted a picture of how software was being developed in Chile in the early 1970s. He felt the Chilean team gave too much attention to programming and not enough time to the administrative aspects of the software project. "We would allow and expect 20 percent of the effort [on Cyberstride] being expended in project administration—overall planning, organizing the effort, preparing detailed work programs, recording usage of time and progress, and progress reporting and progress meeting," he wrote. Hemmings also chastised the Chilean programmers for not properly documenting the programs they coded and for not having a standardized procedure to test the code they generated. "It is difficult to judge the status of the programming . . . because the documentation and development procedures which are to be followed are not clearly defined," he observed. "With regard to program testing there are no standards of which we are aware."[17] He quickly realized that the Andersen consultants needed to teach these skills to their Chilean counterparts if such practices were to become part of Cyberstride's development in the future.

The Andersen consultants thus taught the Chilean programmers practices that were standard in the British computer industry but were not yet standard practice in Chile. This included how to document code, write testing programs, number punch cards, prepare biweekly progress reports, write a general description of the system in the form of a manual, and prepare work programs that listed individual tasks, the person responsible, and the estimated date of completion. According to Benadof, the skills imparted by the Andersen consultants were invaluable: "They gave us a structure, how to work with discipline in order to have a good product at the end with quality assurance." He added that this approach was "not like the Chilean way," a reference to the unstructured, undocumented trial-and-error approach that had been in place at the National Computer Corporation. Yet the Chileans did not embrace the British approach fully. Benadof enjoyed working alongside the Andersen consultants but found their demeanor more formal than what he was accustomed to, qualities he lumped under the heading of "too British."[18]

Scholarship on technology transfer has shown that artifacts are not the only things needed in order for a technology to be taken up elsewhere: people, patents, expertise, manufacturing capabilities, networks of support, economic and legal frameworks, political aims, and cultural values also play a fundamental role. In the Chilean case, developing software required not only the acquisition of mainframe technology and the training of programmers to use that technology, both of which began in the 1960s, but also the movement of people, in this instance between Chile and England, and the sharing of work practices, which improved the quality of the software and the speed of its completion. In the process, the Chilean programmers learned skills that were not necessarily technical—such as producing documentation—but that were nonetheless necessary parts of successful software development. The exchanges that occurred between the Chilean programmers and the Andersen consultants raise important points. First, although the physical transfer of mainframe technology took place in the 1960s, the transfer of technological capability was an ongoing process that extended well beyond the acquisition of computer technology and its use by the Chilean government. Second, although the Cyberstride software had a short lifespan, the practices taught by the Andersen consultants were internalized by the Chileans, who taught them to subsequent generations of programmers. Such practices, which according to Benadof were not standard at the National Computer Corporation before the arrival of the Andersen consultants, are among the more valuable legacies of Project Cybersyn.

The work completed by the Arthur Andersen consultants came in under budget. After the Chilean government paid the bill and closed the contract, the consultants remained intrigued by the unorthodox computer system they had helped build. "We hope the project continues to go as it should," wrote senior consultant David Kaye to his friend Beer. "We are of course enormously interested to know how it develops and any progress reports would be most gratefully received."[19] Beer thanked Kaye for the professionalism displayed by the Andersen consultants and predicted that by late October the system would be "handling some two-thirds of the economy through Cyberstride."

Although Cyberstride is an example of how technology transfer occurred during the Allende period, the emphasis I have placed on the role of the British consultants should not detract from the accomplishments of the Chilean programmers. By early July, Benadof and his team had the temporary suite software checking thirty production indicators for anomalies—significant progress but still a far cry from the "two-thirds of the economy" that Beer predicted would be running through the system by October. Real-time data-processing remained a pipe dream, but the team found a way to shorten the time it took to process factory data. Thus far, Project Cybersyn had used one of the government's top-performing computers, an IBM System/360 mainframe. But the government used this machine for a range of data-processing tasks other than Project Cybersyn, and it was constantly in use at the National Computer Corporation. Due to this high demand for the machine, the agency could not process the indicators it collected from the enterprises for twenty-four to forty-eight hours after they were received. If an emergency arose, the government would be unable to process useful data until a computer became available. To surmount this problem, Benadof worked night and day to rewrite the temporary suite code so that it might be run on the less-used Burroughs 3500 mainframe.[20]

Beer also recognized the accomplishments of the Chilean data management team. In his August letter to Kaye he praised Benadof's recoding of the temporary suite for the Burroughs mainframe. Beer also recognized the work of Hernán Santa María, the head of the data management team, who successfully oversaw the writing of software code to analyze production data from three textile enterprises, one cement enterprise, and one coal mine. Santa María's team then "tuned" these statistical programs, or tweaked them, so that they could reproduce the past behavior of an indicator. Once tuned, the program would be used to predict the future behavior of the indicator. "Hernan [Santa María] and his men have really advanced the theory of 'tuning' the series, picking up where Alan [Dunsmuir] left off; they will contribute an important new chapter to the Bayesian theory in general, if I ever give them time to write it," Beer told Kaye.[21]

Technology transfer from Britain to Chile also played a central role in building the CHECO simulator. Members of the CHECO team aimed to map the larger macroeconomic picture and create a functioning model of the Chilean economy. The model went beyond production to include such considerations as the currency supply, investment, and inflation. It also included factors more directly related to production, such as demand and industrial productivity levels. The CHECO modelers looked at the general behavior of the entire economy and hoped to gradually increase the simulator's specificity by modeling additional economic factors.

Until now most of the work on coding the CHECO simulator had taken place at Queen Mary College in London. In Chile, Mario Grandi and the rest of the CHECO team were still mastering concepts from economics, cybernetics, and industrial dynamics. This changed in May when Espejo wrote to Beer, "We are interested in developing our own simulation language for the Chilean economic characteristics."[22] Beer suggested that the Chilean government send someone to London to study the DYNAMO programming language with Ron Anderton. The government chose Hernán Avilés.

Beer's records suggest that Avilés became well versed in both the DYNAMO programming language and the CHECO model during his stay in England. He worked from 3:30 p.m. to 11:00 p.m., the only period when he could get time on the university computer. He also worked closely with Anderton and even lived with him for a stretch while the two prepared a report on CHECO for Avilés to take back to Santiago. Anticipating Avilés's return to Chile at the beginning of July, Anderton observed, "I think we can achieve shortly the aim of this first phase—the 'take-off' into self-sustained activity of the Santiago team."[23] His use of the term *take-off* echoed the rhetoric of many development policies implemented in Latin America during this time, based on the idea that transferring technologies from the developed world to the developing enabled poorer nations to take the path to progress pioneered by nations such as the United States and England.

After Hernán Avilés returned from Queen Mary College, he resumed his work with the Santiago CHECO team. Perhaps because the team now had someone who felt comfortable with the technical aspects of building dynamic models, members began to focus greater energy on understanding the complexities of the Chilean economy. They expanded the project team to include an economist and an economics student, as well as experts in engineering, systems analysis, statistics, and psychology—almost the same disciplinary range found in the larger Cybersyn Project. They held twice-weekly seminars in which members of the team led discussions of economic theory, and they started studying structuralist inflation models that linked inflation to insufficient production levels rather than to an increase in the money supply.

The CHECO team also started to recognize the fundamental reasons for the difficulty of modeling Chile's socialist economy, which had nothing to do with mastering a new computer language. Instead, the main problem was that the team could not acquire the economic information it needed to build a model and test the model's accuracy. Nor could the information the team collected accurately capture the rapid changes taking place in the Chilean economy. In some cases, the team had to use data from 1964 to 1970, the period marked by the presidency of Allende's predecessor, Eduardo Frei, and predating the economic changes set in motion by Popular Unity. In some cases the information simply did not exist, for the new structure of the state-controlled economy grouped together enterprises that had never been under the same management before. Little was known about "the functioning of the sectors taken separately and about the existent relationships among the different sectors of the Branch."[24] How, Grandi wondered, could his team accurately model the behavior of economic divisions that had not existed nineteen months earlier?

In mid-August the team wrote, "It is very difficult to obtain economic information when in the middle of a revolutionary process such as the present one in which the fight is given in [sic] many fronts. . . . There are not efficient information centers and we cannot even glimpse the possibility of having them available in the near future, although we are making efforts to do so."[25] Before the Cybernet telex network was up and running, the data available on Chilean industrial performance lagged by a year. Macroeconomic data and mining data lagged by two years, and data on the agricultural sector were scarce. Although copper mining and agriculture were not part of Cyberstride, they formed a key part of Chile's economic activity and shaped Chilean import-export activity. Therefore the CHECO economic model needed to include data from these areas. The information available on industry, mining, and agriculture was often scattered among internal documents and reports published by a multitude of government agencies and offices. Much of the team's time was spent locating these data and figuring out ways to make use of incomplete or contradictory data sets. Although the transfer of expertise from Anderton to Avilés helped the Chilean team master the DYNAMO programming language, such expertise was of limited value if Grandi's team could not amass the data needed for economic model building.

The Chileans remained in contact with Anderton as they built a simple model of inflation. The team planned to gradually increase the complexity of the model as it shed light on the inflationary process. In their correspondence with Anderton the Chileans now displayed a more nuanced understanding of the Chilean economy, and how to model it, than their British mentor. For example, in September 1972 they identified sixteen rules for modeling inflation specifically in the Chilean context.[26]

Anderton still advised the Chileans to pursue basic principles, such as locating which factors created exponential changes in economic behavior, which factors contributed to economic stability, and which changes could not be measured with the data available. "As I see it from 8,000 miles away," Anderton wrote, "the center of the problem seems to be in the response of investment to shortages and needs."[27] And from his vantage point across the Atlantic, he thought that rectifying consumer shortages might be possible if the administration focused its investment in the right areas—and the CHECO models might assist in the identification of those areas.

Something Anderton couldn't know, but which was becoming increasingly clear to those living in Santiago, was that the absence of investment, rather than its improper use, was at the root of the problem. And the problem had been caused by the unseen hand of the U.S. government. Decreases in foreign aid and foreign credit, the flight of foreign capital, plummeting international demand for Chilean copper (which had drastically cut the funds available for Chilean foreign trade), and the unwillingness of

U.S. companies to sell machinery and spare parts to Chilean industries all contributed to consumer shortages. Chilean industries had historically relied on imported machinery, much of it from the United States, but the U.S. government had cut economic aid to Chile from $80.8 million in 1969 to $3.8 million in 1973.[28] Moreover, the U.S. government also put pressure on banks to cut credit to Chile. For example, in 1970 the U.S. Export-Import Bank dropped Chile to its lowest credit rating category. The level of available short-term U.S. commercial credits dropped from $300 million during the Frei government to $30 million in 1972. The U.S. Export-Import Bank itself cut credit to Chile from $28.7 million in 1969 to $3.3 million in 1970 to zero in 1971.[29] The inability to secure foreign credit forced the Allende government to pay for imports using cash from its foreign exchange. This put the government in a difficult situation. As mentioned earlier, wage increases from Allende's income redistribution program had created a dramatic increase in demand for many consumer goods. To meet this demand, the government increased its importation of food, fuel, and other goods and, in the process, quickly depleted Chile's foreign exchange, which the government could not replenish because of falling copper prices. While the economic policies put in place by Popular Unity were in part responsible for this imbalance of supply and demand, consumer shortages also stemmed from factors that were beyond the control of the Chilean government, including the openly hostile stance the United States had taken toward Chile.

Even if members of the CHECO team had somehow been able to identify the extent of U.S. meddling in Chile's economy, how could they have modeled it? By September 1972, the economic model described by the CHECO team, which by its own admission was "relatively simple and incomplete," included an inflation model that took into account the levels of goods and services, productive capital, available capital, investment funds, prices, and total currency in the economy. But the inflation model was based on assumptions of structuralist economics—"inflation is generated when the quantity of goods demanded cannot be equalized by production"—and ignored other causes of inflation, such as the government's printing money to make up for the shortages in industrial investment caused by U.S. economic sabotage.[30] Furthermore, these models did not take into account other causes of Chilean consumer shortages, such as black-market hoarding and labor strikes that slowed production.

But Anderton, back in London, was unaware of what was happening to Chile's economy, much less why, and persisted in his efforts at technology transfer, even as it was dawning on the Chilean team that what he was recommending did not apply to their situation. Anderton had described training Avilés as a form of "take-off" because it allowed British expertise in the DYNAMO programming language to travel to Chile. He believed this transfer would give Chileans the skills to build economic models on their own and subsequently improve the productive capabilities of their country. Implicit in this framing are the beliefs that advanced computer-modeling technologies could make Chilean life better and that Chilean technological competence in this area would be able to improve the government's ability to formulate sound economic policies. However, members of the CHECO team could not make full use of the techniques Avilés passed on if they could not amass the data they needed to build and test a model. Nor was Chile fully in control of its own destiny; rather, it was subject to foreign policy (and dependent on money) from nations that openly wanted the Chilean socialist experiment to fail.

Were the CHECO models useful to the Chileans even so? In his account of Project Cybersyn, Beer notes that by September 1972 the CHECO team was running experimental models of national income, inflation, and foreign exchange, as well as a more general model of the entire economy. They had also started building models of the light industry branch and the automotive sector that the team hoped to eventually transform into components of the macroeconomic models. These are substantial accomplishments, considering the short time frame for the project, and the team ran simulations showing what would happen years in the future. Yet the team viewed the simulations as more of a learning experience than hard numbers on which to base policy. According to Grandi, CHECO was "extraordinarily useful for understanding dynamic systems with positive and negative feedback." But as a mathematical model, CHECO "was a failure."[31] Beer agreed, stating that "no one was anxious to place reliance on the results."[32]

Cyberstride and CHECO illustrate how difficult it was for Chile to dismantle relationships of imperialism. Foreign expertise played a central role in both projects, even though the goal of Project Cybersyn was to help manage a growing nationalized sector of the economy, increase national production levels, and diminish Chile's economic dependency on other nations. Moreover, Anderton and the consultants from Arthur Andersen viewed as part of their contract the training of Chilean technologists to imitate practices and use technologies that originated in other parts of the world. The tension between the desire for greater economic independence and the continued reliance on foreign expertise and foreign technology also appeared in the Popular Unity program. Although Allende emphasized the need to develop Chilean capabilities in science and technology and to better harness the use of national resources in Chilean industrial production, he also recognized, as shown in his speech at UNCTAD III, that bringing foreign experts and foreign technology to Chile was essential to national development.

Project Cybersyn needed to draw heavily on foreign expertise and imported technology. But as the history of the CHECO project shows, Chileans could not simply imitate the techniques used in more industrial nations. Chilean modelers could not follow Anderton's recommendations because Chile had different recordkeeping practices than Britain and had less control over its domestic affairs due to U.S. attempts to set up the overthrow of Allende. Through its international exchanges Chile succeeded in creating and strengthening its national technological capabilities, per Allende's dictum. However, the techniques and technologies that Chileans studied were not necessarily suited for the Chilean political context.

Socialism by Design

Of the four subprojects that composed Project Cybersyn, the operations room best captured the vision of an alternative socialist modernity that the project represented. The futuristic design of the room, and the attention it paid to its human user, would never have come about if the State Technology Institute had not had its own team of professional designers that it could assign to the project. Because this team did not exist before Allende's election, it is worth taking a moment to describe how it came to be and the role industrial design played in the creation of Chilean socialism.

The industrial production of goods for mass consumption constituted one of the central goals of CORFO under Allende. Beginning in 1971, the agency pursued a number of programs to "augment the production capacity of goods for popular consumption," including plans for the design and manufacture of low-cost automobiles, bicycles, motorcycles, sewing machines, household electronics, and furniture, among other items.[33] For example, Citroën of Arica began constructing a new "automobile for the people" at the government's request, a Chilean version of the German Volkswagen.[34] Using funding and technology from its parent company, the Chilean Citroën plant drew up plans for a utility vehicle modeled after the Citroën Baby Brousse, a jeeplike conveyance that the French manufacturer had designed for public transportation in Vietnam. Citroën christened the new design Yagán, after a Chilean Indian tribe indigenous to Tierra del Fuego (figure 4.2). Cristián Lyon, then director of Citroën Arica, remembered that the designers "wanted to see [a vehicle] that was native like the Yagáns."[35] Another example was the manufacture of low-cost televisions for popular consumption produced between 1971 and 1972 by the mixed-area enterprise Industria de Radio y Televisión S.A., or IRT.[36] The IRT Antú was a black-and-white unit with an eleven-inch screen. Production of the Antú meant that television, previously obtainable only by well-to-do Chileans, became available to the masses for the first time.

Projects such as the Antú television and the Citroën Yagán paralleled UP policies for income redistribution and represented a "diversification and decentralization" of property, distribution patterns, and commercialization practices within Chilean industrial firms.[37] As a result of these efforts, poor Chileans and members of the working classes gained access to products and services previously reserved for the elite, a maneuver that raised levels of popular support for the UP, particularly during 1971 and early 1972.

The State Technology Institute also wanted to change Chilean material culture to reflect the goals of Chilean socialism. In an interview with *Science* magazine reporter

Figure 4.2
Pedro Medina sits in the driver's seat of the Citroën Yagán. Image used with permission from Editorial Planeta.

Nigel Hawkes, the deputy director of the State Technology Institute explained, "it is important for Chile to be selective about the technologies it adopts, because in the long run they may determine social values and the shape of society—as the automobile has in the United States, for example."[38] In addition to fostering the manufacture of low-cost, durable goods for popular consumption, Popular Unity's technological goals included decreasing Chilean expenditures on imported technologies and foreign patents, using science and technology to satisfy the specific biological and social needs of the Chilean people, producing a greater number of consumer and capital goods domestically, and improving both education and the dissemination of technical knowledge at Chilean universities, industries, and research institutes.

The State Technology Institute created the Industrial Design Group to assist with these efforts. In her study of the history of design education in Latin America, Silvia Fernández writes that Chile during the Popular Unity period was "the most advanced example in Latin America of design successfully integrated into a political-economic project in support of a social program."[39] The state support for design during the Allende years and its place in the Popular Unity program resulted from a series of coincidences and personal connections—although in hindsight design clearly forms part of a larger set of political, economic, social, and technological changes that were linked to Chile's revolutionary process.

Gui Bonsiepe, the head designer of the operations room, had studied at the Ulm School of Design (Hochschule für Gestaltung Ulm) in Germany beginning in the mid-1950s. One of the most influential design schools in Germany, perhaps second only to the Bauhaus, the Ulm School began in 1953 as a center for design education in industrial design, visual communication, industrialized architecture, and information design. From its inception, the school melded design education and practice with the social and political goals of European postwar reconstruction, including the promotion of democracy. The Ulm School also argued that design should be integrated into industrial production processes, where it would improve the production and use of material artifacts ranging from "the coffee cup to the housing estate."[40] The Ulm School moved design closer to science and technology and melded the visual aspects of design with scientific ideas, mathematical analyses, and user studies. Cybernetics, semiotics, systems theory, operations research, analytic philosophy of language, and Gestalt psychology all influenced the design methodology practiced at the school. The regular arrival of new guest instructors and visiting lecturers, such as Norbert Wiener and R. Buckminster Fuller, made student education in this range of areas possible.

Bonsiepe studied in the Design of Information Department, a program that taught the design of products and forms of visual communication. He first encountered cybernetics there. After he graduated from the program, he continued to work in a research and development group at the Ulm School and designed one of the first interfaces for an Olivetti mainframe computer.[41] Ulm professor and fellow designer Tomás Maldonado was Bonsiepe's intellectual mentor, and he made his first trip from Germany to Maldonado's home country, Argentina, in 1964 to work on design projects. Bonsiepe returned to Latin America for four months in 1966 as a consultant for the United Nations International Labor Organization (ILO). During this time he gave a seminar on packaging design and developed a curriculum for an Argentine school of design.[42] "In Latin America I discovered the political dimension of design," Bonsiepe said, "not in the sense of political parties, but in the sense that professional work [in this area] can have a social dimension."[43]

In 1968 Bonsiepe accepted a more permanent position with the International Labor Organization to work with Chile's State Development Corporation to introduce industrial design in small- and medium-sized Chilean industries.[44] (His departure coincided with the closing of the Ulm School.)[45] Industrial design was a new field in Chile, and at the University of Chile it was being developed by a core group of undergraduate students who lacked a formal mentor. Fernando Shultz, Alfonso Gómez, Rodrigo Walker, and Guillermo Capdevilla were students at the College of Applied Art at the University of Chile, which had advertised a program in design. Only after they arrived on campus did they learn that the program existed in name only, there was no curriculum, and they were among its first students.[46] Since the college did not have a good understanding of design, the students bore the burden of forming their own program. The new design students faced a considerable challenge: none of the faculty at the College of Applied Arts specialized in design or had a design background (most worked in the fine arts or architecture). The university "didn't know what design was, and we didn't have a clear idea either," Shultz said. "But we [the design students] knew that there was something else; that there was another alternative. And that was what we were looking for, to be designers."[47] They pushed the university to create a design department with programs in textile and garment design, landscape design, interior design, graphic design, and industrial design.[48] The students found faculty from various parts of the university to teach classes in all these areas but one: industrial design, the area that most interested them. They realized they needed to look beyond their home institution for the education they wanted.

After meeting Maldonado at a 1968 UNESCO-sponsored conference in Buenos Aires, the students learned of Bonsiepe's impending arrival in Chile. When Bonsiepe's boat arrived at the port city of Valparaíso, the four students were there to meet him. They convinced him to take a role in their education, and he, in turn, became a demanding taskmaster who pushed them to read widely and cultivate competencies in a range of areas, including engineering, economics, the social sciences, and design.

In 1970 Bonsiepe accepted an offer to teach design at the School of Engineering of the Catholic University. Bonsiepe's move presented new opportunities for this particular group of design students. They began working as teaching assistants for engineering classes at the Catholic University, even though they were officially enrolled as students at the University of Chile, a rival institution. Teaching engineers led them to appreciate the benefits of combining design with engineering. "The engineers had the know-how," Shultz noted, but in his opinion they were like catalogs that contained a rigid set of solutions. In contrast, designers looked for different solutions but lacked the technical expertise the engineers possessed.

While at the Catholic University, Bonsiepe extended his role as teacher and mentor to a group of four graphic design students from the School of Communications. Unlike the industrial design students and the majority of students at Catholic University's engineering school, the four graphic design students—Eddy Carmona, Jessie Cintolesi, Pepa Foncea, and Lucía Wormald—were all female (figure 4.3). "In the school where we studied [the School of Communications], there were almost no men," said Foncea. "So, rightly, we were girls, just like they [the industrial design students] were the ones who worked with hard things, materials." In Foncea's opinion, this gender divide was "part of a [social] reality that, in a certain form, still exists today in Chile," where science and engineering are male-dominated fields.[49] These two groups of students, the industrial design students and the graphic design students, would contribute to the design and construction of the Cybersyn operations room.

In 1970, Flores was still the director of the engineering school at the Catholic University, and he met Bonsiepe through a mutual friend. Years later Flores confessed to

Figure 4.3
Graphic design students (left to right): Pepa Foncea, Lucía Wormald, Eddy Carmona, and Jessie Cintolesi. Personal archive of Pepa Foncea. Image used with permission from Pepa Foncea.

Bonsiepe that he did not have a high opinion of the design profession until he visited Bonsiepe's home and saw one of Stafford Beer's books on Bonsiepe's bookshelf. As Bonsiepe tells it, Flores remarked, "'There were probably only two people in Chile who knew this book at that moment [Bonsiepe and Flores], and I thought that if a designer reads Stafford Beer, the design profession must have something serious in it.'"[50] Bonsiepe credits Flores for promoting industrial design education in Chile when it was still in its infancy. "This also happened in Brazil and Argentina," Bonsiepe noted. "Engineers with decision-making power created the conditions for the field of industrial design. This is not a well-known historical fact."[51]

When Allende came to power, Flores used his positions as both general technical director of CORFO and president of the board of the State Technology Institute to create the first state-sponsored industrial design group, which was to be housed at the State Technology Institute and led by Bonsiepe. The four industrial design students also moved to the institute. For Shultz the move meant not finishing his undergraduate degree at the University of Chile, a sacrifice he was willing to make. Higher education was far less attractive to him than the possibility of contributing to the Chilean road to socialism. Shultz noted that at the time finishing a degree was seen as bourgeois, or akin to having a "title of nobility," which was not appealing to the young design student. In addition to Capdevilla, Walker, Schultz, and Gómez, Bonsiepe assigned additional designers and mechanical engineers to the Industrial Design Group, including three Ulm School graduates (figure 4.4). Outside the institute Bonsiepe continued to work with the four graphic design students from the Catholic University; the four women contributed to several institute projects from 1970 to 1973, including the design of the institute's logo. Although the State Technology Institute benefited from the contributions of the graphic designers, the four women were not formally invited to join the institute. Foncea believes this was because graphic design had a less obvious connection to improving Chilean production capabilities than the field of industrial design.[52]

From 1971 to 1973 the State Technology Institute developed nearly twenty products, including inexpensive cases for electronic calculators; agricultural machinery for sowing and reaping that furthered the agrarian reform by raising the productivity of the land; spoons for measuring rations of powdered milk given to children through the National Milk Plan; a collection of inexpensive, durable furniture for use in public housing projects and playgrounds; and a record player inexpensive enough for popular use (figure 4.5). These goods were simple in design, easy to construct, inexpensive, and

Figure 4.4
The State Technology Institute (INTEC) Industrial Design Group. Front row (seated, from left): Rodrigo Walker, Gustavo Cintolesi, and Fernando Shultz Morales. Second row: Alfonso Gómez. Back row (seated, from left): Gui Bonsiepe, Pedro Domancic, Werner Zemp, and Guillermo Capdevila. Not pictured: Michael Weiss and Wolfgang Eberhagen. Image used with permission from Gui Bonsiepe.

Figure 4.5
An inexpensive record player designed by the Industrial Design Group. Image used with permission from Gui Bonsiepe.

of good quality, all important considerations for the majority of Chilean consumers. These products also illustrated the political dimensions of design. A piece of agricultural machinery that cut grass to feed livestock was Bonsiepe's favorite product "because it was directly related to the production of food—in this case, milk," and would raise levels of Chilean nutrition.[53] Taken together, these projects illustrate a shift in the definition of industrial success and the considerations driving technological innovation. Instead of giving priority to the production of capital-intensive goods and the maximization of profit, as private companies had in the past, the government emphasized accessibility, use value, and the geographic origin of component parts. These new considerations reflected the economic policies of Popular Unity and the social goals of the Chilean revolution. Far from being neutral, the technologies described here intentionally reflected the philosophy of the Allende administration and became tools for revolution.

Building the Opsroom

The Cybersyn operations room fit with the political mandate of the Industrial Design Group, but it was unlike anything else it created. While its other projects were closely tied to the day-to-day life of the Chilean people, the room was more of a futuristic dream. However, it did incorporate elements characteristic of the Ulm School of design and reflected the merging of engineering and design that had taken place at the Catholic University. The designers paid great attention to ergonomics and concerned

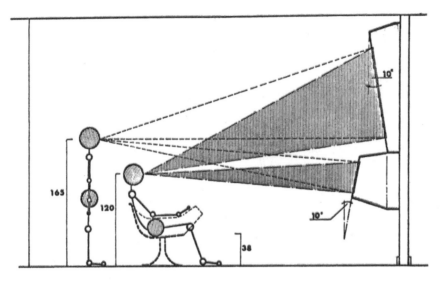

Figure 4.6
Design sketch for the Cybersyn operations room. Image used with permission from the State Technology Institute, Santiago, Chile; Gui Bonsiepe; and Constantin Malik.

themselves with such questions as the best angles for a user to read a display screen (figure 4.6). They studied aspects of information visualization and wondered how they could use color, size, and movement to increase comprehension or how much text could be displayed on a screen while maintaining legibility. The operations room offered a new image of Chilean modernity under socialism, a futuristic environment for control that meshed with other, simultaneous efforts to create a material culture that Chileans could call their own.

Beer gave the design team general instructions about the type of control environment he wanted to create. He asked Bonsiepe to create a relaxing environment, akin to a British gentlemen's club. The designers drew up plans for a "relax room" that used indirect lighting to simulate a "saloon" atmosphere.[54] The plans included space for a bar where room occupants could make pisco sours, a popular Chilean cocktail. The design also represented the future of Chilean socialism. "I believe that the original idea was Stafford's own," said designer Fernando Shultz, "that we are looking toward the future," and creating an aesthetic that would break with the way things were done in the past.[55] Rather than replicating old designs of control rooms or gentlemen's clubs, the designers gave the room a futuristic flair. For example, they proposed that the chairs and screen cases be made out of fiberglass, a relatively new construction material that lent itself to organic curved shapes that were difficult to achieve with more traditional building materials.

Figure 4.7
Design sketch by Werner Zemp showing ten chairs placed around a single control mechanism.
Image used with permission from Gui Bonsiepe and Constantin Malik.

In April Bonsiepe sent Beer sketches of a circular room with ten chairs placed around a single control mechanism (figure 4.7). The circular arrangement meant the seating arrangement could not be hierarchical, and the central control mechanism determined which data sets appeared on the wall displays. One wall contained a representation of Beer's five-tier Viable System Model. A series of slide projectors placed behind a wall projected slides of economic data onto acrylic screens, which Beer called "datafeed." These back projections created the effect of a high-tech flat panel display.

By mid-June the team had located a small space (approximately 24 feet by 12 feet) where the room could be housed. The small dimensions required the industrial design group to rethink its original layout (figure 4.8). Among the changes they made, the designers put the screen for the five-tier Viable System Model on a rail so that it could easily be moved out of the way; they reduced the number of chairs from ten to no more than four; and they nixed the bar. These changes concerned Beer, who described the new space as claustrophobic and unable to accommodate enough people in decision making. Moreover, he felt the smaller space did not do an adequate job of selling the project. "We already have a selling problem in principle," Beer wrote. "This [small room] aggravates it."[56] As Beer saw it, Project Cybersyn aspired to fundamentally change management practices in the enterprises and government offices. People would need to be convinced of the superiority of this cybernetic approach, and he hoped the modern-looking control room would offer an effective form of visual persuasion.

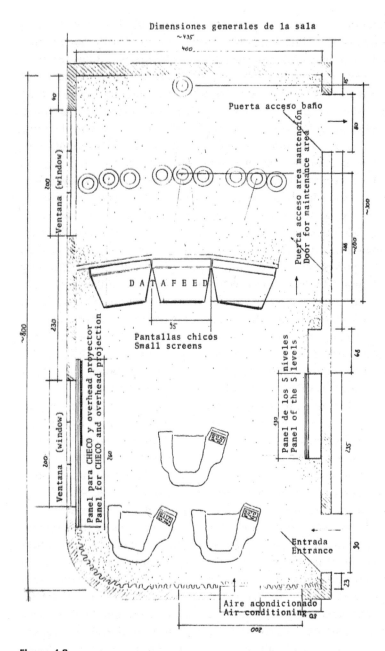

Figure 4.8
An alternative design to make the operations room fit in a small space. Reproduced with permission from Constantin Malik. Original kept at Liverpool John Moores University, Learning and Information Services, Special Collections and Archives.

In August the team finally located a more suitable space for the operations room, an interior patio of a downtown building that previously had been used to display automobiles. The space offered a number of advantages, including four hundred square meters (4,303 square feet) of open space with no columns, the opportunity to construct a ceiling at any height necessary, and a central Santiago location in a building several stories tall "so nobody will be able to actually see us working" in the patio area.[57] As an added perk, the National Telecommunications Enterprise (ENTEL) owned space in the same building and had wired it with telecommunications capabilities. CORFO arranged for the room's construction, and Bonsiepe began working with the architect on the room's design, which could now accommodate a greater number of people and display screens than would have been possible in the tiny space the team had found back in June.

The new design allowed for seven chairs arranged in a circle in the middle of the room. Putting an uneven number of individuals in the room meant there would be no tied votes. In deciding on this number, the team also drew from the influential 1956 paper "The Magical Number Seven, Plus or Minus Two: Some Limits on Our Capacity for Processing Information," by Princeton psychologist George A. Miller. Miller suggested that human beings could best process five to nine information channels, seven on average.[58] The team felt that limiting the number of occupants to seven would allow a diversity of opinion but still permit each voice to be heard. Paper was explicitly banned from the room, and the designers did not provide a table or other area for writing. Beer believed the use of paper detracted from, or even prevented, the process of communication; writing was strictly prohibited in the operations room.

The designers originally wanted to make the room circular as well, but when this proved difficult, they opted for a hexagon, a configuration that permitted five distinct wall spaces for display screens plus an entrance (figure 4.9).[59] Upon entering the room, a visitor would find that the first wall to the right opened up into a small kitchen. Continuing to the right, the second wall contained a series of four "datafeed" screens, one large and three small, all housed in individual fiberglass cabinets (figure 4.10). The large screen was positioned above the three smaller screens and displayed the combination of buttons a user needed to push on the armrest of his chair to change the data and images displayed on the three screens below. The armrest also included a hold button that, when pushed, gave that user control over the displays until the button was released. Although the dimensions of the room had changed, the new space still placed a series of slide projectors behind the wall and used them to back-project slide images onto the datafeed screens, thus simulating flat-panel displays. The armrest buttons sent signals to the different projectors and controlled the position of the slide carrousel. Slides displayed economic data or photographs of production in the state-run factories.[60] Rodrigo Walker, a member of the Industrial Design Group who worked on the design and construction of the operations room, said the user's ability to create his own path through the data was "like a hypertext" but one that preceded the invention of the World Wide Web by more than twenty years. While the parallel with the Web is not

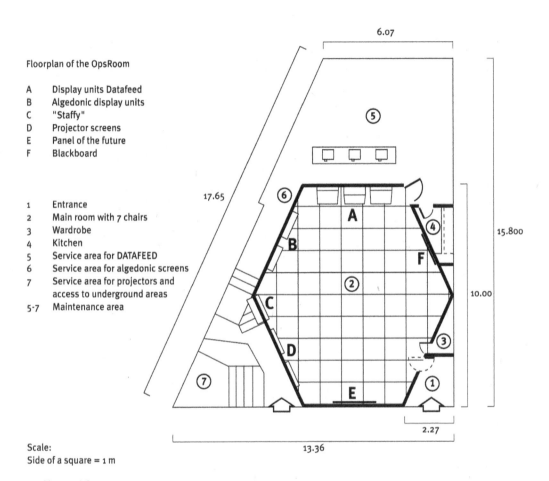

Floorplan of the OpsRoom

A   Display units Datafeed
B   Algedonic display units
C   "Staffy"
D   Projector screens
E   Panel of the future
F   Blackboard

1   Entrance
2   Main room with 7 chairs
3   Wardrobe
4   Kitchen
5   Service area for DATAFEED
6   Service area for algedonic screens
7   Service area for projectors and
     access to underground areas
5-7 Maintenance area

Scale:
Side of a square = 1 m

Figure 4.9
Floor plan for the final version of the Cybersyn Opsroom. Image redrawn and translated from the original. Image used with permission from Gui Bonsiepe.

exact, the room did offer a nonlinear way of seeing the Chilean economy that broke from the presentation of data in traditional paper reports. The three screens contained a mix of flow diagrams, graphs of actual and potential production capacities, and factory photographs, an intentional mix of quantitative and qualitative data designed to give the occupant a "physical relationship" to the enterprise being discussed.[61]

The third wall held two screens for recording Beer's algedonic signals, which would warn of trouble in the system. The screens displayed the overall production trends within different industrial sectors and listed urgent problems in need of government attention. A series of red lights appeared on the right-hand side of each screen and blinked with a frequency that reflected the level of urgency that a given problem posed (figure 4.11).

Figure 4.10
Close-up image of the datafeed screens. Image used with permission from Gui Bonsiepe.

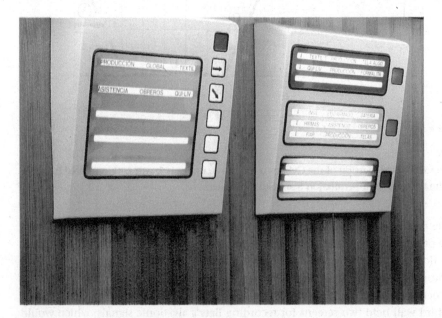

Figure 4.11
The algedonic screens from the Cybersyn operations room. Image used with permission from Gui Bonsiepe.

The fourth wall held a board with a large reproduction of Beer's Viable System Model (figure 4.12) and two large screens that could show additional information of use to the occupants. Beer insisted that the Viable System Model appear in the room to help participants remember the cybernetic principles that supposedly guided their decision-making processes. However, interviews revealed that few team members—let alone factory managers and CORFO employees not directly involved in the project—truly understood the Viable System Model. Some found it strange that such a theoretical representation appeared in a room dedicated to concrete representations of data and decision making. The board was so closely associated with Stafford Beer that the project team referred to it as "Staffy."

Occupying the final wall was a large metal board covered in fabric (figure 4.13). Here users could change the configuration of magnets cut in various iconic forms, each of which represented a component or function of the Chilean economy. This physical model served the same basic purpose as the model being developed by the CHECO team; both offered policy makers an opportunity to play with their policies and visualize different outcomes, but unlike CHECO the metal board was the epitome of low tech.

The British company Technomation completed four screens for the datafeed display. However, import licenses were difficult to acquire from the Central Bank: "I have had the [word] IMPOSSIBLE written in red tape and with flashing lights on every step of the bureaucratic way," Cañete complained, alluding to the flashing red lights in the operations room that signaled trouble.[62] He thus conceived of an elaborate plan to smuggle the screens into Chile marked as donations from "Artorga," a reference to the British cybernetic investment club ARTORGA (the Artificial Organism Research Group) to which Beer belonged. But at the eleventh hour the Central Bank came through with the import licenses, and the screens reached Chile in September.[63]

The Chilean government dedicated some of its best resources to the room's completion. Its futuristic design, which borders on science fiction, was unlike anything being built in Chile at the time. It is often compared with the style of design found in Stanley Kubrick's classic movie *2001: A Space Odyssey* (1968), although the designers vehemently dispute that they were influenced by sci-fi films. "There was no reference point for this project," asserted Rodrigo Walker. "If I told you, 'Let's go build a movie theater,' you would have a reference point, you could begin to imagine what it would look like. But there was no operations room [in Chile], there was nothing that we could look at."[64] So they looked at design styles elsewhere and found inspiration in the work of Italian designers who used unorthodox materials, such as plastic and fiberglass, to create furniture with a sleek organic form. Only a few people in Chile knew how to work with fiberglass, and it had previously been used to construct swimming pools, not furniture, but the designers felt the material gave them the practical and stylistic elements they desired. "I think the room looked the way that it did because of the

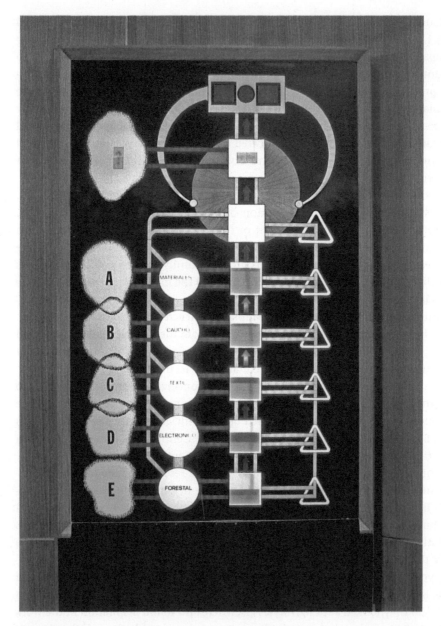

Figure 4.12
The operations room housed a reproduction of the Viable System Model, informally known as "Staffy." Image used with permission from Gui Bonsiepe.

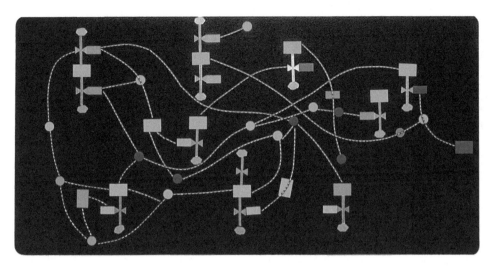

Figure 4.13
The team constructed a low-tech economic simulator using magnetic pieces on a cloth-covered metal board. Image used with permission from Gui Bonsiepe.

materials that we used . . . polyester with fiberglass, an organic material that allows you to do anything that you want," Walker noted.[65] Using these new materials allowed the designers to project a new image of socialist modernity that rivaled science fiction.[66]

The operations room also gave the designers opportunities to form new working relationships, which they viewed through the lens of socialist change. For example, the designers wanted to attach the fiberglass form of the seat to a metallic base that swiveled. However, the swivel mechanism they envisioned was not manufactured in Chile, and the designers could not import the mechanism because of the government's shortages of foreign credit and the invisible blockade. So the designers consulted with workers in their metal shop, who devised an alternative design that used grease alone and allowed the upper part of the chair to move without friction. Thus, Chilean socialism not only inspired the use of new materials but forced Chileans to develop innovative ways of working with old materials. Ideas that originated on the shop floor mixed with those of the professional designers, and, in the context of the Chilean road to socialism, this mixing had new significance. One designer, Fernando Shultz, said that Chilean socialism opened up a new awareness of worker participation that was "very subtle" but still part of the government's program. For Shultz, asking for workers' suggestions to improve the design team's work was not a simple act but rather the result of "a mental process, a process of conscience and commitment" that was set in motion by the Popular Unity government.[67] In the area of industrial design, Cybersyn thus resulted in more inclusive and participatory design practices.

Work on the slides showing production data and factory photographs was supposed to start in August, and the team secured one of the top photographers in Chile to assist with their production. But the team was not sure how to create a clear, homogeneous representation of factory data that managers and government administrators could easily understand. This uncertainty delayed production of the slides, and the team worried that the photographer would be otherwise engaged by the time they were ready for him.

The slides provided a way for the design team to update the data displayed in the operations room. But the team did not use a computer to generate these visual displays of data, as they would today. Instead, Bonsiepe enlisted the four female graphic design students from the Catholic University to create, by hand, camera-ready versions of the flow charts and graphs that the photographer could convert into slides (figure 4.14). The graphic designers completed the first flow charts showing production activities in September; these gave an overview of production in several nationalized textile enterprises.[68]

Although the operations room presented a sleek, futuristic vision of socialist modernity in which an occupant could control the economy with the touch of a button, maintaining this illusion required a tremendous amount of human labor. In this case,

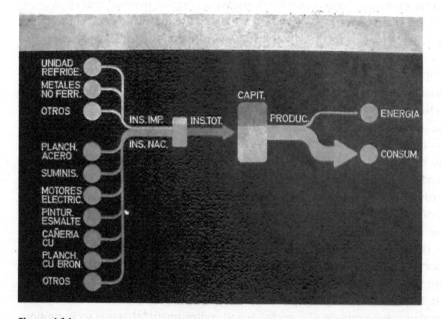

Figure 4.14
A slide image used in the Cybersyn operations room. These flow diagrams were drawn by hand by the four graphic designers. Image used with permission by Constantin Malik.

it required some of Chile's best graphic designers to draw by hand every graph and chart the room displayed. These images needed to change regularly to permit the form of dynamic control Beer imagined, yet there were no plans to automate this process in the future. Although Allende believed that Chile would have a revolution with "red wine and empanadas," this assertion failed to account for the actual complexity that the process entailed. In the same way, the clean, futuristic appearance of the control room obscured the vast network of individuals, materials, expertise, and information required to make economic management appear simple.

Design for Values

Beer and the Industrial Design Group were well aware that design could reflect social values. For example, Beer found the early design sketches for the operations room, which placed a single control mechanism in the middle, to be lacking because the design inhibited democratic participation. As a result Bonsiepe sent Beer a new set of sketches that put the mechanism for controlling the content of the datafeed display screens in the armrest of each chair. Occupants could thus change the data displayed by pushing different combinations of geometric buttons (figures 4.15–4.17). This new design gave all occupants equal access to the data and allowed them to control what was displayed inside the room. The geometric buttons also made the room more inviting by replacing a more traditional mechanism, the keyboard. Beer imagined that the

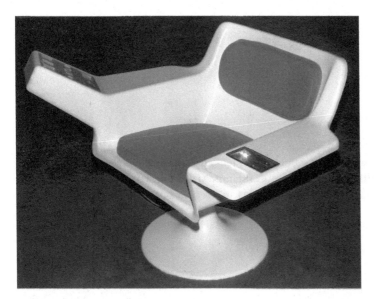

Figure 4.15
The operations room chair. Image used with permission from Gui Bonsiepe.

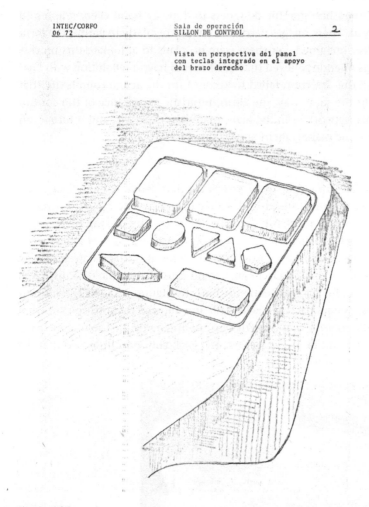

INTEC/CORFO   Sala de operación
06 72   SILLON DE CONTROL   2

                   Vista en perspectiva del panel
                   con teclas integrado en el apoyo
                   del brazo derecho

Figure 4.16
A design sketch for the armrest of the operations room chair showing the geometric "big hand"
buttons. Reproduced with permission from Constantin Malik. Original kept at Liverpool John
Moores University, Learning and Information Services, Special Collections and Archives.

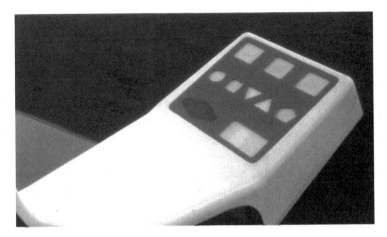

Figure 4.17
A photo of the armrest of the operations room chair. Reproduced with permission from Gui Bonsiepe.

individuals sitting in the operations room would be either members of the government elite or factory workers, individuals who did not know how to type—a skill typically possessed by trained female secretaries. With little instruction, occupants could use the large "big-hand" buttons on each armrest. Participants could also "thump" these buttons if they wished to emphasize a point. Beer claimed that an interface of large, geometrical buttons made the room more accessible for workers and prevented it from being a "*sanctum sanctorum* for a government elite." Through this design decision, the system allowed for worker participation.[69]

While politics favoring class equality influenced the design decision to use the buttons, this design decision was also gendered. Beer stated that the decision to eliminate the need for a keyboard literally eliminated the "girl between themselves and the machinery" and thus brought the users closer to the machine.[70] He was referring to a literal woman, a typist who would navigate the keyboard interface on behalf of the bureaucrats or factory workers occupying the operations room chairs. Other gendered assumptions also entered into the design of the control environment. In addition to eliminating female clerical work, the room was explicitly modeled after a gentlemen's club. It also encouraged a form of communication that bears a closer resemblance to masculine aggression ("thumping") than to a form of gender-neutral or feminine expression. Bonsiepe later acknowledged that "in hindsight I can see a gender bias" in the room's design.[71]

The characteristics ascribed to the room's future occupants reveal assumptions about who would hold power within the Chilean revolution and who constituted a "worker." Generally speaking, factory workers and bureaucrats would have the ability to make decisions affecting the direction of the country; clerical workers, women, and those operating outside the formal economy would not.[72] The operations room also offers a valuable counterexample in the history of technology, a field filled with examples that link female labor to the routinization of work and unskilled labor. Here we see an opposite but no less interesting phenomenon: Beer and the designers viewed female clerical work as *too* skilled; it therefore needed to be eliminated to make the room accessible.

The design of the operations room illustrates that even futuristic visions of modernity carry assumptions about gender and class. Moreover, the design of this control space shows how cultural and political givens limit technological innovation. By treating the design of the operations room as a historical text, we can see how the Allende government framed its revolutionary subjects and ultimately limited the redistribution of power within Chile's socialist revolution.

Politics and Practice

The operations room clearly illustrates how members of the Cybersyn team tried to engineer Chilean socialism into the design of the Cybersyn system. However, in some cases the practices Chilean technologists used to implement the system did not match the politics of the Popular Unity government. Such practices show that historical actors were not consistent in how they portrayed the relationship of technology and politics in Project Cybersyn and bring to light a disconnection between rhetoric and praxis. In some cases, Cybersyn engineers intentionally framed the system as apolitical and technocratic. This helped them persuade members of the opposition to support the project. In other cases, Cybersyn engineers assumed that their own practices were scientific and thus neutral, without recognizing that these scientific techniques also had an implicit bias that ran counter to the aims of the Allende government.

The inconsistent relationship between technology and politics is best seen in the work of the Chilean engineers charged with building models of production in the state-run enterprises. Most of these engineers worked for the State Technology Institute. The models they created identified key production indicators and their range of acceptable values, which were then used as parameters in the Cyberstride software code.

By the end of June Cybersyn engineers had visited enterprises in the textile and agroindustrial sectors and enterprises in the light industry branch. By the end of September engineers at the State Technology Institute had modeled or were still modeling at least forty-eight enterprises and twenty-three plants, models that would later be used to code the Cyberstride permanent suite.[73] Although engineers from the State Technology Institute described the modeling process as "just looking at what was going on," project reports reveal a more complicated process that highlights the marginal role played by workers in Cybersyn's implementation, despite Allende's insistence that the system encourage worker participation.[74]

The engineers began the modeling process by contacting the upper management of an enterprise and arranging to give a presentation to the interventors and the general managers. During this presentation the engineers used a simplified version of the Viable System Model and explained Project Cybersyn. While the presentations were intended to explain Cybersyn, they also were designed to persuade the managers to support the modeling process and recognize the value of the project. The engineers then explained the project to lower levels of management and worked their way down until they reached the production engineers on the factory floor.

The Cybersyn engineers talked to a factory's production engineers and then followed the flows of raw materials and their gradual conversion into finished products. The Cybersyn team next created a quantified flow chart of production in the enterprise, which they gave to the interventor.[75] The flow charts helped the modelers identify, on average, the ten most important indicators of factory performance, typically some combination of raw materials, finished materials, energy used, and labor absenteeism.[76]

It is important to note that the Cybersyn engineers were not interested in financial information. With the exception of the CHECO simulator, Cybersyn focused exclusively on industrial production and thus echoed the socialist accounting practices adopted by CORFO as a whole. Such practices gave priority to increased production over profit and accepted financial losses as part of government price freezes. Cybersyn factory models were therefore intended to help the government identify ways to raise production levels, independent of a market and without concern for prices. Since Cybersyn was designed to fight "the battle of production," the bulk of the system did not take considerations such as the price index or the rate of inflation into account.

After the engineers identified the key production indicators, they needed to identify how to collect such data on a regular basis. In many cases, such information collection systems simply did not exist at the enterprise level. The engineers also needed to determine the range of acceptable values for the indicator, as well as how much time the enterprise should be given to correct the indicators that fell outside this range before CORFO intervened from above. Finally, the engineers needed to determine two additional values for each indicator: the "potentiality" value and the "capability" value. Beer defined the capability value as "what we *could* be doing . . . with existing resources, under existing constraints, if we really worked at it." The capability value was the best possible value of the indicator under current conditions. He defined the potentiality value as "what we *ought* to be doing by developing our resources and removing constraints, although still operating within the bounds of what is already feasible."[77] Thus, the potentiality value was the best possible value of the indicator under the best possible conditions. The engineers gave these two values to the Cybersyn computer programmers, who coded them into the Cyberstride software. The computer program could then compare current, or "actual," data with these optimal numbers and create a unitless percentage that showed how close present enterprise performance was to

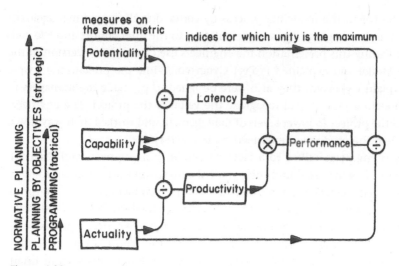

Figure 4.18
Diagram showing how Beer created unitless measures of achievement from actuality, potentiality, and capability values. Reprinted from Stafford Beer, "Fanfare for Effective Freedom: Cybernetic Praxis in Government," in his *Platform for Change* (New York: J. Wiley, 1975), 437. Image reproduced with permission from Constantin Malik.

its ideal (figure 4.18). Beer reasoned that government administrators, with little background information, would be able to quickly grasp these unitless measurements.

A study of the Easton Furniture factory reveals how complicated the modeling process could be. In this report the four coauthors begin their analysis by describing in detail the process of building wooden furniture, each of the machines involved, the humidity levels of the wood, how to apply varnish, and so forth. In addition to a narrative description of the process and a flow diagram, the report includes various tables showing the exact time required for each stage of the production process for 13 of the 150 different products the factory produced. These measurements were then averaged to create a "typical product" and to calculate the idealized capability values. Pages of statistical analysis determine the range of normality for each indicator.[78]

Modeling factories required university-level training in operations research. Although the State Technical Institute employed a number of individuals with this expertise, it did not have a labor pool sufficient to complete the task in the time allotted. In a July report Humberto Gabella complained that he had requested three engineers to model enterprises in the forestry sector and three engineers to model enterprises in the building materials sector but so far had received only two engineers for the forestry sector and none for building materials.[79] To solve this problem, the Cybersyn team recruited engineers from within the enterprises or sectors being modeled or from private consulting firms. The additional hands helped, but it made consistency in the modeling process difficult because engineers used different methodologies to study production and identify key production indicators.[80]

Data collection also proved difficult. Modelers sometimes needed data that the enterprise did not collect, or needed data from the companies that supplied the enterprise with raw materials or component parts. Project notes state that at least one enterprise could not be modeled because of "internal organization problems," a cryptic line that could have referred to a number of scenarios, from a labor force on strike to political battles for representation on enterprise committees that negatively affected factory management.[81]

The engineers also needed to convince the enterprises and the sector committees to support Project Cybersyn, but they were not particularly skilled at public relations. Modeler Tomás Kohn speculated that his presence probably "pissed off" several managers. "We were fairly young at the time," Kohn said. "For most of us it was probably our first job. We were pretty arrogant, not because of any political position but because we thought we had a good model, and we firmly believed in this approach. . . . I suspect that people were really turned off by this group of youngsters."[82] The modelers quickly learned that portraying the project as technocratic rather than political made it easier to gain the managers' participation. Kohn recalled one textile plant manager who, having already spent several years reaching his senior position, was not happy with the changes introduced by the Allende administration. The plant manager was "difficult to deal with," Kohn said, but "when it came to the more technical aspects, he could work quite openly."[83] Other modelers shared similar stories. Although enterprises were often run by Allende appointees (the interventors), much of the management structure within the enterprises had been in place before Allende was elected. These managers had expertise that was important to the modeling process, but political speeches would not convince them to support the Cybersyn project.

In theory, Cybersyn engineers also consulted with members of the rank-and-file. Beer writes that the engineers were expected to create "quantified flowchart models with the *help* and the *agreement* of workers' committees" and to determine the "recovery times for each index on the same terms: that is with help and agreement."[84] The modelers did talk to committees of workers in some cases but not as a rule. More often technocracy eclipsed ideology on the factory floor. Despite the explicit instructions the engineers received to work with worker committees, often the converse occurred, and the engineer treated the workers with condescension or would ignore the workers altogether and deal directly with management. Moreover, the engineers frequently hid or overlooked the political facets of the project in favor of emphasizing its technological benefits, thereby avoiding potential conflicts.[85]

My interviews of Cybersyn engineers, interventors, and workers yielded little evidence that workers were involved in shaping the modeling process.[86] Kohn described the process of modeling a factory as "a fairly technocratic approach," one that was "top down" and did not involve "speaking to the guy who was actually working on the mill or the spinning machine or whatever." Eugenio Balmaceda, another engineer from the State Technology Institute who modeled enterprises within the forestry and construction sector, also reported working exclusively with the directors of the firm, not the workers. Like Kohn, Balmaceda found it easier to avoid the political aspects of the project and concentrate solely on the technical aspects. He remembered giving a general description of the project to groups of workers and that "they were totally in favor of the ideas we wanted to implement." But later in our conversation he told me, "The workers could not have many doubts [about the system] because it was a highly technical subject."[87] In essence, the technical sophistication of the cybernetic system prevented the participation of workers, if they even knew it existed.[88]

Looked at from a different angle, the Cybersyn system could even be read as disempowering Chilean workers. The timing charts printed in the study of the Easton Furniture factory are reminiscent of the time studies that characterized the Taylor system of management, which had been introduced in a number of Chilean factories before Allende came to power. In the 1960s Chilean workers went on strike to protest the accelerated pace of production that Taylorism demanded; it pushed workers to perform beyond their capabilities and worsened factory working conditions.[89] The study of Easton Furniture thus reveals a contradiction in Chile's revolutionary process: although the Allende government wanted to increase worker involvement in decision making, Cybersyn shows that it also continued management practices that had disempowered and dehumanized workers in the past. For example, managers could use the capability values calculated from timing charts to control the means of production. Cybersyn could also give Chilean managers the ability to exert control over labor through an abstract technological system instead of a shop floor manager with a stop watch. In this sense Cybersyn could have followed a path similar to that of numerical control technology in the United States, which gave management greater control of production and disempowered labor—the very thing the Allende government sought to undo.[90]

Social and political considerations clearly entered into the model-building process, prioritizing which factories to model and which elements, such as labor, appeared in the quantitative flow charts. However, the specific techniques used to build these models also had politics, in the sense that they could empower some groups and disempower others—techniques that the young engineers probably learned in their university operations research classes and saw as strictly technical and thus neutral.

Since Project Cybersyn never reached completion, it is impossible to know how such a system would have affected the lives of the rank-and-file or how it might have changed power relations on the shop floor. But it would have been much harder for workers to organize against an abstract technological system, or a factory model, than to stage a protest against a visible production manager holding a stopwatch.

Cybersyn engineers were not consistent in how they portrayed the relationship of technology and politics in Project Cybersyn. Beer believed the system could provide a way to change how white-collar technologists interacted with blue-collar workers, but it was impossible to undo long-standing class prejudices overnight. The State Technology Institute had a rather sophisticated understanding of how technological artifacts could uphold particular configurations of power, either by enriching one class at the expense of another or by promoting unjust economic relations between developed and developing nations. But engineers from the State Technology Institute did not extend such criticism to the scientific techniques they used, which they viewed as free of political bias.

Populist Technology

To increase the political appeal of Project Cybersyn, Beer began developing ways to lay populist overtones on his cybernetic system for economic management. In addition to working with some of Chile's best designers, engineers, and computer scientists, he also formed ties with one of Chile's best-known musicians, Angel Parra. Music gave Beer not only a better sense of Chilean life and culture but also a better idea of how Chileans experienced the revolution taking place around them. By the early 1970s, folk music in particular had proved to be exceptionally powerful for conveying political messages in Chile and throughout the western hemisphere. Folk music presented Beer with new opportunities to translate his cybernetics into forms better understood by the Chilean people.

Angel Parra was a member of one of Chile's most beloved musical families. His mother was Violetta Parra, one of the most famous Latin American folk musicians. In 1965 Angel and his sister Isabel established the Peña de los Parra in Santiago, an artistic space where they could sing for a small audience and experiment with the Nueva Canción (new song) movement, a form of music that linked Chilean folk traditions to the social and political movements of the time. Whereas traditional folk music was suitable for parties or dancing, music in the Nueva Canción vein reflected the lives of Chilean workers, peasants, and shantytown dwellers, and the difficulties they faced, as well as themes such as world peace, friendship, and solidarity.[91] When Allende came to power, the Parra family and the Peña de los Parra became a cultural center for the left and a musical inspiration for the entire country.

Parra was used to meeting famous people and later described himself as "a young person, insolent, and without respect." When Stafford Beer first wandered into the Peña, Parra was not impressed with Beer's reputation as an international scientific consultant. But Beer still managed to make a lasting impression. "He was like how one imagines Santa Claus," Parra recalled: tall, with a white beard, and "bringing this hidden gift, cybernetics," which Parra did not understand.[92] Beer kept coming to the Peña de los Parra with increasing frequency and started hanging out with a small, select group of Angel Parra's friends, including José Miguel Insulza, the future vice president of Chile and secretary general of the Organization of American States.[93] Parra did not

speak English, but others at the Peña de los Parra did, including Cañete, who sometimes accompanied Beer and served as his translator. "Beer asked me if I would write
a song for [Project Cybersyn]," Parra said. "For me the project was like a pregnancy, a
pregnancy of Popular Unity." He deepened the comparison: "If you bring a child into
the world, you have to be responsible, you cannot abandon it. I was saying that the
computer system was also going to be like this."[94]

In June 1972 Parra completed the lyrics for a song that he wrote in honor of the
Cybersyn Project. He titled it "Litany for a Computer and a Baby about to Be Born." As
a whole, the song emphasized the importance of technology in bringing about social
change and its potential for eliminating political corruption. The chorus of the song
similarly conveyed the political intentions of the project:

Hay que parar al que no quiera
que el pueblo gane esta pelea
Hay que juntar toda la ciencia
antes que acabe la paciencia.

Let us stop those who do not want
the people to win this fight,
Let us bring together all of science
before we exhaust our patience.[95]

The lyrics constituted a rallying cry as well as a prophetic warning.

Parra never recorded the song but remembers singing it in the Peña de los Parra,
and its lyrics remain scrawled in a notebook that holds many of Parra's songs from the
Popular Unity era. Beer had greater ambitions for the song, hoping that it would make
cybernetics and the Cybersyn Project more accessible and appealing to Chilean workers. As one of the most recognizable voices of the revolution, Parra's voice would frame
the system as a form of science for the people, something that was culturally Chilean
and that could connect the project to the broader social changes that were taking place.
It would also present Cybersyn as a technology that workers could understand and use
for their own empowerment.

Implementing Cybersyn went beyond coding software or modeling factory production; Beer felt he needed to link the project explicitly to other forms of Chilean political
life. Flores shared this position, and in late September he held a meeting that brought
together the diverse groups at work on the project as well as others who were connected
to it peripherally.

According to Beer, both he and Flores stressed the political aspects of the project
during the meeting. This message distressed many of the professionals involved, who
viewed Cybersyn as a highly technical project that was politically neutral.[96] "It became
obvious that there would have to be major changes in the management team that
was actually implementing the results of the cybernetics," Beer wrote.[97] He and Flores

started discussing how they might make Cybersyn less technocratic and more political. These opposing interpretations of Project Cybersyn would resurface repeatedly in the months ahead.

Beer began to explore how concepts and language from the Chilean revolution might be used to communicate ideas from management cybernetics. In September he drafted a small, illustrated booklet titled *Five Principles for the People toward Good Government* that explored how cybernetic thinking could improve government practices in ways that went beyond economic management. The principles contained in the booklet reflected common themes in Beer's writings: the booklet called for an end to bureaucracy, greater transparency, increased personal responsibility, clearer government organization, and planning for the future. Technology played an important role in achieving these goals. "The wishes of the people will be made known to the Government at all times," it read. "We shall use TECHNOLOGY, which belongs to the people, to do it."[98] Beer viewed the booklet much as he viewed the folksong that Angel Parra wrote about cybernetics and social change—another attempt to educate the Chilean people about the promise of cybernetics by putting it into a language that people could understand. For Beer, making Cybersyn populist was central to making Cybersyn socialist.

"Programme Beat-the-Clock"

Thus far I have traced the progress the project team made coding the Cyberstride software, building the CHECO models, and constructing the operations room. From April to September 1972, the telex network (Cybernet) also continued to grow. By early July, the telex network had connected the ministers of economics and finance, the subsecretary of economics, the Central Bank, the National Directorate of Industry and Commerce, the National Computer Corporation, the State Development Corporation, and the National Technology Institute, as well as eight sector committees and forty-nine plants.[99] By August, Benadof and Améstica had started developing software to allow the computer to read signals directly from the telex machines. They hoped such software would eventually eliminate the need for human operators to collect the data from the telex machines and reenter it into the mainframe for processing.[100]

Time was of the essence. The precarious position of the Allende administration and the gravity of the national economic situation pushed the team to work harder. In July, Beer revised the project's work schedule through the end of October 1972 and called the new plan "Programme Beat-the-Clock" (figure 4.19). Among other things, the plan called for a functioning operations room by mid-October. Beer hoped this ambitious schedule would help the administration withstand the opposition's destabilization efforts, and the title of the document was meant as a reminder that the administration was, quite literally, under the gun.

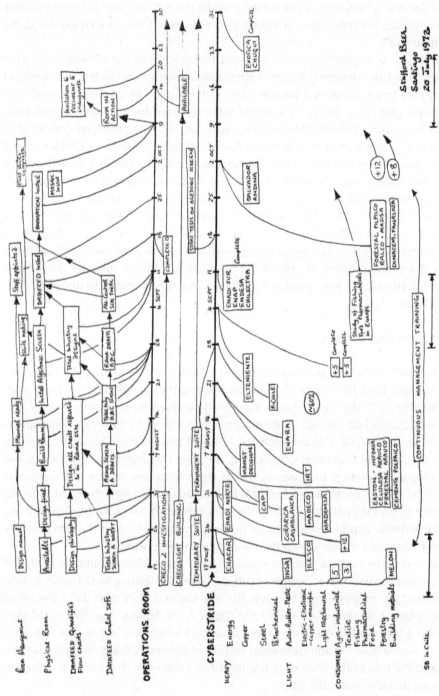

Figure 4.19

The project schedule drafted by Beer in July 1972. Reproduced with permission from Constantin Malik. Original kept at Liverpool John Moores University, Learning and Information Services, Special Collections and Archives.

Nationalization continued to incite controversy and deepen political fissures. In June 1972, the Christian Democratic Party and the Popular Unity coalition failed to reach a consensus on the nationalization issue. This failure to reach a compromise heightened the levels of counterrevolutionary activity in the country, and these oppositional activities increasingly took place in the streets in addition to the Chilean Congress. Yet the nationalization process still continued at a rapid clip. In July and August 1972, the administration brought twenty-five additional enterprises into the Social Property Area. "We have kept on nationalizing industries at a steady pace," Cañete reported to Beer. "The poor owners of industries related to the light industry [branch] do not know what hit them and are right now reeling under a continuous series of blows."[101] Allende continued to support a moderate approach to nationalization and promised the owners of small- and medium-sized businesses that the government would not take their property.[102] But his own Socialist Party did not agree with the president's restrained approach and pushed to accelerate the pace of nationalization and increase government control of the private sector. This gave owners of these businesses another reason to distrust Allende's promises and to align themselves with the opposition.

Chile teetered on the brink of political violence. By August 1972 rumors of a rightwing coup had begun to circulate and continued to gain strength, and they were grounded in truth. In August demonstrations against the government resulted in arrests and injuries and forced the government to declare a state of emergency in the capital city. In September the president publicly denounced an aborted plot by rightist factions to overthrow the government. For the first time Beer started to worry about his safety. On 28 September he telexed Cañete, asking, "Do you regard my [upcoming] trip as secure?"[103] Cañete telexed back immediately, "General news . . . not better nor worse than in any of your previous visits. Your safety absolutely and utterly guaranteed." Trying to make the conversation lighter, Cañete then wrote, "Remember we are starting our spring so there are more interesting matters to worry about. Be sure to bring swimming trunks and light clothes."[104] Beer returned to Chile the following month, after asking his assistant, Sonia Mordojovich, to book him a poolside room at the Sheraton.

Political Challenges, Engineering Challenges

Members of the Cybersyn project team set out to make Cybersyn a socialist technology and accomplished this in multiple ways. In the area of design, the project formed part of a larger effort by the Industrial Design Group to create a new material culture that furthered the aims of Chilean socialism and broke from the aesthetic of the past. The context of socialism also encouraged Chilean industrial designers to solicit worker opinions and incorporate them into the design and construction of the operations room. Unexamined assumptions about who held decision-making power in the Chilean revolution also shaped the design of the operations room. It was inclusive in the sense that it accommodated both workers and high-ranking government bureaucrats. At the same time the room was designed as a gendered space that explicitly encouraged masculine forms of communication, was modeled on a gentleman's club, and eliminated female clerical work. The design of the operations room reveals the gendered limits of power redistribution on the Chilean road to socialism and how preexisting ideas about gender and class restricted the way historical actors imagined the future, even when their visions bordered on science fiction. Beer's own gendered assumptions about decision-making behavior are also evident here.

In addition, Beer attempted to instill political values in Project Cybersyn through sociotechnical engineering. In some instances he designed Cybersyn's technology to encourage certain desired social interactions. For example, he rejected having the display screens in the operations room connected to a single, centralized control mechanism and instead insisted that control mechanisms be built into the armrest of every chair, a design he felt encouraged broader participation in decision making. Beer also tried to engineer the social relationships in Cybersyn's construction by encouraging Chilean engineers from the State Technology Institute to seek input from Chilean workers when creating models of the state-run factories. But, as we have seen, Cybersyn engineers preferred to work with the other white-collar professionals in the state-run factories. In most cases they did not discuss their work with Chilean workers, or if they did, they presented their model building as a technical endeavor that the workers could not understand or question. Class prejudices could not be undone by political revolution or by sociotechnical engineering, despite Beer's considerable influence within the project team.

Project Cybersyn was political in other ways: it advanced Allende's goal of improving Chilean capabilities in science and technology through the transfer of technological expertise to Chile from more developed nations. Examples abound of how Chileans acquired technical expertise through their interactions with British consultants and academics as part of their work on the project, but U.S. and British ideas about dynamic economic modeling were of limited use to Chile. The South American nation had different recordkeeping practices than Britain, had a political and economic context without precedent (which therefore could not be modeled), and was a target of foreign intervention and sabotage. Furthermore, the history of Project Cybersyn suggests a different model of technology transfer, one that was not based on imitation and appropriation. With friendship, collaboration, and mutual respect, Beer and his Chilean colleagues worked together and produced something new.

Constructing Cybersyn posed a number of challenges, some of which are part of any high-risk engineering project, regardless of where it is built or its political context. Like the leaders of Cybersyn, many project directors have to create a work culture that encourages creativity, productivity, risk taking, and teamwork. Yet, as noted previously, Cybersyn technologists also confronted challenges that were related to Chile's status as a Latin American nation. For example, project team members needed to establish channels for technology transfer. Foreign experts such as Beer, Bonsiepe, Anderton, and the Arthur Andersen consultants all played a central role in the construction of the project. Chile's limited technical resources also necessitated creative design solutions.

However, it is important to realize that those involved in constructing Project Cybersyn were also facing extraordinary challenges, which were directly related to Chile's political project. The U.S.-led economic blockade prevented the Chilean government from acquiring the U.S.-made technologies and spare parts on which the Chilean economy had depended before 1970. This lack of resources presented serious obstacles to Cybersyn's design, as well as to the government's winning the battle of production and achieving Chilean economic stability. The U.S. government also supported the activities of the political opposition and threatened Chile's long-standing history of political stability. As rumors of a military coup began to circulate, Cybersyn team members realized that even though they had made substantial progress, they were still engineering against the clock. Ironically, the Chilean political context that had led to the creation of Project Cybersyn also created the most difficult challenges that the Cybersyn technologists faced.

5 The October Strike

This is our hour of truth, and yours too.
—Fernando Flores, quoted in a letter from Herman Schwember to Stafford Beer, November 1972

When Beer returned to Chile on 10 October 1972, he saw the fruits of almost a year's worth of intensive labor. The display screens for the operations room had arrived from England. The industrial design team had drafted fourteen different production flow charts for display in the operations room. Seven operations room chairs were being completed. Raúl Espejo, the Cybersyn project director, had hired additional contractors to model the state-controlled enterprises, especially in the sectors of light industry and building materials. Flores continued to oversee many aspects of the project, and he and Beer remained in close contact. Beer arrived in Santiago at noon, and he met with Flores that night. Cybersyn was moving toward fruition.

But within a month, a watershed event would transform the Allende government and Project Cybersyn, and would shake both Beer's and Flores's views of the role of technology in the Chilean revolution and its potential to revolutionize the structure of Chilean society. A national strike begun by thousands of Chilean truck owners would throw the country into a state of emergency. The strike was intended to demonstrate the power of the bourgeoisie, bring the economy to a halt, and set up the conditions for a coup. While the Allende government survived the strike, it was forced into a permanent defensive position from which it struggled simply to stay in power.

The October Strike (El Paro de Octubre, as it came to be known) was a milestone in cybernetic history. To survive the strike, the Allende government needed a way to maintain the distribution of essential goods throughout the country. In this context of crisis the government decided to use the telex network created for Project Cybersyn. It expanded this network beyond the industrial sector to send messages quickly and reliably from the northernmost to the southernmost regions of the country (about 5,152 kilometers or 3,201 miles), from Arica to Punta Arenas. The existence of this network gave the government a new way to respond to the effects of the strike and ultimately helped it survive. The October Strike provides a clear example of how a national government benefited from cybernetic ideas of control and viability and of the successful use of cybernetics to manage a crisis.

The October Strike also changed how Beer and Flores viewed the relationship of technology and politics. Although Flores still felt that Cybersyn was useful, he came to see that it was incapable of regulating the size and scope of Chile's economic and political problems or of changing the structure of Chilean society. As he continued to assume positions of increasing power within the Allende government, he moved from viewing science and technology as a key part of Chile's revolutionary process to seeing the limitations of both when faced with the real possibility of a military coup.

Beer, in contrast, came to believe after the strike that cybernetics could benefit many aspects of Chilean socialism beyond production management. In the months after the strike he envisioned new ways of embedding socialist values in the design and construction of Cybersyn, and he theorized that such embedded values could change social relations in Chilean factories and encourage broader use of the system. He even urged the government to feature Cybersyn in government propaganda as a symbol of Chilean technological prowess under socialism.

The strike was also a turning point for Beer personally and professionally. His time in Chile and his friendships with Chilean revolutionaries forced the cybernetician— who at the time of the strike was ensconced in a poolside room at the Sheraton—to reconsider his materialist lifestyle and how best to prioritize his ideals, his science, and his family. While he and Flores were both deeply dedicated to the success of Chilean socialism, by the end of December they had diverging ideas on how Cybersyn fit into the larger picture of Chilean socialist change and how to design or use it to achieve the political goals of Popular Unity. Tracing this divergence illuminates the symbiotic relationship of technology and politics, and illustrates the myriad ways that technologies have politics.

Politics and the Cybersyn Team

Politics was a pervasive part of Chilean life, and, for some members of the project team, politics became a more important part of Project Cybersyn as it progressed. For these members of the group, including Beer, *technocracy* became an increasingly pejorative term. In early October Flores, now undersecretary of economics, brought two new people in to work with Raúl Espejo, who directed Cybersyn's day-to-day technical operations. Flores charged Enrique Farné and Herman Schwember with thinking beyond Cybersyn's technology to insert the project in the flow of Chile's broader political, economic, and social transformations.

Farné was already playing an active role in the economic nationalization process and had a proven ability to get things done. He and Flores had known each other since they were both thirteen and living in Talca. Now, at twenty-nine, Farné had experience in mining, finance, tourism, computing, and the automobile industry.[1] When Allende came to power, Pedro Vuskovic, then the minister of the economy, had put Farné in charge of bringing the sale of automobiles under state control. While Farné had voted for Allende and sympathized with the left, he was not a member of any party and thus had the freedom to negotiate with different parties, including those in the opposition, such as Christian Democracy. Farné also possessed exceptional people skills, had a flair for languages, and was a talented political operator. In early October 1972, Flores asked for Farné's ideas about how to implement Cybersyn. This included figuring out how to deal with union leaders, determining who would occupy the operations room, and convincing the different political parties within the state-controlled enterprises to support and use the system. Flores asked Farné to manage these aspects of the project, which required an ability to meld the technical aspects of the system to the nuances of the Chilean political landscape.

Schwember was Flores's friend and confidant. Although Schwember had tutored Beer in Chilean politics and economics during the cybernetician's first trip to Chile in November 1971, he had not had an official role with the Project Cybersyn team until now. He worked as an engineer for CODELCO, the national copper company, and he had an excellent understanding of the Chilean political landscape. Flores asked Schwember to think about how Cybersyn fit into the larger political picture of Chilean socialism, including how to build political support for the project and how to use it to strengthen the government's position.

This new managerial relationship positioned Flores, Schwember, and Farné as Systems Five, Four, and Three of Beer's Viable System Model. Flores occupied System Five, the chief executive position, and decided how the system could be used to further the goals of the Popular Unity government. Schwember occupied level four, the level dedicated to future planning. As System Three, Farné determined the feasibility of Flores's policies and ways to implement them (figure 5.1). Flores and Beer saw this new management structure as complementing Espejo's management of the technical aspects of Cybersyn's development. But it was an uneasy relationship because Schwember and Farné both regarded Espejo as a technocrat.[2]

As for Beer, he now gave greater attention to the nontechnology aspects of Cybersyn. One problem in particular caught his attention: how to get industrial managers to incorporate Cybersyn in their management practices. This problem once more directed Beer's focus to the tension between centralized control and individual autonomy, and this time Beer's views explicitly shifted in favor of centralized control. In an October report on the extension of the cybernetic management system to the state-run enterprises, a report that reflects his pre-strike thinking, Beer proposes three ways of addressing the adoption problem, dubbing these approaches prudence, selling, and decision.[3] Prudence gave top priority to factory autonomy, although Beer does not state this explicitly. His report called for the team to establish a model enterprise for members of

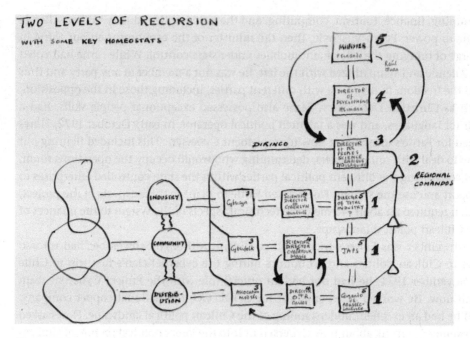

Figure 5.1
A drawing by Beer of the Viable System Model incorporating the roles of Herman Schwember and Enrique Farné. Image reproduced with permission from Constantin Malik. Original kept at Liverpool John Moores University, Learning and Information Services, Special Collections and Archives.

other enterprises to visit and learn from. Visitors could then take these new ideas back to their enterprises and implement them as they saw fit. But this approach, while preferable, would take too long to implement—five to ten years by Beer's estimation—and the government did not have that long.[4] Beer's second approach, selling, recognized factory autonomy but called for team members to convince managers to adopt the system. The team had been using this method all along, and Beer noted that it was the usual approach in capitalist countries. Now he began to wonder whether it was the right one for a socialist Chile.

Instead, Beer proposed that the government adopt a "method of decision," with top-down leadership and decision making. Rather than selling the idea to managers, the government should make adopting Cybersyn a matter of national policy. This change in emphasis paralleled Allende's desire to lead the Chilean socialist revolution from above, especially during times of crisis. During the October Strike, the president insisted, "It is the government that will give the directives for their [workers'] actions," adding that workers must demonstrate "the highest level of social discipline."[5] For both Beer and Allende, the urgency of the Chilean political situation was beginning to make decentralized control seem more like a luxury than the most useful approach for regulating change.

Beer also advised the government to start a national campaign to introduce Cybersyn to the Chilean people. His October report pushed the government for the first time to tout aggressively a project that had been kept low profile. He suggested that the government do so "with maximum noise" in January 1973 in order to influence the upcoming March elections. For the cybernetician, Project Cybersyn was not only a means to regulate production; it could also serve as positive political propaganda.[6]

However, Schwember, now charged with considering the larger political ramifications of Cybersyn, urged that the government proceed with caution. If the government made such an announcement, he warned, "the opposition will certainly attempt to distort it as a distracting gas balloon, while contrasting it to the practical failures of present management." Schwember also worried that publicizing Cybersyn could generate opposition from "political or professional groups that consider themselves under jeopardy," in particular, the National Planning Ministry, ODEPLAN. He also warned that a public announcement might hype expectations and cause people to ask for results "the very same day."[7] These objections to drawing more attention to the project show that Schwember had a more sophisticated understanding of the political landscape than Beer did.[8] In a 2002 interview Schwember added that Flores also knew he needed "to be careful with the cards he's playing [and] . . . you don't want to make announcements before you have something to show."[9]

In many ways its relative obscurity had benefited Cybersyn. The team had enjoyed a high degree of autonomy that was rarely challenged. Using his informal web of contacts, Flores had found it fairly easy to secure most of the financial, human, and material resources that the project needed and had done so without bureaucratic delays. Both factors helped the team make rapid progress. Making the project public and political could actually have impeded its adoption in the state-controlled enterprises and have had detrimental effects on the work under way. However, part of the project was about to become very public through a series of events that would dramatically change the path of Cybersyn's development.

El Paro de Octubre

A month before, in September 1972, rumors of a coup had become so strong that Popular Unity was waiting for an opposition attempt to overthrow the government. The opposition, meanwhile, was waiting for the right opportunity to do so, although its members disagreed on how they wanted to remove Allende from power. The right, including many members of the economic elite, hoped to create the conditions for a military coup. In contrast, the Christian Democrats hoped the opposition would win a landslide victory in the upcoming March 1973 congressional elections and thus have the congressional majority it needed to impeach Allende.

In October members of the Chilean economic elite found the moment they had been waiting for. A provincial truck owners' *gremio*, or business association, in the small southern province of Aysén went on strike to protest the government's creating a parallel state-owned trucking firm in the province, which the government claimed was meant to increase transportation to an isolated part of the country. The economic elite saw the strike as the moment to put more than a year's worth of planning and organization into action. They joined forces with middle-class *gremios* across the country, and within days truck owners throughout Chile struck in sympathy.

By 10 October 1972, twelve thousand truck owners were on strike, and that number quickly grew to forty thousand nationwide, a pace that shows the level of organization behind this national stoppage.[10] While the opposition promoted the strike as an effort to defend the private sector and ensure its continuance, the bourgeoisie was using the strike as a public demonstration of class power.

The truck owners refused to distribute food, fuel, or raw materials for factory production, as well as other essential goods, and they blocked roads, sometimes violently, thus prohibiting others from passing. Additional *gremio* organizations voiced their support for the truck owners in the days that followed, and locked out their own workers and clients. For example, the retail merchants' *gremio* closed retail and food stores throughout the country. Enforcement squads attacked businesses that refused to close their doors. By one newspaper estimate, the strike closed 80 percent of the stores in Valparaíso and 90 percent of the stores in the neighboring city of Viña del Mar.[11] Approximately 70 percent of the privately owned buses stopped running in Santiago during the strike, and city residents clung to the outside of the few buses that continued to operate.[12] The National Agriculture Society voiced its support for the strike, as did the centrist Christian Democratic Party and the rightist National Party.

Professional guilds of doctors, lawyers, and engineers also went on strike, making it extremely difficult for Chileans to gain access to their services. The loss of the engineers proved particularly challenging to the industrial sector. Factory managers distributed the few engineers who were loyal to the government across the state-controlled enterprises, with some engineers being assigned four or five plants to handle simultaneously. Members of the National Manufacturers' Association locked workers out of their factories to forcibly shut down production, and some even offered to pay workers not to come to work.[13]

At the same time, members of the right stepped up their efforts to hoard or destroy basic consumer goods, exacerbating consumer shortages and antigovernment sentiment among the Chilean people. With substantial financial support from the U.S. government, the strikers appeared poised to make good on their promise to shut down the country indefinitely.[14]

President Allende denounced the strike as "absolutely and totally illegal."[15] He declared a state of emergency from the coastal province of Valparaíso down to the Bío Bío province in southern Chile. The military therefore took control of twelve provinces in all, including Santiago. On national television and radio Allende declared that the strike "will not paralyze Chile," and indeed, Chilean factories continued to operate.[16] Undeterred, workers reported to their jobs as usual, despite the transportation difficulties, and forcibly opened factories closed by their owners. To maintain production, the government subsequently requisitioned more than fifty of these factories during the strike period; later only fifteen were returned to their owners.[17] To counteract black-market hoarding, some factories began distributing goods directly to the Chilean people, bypassing their traditional private-sector distribution systems.

Workers loyal to Allende used trucks from their factories to ameliorate the national transportation problem. These and other vehicles owned by Popular Unity sympathizers served as impromptu buses and helped the government distribute raw materials, spare parts, food, and other consumer necessities. The government also nationalized trucks to help with distribution. Because of the strike, neighboring factories banded together and began trading supplies and raw materials to maintain production. These *cordones industriales*, or organized industrial belts, worked with other community organizations, such as Mothers' Centers and student groups, to create new locally run supply-and-distribution networks. The strike also had the effect of radicalizing factions of the left, some of which began preparing for armed conflict. Political scientist Arturo Valenzuela notes: "ironically, it was the counter-mobilization of the petite bourgeoisie responding to real, contrived, and imaginary threats which finally engendered, in dialectical fashion, a significant and autonomous mobilization of the working class."[18] Rather than bringing an end to Chilean socialism, the strike pitted workers against small-business owners and members of the industrial bourgeoisie and created the class war that the right openly feared.

By the end of October the strike was at a stalemate. The government had failed to end the strike, but the opposition had also failed to stop production and distribution, largely because of the improvisational efforts taking place in Chilean factories and communities. The government decided to broker a compromise to end the strike. In a move designed to mollify the administration's political opponents, it reached out to the military and offered to include representatives from each of the three branches of the armed forces in the cabinet. On 2 November, Allende appointed General Carlos Prats of the army as his new minister of the interior and vice president. Members of the military also took over as minister of public works and minister of mining. The military, now an active participant in Chilean political life, declared the strike over, and the right agreed, largely because its members did not want a conflict with the military. Despite the best efforts of the opposition, Allende remained in power.

Cybersyn and the Strike

Scholars of the Allende period widely recognize the October Strike as a turning point for Allende and Popular Unity. Barbara Stallings, for example, writes, "Before October, the Allende government was on the offensive, generally in control of the situation; after October, the government essentially limited itself to reacting to the initiatives of others."[19] The actions of the opposition and the response of government loyalists, which are chronicled briefly here, are well documented. Less known is the role of cybernetics during the strike and its important contribution to the government's survival.

On the evening of Sunday, 15 October, Flores and Mario Grandi, the director of the CHECO project, found themselves alone together in Flores's office. Flores acknowledged that if things continued the way they had been going, the government would not survive. According to Grandi, Flores asked, "Why don't we apply what we've learned from Project Cybersyn to manage to strike?"[20] The two spent the evening designing a new command system for the government that used the telex network created for Project Cybersyn as its backbone. The next morning Flores presented the idea to Allende and his cabinet.

Flores proposed setting up a central command center in the presidential palace that would bring together the president, the cabinet, the heads of the political parties in the Popular Unity coalition, and representatives from the National Labor Federation—approximately thirty-five people by Grandi's estimation. Once these key people were brought together in one place and apprised of the national situation, Flores reasoned, they could then reach out to the networks of decision makers in their home institutions and get things done. This human network would help the government make decisions quickly and thus allow it to adapt to a rapidly changing situation. "Forget technology," Flores said—this network consisted of "normal people," a point that is well taken but also oversimplistic.[21] The solution he proposed was social *and* technical, as it configured machines and human beings in a way that could help the government adapt and survive.

In addition to the central command hub in the presidential palace, Flores established a number of specialized command centers dedicated to transportation, industry, energy, banking, agriculture, health, and the supply of goods. Telex machines, many of which were already in place for Project Cybersyn, connected these specialized command centers to the presidential palace.[22] Flores also created a secret telephone network consisting of eighty-four numbers and linking some of the most important people in the government, including members of the Popular Unity coalition and the National Labor Federation. According to Grandi, this phone network remained active throughout the remainder of Allende's presidency.[23]

Both the telex and the telephone network allowed the command centers to receive upward flows of current information from across the country and to disseminate government orders back down, bypassing the bureaucracy. Flores assembled a team at the presidential palace that would analyze the data sent over the network and compile these data into reports. High-ranking members of government used these reports to inform their decisions, which Flores's team then communicated using the telex and telephone networks. This arrangement gave the government the ability to make more dynamic decisions.

The Project Cybersyn telex room, housed in the State Development Corporation (CORFO), served as the industrial command center during the strike. In addition to transmitting the daily production data needed for the Cyberstride software, the CORFO telex machines now carried urgent messages about factory production. "There were enterprises that reported shortages of fuel," Espejo recalled. Using the network, those in the industrial command center could "distribute this message to the enterprises that could help."[24] The network also enabled the government to address distribution problems, such as locating trucks that were available to carry the raw materials and spare parts needed to maintain production in Chilean factories, or determining which roads remained clear of obstructionist strike activity. Espejo recalled, "The sector committees were able to ask the enterprises to send raw materials, transport vehicles, or whatever to another enterprise" that needed them. At the same time, enterprises could send requests to the sector committees and have these requests addressed immediately. "It was a very practical thing," Espejo continued, referring in particular to the state-appointed managers known as interventors. "You are the interventor of an enterprise, you are running out of fuel, you ask the corresponding sector committee. . . . Or [the interventors] know that the raw materials they need are available in Valparaíso and that they need a truck to go and get it. With bureaucratic procedures it would have been more difficult to resolve these situations."[25]

Gustavo Silva, an employee in the energy sector of CORFO, used the telex and telephone networks at the energy command center. This technological infrastructure helped Silva keep track of the trucks that left oil distribution points and determine whether they reached their destination. "We knew exactly how many trucks we needed, so each time we lost one we were able to requisition another," Silva explained. Silva's experience with the telex network in particular left a lasting impression. After the strike, Silva said, "two concepts stayed in our mind: that information helps you make decisions and, above all, that it [the telex machine] helps you keep a record of this information, which is different from making a telephone call. [Having this record] lets you correct your mistakes and see why things happened." Silva added that the energy command center relied primarily on the telex network because it gave up-to-the-minute information, but if those in the command center could not reach someone by telex, they used the telephone. "I remember that a message would arrive from the presidential palace saying that in this community [*población*] there was no kerosene, or natural gas, or gasoline. We would look and say, 'But why? We sent a truck there.'"

Then Silva and his co-workers would have to figure out what happened and requisition another truck if necessary.[26]

The telex network thus extended the reach of the social network that Flores had assembled in the presidential command center and created a sociotechnical network in the most literal sense. Moreover, the network connected the vertical command of the government to the horizontal activities that were taking place on the shop floor. To put it another way, the network offered a communications infrastructure to link the revolution from above, led by Allende, to the revolution from below, led by Chilean workers and members of grassroots organizations, and helped coordinate the activities of both in a time of crisis. During the strike, workers in the state-run factories found ways to maintain production while simultaneously defending their workplaces from attack. They also transformed factory machine shops into spaces for repairing the trucks the government owned or requisitioned. Meanwhile, the telex network helped the government direct raw materials, fuel, and transportation resources to the places that most needed them. It also helped the government keep track of its trucks and provided information about which roads were blocked and which roads were open.

Beer estimated that the telex network transmitted two thousand messages daily during the strike. "The noise was indescribable," Beer said, referring to the simultaneous clacking of twenty telex machines in the industrial command center.[27] In the presidential palace, high-ranking members of the government, including Flores, slept in the central command center to make sure they caught all the high-priority information being transmitted that could be used to manage the strike. Beer was in Santiago for the first week of the strike, but then needed to return to London. However, he stayed in touch with the telex team—Schwember, Roberto Cañete, Espejo, and Sonia Mordojovich—by telex as the strike continued.

Besides helping the government react to many of the emergencies caused by the strike, the telex network allowed the Cybersyn team to create an overview of national production based on a closer approximation of real-time data than the government had been able to assemble in the past. "During the strike, we worked very late gathering and processing telexes so that we could see the bigger picture," Espejo recalled. These data were compiled into reports that went first to the sector committees at CORFO and later, if necessary, to the presidential palace.[28] Both Cybersyn team members involved with the telex network and people outside the project team who used the network during the strike agree that the telex helped the government survive the October Strike until it ended on November 2.

Nevertheless, Cybersyn participants had differing views of the role the network played in bringing the strike to a conclusion. In his account of the Cybersyn project, Beer writes that one senior minister "said flatly that the government would have collapsed that night [17 October] if it had not had the cybernetic tool."[29] In 2001 he described the October Strike as something "we absolutely defeated by using computers and telex machines, of all things."[30] Espejo took a more moderate view: "I think [the telex network] played an important role" during the strike, but "naturally other factors also came into play," including the mobilization of people in neighborhoods and workers in factories and the government's decision to include the military in the cabinet. "It would be presumptuous to say that the strike ended [only] because of what we did," Espejo concluded.[31] Scholars of Chilean history also disagree with Beer's view, and instead credit the popular mobilization from below that stalemated the strike and the government's decision to bring the military into the cabinet as the primary reasons the strike ended.[32]

Still, participants concur that the telex network helped the government counteract the effects of forty thousand striking truck drivers, so its omission from previous studies of the Allende period is curious. Since the network formed part of Chile's technological infrastructure, perhaps it simply faded into the background, as infrastructure often does. As a technological system, it also might be viewed as playing second fiddle to the human protagonists and the decisions that they made. Both views are understandable.

However, the role of the telex network during the October Strike is a good example of the value of including technology in political history and analysis. Simply put, the existence of the telex network gave the government options that it would not have had otherwise. It allowed those in the presidential palace, representatives of the State Development Corporation, those in the state-controlled enterprises, and those in the other command centers to act in ways they could not have previously. While the network alone did not bring an end to the strike, it did shape an event that is widely acknowledged as a watershed for the Allende administration. To fully understand the dynamics of the strike requires the documentation of what was taking place in Chilean factories, in Chilean communities, and in meetings of industrialists and government officials. It also requires understanding the technological infrastructure that, in part, made these actions possible.

Furthermore, the government's use of the telex network during the strike is important from the perspective of cybernetics and management. Using telex technology during this crisis allowed the Chilean government to transform the nation into an information system that top officials could manage through real-time data exchange. The network helped the Chilean government assess the rapidly changing strike environment as well as adapt and survive—much like the biological organisms from which Beer drew inspiration in his cybernetics. In Chile, cybernetic thinking shaped the path of history.

The New Minister

The events of the October Strike led to a new role in the Allende administration for Fernando Flores. The president named the twenty-nine-year-old to be the new minister of economics.

Flores believed his use of technology helped him secure this cabinet-level position, and he felt that further cultivating his image as a science and technology expert might give him an edge politically, especially since he was still relatively unknown to the opposition. During the strike he had managed to form ties with members of the military and with key members of the Communist Party, and he wanted to broaden his base of support beyond his small party, the MAPU, and the Popular Unity coalition. But he recognized that he had little time in which to do so. At Flores's request, Schwember wrote to Beer, who at that moment was in England, asking the cybernetician for help. Schwember writes that when Flores was appointed to the cabinet, "his prestige was very high," in large part because "he had a very essential role in . . . the solution of the [October] crisis."[33] But to get things done, the new minister also needed some support from the opposition. To bridge the political gap, Flores proposed developing "a certain myth around his scientific qualifications." Schwember asked whether Beer could have Flores "appointed to one of the scientific societies or clubs, or better still, to get an honorary degree from one of the universities or boards where you have some influence."[34]

In addition to leveraging his image as a scientist, Flores began his tenure as economics minister by planning how to use the tools he had developed with Beer. He, and other members of the government, continued to use the telex network, if not at the same frenzied level of activity as during the strike. Flores also moved the CHECO project, the economic stimulator, into the Ministry of Economics. He planned to use economic models to inform policy by locating the five or six specific parameters that had the greatest effect on the Chilean economy. In addition, Flores asked Beer for a "new and more intensive commitment" to the Chile contract, which would mean relocating Beer and his family to Chile. In early November Schwember conveyed Flores's invitation and assured the cybernetician that "the growth of our actual influence and power has exceeded our best imagination."[35] While Flores's desire to portray himself as a technical expert was in part window dressing, he clearly believed, along with Beer, that science, technology, and cybernetics could assist the Allende government and its economic program.

Flores was not the first to use science and technology to justify his claim to political power. Given the contentious, ideologically charged environment of Chilean politics, it is easy to see why the new minister would want to ground his actions in scientific objectivity and why he might view "scientific" solutions as superior to "political" ones. This approach had in fact been used by the Christian Democrats during the presidency of Allende's predecessor, Eduardo Frei, to justify government policies and present them as politically neutral. While this strategy helped the Christian Democrats rule as a single party initially, it eventually alienated members of other parties who were put off by the use of highly technical language and who felt frustrated at the unwillingness of the Christian Democrats to compromise. Similarly, Flores soon learned that technical expertise had questionable value in the upper echelons of Chilean politics.

By December 1972, Flores had started to wonder about the value of cybernetics to Chilean socialism. From his office in the Ministry of Economics, he had a macroscopic view of the Chilean revolution and the growing counterrevolution. In addition, he was further removed from Project Cybersyn institutionally than he had been in the past and could no longer be as involved as he once was. This new vantage point caused him to reconsider the utility of the project, and of cybernetics, as a way to regulate the complexity of the Chilean revolution. After the October Strike, "we [the cabinet] felt the pressure of the next coup, the successful coup," Flores said. "I was not a fool, I knew that clearly. I knew that we could win a lot during the October Strike [by] using my room, but . . . the room was not going to stop tanks and planes and bigger strikes." Flores felt that cybernetics was valuable in situations in which your enemy is not trying to kill you, but "if they are killing you, the concept is worthless."[36] Although Flores made these comments with the benefit of thirty years' hindsight, Beer also writes in *The Brain of the Firm* that by December 1972 Flores had begun to distance himself from the project because other, more pressing emergencies demanded his attention on a daily basis.[37] Schwember described the situation thus: "Flores became a full-fledged politician. The things that had been central to him [such as Project Cybersyn] became not so central."[38]

As 1972 drew to a close, Flores was increasingly absent from the project but continued to affiliate himself peripherally with the work. According to Beer, Flores's absence created mixed reactions: "The consternation was felt by those who regarded Cybersyn as a political instrument, and who thought they saw political support incipiently withheld." On the other hand, "the technocratically minded, who wanted effective management regardless of the political framework," viewed Flores's absence with pleasure.[39] Although Flores saw value in the telex network, he had started to see Cybersyn as an instrument with limited possibilities. Beer, on the other hand, saw the success of the telex network during the strike as reason to begin recasting Chile's myriad problems in cybernetic terms.

Beer's New Level of Recursion

The October Strike caused Beer, like Flores, to look at the larger political picture. On 20 October, a week after the strike started, Beer drew a diagram titled "Cybernetic and Political Analysis" (figure 5.2) that showed how to change the way Chileans interacted with their government and positioned Cybersyn as only one small part of a large, multi-sited program to introduce cybernetic thinking in Chilean life.[40]

Beer returned to London on 21 October, while the strike was still in progress. He learned via telex that the use of the telex network during the strike had elevated the status of Project Cybersyn and those involved in its creation. On 27 October, Schwember wrote, "The whole project is gaining momentum in spite of obvious environmental

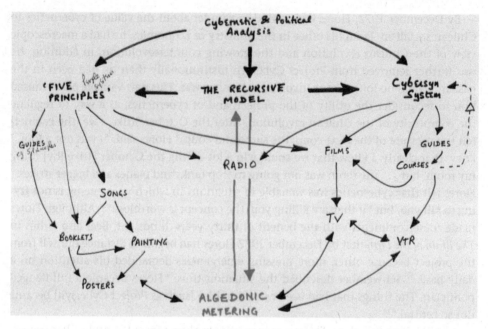

Figure 5.2
Diagram showing how Beer envisioned the scope of his work in Chile and its connection to the political context. Image reproduced with permission from Constantin Malik. Original kept at Liverpool John Moores University, Learning and Information Services, Special Collections and Archives.

troubles."[41] News of Flores's cabinet appointment also reached Beer. Such reports made Beer euphoric and galvanized his ambitions for the project. Several days after the strike ended, he telexed Espejo: "We are only just beginning the reformation of the whole process of government. I do not exaggerate to say that the total concept is two orders of magnitude bigger than cybersynergy."[42] Beer began to think about how he might apply cybernetics in areas other than industrial production and in ways that went beyond Project Cybersyn. However, the strike had also made clear the seriousness of the Chilean political climate and the opposition's determination to end the Allende government. As a precaution Beer instructed his assistant, Mordojovich, to encode her telexes to him in case members of the opposition were spying on his correspondence (figure 5.3 and figure 5.4).

But the work in Chile was also magnifying Beer's internal conflicts. On the one hand, he told Espejo, it was allowing him to "enter another world of scientific creativity and genuine influence."[43] On the other, his political ideals and scientific ambitions were increasingly in conflict with his more-than-comfortable lifestyle and responsibilities to his wife and children.

ANY MORE MESSAGES PLEASE

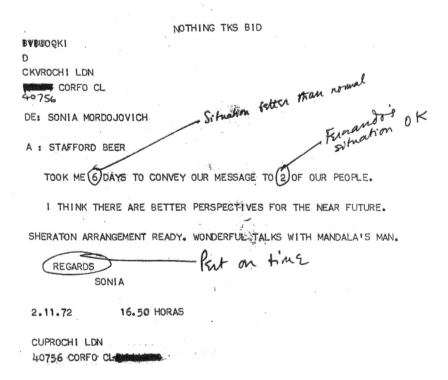

NOTHING TKS BID

BVBWOQKI

D

CKVROCHI LDN

CORFO CL

40756

DE: SONIA MORDOJOVICH

Situation better than normal

A : STAFFORD BEER

Fernando's situation OK

TOOK ME ⑥ DAYS TO CONVEY OUR MESSAGE TO ② OF OUR PEOPLE.

I THINK THERE ARE BETTER PERSPECTIVES FOR THE NEAR FUTURE.

SHERATON ARRANGEMENT READY. WONDERFUL TALKS WITH MANDALA'S MAN.

REGARDS *Put on time*

SONIA

2.11.72   16.50 HORAS

CUPROCHI LDN

40756 CORFO CL

Figure 5.3
An example of a coded telex between Beer and Mordojovich. Image reproduced with permission from Constantin Malik. Original kept at Liverpool John Moores University, Learning and Information Services, Special Collections and Archives.

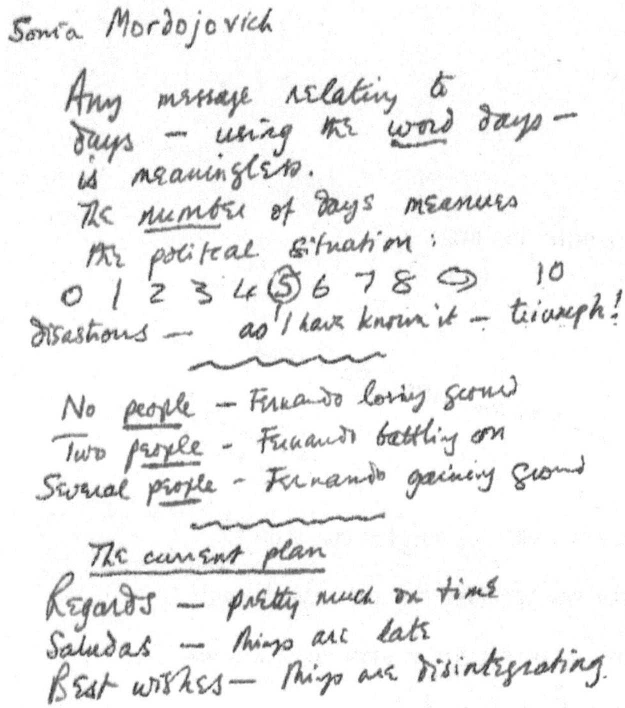

Sonia Mordojovich

Any message relating to days — using the word days — is meaningless.
The number of days measures the political situation:
0 1 2 3 4 ⑤ 6 7 8 ⑨ 10
Disastrous — as I have known it — triumph!

No people — Fernando losing ground
Two people — Fernando battling on
Several people — Fernando gaining ground

The current plan
Regards — pretty much on time
Saludas — things are late
Best wishes — things are disintegrating.

Figure 5.4
A page from Beer's personal code book. Image reproduced with permission from Constantin Malik. Original kept at Liverpool John Moores University, Learning and Information Services, Special Collections and Archives.

In a candid November letter to Schwember, Beer confessed that Sallie, his wife, did not approve of his involvement with the Allende government, which might "fail, or will cast me aside without warning," or which, due to political turmoil, could "have me jailed or shot!" She felt the work also prevented Beer from "building a nice respectable consulting practice" and that "a lot of people, ranging from family to friends to prospective clients, regard the UP with disapproval." Moreover, she feared that Beer's contract with the Allende government could cause such clients to "write me off as an advisor, whereupon we shall all starve."[44] Such views were not without basis. Beer himself acknowledged that his work for the Chilean government negatively affected his professional reputation. For example, he believed a U.S. university had rescinded an offer to award him an honorary degree because of his connection to the Allende government.[45] Because of Sallie's disdain for the Chile work, she would not relocate to Chile, thus preventing her husband from doing so as Flores had requested and limiting the amount of time the cybernetician could spend in South America.

Sallie had a second reason for disliking her husband's involvement with the Allende government. Beer admitted to Schwember that his wife found him changed by his time in Chile "in a way she detests" and that these changes were profound. "I feel liberated as a person," Beer wrote. "For the first time in my life I have real friends; for the first time in my professional career I am not staggering under the weight of frustration and bitterness." He also expressed distaste for his expensive lifestyle and the pressure he felt from Sallie to maintain it: "I am sick of England, and sick of my life-style; I would like to start again." But at the same time, he did not feel comfortable gambling the short-term financial future of his wife, ex-wife, and eight children on a government that might be overthrown and thus unable to pay him. "Am I entitled to take the risks involved?" Beer wondered. "Because of my upbringing and the way I have lived I have always worked within the constraints. To do so was what was 'honorable.' But I've talked enough with Fernando [Flores] to realize that it's possible to regard that worldview with actual contempt." Maybe honor was nothing more than a "vast psychological hang-up," he mused, instead of a concept that should guide his actions and set his priorities.[46] Sallie's concern about her husband's ability and resolve to maintain their comfortable standard of living clearly was justified.

Fortunately for her, Beer was not prepared to forsake his income and the life his family then enjoyed, not even for the chance to devote more time to what he must have felt was an extraordinary opportunity for him and his cybernetics. He told Schwember that if the Chilean government wanted to hire him full time, he needed a "compelling letter" from Allende and a salary of £20,000 paid in advance (roughly $304,000 in 2009 dollars) to "clear my money problems for 1973." Beer justified the amount by adding, "My normal fees in the capitalist world are standard 'top consultant' rates of $600 a day [equivalent to $2,900 in 2009 dollars]. Ridiculous, but it accounts for the muddle I am in." Beer was not willing to give up his financial security entirely, but he was willing to compromise. Although the advance he proposed was substantial, he did reduce his rates and was willing to work longer hours than his contract with the Chilean government specified. This proposal also allowed him to sidestep the conflicting demands he felt between his work and his family, at least for now. However, as these figures indicate, his work in Chile was far from philanthropy. Beer eventually received £13,000 [$182,000 in 2009 dollars] from the Chilean government for his work in 1973, but he was not paid until April, a delay that stressed the cybernetician financially. He was also unable to clear his schedule of other commitments, including his teaching duties at the University of Manchester Business School.[47]

Beer returned to Chile on 28 November, less than two weeks after the death of his mentor, the British cybernetician W. Ross Ashby, on 15 November. The news devastated Beer, and perhaps losing his mentor inspired him to push his cybernetic thinking even further. During this period he reimagined the scope of his cybernetic work, so that it went well beyond the diagram he had submitted to Flores in October. On 12 December

Beer drafted the report "One Year of (Relative) Solitude: The Second Level of Recursion." The title was a thinly veiled allusion to the Gabriel García Márquez novel that had introduced Beer to the magic realism of South American life as well as to Beer's own recent struggles to understand the changes he had witnessed in Chile as part of its transition to socialism.

In the report Beer viewed the relationship of cybernetics, technology, and politics in three key ways. First, he envisioned a greater role for cybernetics in the Chilean transition to socialism, a change in scope that he tied to Flores's being named economic minister.[48] Cybersyn had used cybernetics to control industrial production while enterprises in the public and mixed sectors of the Chilean economy shifted from private ownership to state control. But this limited approach "could not account for the changes in economic management that had nothing to do with ownership in the legal sense," Beer wrote later.[49] For example, Cybersyn did not address changes in distribution and consumption, although each had played a crucial role in the state of the Chilean economy during the October Strike. Instead of limiting cybernetic management to the area of production, Beer argued, the government should use cybernetic theories and techniques from operations research to also regulate distribution and consumption.

For example, he suggested that the government should conduct operations research studies of Chilean distribution networks and establish an operations research department to monitor supplies of consumer goods. He advised the government to ask the Chilean people what goods they considered essential, the quantity they desired, and the quantity that they already had, and use that information to determine which goods were of "primary necessity." That information would also supply a measure of the gap between supply and demand. Beer further suggested that the Cyberstride software could be tweaked to predict how the relationship of supply and demand might change in the future.

Second, Beer envisioned new ways for science, technology, and cybernetics to serve as forms of pro-government propaganda. He urged the government to use the pamphlet he had developed and Angel Parra's folk song to teach the Chilean people about cybernetic thinking in government and to promote the government's use of science and technology in the service of the Chilean people. He pushed the government to create a "proper proletarian channel" for Chilean television and radio that could shape public opinion of the government and offset the influence of the media outlets run by the opposition and funded by the CIA. He also suggested that the government create the positions of director and deputy director of the "people's science," offices he saw as serving a practical purpose but that also made a political statement. Such titles "have the same impact as slogans: we can really put them to use," he wrote in the report.

Third, Beer proposed new ways to explicitly embed socialist values in the design and construction of Project Cybersyn, especially the value of worker participation, and to change the social organization that surrounded the Cybersyn technology.[50] For starters, Beer insisted that workers should control the use of Cybersyn and argued that this was within their capabilities. Since he reasoned that Cybersyn was like any other "automated machine tool," he concluded that Chilean workers could reasonably use the system "without understanding the electronics," such as the mainframe computer. Beer also felt that the operations room should function as "the shop-floor of Total Industry" and reiterated that it should be "a place for the workers." In addition, Beer wanted to change the power relations between Chilean technical experts and Chilean workers: he proposed reducing the role of Chilean scientists and technologists to that of advising the workers when needed and performing supporting roles, such as system maintenance. At the same time, he wanted to create new leadership roles for members of the rank and file. For example, Beer suggested that CORFO, the state development agency, create a director of total industry and fill the position with a worker who understood both politics and industrial management and was not frightened by technology.[51]

The cybernetician did not understand that creating such a position would, in essence, undermine the authority of Pedro Vuskovic, the current CORFO vice president and acting director of Chilean national industry, and was therefore unlikely to gain approval from the development agency. Beer also did not consider that Chilean technical experts would object to the subservient role he was proposing. Many of Chile's technical experts were affiliated with opposition parties such as Christian Democracy and thus would not embrace the ideological reasons Beer gave for subordinating their technical expertise and education to the decisions of less educated workers.

Moreover, Beer wanted Chilean workers to contribute to the internal design of the system and suggested a radical change to the factory modeling process. Instead of having trained engineers and operations research scientists build models of the state-controlled factories, Beer recommended that the government should assign this task to the workers. "There is no-one better qualified to model a plant than the man whose life is spent working in it. He *knows*," Beer wrote in the report. In this scenario, Chilean programmers would then transform the production models built by the workers into parameters for the Cyberstride software. Worker knowledge would thus contribute to factory management through Cyberysn—by solidifying workers' participation in management, not only by putting the workers in charge of the system but also by incorporating worker knowledge in its software. Beer hypothesized that once Chilean workers understood these tools for cybernetic management, and mastered them, "they will see [Cybersyn's] value" and "will *ask us* for Cybersyn." He then imagined the workers' taking action to dismantle the Chilean bureaucracy themselves and even dissolving the sector committees.[52]

Beer was spinning ideas in "One Year of (Relative) Solitude," but he was aiming for a new technological approach to the worker participation question that would create a more democratic and less stratified workplace. And he concluded that giving workers control of technology, both its use and its design, could constitute a new form of worker empowerment.

This assertion differed substantially from how other industrial studies of the day approached the relationship of computer technology and labor in twentieth-century production. Such studies, especially those inspired by Marxist analysis, often presented computers and computer-controlled machinery as tools of capital that automated labor, led to worker deskilling, and gave management greater control of the shop floor. In *Labor and Monopoly Capital* (1974), Harry Braverman credits such machinery "*as the prime means whereby production may be controlled not by the direct producer but by the owner and representatives of capital*" and cites computer technology as routinizing even highly skilled professions such as engineering.[53]

In the 1980s, historian David Noble also argued that the introduction of numerical control technology in factory work stripped workers of their abilities to mentally and physically control factory machinery and gave management greater control of labor. "Because technology is political, it must be recognized that . . . new technologies will invariably constitute extensions of power and control," namely, of managers over workers. That such technologies "might be turned to humane ends is a dangerous delusion," he concluded.[54]

Studies of computing and labor on the shop floor that were not inspired by Marx also linked computers to automation, worker deskilling, and management control. For example, in the 1980s, an ethnographic study by Shoshana Zuboff, a Harvard Business School professor, found that the introduction of microprocessor-based control systems in the Piney Wood pulp mill created hierarchical forms of centralized control. These control systems replaced workers' tacit knowledge with intelligent sensors. Now dominated by a "smart machine," mill workers became machine operators with little control or knowledge of the systems they used. As one Piney Wood plant manager described it, the worker is "simply another variable in the process that we manage in the way we manage all of the mechanical variables."[55] Similar interpretations also appear in early discussions of cybernetics. In the 1950s Norbert Wiener, author of *Cybernetics*, believed computers would usher in a second industrial revolution and lead to the creation of an automatic factory. In *The Human Use of Human Beings* (1954), he worries that automated machinery "is the precise economic equivalent of slave labor. Any labor which competes with slave labor must accept the economic conditions of slave labor."[56] These anxieties were also being expressed in Chile, where imported capital technologies were viewed not only as a means of controlling labor but also as signs of economic domination by the United States and Europe.

Such studies of computing and labor have treated computer technology as a form of worker disempowerment and worker deskilling, instead of a means to increase participation, as Beer suggested. They also have viewed the concept of worker participation with some skepticism. Braverman, for example, noted that in the 1970s worker participation in the United States was "a gracious liberality in allowing the worker to adjust a machine, replace a light bulb, move from one fractional job to another, and then have the illusion of making decisions by choosing among fixed and limited alternatives designed by management which deliberately leaves insignificant matters open to choice."[57] In contrast, Beer's report envisioned a more substantial form of participation. He wanted to change how management decisions were made, whose knowledge was used to make these decisions, and how workers, technologists, and managers interacted. And he believed that Project Cybersyn could change all this for the better.

Two factors explain the difference between Beer and Braverman, who were writing at about the same time. First, the computer system Beer designed did not automate labor. Given the Popular Unity commitment to raising employment levels, automating labor would not have made political sense. Second, Beer was writing and working in a different political context than Braverman. The context of Chilean socialism inspired Beer and gave him the freedom to envision new forms of worker participation that were more substantial than what Braverman saw in the United States. It also allowed Beer to see computer technology as something other than an abusive capitalist tool used by management to control labor. Beer's approach also reflected his position as a hired science and technology consultant. His use of technology to address worker participation differed from the contemporaneous efforts of the Allende government on this issue, efforts that had focused on devising new governing committees within the industrial sector and electing worker representatives.

Beer's proposal bears a close resemblance to the work on participatory design that emerged from the social democratic governments in Scandinavia in the 1970s. The history of participatory design is often tied to Scandinavian trade union efforts to empower workers during that decade, and thus to create a more equitable power relationship between labor and capital in Scandinavian factories.[58] These efforts were either contemporaneous to Beer's December report or began several years later, depending on historical interpretation. Like the aforementioned automation studies, early participatory design work viewed technologies such as computer systems as representing the interests of management, not labor. However, participatory design used the primacy of management as a starting point and then tried to change the dynamics of the labor-capital relationship by changing the social practices surrounding the design and use of technology. Initially, this involved educating workers about the technology in use in the workplace so that they could participate in decisions about its use. During the 1980s and 1990s, though, participatory design evolved into a set of methods, theories, and practices for involving workers in the design of the computer systems they used. Proponents of participatory design argued that such practices resulted not only in the creation of better computer systems, in the sense that they better suited workers' needs and increased their ability to get the job done, but also in the creation of more ethical systems that took into account the interests of stakeholders other than management.

Beer's proposal resembled participatory design even before that field had become a recognized area of research. His December report thus shows that ideas about participatory design originated on multiple continents and were inspired by different contexts of democratic socialism.[59]

At the same time, Chilean and Scandinavian ideas on participatory design had a different genealogy, and Popular Unity ideas about worker participation were not shaped by the Scandinavian experience.[60] Whether these different genealogies of worker participation resulted in different participatory design practices is a topic for future study. Chilean ideas about worker participation did affect the activities of the INTEC industrial designers and increased their willingness to include workers' suggestions in the design process. Also, Beer was inspired by what was taking place in Chilean factories as well as by Chilean government efforts to increase worker participation in industrial management.[61] He extended these ideas about participation in a different direction, to the design of a management information system. And he saw the system as a way to help the government achieve its goal of including worker participation at all levels of national economic management.

However, Beer did not have a complete understanding of the Chilean shop floor. This is especially apparent in the December report, where he treats Chilean workers as a homogeneous group. Although the events of the October Strike did much to unify workers and raise class consciousness, sectarian politics divided the rank and file as well as the political leadership. Moreover, Chilean political parties had different stances on worker participation—even within the Popular Unity coalition. For example, the Communist Party, which preferred hierarchical, top-down party-controlled union leadership, had a stronger power base in the unions and was less supportive of nonunion worker-participation initiatives. In contrast, members of the Socialist Party were more open to worker participation initiatives that challenged Communist power in the unions.

This difference highlights another oversight in Beer's proposal: his sole focus on "workers" also failed to include the role labor unions played within the state-controlled factories. The Popular Unity government charged the unions with developing new forms of worker governance in the state-controlled enterprises, but union leaders sometimes viewed these initiatives as a threat to their power and did not encourage them. Union leaders also viewed developments such as the growth of the *cordones industriales* during the October Strike as a potential threat to their position. They might have considered the building of factory models with similar suspicion, since it was an activity completely outside their purview.[62]

Furthermore, appointing worker representatives to control the use of Cybersyn would not guarantee that the system would be used in a way that represented the best interests of the rank and file. Studies of worker participation have shown that worker representatives often separate themselves from their co-workers on the shop floor and form a new group of administrators. As Juan Espinosa and Andrew Zimbalist write in their study of worker participation in Allende's Chile, "It has been the historical experience, with a few exceptions, that those interpreting workers' priorities and needs have grown apart from the workers they are supposed to represent. . . . [They] become a new class of privileged administrators."[63] Simply put, it would be impossible to give "the workers" control of Cybersyn as Beer suggested, even if Chilean workers possessed the skills to use the technology or build the factory models.

Despite these oversights, Beer did realize that the October Strike was a transformative event for Chilean workers. Their self-organization and improvisation during the strike played a central role in maintaining production, transportation, and distribution across the country. During the strike, workers organized to defend their factories from paramilitary attacks, retooled their machines to perform new tasks, and set up new community networks to distribute essential goods directly to the Chilean people. Members of larger industrial belts collaborated with other groups of workers to seize private-sector enterprises that had stopped production during the strike. Historian Peter Winn notes that during the strike workers came together regardless of politics, industrial sector, factory, or status, thus "generating the dynamism, organization, and will to stalemate the counterrevolutionary offensive and transform it into an opportunity for revolutionary advance."[64] In short, the strike transformed the mindset of the Chilean working class and showed that workers could take control of their destiny and accelerate the revolutionary process.

Although his information was limited, Beer was aware of workers' activities during the strike, and was excited by them. In fact, the ideas he presented in his December report, "One Year of (Relative) Solitude," were designed to support the "people's autonomy." Beer wrote, "The new task [outlined in the report] is to try and get all this, plus the spontaneous things that I know are happening [such as the *cordones industriales*] together."[65] From his perspective, it looked as if Chilean workers were self-organizing to keep the larger revolutionary project viable. It is important to stress, especially given the criticism he would receive in the months that followed, that Beer viewed his role as using science and technology to help support these bottom-up initiatives.

Although Beer's take on participatory design was inspired by the events of the October Strike, it also came from his understandings of cybernetics. "The basic answer of cybernetics to the question of how the system should be organized is that it ought to organize itself," Beer writes in the pages of *Decision and Control*.[66] In his writings Beer often cited nature as a complex system that remains viable through its self-organization. He argued that such systems do not need to be designed because they already exist. To modify the behavior of such a system, one need not control its every aspect but rather change one subsystem so that the overall system naturally drifts toward the desired goal. Perhaps the injection of worker action could drive Chile toward a new point of homeostatic equilibrium, one that was congruent with the overall goal of socialist transformation. Worker improvisation on the ground could, moreover, supplement Allende's directives from above. Beer viewed this redundancy as another prerequisite for self-organization and system viability. He wanted to encourage self-organization both by having Chilean workers participate in the actual design of Cybersyn and by using cybernetics to enhance the new forms of participation that were developing in Chilean communities. Such participatory activities would not only increase worker freedom but also create a more participatory working life and a more democratic society.[67]

Beer noted that his Chilean colleagues did not share his enthusiasm for the ideas he proposed in the December report.[68] He blamed this cool response on the attention the government was giving to sectarian politics during the period, and felt it did not signal a lack of interest in his cybernetics. However, it also seems that Beer did not fully understand the magnitude of what he was proposing or how difficult it would be for the government to implement these ideas, given the growing public support for the opposition and the magnitude of the Chilean economic crisis. Making Chile cybernetic in the way Beer described would require the creation of new communication networks, the reorganization of existing management hierarchies, and the introduction of radically different work practices. While some of these changes might have been possible early in Allende's presidency, by December 1972 they no longer were. Enrique Farné, who was then managing the implementation of Cybersyn, described Chile under Allende as "a time when people were talking about empty pots and shortages, a time when subversive groups like Fatherland and Liberty [a radical right-wing political group] were open to terrorism, a time when money from foreign multinationals or from the CIA financed militants to buy sugar and throw it in the river" and thus exacerbate existing consumer shortages.[69] On the shop floor, workers were consumed with political power struggles and making just-in-time innovations simply to keep production going. It would be unreasonable, even impossible, to have workers also learn to draft factory models, use statistical software, and run economic simulators, with the expectation that they could do all this *without* decreasing production levels.

Although Beer had begun to pay greater attention to the political dimensions of his work, in some ways he was still thinking like a technologist. Farné felt that Beer did not fully understand how Project Cybersyn fit into the context of Chilean politics because he was involved only in the technocratic and intellectual aspects of Chilean economic management: the theory, not the practice; the technology, not the politics. Whereas Beer criticized his Chilean colleagues for making Cybersyn technocratic, not political, others viewed Beer's reading of how Cybersyn meshed with Chilean politics as divorced from the nitty-gritty of the Chilean revolutionary process. Still, at a basic level Flores and Beer agreed on what the government needed to do. Flores saw the government as playing a defensive game in which his role was to resolve short-term emergencies to keep Allende in power. Beer wanted to transform the Chilean state into a cybernetic organism, one that could adapt to a dynamically changing environment and ultimately survive. These goals, while remarkably similar in theory, differed dramatically in their execution.

A Technology of Contradictions

While Beer was discussing how to make Cybersyn more political, the State Development Corporation increasingly separated the project from its cybernetic underpinnings. Work on Project Cybersyn accelerated after the strike, but more and more it was viewed as a collection of tools instead of as a synergistic, holistic endeavor grounded in cybernetic principles. This was especially true of the telex network. After the strike, the telex network had "its own dynamic," Flores said. "Most people did not see the telex as part of Cybersyn" but rather "as a very astute idea to produce coordination and communication."[70] The government continued to use the network and planned for its expansion. Before the strike, the team had installed ninety-nine telex machines across the country and connected them to the Cybernet network.[71] CORFO approved the purchase of additional telex machines to accommodate the five hundred new subscribers to the network that the agency predicted for 1973.[72] Despite this increased role, the government did not bring Project Cybersyn to the attention of the Chilean public, nor did it use Cybersyn as a form of government propaganda as Beer desired.

After the October Strike, CORFO carved out a new informatics directorate under the control of Espejo, who also continued to head Project Cybersyn and direct its day-to-day operations. From one perspective, the creation of the informatics directorate reflected CORFO's appreciation of the telex network and, by extension, of Cybersyn. However, the new directorate also reflected an organizational maturation of the project and a desire to end the flexible accounting practices that formerly were used to fund the project. When Flores had been at CORFO, he had used his network of professional and personal contacts to secure resources informally. When Flores left CORFO, Espejo inherited fiscal responsibility for the project, and he wanted to put the bookkeeping in order. "Each day I became more and more worried," Espejo remembered. "I saw that politically things were going from bad to worse and that if we did not straighten the accounts out, the opposition could charge Fernando [Flores] with misappropriating funds."[73] Espejo put together a formal budget for Cybersyn and sought approval from the board of directors of CORFO, which included members of the extreme right. Because the project had such a strong association with science and technology rather than with politics, the board approved the budget with little discussion.[74] This approval might not have been possible had the government followed Beer's advice and made Cybersyn a public component of its political program.

Although the project now had more formal support from CORFO, CORFO employees still did not have a good understanding of Cybersyn. Nor did CORFO integrate the project into its existing management and industrial planning practices. These shortcomings were due in part to the organizational philosophy of Beer's management cybernetics, for adopting Project Cybersyn in the way Beer imagined would require CORFO to change its industrial management practices in substantial ways. The large size of CORFO also played a role. Espejo estimated that the agency had about 2,500 employees at that point; thus, most people working for CORFO did not know about Project Cybersyn because it was so small in comparison.

This continued to be true even as the project team expanded after the strike, in part because Cybersyn grew in a way that Espejo described as "more opportunist than institutional. For example, [team members would ask,] 'we need production indicators from the petrochemical sector; who do we know that could do this?'"[75] This approach did not create a unified team within CORFO that could instantiate Cybersyn's brand of management within CORFO's existing planning and management activities. Because the team grew in this decentralized, "opportunistic" way, most new recruits were not introduced to Beer and had little or no awareness, let alone understanding, of cybernetic principles such as the Viable System Model or the Law of Requisite Variety. Nor did they understand how Beer's approach to decentralized control was congruent with the principles of Allende's democratic socialism. Increasingly, Cybersyn was becoming a technological project divorced from its cybernetic and political origins. The best-known component of the project, the telex network, was not even associated with the overall Cybersyn system, let alone with Beer's ideas about management cybernetics.

In contrast, members of the core group had become serious students of cybernetics. Several months earlier they had formed a small study group known as the Group of 14 and tasked themselves with learning more about cybernetics and related scientific work in psychology, biology, computer science, and information theory. They read the work of Warren Weaver, Claude Shannon, Heinz von Foerster, and Herbert Simon and invited Chilean biologists Humberto Maturana and Francisco Varela to speak to the group (both accepted). Maturana was arguably the first substantial connection between Chile and the international cybernetics community. In 1959, while a graduate student at Harvard, he had coauthored an important paper, "What the Frog's Eye Tells the Frog's Brain," with Warren McCulloch, Jerome Lettvin, and Walter Pitts, all of whom were important figures in the growing field of cybernetics.[76]

In 1972 Heinz von Foerster, director of the Biological Computer Laboratory at the University of Illinois and editor of the Macy conference proceedings, traveled to Chile to visit Maturana. Von Foerster was also a friend of Beer, and through this connection von Foerster began giving lectures to the Group of 14.[77] "Heinz was very, very exciting and with Humberto [Maturana] we are discussing the possibility of having him [von Foerster] for a semester or so in 1973. It might be very helpful to us in many respects," Schwember wrote Beer after one of von Foerster's lectures in November 1972.[78] Beer, von Foerster, Maturana, and Varela—all significant in the international cybernetics community—spent time stimulating the thinking of this small group of Chileans, which made their involvement with Project Cybersyn all the more exhilarating.

By the end of December 1972 Cybersyn had become a project of paradoxes. Beer, the scientist, saw Cybersyn as just the beginning of socialist cybernetics in Chile and increasingly emphasized the political dimensions of his cybernetic work. Flores, the politician, saw Cybersyn as useful in a limited way but not capable of solving the larger problems that the nation faced. Cybersyn now had an institutional home in the informatics directorate of the development agency. However, CORFO did not incorporate the project in its industrial planning activities, and most of the agency staff did not even know it existed. The telex network created for Project Cybersyn had helped the government survive a national strike, but few people knew that this network formed part of a larger cybernetic project for economic management. The project team continued to grow in size, but for most of these people Cybersyn had nothing to do with cybernetics. Yet for a smaller group of Chilean team members, Cybersyn had served as a vehicle not only for learning about cybernetics but also for meeting and learning from prominent members of the international cybernetics community. Espejo perhaps summarized it best when he wrote in his December progress report, "This last month has probably been one the most contradictory months concerning with [sic] the development of our work."[79]

All the while, the work on the project progressed at an impressive rate. The CHECO group, now in the Ministry of Economics, continued to build macroeconomic models to "relate the most relevant variables in the Chilean economy."[80] Cyberstride too had momentum. In November the permanent suite generated its first print-out, an analysis of select production indicators. By the end of November the temporary suite was checking 74 production indicators for anomalies. The data management team also had 26 indicators ready for the permanent suite and had an additional 180 indicators in various stages of preparation.[81] Beer asked his son Simon, an electronics expert, to draw up design schematics for the algedonic meters Beer had proposed in Project Cyberfolk. The Center for Studies on National Reality, the leftist research center at the Catholic University in Santiago, agreed to test the prototype meters once they were built. Beer also developed plans for a series of training films on cybernetic management to educate sixty people at a time (including workers, senior managers, and operations research scientists) over a ten-day period in order to drive home the message that "we are engaged in an economic war."[82] The training program received verbal support from Flores and Schwember, but serious obstacles—chief among them that the team could not lay its hands on film, 16mm cameras, or editing equipment—nonetheless blocked its realization in the way Beer envisioned.[83]

Meanwhile, construction of the operations room had encountered several initial setbacks.[84] In mid-November the owner of the site that had been selected for the room backed out, refusing to let the government use his property. The team managed to find a new space for the project in a building that had once housed *Readers' Digest*, but then they had to redraw the blueprints. By the end of November the team had relocated all the hardware for the room to the basement of the new building, allowing work to progress quickly. The operations room was near completion by the end of December.

Beer proposed that Allende inaugurate the room, and even drafted a sample speech for the president to deliver at the event, but it would never be given. The speech contained such sentiments as "[We] set out courageously to build our own system in our own spirit. What you will hear about today is revolutionary—not simply because this is the first time it has been done anywhere in the world. It is revolutionary because we are making a deliberate effort to hand to the people the power that science commands, in a form in which the people can use it."[85] This speech perhaps embodies one of the greatest contradictions of Project Cybersyn: in it Beer, a foreign scientific expert, would have the Chilean president describe the operations room as a Chilean technology that embodies the spirit of the Chilean people. Never mind that Beer had conceived of it in general terms before he ever set foot in Chile. The speech also shows Beer, a British national, pushing for Cybersyn to become a symbol of Chilean nationalism. Yet, as this chapter has shown, he was the only member of the top Cybersyn leadership to adopt this position at this time. In contrast, Chilean members of the Cybersyn team, like Espejo, found it more useful to present Cybersyn as a technology devoid of politics.

Allende never inaugurated the Cybersyn operations room, but he did visit the space at the end of 1972, as I related in the prologue. On 30 December Flores brought Allende and General Carlos Prats, the minister of the interior, to the operations room. The president sat in one of the futuristic chairs and pushed a button on the armrest. A small moment, yes, but one that presents a new reading of Chilean socialism because it differs from the images of protests, public speeches, and community activities that typically define the Allende period.[86]

The October Strike had had a dramatic impact on Beer and Flores, on Cybersyn, and on the nation. As a moment of economic and political crisis, the strike pushed the Chilean government to use technology in new ways. The gravity of the situation also pushed Beer and Flores to reevaluate how they viewed the relationship of technology and politics and the role of Project Cybersyn in the Chilean revolution. Beer saw a convergence of his cybernetic ideas and the organized activity of Chilean workers during the strike. This convergence, combined with Flores's promotion to minister of economics, encouraged Beer to broaden the scope of his cybernetic work and took him to a new place professionally and personally. Flores, however, had a different perspective from his office in the Ministry of Economics, where he experienced on a daily basis the precariousness of the government's position. While he remained interested in cybernetics, he was more pragmatic about its application and more aware of its limitations. While Beer was blossoming intellectually, Flores knew the October Strike might have signaled the beginning of the end. Examining how Beer's and Flores's views changed in the aftermath of the strike shows that individual experiences, historical moments, and geographies all contribute to the ways that technologies have politics and politics are shaped by technology.

Moreover, a cybernetic history of the October Strike shows how technological systems can influence the direction of political events by giving governments opportunities that they may not have had otherwise. The telex network created for Project Cybersyn enabled the Allende government to construct a partial map of national economic activity that was based on current information. These data helped the government to make informed decisions in a time of crisis, to convey them with an extreme rapidity that would have been impossible otherwise, and ultimately to survive. The history of Project Cybersyn thus moves us beyond a framework of social construction, where social considerations influence technology, and draws our attention to the way that technologies matter in shaping the course of history.

6   Cybersyn Goes Public

Does it take more courage to be a cybernetician than to be a gunman?
—Stafford Beer, April 1973

The Cybersyn team began 1973 on a high note. By this point, both the temporary and permanent suites were running and processing production indicators from select factories. The CHECO economic models remained simple, but the economic modeling team had also made significant strides and no longer needed guidance from Ron Anderton in London. And the operations room was a functioning prototype by 10 January.

Flores was still a member of Allende's cabinet, but around the first of the year he left his post as minister of economics, to which he had been appointed only two months earlier, to become minister of finance. This latest presidential appointment took Flores even further from Project Cybersyn, although the Cybersyn team had not yet felt the full ramifications of losing his political leadership. Raúl Espejo began 1973 as head of the newly formed informatics directorate in the State Development Corporation and had secured financing for the project from the agency. The number of people working on Cybersyn continued to grow.

These positive developments stood in sharp contrast to the deteriorating political and economic situation that confronted the Popular Unity government. Chile started 1973 with a trade deficit of $438 million, declining production, and a 180.3 percent increase in prices in the previous twelve months.[1] The class war intensified in the aftermath of the October Strike, exacerbating political polarization. As more Chileans moved from the center to the right, either civil war or a military coup became an increasingly real possibility. Members of the opposition vowed to take back the country, either in the upcoming congressional elections in March 1973 or through tactics of economic sabotage, political and legal obstructionism, and violence. Yet those working on Project Cybersyn felt their efforts might still help the Popular Unity government, the Chilean economy, and the Chilean nation.

Back in Britain, Stafford Beer also began the new year with a positive outlook. Now that cybernetic thinking had produced concrete benefits for the Chilean government through the use of the telex network, the cybernetician believed he would have new opportunities to apply his ideas. While cybernetics had already proved useful to the government in managing Chile's "war economy" during the October Strike, it also held the potential to advance the social transformations taking place on the shop floor and in Chilean communities. Beer believed his cybernetic science could help Chilean workers increase their role in factory management as well as enable the Chilean people to have a greater role in national governance. He planned to continue developing these ideas in 1973 and to push for their implementation.

Beer was also excited because the Chilean government had finally given him permission to make his work on Project Cybersyn public. For months he and the Chilean team had debated making a public announcement, but the Chileans had always concluded the timing was not right. They worried an announcement would draw fire from the opposition and result in negative coverage of the system in the opposition-controlled press. To counter this bias, Beer and the Chilean team decided they would announce the system in Britain and Chile simultaneously, with the hope that positive coverage of Cybersyn in the British press would balance the Chilean coverage and improve international perceptions of the Allende government. Thus, they regarded acquiring support from the international community as a key to making the system successful in Chile. International support might also help the team address another long-standing problem: how to persuade Chilean industrial managers to actually use Project Cybersyn. Although the State Development Corporation, CORFO, continued to use the telex network, the system as a whole was not widely known and remained marginalized. Perhaps public support for the system from other countries could change this. Beer and the team set the announcement for 14 February 1973, when Beer was scheduled to give the prestigious third Richard Goodman Memorial Lecture at Brighton Polytechnic outside London.

Making the project public would open the system and the efforts of the project team to public scrutiny. Yet, judging from the archived source materials, it does not seem that the team worried much about how the British would view Project Cybersyn. Both Beer and the Chilean team were proud of their accomplishments, especially considering that they had created a prototype of a new computer system for economic management using modest technologies such as telex machines and slide projectors in innovative ways. The team seemed poised to deliver on Beer's November 1971 promise to President Allende—that a system based on a firm understanding of cybernetic principles could accomplish technical feats deemed impossible in the developed world, even with Chile's limited technological resources. The team believed that Project Cybersyn was proof of Chilean technological prowess under socialism.[2]

Moreover, Beer believed the system was different from earlier Soviet attempts to build a computer system for economic management and that Cybersyn was not vulnerable to the same criticisms of overcentralization and authoritarian control. He had designed the system to preserve factory autonomy and increase worker participation in management—the very values that set the Chilean revolution apart from that of the Soviet Union. He also viewed Cybersyn as a weapon against state bureaucracy. In contrast to the centralized Soviet approach, which sent large quantities of data to a central command point, Cybersyn selectively gave government decision makers limited quantities of data deemed vital to their decision making. In Beer's mind, Cybersyn went beyond offering a new form of decentralized, adaptive control that respected individual freedom without sacrificing the collective good; it also demonstrated that it was possible to marry the sociopolitical to the technological with the goal of creating a new society. He expected that other nations would view the system on those terms. But things did not work out in the way that Beer or the Chilean team imagined.

The first blow came on 7 January when the *Observer*, the United Kingdom's oldest Sunday newspaper, scooped both Beer and the Chilean government and brought Project Cybersyn to the attention of the English-speaking public with the provocative headline "Chile Run by Computer." Beer suspected that the news leaked after he talked to someone "on the condition that nothing was said until the Goodman lecture, and he betrayed me on that."[3] The *Observer* article portrayed the system in a way that was both damaging and untrue. It claimed, "The first computer system designed to control an entire economy has been secretly brought into operation in Chile," and described it as having been "assembled in some secrecy so as to avoid opposition charges of 'Big Brother' tactics."[4] Neither archival source materials nor the interviews I conducted with key project participants suggest that Cybersyn was ever a covert government initiative. Nor do any of these sources suggest that the project team worried it might be accused of creating an Orwellian state through Cybersyn. The Popular Unity approach to socialism was, in fact, quite different from the totalitarianism the British socialist George Orwell criticized with his novel *1984*. Nevertheless, this early misreading of Project Cybersyn proved extremely difficult for Beer to correct. It also demonstrates how international geopolitics politicized views of this technological system, causing Cybersyn to become a canvas on which historical actors painted their cold war anxieties.

Polemicizing Project Cybersyn

Beer arrived in Chile on 9 January—two days after the *Observer* story broke in Britain. The trip began with a gesture of friendship that so surprised Beer that he telexed London soon after he arrived: "Astonished to be embraced by [the eminent biologist Humberto] Maturana on the Tarmac."[5] But the trip quickly took a more serious turn. In a letter to Ron Anderton, Beer wrote that the *Observer* article "led to a cabinet crisis while I was there [in Santiago]—but don't tell anyone."[6] Strangely, Beer kept few documents from his January trip. Perhaps his, or even the government's, desire to keep these events private affected Beer's record-keeping practices.

The next blow came on 10 January, three days after the *Observer* broke the story, when Flores announced to the public a new program to give the government greater control of the national distribution of goods. The government planned to control the distribution of thirty essential goods, including flour, rice, tea, and sugar. This was a radical move to increase government control of the economy and, according to some interpretations, to prepare for the conflict to come. Flores felt that the program could help counteract the effects of the expanding black market, falling production levels, and consumer shortages, all of which were exacerbating the economic crisis.

Flores's announcement came less than two months before the congressional election, when political tensions were already running high. The opposition happily used the new program as fodder for a round of attacks against the government. *El Mercurio*, the opposition-owned newspaper, claimed the new program would destroy small- and medium-sized businesses. Accusing the government of using the program to requisition merchants' inventories, the newspaper claimed that government rationing would allocate inadequate quantities of goods to store owners, making it impossible for them to earn a living. The opposition also blamed government policies for police violence against Chileans whom the police suspected of hoarding. One *Mercurio* article claimed a police officer violently expelled from a supermarket a woman who was eight months pregnant. The officer accused her of hoarding because she had two cans of condensed milk instead of one.[7] This article illustrates how the opposition-owned *Mercurio* was trying to turn the Chilean public against the Allende government by cultivating feelings of fear and outrage. Whether true or not, these stories fueled criticism of the new government distribution program and of Flores. They also heightened anxieties about the availability of consumer goods. Chileans rushed to the stores to purchase goods they feared the government would ration in the future, further exacerbating the consumer shortages. The distribution program also hurt the increasingly fragile relationship between the government and the military. The military openly disapproved of the program, and one military member of the cabinet resigned in protest.

To further complicate matters, Flores made the announcement before the government was even able to control a national distribution network. Allende's minister of mining, Sergio Bitar, writes that "an apparatus capable of administering the direct distribution of even two or three products had never been assembled, to say nothing of one that could manage thirty."[8] Despite Flores's extreme care about not announcing Project Cybersyn before he had something to show, he had not exhibited the same level of caution with his national distribution program. As a result, he announced a plan that was considered technically impossible, handed propaganda bullets to the opposition, and suffered the consequences.

On 12 January, two days after Flores announced the rationing plan in Chile, news of Project Cybersyn appeared in the British publication *Latin America*. Like the *Observer*, *Latin America* linked Cybersyn to the creation of an Orwellian state.[9] Meanwhile the

Figure 6.1
Joe Tonelli, editorial cartoon, *St. Petersburg Times*, 17 January 1973. Image used with permission from Joe Tonelli.

Observer story continued to spread in the English-speaking world. In the United States, the *St. Petersburg Times* reprinted the *Observer* story but added its own embellishment: a cartoon mainframe computer using binoculars to watch a small man in a Mexican sombrero—a misrepresentation of both Project Cybersyn and the Chilean people (figure 6.1).[10] Besides reflecting U.S. fears of Soviet expansion in developing nations such as those in Latin America, the image presented a racialized view of computer technology. The mainframe computer can be read as representing a centralized, all-knowing state apparatus, while the small man in the Mexican sombrero represents a stereotype about people from the developing world, who in this image are being watched, controlled, and manipulated by an authoritarian state.

On 23 January, several days after Beer returned to London, the centrist Chilean newsmagazine *Ercilla* broke the Cybersyn story to the Chilean public under the headline "Mr. Beer's Big Brother." The article appeared a full three weeks before the simultaneous public announcement the team had planned for Brighton and Santiago—and

that it still planned to make as scheduled. The *Ercilla* article cited the British publication *Latin America* as its source, which was reflected in the headline and content of the
article, and repeated the charges of secrecy.[11] It did not help that *Ercilla* had learned
of Project Cybersyn from the British press instead of from the Chilean government, a
chain of events that seemed to substantiate the secrecy charges.

The article also mentioned Flores's central role in the project and described the finance minister as someone who had "searched fruitlessly for a chance to use his futuristic plans."[12] This was, perhaps, a thinly veiled reference to the rationing debacle and
the government's inability to control the distribution of consumer goods on a national
scale. *Ercilla* ran a separate article on the proposed distribution program in the same
issue, accompanied by a cartoon drawing of Flores saying, "The poor eat bread and the
rich eat shit, shit. I have spoken."[13] *Ercilla* thus introduced Project Cybersyn as something that could deprive the Chilean people of their civil liberties, and similarly suggested that Flores's distribution program might be a way for Popular Unity to deprive
the Chilean people of essential consumer items. *Ercilla*'s centrist reputation arguably
gave such criticism even more weight. Cybersyn had now been politicized in ways that
reflected the ongoing political struggle between the government and the opposition.

Beer pushed the Chilean team to respond to the negative press. On 29 January he
telexed Espejo to say that inaccurate and misleading reports of the system had now
appeared in the Toronto and Johannesburg press and that, in his opinion, "silence is a
mistake."[14] Beer proposed that the government give a televised tour of the operations
room. If the public saw the room, he reasoned, people would not think it was something secretive and thus sinister.

But the Chileans rejected his proposal. According to Beer, they countered that giving a televised tour of the operations room made the room vulnerable to sabotage by
the opposition. Beer respected the wishes of his Chilean colleagues—in the 29 January
telex he writes, "Am still refusing to speak until [February] 14th"—the announcement
date the team was sticking to despite the stories that were appearing about Cybersyn—
but he clearly believed the Chileans did not understand the consequences of allowing
such misinformation to go unchallenged.

The cybernetician was particularly frustrated with Flores, who, he felt, "virtually
disregarded" the media situation all together.[15] From Beer's point of view, responding to
the negative press made sense. As an international business consultant, he understandably did not want his work, or the work of his colleagues, to be portrayed incorrectly
in the international media. On the other hand, Flores's reaction may make sense as
well, especially if he wanted to avoid additional media attention and charges of having
futuristic ideas or if he was consumed with matters he deemed more important than
Project Cybersyn. Unfortunately, by refusing to respond to the press reports, Flores
and the rest of the Chilean team allowed the negative impressions of Cybersyn to gain
momentum.

The speed with which the international and Chilean press associated Cybersyn with totalitarianism is surprising, given the explicit efforts of Beer and the Chilean team to embed in its design political values that were the exact opposite of totalitarian control. These initial press accounts illustrate a finding from science studies research, namely, that for a technology to be successful it must be taken up by people other than the inventors. What Bruno Latour, a sociologist of science, writes of scientific ideas also holds true for technologies: "You need *them*, to make *your* [scientific] paper a decisive one."[16] However, this appropriation creates a dangerous situation. Engineers need others to support their technologies so that the technology will be successful, but in the process the engineers lose control of their invention. Latour warns, "The total movement . . . of a statement, of an artefact, will depend to some extent on your action but to a much greater extent on that of a crowd over which you have little control."[17] As Latour observes, others may decide to accept the technology as it is, but they could also dismiss, appropriate, or change the technology in fundamental ways.

Latour's observation illuminates what happened to Project Cybersyn in early 1973 and provides a framework for understanding how difficult it is to embed a political value in a technological system. The Cybersyn team needed a groundswell of support for the system for it to gain acceptance in Chilean industry. The team decided to make Cybersyn public in order to increase the support for its labors within Chile and the international community, and team members viewed international support as necessary for Cybersyn's success. But having more people aware of Cybersyn meant that the project team could no longer control how the project was presented to the public or how the public perceived the team's work, and this lack of control was exacerbated by the *Observer* story containing misinformation and by the team's decision not to counteract such negative depictions before the Goodman lecture. Instead of immediately enrolling others to support Project Cybersyn and the Allende government, the project team left the project vulnerable to competing interpretations and competing political interests. It was remarkably easy for critics to separate the technology from the beliefs that had guided its creation. Keeping a technological project tied to a particular political project was not a simple affair. This fragile relationship could be derailed at any point along the way.

The Goodman Lecture

The Goodman lecture on 14 February served multiple purposes for Beer. First, it allowed him to respond to his British critics by demonstrating the value of his cybernetic approach to management and proving that his ideas could be put into practice. In the lecture Beer outlines, then refutes, several "British objections" to his ideas, which he claims to have heard from British economists, managers, civil servants, and ministers before his work in Chile on Project Cybersyn. Among these objections were charges that using computers for real-time management was the stuff of science fiction, that its software would take hundreds of human-years to write and debug, that such a system would implement a form of Orwellian abuse, and that it could be built only in the United States—the recognized world leader in computer technology.

To these criticisms, Beer responded that the system used simple technologies such as telex machines, drew from excellent programming talent in London and Santiago, and relied on many "human interfaces," meaning it was not automated. He also said that he was tired of hearing the assertion that such a system could be built only in the United States, and stressed that building the futuristic control room required only "the managerial acceptance of the idea, plus the will to see it realized."[18] But, he added, "I finally found both the acceptance and the will—on the other side of the world."[19] This final comment was a not-so-subtle jab at his British compatriots, who over the years had questioned the legitimacy and feasibility of his cybernetic ideas.

Second, the Goodman lecture gave Beer an opportunity to present his own interpretation of the Allende government and Project Cybersyn. Beer had spent part of January carefully preparing his remarks for the lecture, which, given the negative press, now took on a new level of importance. He sent the first ten pages of his planned remarks to Flores, Schwember, and Espejo for their comments. On 2 February Espejo telexed Beer the feedback from the group, noting that Beer would be able to guess who in the group had made which comment. Like Beer, the Chileans wanted the Allende government to be portrayed in a positive light. They asked that Beer refrain from mentioning the severity of the food shortages, and the cybernetician agreed.

Instead, Beer informed his British audience that Chile's main problems were not food shortages and public demonstrations but an international economic blockade that prevented the nation from exporting its copper and from importing the machinery and spare parts that its agricultural and industrial sectors needed. He stressed that the Allende government respected Chilean law and that Chile's revolution was one without bloodshed. He told the audience that much of the misinformation coming out of Chile was the result of the government's honoring the liberty of free speech and that many claims printed in the international media had been copied uncritically from media outlets controlled by the Chilean opposition. Beer hoped to generate a more favorable disposition toward the Allende government among members of the audience. The British government, then led by the Conservative prime minister Edward Heath, had clashed with British trade unions and tried, unsuccessfully, to curb the growing power of the labor movement. Strikes, blackouts, worker conflicts with the police, and inflation also characterized British life in the early 1970s. To some British observers, the economic and social disorder of Allende's Chile represented what the future might hold for Britain.[20] Beer hoped to counter these fears.

Beer told the audience that he was proud of what he had accomplished in Chile. Project Cybersyn offered a humane form of management that recognized human beings as "independent viable systems with a right of individual choice" who belonged to "a coherent society which in turn has a right of collective choice."[21] His cybernetic approach to management would empower the Chilean people and put the power of science at their disposal: "I know that I am making the maximum effort towards the devolution of power. The government made their revolution about it; I find it good cybernetics." Beer stressed that the tools he was developing in Chile were the "people's tools" and that his systems were designed for and in consultation with Chilean workers.[22]

Beer's desire to put a positive spin on his work pushed him to exaggerate his claims. For example, he stated that the Allende government had approached him with the question, *"How should cybernetics be used in the exercise of national government?* You will note that the question [of] whether cybernetics had any relevance to the problems of society and of government had already been answered affirmatively."[23] This claim was not exactly true. As we now know, Flores had been working on his own initiative when he invited Beer to Chile to address a much narrower problem: how to improve the management of the state-controlled enterprises. Moreover, most Chileans who were involved with the project had a very limited understanding of cybernetics and its application when Beer first arrived in Santiago.

Beer also gave the impression that Cybersyn was much closer to being a fully functional, real-time system of economic management than it actually was. He explained why it is important for a government to have an economic simulator to play with, but he did not tell his audience that the models designed for the CHECO project were too simple to provide substantial economic insight or to drive policy. When discussing the operations room, Beer said, "It is not science fiction; it is science fact. It exists, and it works; it exists and it works for the worker as well as for the minister."[24] But this too is a half-truth. The room worked in the sense that the team had installed the equipment and had a functioning prototype. However, it was not a space that CORFO used for decision making, nor was the room being used by teams of workers or managers from the state-controlled enterprises. At this point it was still impossible to know whether the room "worked" for workers or for managers as a space for decision making. Beer did say that the system was still unproved, but he did not detail how much work remained before the actual system would match the archetype he described in the lecture. Beer used the Goodman lecture to give his side of the story, but his presentation of Cybersyn also contained instances of hyperbole that could be construed as misrepresentation.

But Beer's critics did not latch onto Beer's exaggerations. Instead, they gravitated to two other aspects of the lecture, namely, Beer's claim that his work on Cybersyn was not technocratic and his insistence that Cybersyn, a technology for control, promoted freedom. Although these were common threads in Beer's writing, such claims seemed to defy logic for those unfamiliar with the nuances of his work.

In the lecture Beer positioned technocracy as an enemy but one that could be defeated through cybernetic thinking. "I am a scientist; but to be a technocrat would put me out of business as a man," Beer said, demonstrating the depths of his loathing for technocracy and his commitment to creating human-centered technologies that allowed Chilean workers and everyday citizens to participate in government.[25] Beer viewed technocracy as a symptom of bureaucracy, the epitome of organizational inefficiency, and he used it as a common foil in his cybernetic writings. Besides rejecting technocracy, Beer said he was working against "the image of exploitation that high science and the electronic computer by now represents." He cast Cybersyn as a solution. But in doing so, he positioned technology as both problem and savior and adopted a technology-centered view of the Chilean revolutionary process that was easier to confuse with technocracy.[26] By emphasizing technology instead of Cybersyn's relationship to the social and economic goals of Allende's nationalization program, Beer failed to definitively separate himself from the technocrats he criticized.

Espejo, Flores, and Schwember had warned Beer of this pitfall in the 2 February telex they sent the cybernetician.[27] The Chileans questioned the distinction Beer drew between technocracy and what he was doing. Beer felt his work was not technocratic because (at least in theory) it used science to empower people—in particular, Chilean workers—rather than to aid the government elite. Espejo countered that "one can be scientific and technocratic at the same time. Having shaped up a government machine in itself can be interpreted as a merely technocratic thing."[28] Espejo telexed that Beer would further distance himself from charges of technocracy if he adopted an explicit ideological position in his remarks. This comment about ideology probably came from either Schwember or Flores, given the attention both men had placed on developing the political aspects of the project. Yet Beer refused to give the lecture a more ideological tone: "I want to carry my audience with me and will lose all credibility if I go too far at once," he wrote. "This was a matter of judgment but I do know my public and press."[29] Considering that the right in Britain was not supportive of Allende's politics and the British left had mixed reactions to the Chilean government, Beer was probably right to be cautious. Still, given his willingness to embrace and even amplify the ideological aspects of Project Cybersyn in Chile, his reticence to do the same in Britain is telling: it shows that Beer changed his presentation of Project Cybersyn and Chilean socialism according to his goals and his audience.

The comments Espejo, Flores, and Schwember telexed to Beer show that they objected to other facets of the speech as drafted. They wrote that, while they agreed that cybernetic thinking might help the government increase social stability, they also wondered whether instability might be an important part of social progress. "Historical development is a succession of equilibriums and unequilibriums [sic]," Espejo telexed. Disequilibrium "might be indispensable." This is an interesting observation, although it was not raised as an objection to Cybersyn in subsequent press accounts. The Chileans also challenged Beer's framing of the Chilean revolution as a control problem. "The social phenomena goes [sic] further than the control problem," Espejo wrote; "there is for instance the problem of power." If cybernetics looked only at control and ignored power relationships, "there is the danger that cybernetics might be used for social repression," Espejo continued, echoing the fears that had already appeared in the press. Beer responded: "I cannot write the next book in this one lecture."[30] But perhaps Beer would have given greater thought to this issue had he known that his critics would be most concerned with whether Cybersyn facilitated social repression.

Instead, Beer chose to address this issue by asserting that Project Cybersyn promoted freedom. However, he did not use the word *freedom* in the common sense of being exempt from authority, and this difference led to further confusion and more criticism. Beer argued that Cybersyn promoted "effective freedom" because it made it possible to compute the maximum amount of autonomy an enterprise could have without threatening the overall viability of the national economy. (He even titled the Goodman lecture "Fanfare for Effective Freedom: Cybernetic Praxis in Government.") Beer writes that "the polarity between centralization and decentralization—one masquerading as oppression and the other as freedom—is a myth. Even if the homeostatic balance point turns out not to be always computable, it surely exists. The poles are two absurdities for any viable system, as our own bodies will tell us."[31] The algedonic, or warning, signals that Cybersyn sent to alert higher management constituted a threat to factory freedom but it was a necessary one, for not alerting higher management might pose a greater threat to system survival. "The body politic cannot sustain the risk of autonomic inaction any more than we can as human beings," Beer observed.[32] In proposing the idea of effective freedom, Beer was arguing (1) that freedom was something that could be calculated and (2) that freedom should be quantitatively circumscribed to ensure the stability of the overall system. For those who had followed Beer's work over the years, *effective freedom* was a new term to describe the balance of centralized and decentralized control that Beer had advocated for more than a decade. It also reflected the same principles as Allende's democratic socialism, which increased state power but preserved civil liberties. But for the uninitiated, the claim that a control system that explicitly limited freedom actually preserved and promoted freedom must have seemed like a political slogan straight out of *1984*.[33]

Beer hoped that the Goodman lecture would put to rest the "Big Brother" charges that had appeared in the international media, and by his own account the lecture went well. On 16 February he telexed project coordinator Sonia Mordojovich: "The Brighton Lecture was a huge success. 300 people came. Chilean ambassador was delighted. Also his wife."[34] On 17 February he wrote to Flores, "The Goodman Lecture went off extremely well, and has attracted much attention. I have given six radio interviews about it."[35] But, unfortunately for Beer and the Chilean team, journalists and technologists latched onto the seeming contradictions and read them through the lens of the cold war.

Public Readings

On 15 February, the day after Beer's Goodman lecture, the British publication *New Scientist* ran an article and an editorial about Project Cybersyn, both written by Joseph Hanlon.[36] Beer telexed Mordojovich that he deemed the *New Scientist* article "quite good."[37] But Hanlon's editorial was damning. He called Beer a "technological power broker" and mused, "if this [Project Cybersyn] is successful, Beer will have created one of the most powerful weapons in history."[38] Placing emphasis on Beer's bourgeois lifestyle, Hanlon implied that it was hypocritical for someone who claimed to support the socialist government in Chile to live so comfortably. Hanlon also challenged Beer's assertion that he was different from the technocrats he criticized. The reporter took issue with Beer's claim that Chilean workers and managers, not the technical elite, would use Cybersyn and argued that this did not absolve the cybernetician of creating a more centralized state or of expanding the role of technical experts within the Chilean government at the expense of the Chilean people. Nor did Hanlon view the safeguards Beer built into the system as sufficient for preventing government abuse. "Many people . . . will think Beer the super-technocrat of them all," Hanlon concluded.[39] Beer's response was swift. In a letter to the editor published 22 February, Beer characterized Hanlon's charges as a "hysterical verbal onslaught" and an ad hominem attack.[40] Ironically, Hanlon and Beer were being critical of the same thing in their opposite readings of Project Cybersyn: they were both against a Soviet style of socialism in which the regimented actions of the worker formed part of the state machine and technology was used to maintain a top-down form of centralized control.

Beer viewed the reaction of *New Scientist* as evidence that the British press was "totally prostituted," but he worried that the article could have negative ramifications for his friends in Chile. He told Flores, "If anyone raises this with you, I would advise you to laugh and say you know all about it, it is just what we both expected of the British press, and that it is simply a personal attack on me."[41] Beer knew he had his share of critics in Britain, but despite the bravado in his message to Flores, this was not how he had envisioned the public's reaction to his work.

Although Beer viewed Hanlon's portrayal of Cybersyn as a personal attack, *New Scientist* may genuinely have viewed Project Cybersyn as implementing a Soviet form of top-down control for other reasons. From the late 1950s into the 1960s, the Soviet Union saw cybernetics as the unifying language for its scientific program. According to historian Slava Gerovitch, this "cybernetization" of Soviet science entailed bringing the objective language of mathematics and computing to bear on the social and life sciences, what Gerovitch refers to as "cyberspeak."[42] The attention the Soviets gave to cybernetics made members of the U.S. intelligence community worry that the Soviet Union might eclipse the United States in such areas as computing and automation. John Ford, an expert on Soviet science working in the CIA Office of Scientific Intelligence, was monitoring Soviet cybernetic activity as early as 1959 and warned the U.S.

government in 1965 of a potential cybernetics gap between the United States and the Soviet Union.[43] In the 1960s Ford played a central role in promoting cybernetics among members of the U.S. scientific community; he also helped to form the American Society for Cybernetics in 1964.[44] While Hanlon had no way of knowing how the U.S. government viewed cybernetics during the cold war, he could have known about the central role cybernetics was playing in the Soviet science program. He also might have known that Soviet cybernetics emphasized using computers for administrative decision making and that the Soviets had been working since early 1959 on ways to use computers for centralized economic planning. Any of these considerations might have pushed Hanlon to associate Project Cybersyn with the Soviet experience.

Hanlon might have had still other reasons for challenging Beer's presentation of Cybersyn as a human-centered technology. In the early 1970s, studies of job dissatisfaction had become a fashionable topic, and management consulting companies began recommending ways to "humanize" work. Members of the intellectual left viewed such approaches with suspicion. For example, in 1974 Harry Braverman observed that "a number of management consulting firms have taken this sort of 'humanization' as their field and are pressing schemes upon managers. . . . Whatever their phraseology, these consulting organizations have only one function: cutting costs, improving 'efficiency,' raising productivity."[45] While Braverman does not cite Beer's work in particular—he may not have known of Beer's work in Chile—his comments do illustrate that Beer was not the only management consultant arguing that rationalization could make work more humane. Braverman's comments also show that some viewed such approaches as an indirect way to give management greater control over labor.

The ease with which Hanlon painted Cybersyn as upholding political values that were the opposite of those of Chilean democratic socialism is a good example of the difficulty engineers and other technologists face in designing political values in a technological system. In fact, Hanlon was not alone in recognizing Cybersyn's potential for centralized control. On 1 March Beer telexed to Espejo, "Accusations come from Britain and the USA. Invitations [to build comparable systems] come from Brazil and South Africa." Considering the repressive governments that were in power in Brazil and South Africa in the early 1970s, it is easy to sympathize with Beer's lament: "You can see what a false position I am in."[46] Beer was understandably frustrated with these international misinterpretations of his cybernetic work.

However, it took little political imagination to see how putting Cybersyn in a different social, political, and organizational context could make the system an instrument of centralized control. Beer had tried to embed political values in Cybersyn's design, but he engineered them in the social and organizational aspects of the Cybersyn system, in addition to the technology itself. As safeguards, these social and organizational arrangements were not very strong. Archived telexes from the project team show that if the Cyberstride software detected a production indicator outside the accepted range of values, a member of the National Computer Corporation (ECOM) alerted the affected enterprise, those in the central telex room in CORFO, and Espejo in the CORFO informatics directorate—all at the same time.[47] Beer's design allowed an enterprise a limited window within which to address the production problem identified before higher management in CORFO intervened. Yet CORFO staffers were apprised of anomalous factory activity, such as raw materials shortages and high worker absenteeism, from the outset. The autonomy of an enterprise therefore depended on a CORFO staff member's not sharing this information with colleagues. In addition, Cybersyn's being run by and physically located in the institution charged with national industrial management could have threatened the preservation of factory autonomy, whether deliberately or otherwise. Dismantling one of the primary safeguards of that autonomy might have been as easy as having someone from the telex room walk down the hall.

Because Cybersyn never reached completion, I cannot say with absolute certainty whether the system would have empowered Chilean workers or whether it would have increased the influence of a small group of government technologists. We do know that worker involvement in Cybersyn was minimal and that the project did little to increase worker participation on the shop floor. Nevertheless, in CORFO's March 1973 comprehensive report on Project Cybersyn, Espejo echoed Beer's claim that Chilean workers were in the best position to build the factory models because they had intimate knowledge of factory production processes. He also asserted that building such models would improve workers' understandings of production and investment.[48]

But such statements were more rhetoric than real. In a 2006 interview, Espejo said that worker participation was extremely important "at a declarative level" but not at "the operational level, the level of action." Later in the interview Espejo gave a more cybernetic description of how worker participation figured into the project: it was "activity in the brain with no muscular connection."[49] Oral and archived source materials show that by March 1973 Cybersyn had done little or nothing to empower Chilean workers, while at the same time the number of engineers involved in the factory modeling process continued to grow. It is also telling that in March 1973 CORFO published a report detailing how to build quantified factory models for Project Cybersyn. The report was more than ninety pages long and was clearly written for an audience that had a university education in a technical field.[50] Despite Beer's claims that Cybersyn was an instance of the "people's science," the project was clearly run by and for government technologists.

Political Viability, Technological Viability

As 1973 progressed, Chilean socialism and Project Cybersyn came under increasing attack. Now, more than ever, the fate of Project Cybersyn was tied to the fate of Chilean socialism. In 1971 Chile's political innovation had supported technological innovation and generated new approaches to computing and economic management. However, by 1973 Project Cybersyn required political stability to move forward, and yet the possibility of peaceful socialist change decreased with each passing day.

Scholars of the Allende period cite the congressional elections, held on 4 March 1973, as the moment that sealed the fate of the Allende government. Held near the midpoint of Allende's presidency, these elections were the last scheduled before Allende's term ended in 1976; as such, they represented the last chance to change the balance of power in national politics by constitutional means. The elections therefore were of vital importance to both the government and the opposition. The opposition hoped to increase its representation in the legislature to a two-thirds majority—the percentage it needed to impeach Allende or block an executive veto, either of which would render Allende powerless and give the opposition control of the country. The government was simply hoping to prevent the opposition from reaching this goal.

But although the opposition succeeded in securing the majority of seats in the Chilean Congress, the size of that majority fell short of its expectations. Not only did the opposition fail to achieve the two-thirds majority it desired, it actually lost seats to the Popular Unity coalition: the representation of Popular Unity in Congress increased from 36 percent in 1970 to 44 percent in 1973. These results gave the government new hope as it looked toward the next elections in 1976. The government attributed these results to the growing class consciousness of Chilean workers, who showed up at the polls en masse to support their president. In a 6 March letter to Beer, Roberto Cañete wrote, "Nobody, and I mean nobody, had even imagined such a result and I am sure that the great teaching this election leaves us is the tremendous political conscience of the people." Cañete added that, despite inflation, shortages, and the lack of qualified people to run the nationalized industries, "the people made true the phrase 'This Government is shit, but it is my Government.'"[51]

Although the Allende government had defied expectations, the electoral victory came at a high cost: it strengthened the resolve of the opposition, unleashing a counterrevolution whose proponents realized they could not end Chilean socialism by legal means. The opposition stepped up its criticism of the Allende government, challenging the election results and accusing the government of committing electoral fraud. It also repeated earlier criticism of Allende's economic policies. Previously, the opposition had attacked the government nationalization program for decreasing production levels and taking away Chilean civil liberties. After the elections, the opposition cited Project Cybersyn as an additional example of how nationalization threatened individual freedom, heightening the existing fears that members of the Chilean public had about their government. On 15 March, less than two weeks after the congressional elections, the center-right magazine *Qué Pasa* ran an article with the headline "Secret Plan 'Cyberstride': Popular Unity Controls Us by Computer." The article stressed that Project Cybersyn would "not only be used for economic ends, but also for political strategy," and it transformed the cybernetic phrase "communication is control" into something that sounded sinister. The article concluded by taking a jab at the ailing Chilean economy: "It is not clear if inflation, shortages, the black market and long lines have been studied by the 'Cyberstride' computers."[52] Not only did Project Cybersyn, and by extension the Chilean government, threaten political freedom, it also was not qualified to fix the broad scope of Chile's economic ailments.

However, the political interpretations of Project Cybersyn were more complicated than the *Qué Pasa* article suggests. Espejo recalled that after the March elections, "every day more people [technologists] wanted to work on the project. . . . The quantity of work was infinite and it had an intellectual pedigree. For a number of them, it offered a . . . productive way of using their time."[53] Although Cyberysn was a project designed to further the economic changes wrought by Chilean socialism, the project attracted people from the right, left, and center. Some were simply taken with the new approach to computing that the project offered and with the futuristic operations room. Espejo also believed the project offered an alternative for Chilean technologists who wanted to help the government but did not want to march in the streets, conduct acts of civil disobedience, or pick up a rifle and join the workers. The project also appealed to technologists who were sympathetic with the opposition but wanted to improve the national economy. This composition of the project team offers a more nuanced reading of how technology and politics came together in the Chilean revolution and complicates accounts of Cybersyn in the opposition press.[54]

The same day that *Qué Pasa* embroiled Project Cybersyn in opposition criticism of the Allende government, the British publication *New Scientist* published a scathing letter to the editor written by Herb Grosch, a U.S. mainframe computer expert, who questioned whether Project Cybersyn was technologically feasible.[55] Grosch had visited Chile in 1969 as part of a conference on government data-processing and had seen the beginnings of the Chilean State Computer Service Center (EMCO). Judging from what he had seen in 1969, Grosch concluded, "it is absolutely not possible for Stafford Beer, Minister Flores or the Chilean government or industrial computer users to have since then implemented what is described in [*New Scientist*]."[56] Unlike Hanlon, who objected to Cybersyn's political implications, Grosch objected to Cybersyn from a purely technical standpoint. Based on his knowledge of how mainframes were being used for industrial management in the United States and Western Europe, the most advanced areas of the world with respect to computing, he believed that what Beer described was not technologically possible.

Grosch's letter to the editor underlines the assumption that industrialized nations, such as the United States and the nations of Western Europe, pioneered modern computer capabilities; nations of the developing world, such as Chile, did not. In his letter Grosch wrote that Project Cybersyn could not be built in a "strange and primitive hardware and software environment," such as that found in Chile, and in such a short time. He compared Beer's description of Project Cybersyn to contemporaneous European efforts to use computer models in factory management. In particular, he cited a successful effort at a BASF plant in Ludwigshaven, Germany, to use computer models in plant management practices. According to Grosch, the BASF modeling project required "a big, expert team and a very sophisticated top management" and took five years to complete. Since the German effort required greater technological and human resources and substantially more time than what was available in Chile, Grosch concluded Cybersyn must be the stuff of fantasy. "I call the whole concept beastly," Grosch wrote. "It is a good thing for humanity, and for Chile in particular, that it is as yet only a bad dream."[57] Modernization theory posits that technological development follows a universal trajectory and that this trajectory is pioneered by advanced industrialized nations such as Germany or the United States. Grosch's logic displays the hallmarks of such reasoning.

But the international response to Chile's socialist project had deterred, and even prevented, Beer and the Chilean team from imitating the way Germany or the United States or other industrialized nations used computer technology. The economic blockade had prevented the team from acquiring state-of-the-art hardware, and a very different economic program drove the team's use of computer technology.

It could also be argued that Project Cybersyn used computers in ways that could not be replicated in more industrialized nations. In 1973 the Chilean economy was more than twenty times smaller than that of Germany and almost one hundred times smaller than that of the United States. The Chilean economy was also composed of only a few core industries.[58] Building a computer system to manage the Chilean economy was thus a much simpler task than trying to build a comparable system in Germany or the United States, although such a system would not have made much sense outside the context of a socialist economy. The context of political revolution also created a climate in Chile in which people wanted to break from the past and pursue new technological possibilities, including those that were different from what the United States and the Soviet Union were working on. Cybersyn was possible *because* it was built in Chile, not in one of the nations of the industrialized world, during this particular historical moment.

Beer spent March in Britain, teaching at Manchester Business School and defending Project Cybersyn in the British press. Back in Chile, project director Raúl Espejo decided to make Cybersyn public in a different way. In early March he telexed Beer that he had commissioned a series of six reports to formally document the project and give it a "scientific character."[59] Through these reports, Espejo hoped to increase the scientific legitimacy of Project Cybersyn and perhaps boost support for the project within the government. However, Espejo's decision to focus on the scientific aspects of the project upset Schwember, who felt the project director's energy would be better spent trying to convince management in the state-run enterprises to adopt the system. The discussions that followed brought to the surface disagreements about whether to prioritize the technical or the outwardly political aspects of Project Cybersyn, to fully develop the conceptual and scientific aspects of the project, or to do whatever was necessary to put the system into practice. Such disagreements illustrate another key way that the fate of Project Cybersyn was tied to the viability of Chilean socialism.

Schwember blamed Espejo for Cybersyn's marginal role in Chilean industrial management. On 22 March, Schwember wrote Beer that "Enrique [Farné] and I cannot convince Raúl that he is using the wrong tactics. Instead of using the Operations Room . . . he has assigned Juan to study it. He [Espejo] thinks that theory can solve all problems and that at some point the whole of industry will—by an Act of God—fall in the open arms of the robot." Schwember warned: "if we don't have at least one production unit using cyberware rather soon, the whole thing [Project Cybersyn] will fall in disrepute."[60] Schwember's words struck a chord with Beer. On 28 March, Beer telexed Espejo, "I know the problems and do not underrate the work accomplished. But remember my analogy of [a] motor car. We should be driving it however erratically, not inspecting it, polishing the handle, and waiting for extras. . . . Publicity grows and attacks increase. We shall lose credibility if routing information flow in long established links not established quickly."[61]

Although Beer and Schwember both believed the academic aspects of the system should be secondary to getting the system to actually do things in the world, Espejo felt that he did not have the political clout needed to push members of CORFO or Chilean industry to adopt the system. Flores had protected the project politically throughout 1972, but he had now distanced himself from the project institutionally and personally. Flores's absence left Espejo with limited options, which may explain why he decided to spend time advancing the scientific credibility of the project instead of tackling the much more difficult task of promoting the system's use in the state-controlled factories.[62] In addition, Espejo found it difficult to follow Beer's dictum to push the system as something other than a tool for economic centralization, especially since CORFO wanted to centralize its control of national industry and expand the reach of the state apparatus. On 29 March Espejo telexed Beer, "Given that I've had no support from Aureliano [Flores] . . . I see myself forced to sell the ideas," a situation Espjeo viewed as absurd.[63] On 5 April Espejo telexed Beer that Flores needed to commit to the project because he "is the only one who could be listened to at the moment."[64] In a report in mid-April, Espejo repeated that Flores "had nothing to say or to do in connection with the project," and complained that the team lacked political guidance.[65] Without such guidance, the team could not adapt its work to the current political situation.

Enrique Farné and Herman Schwember had also distanced themselves from Espejo. Flores had asked Farné to navigate the political aspects of Cybersyn's implementation, such as how to build support for Project Cybersyn on the shop floor, but he had been consumed by his work for the automotive sector and was further hindered by a broken leg. Farné's absence meant that no one was overseeing this crucial part of the project. Schwember, whom Flores had asked to study how the system fit in the larger picture of Chilean socialism, maintained regular contact with Beer but not with Espejo. Schwember's time also became more limited when he left his technical position in the State Copper Corporation to assume a leadership role in the agroindustrial sector. Flores's decision to direct his attention to his role as finance minister and away from Project Cybersyn also caused him to limit his communication with Espejo (although Flores did continue to stay in touch with Beer). The cabinet position was so stressful that it affected the young finance minister's health, and in March Flores was hospitalized with kidney problems.

While Flores, Farné, and Schwember all had good reasons for not maintaining regular contact with Espejo, it is nevertheless understandable that Espejo felt abandoned. His correspondence makes clear that the project director found himself trapped in a feedback loop. On 16 April, Espejo wrote Flores that even members of the Cybersyn team viewed the project as a "refined technique alien to the political-social process," precisely because they lacked political leadership and could not incorporate the system in this process.[66]

Cybersyn was a working prototype, but it was still not developed enough to be of use to Chilean factory managers. And these managers could ill afford to divert their attention from the daily emergencies on the shop floor in order to support a new technological prototype that was still under development. Although Espejo wrote that the factory modeling conducted for Cybersyn had helped managers improve production processes in the Easton Furniture factory, in general the system did not have much effect on factory activity.[67]

Beer had trumpeted Cybersyn as a real-time control system, yet its actual operation was too slow help the industrial managers. The team often required more than two weeks to collect factory data, process the data using the Cyberstride software, and then send information back to the enterprise. On 29 March, Espejo telexed Beer that "reasons are many" for the two-week delay: "Our mistake was that we did not send these reports back to the enterprises. They [the enterprises] generally delayed [sending] the dispatches [to the Cybersyn team] because they did not realize their value."[68] Such delays made the system useless to factory interventors.

The following anecdote explains why Chilean factory managers did not view the system as useful. An interventor from a cement factory discovered a serious coal shortage in his factory. He decided to visit the supplying coal mine to learn the cause of the problem. He traveled to the mine, personally spoke to the miners, and explained the importance of maintaining the coal supply. He then created a log to show when trains were available that could bring coal to the factory from the mine. Several days after the interventor returned to his cement factory, he received a notice from Project Cybersyn telling him of a potential shortage of coal.[69] The system had correctly identified a problem but had done so too late to be of value. Based on this example, it's no wonder that factory managers did not make sending data to the National Computer Corporation a priority or that Espejo had trouble selling the system to those directly involved in industrial management.

To get data from the factories, employees of the National Computer Corporation had to call the enterprises individually and ask them to send the information through the telex network so that it could be processed by the mainframe, a painstaking process. According to Isaquino Benadof, now the data management director, those at the enterprise responded, "Oh, just wait a minute, wait a minute, I [will] send you [the data] in half an hour," but "in a half an hour you [needed to] call again." The big problem was "not technology, it was not the computer, it was [the] people," he concluded.[70] Cybersyn, a sociotechnical system, depended on more than its hardware and software components. For the system to function, human beings also needed to be disciplined and brought into line. In the case of Cybersyn, integrating human beings into the system, and thus changing their behavior, proved just as difficult as building the telex network or programming the software—or perhaps even more difficult. While the Cybersyn team could exert some degree of control over the computer resources, construction of the operations room, or installation of a telex machine, they had very little control over what was taking place within the factories, including levels of management participation or whether Cybersyn would be integrated into existing management practices. Espejo and Benadof lacked the authority to force the state-run factories to implement Cybersyn, and industrial managers remained unconvinced that it warranted their total compliance.

Espejo could not even convince higher management in his own institution, CORFO, to use the project beyond the telex network. For example, the director of planning at CORFO was openly hostile to Cybersyn because he felt it was unreasonable to connect an economy and factories that were "underdeveloped to a control center that was super-developed."[71] In addition to being attacked by the opposition and ignored by factory management, at this point Project Cybersyn lacked real political support from the government. Without this support, the project was a marginal endeavor languishing in CORFO's informatics directorate.

Cybersyn also lacked support from leftist members of the British scientific community—the very community Beer expected to appreciate the system most. In April 1973 the progressive British publication *Science for People* published an article critical of both Beer and Project Cybersyn. This seemingly paradoxical occurrence again illustrates how easy it was for onlookers to separate the Cybersyn technology from the core political values of its design. It also brings to light the heterogeneity of the British left as well as the complicated relationship Beer had with members of Britain's progressive scientific community.

Science for People was the publication of the British Society for Social Responsibility in Science, an organization that had formed in 1968 partially in response to the biological and chemical warfare research that was taking place on U.S. and British university campuses. Thinking the society's members would be sympathetic to his work in Chile, Beer discussed his work openly with a small group of scientists affiliated with the organization. However, not all members of the society viewed Beer as a kindred spirit. The contradiction between the cybernetician's statements of support for Allende's socialism and his comfortable lifestyle caused some to question Beer's motives. They might have further questioned his politics had they known that by September 1973 the Chilean government had paid Beer nearly £79,000 ($1.1 million in 2009 dollars) for expenses related to Project Cybersyn, including almost £33,000 ($461,000 in 2009 dollars) in personal fees.[72]

Jonathan Rosenhead was a founding member of the British Society for Social Responsibility in Science, and he was familiar with Beer's work. Rosenhead had worked at SIGMA right after Beer left the consulting group. Rosenhead had also approached Beer in January 1972 about going to Chile to work on Project Cybersyn.[73] Although Rosenhead did not attend the meetings that members of the society had with Beer, he said he heard the following anecdote repeated among society members. Stafford "was pulling out his hip flask and taking his whiskey and drinking and smoking his cigar and talking to these hair-shirted socialists," Rosenhead said. At some point someone asked, "'Stafford, do you drive a Rolls Royce?' And he said, 'Well, yes, I do.'" Rosenhead said this line of interrogation continued, eventually leading to the question, "'Stafford, did you say you're a socialist?'" Rosenhead believed that "they perceived a disconnect between what [Beer] said and how he was living" and that this "caused some bad feeling."[74] Beer was right, at least in part, that some of his negative press was ad hominem.

On the other hand, the society's members also had some misgivings about the Allende government and therefore felt some discomfort with Beer's decision to use his scientific expertise to assist Chilean socialism. "The left [in Britain] isn't all one thing," Rosenhead explained. "The BSSRS had a strong mixture of Trotskyism and anarchism and libertarianism, and we were very antiauthoritarian, as indeed the whole new left in Britain was at that stage."[75] Because the members of the society were highly critical of Stalinism and the top-down discipline of the Communist Party, they were suspicious of Chilean socialism, despite Allende's expressed commitment to preserving Chilean civil liberties. On one level, the reading of Chile advanced by Rosenhead and his colleagues was accurate. Although Allende was a socialist and dedicated to the idea of a constitutional revolution, he was also the head of a leftist governing coalition, which included the Communist Party and members of the Socialist Party who wanted to accelerate the pace of revolution beyond what Chilean law allowed. The left was not unified in Chile or in Britain, and this led to multiple interpretations and misapprehensions among the British left about Allende and the Chilean political experiment.

The article in *Science for People* portrayed Cybersyn as a tool to centralize government control and abuse Chilean workers, as its headline made plain: "Chile: Everything

Figure 6.2
Cover image from *Science for People*, April–May 1973.

under Control." This title was reinforced by the publication's cover image of an over-weight Chilean manager lounging comfortably in a chair and lazily pushing a main-frame computer button to move the limbs of a robotic worker (figure 6.2). John Adams, the writer of the article, claimed the Cybersyn system concentrated power in the hands of the president or the people who ran the control room. He was also highly critical of Beer's algedonic warning signals, viewing them not as a way to maximize factory autonomy but to control individual workers. "Should anyone in the lower reaches of the system have different objectives that lead them to stray beyond their 'physiologi-cal limits' and, thereby, constitute a threat to the 'well ordered production machinery,' they will be communicated with 'algedonically,'" Adams wrote, citing phrases from Beer's Goodman lecture.[76] The society thus cast Project Cybersyn as destroying "the inner autonomous man" and making workers part of a well-oiled machine.

Rosenhead speculated that Beer must have viewed the *Science for People* article as a "stab in the back from people who he thought were his friends." Beer's letter to the editor of the publication also conveys his belief that he was treated unjustly. "Take an arbitrary selection of any man's writings. . . . Note down any odd passages that look a bit weird on their own. Disingenuously string these gobbets on a thread of guilt. Could you not make a necklace to hang the man?" the cybernetician asked.[77] In retrospect, Rosenhead felt that the society would have taken a different stance on Cybersyn had they known about the military coup that was to come and the oppressive Pinochet dic-tatorship that would follow. "Then it would have been clear we were on the same side, and we wouldn't have dreamed of doing it," he said.[78] Perhaps the society's members would have changed their position on Cybersyn if they had known the path Chilean history would follow, but their reading of the system in April 1973 reflected the geopolitical context of the cold war and the divisions among the British left.

Beer, however, recognized the real possibility of a military coup. In his letter to the editor of *Science for People*, he considered whether Cybersyn might be altered by an "evil dictator" and used against the workers. Since Cybersyn team members were educating the Chilean people about such risks, he argued, the people could later sabotage these efforts. "Maybe even the dictator himself can be undermined; because 'information constitutes control'—and if the people understand that they may defeat even the dictator's guns," Beer mused.[79] I have found no evidence that members of the Cybersyn team were educating Chilean workers about the risks of using Cybersyn, although they might have been.

More important, I believe, is the level of naiveté displayed in Beer's response, which reveals he did not understand the implications of military dictatorship. But then neither did the Chilean public at that point in time. By the end of 1973, four months after the Pinochet military coup, information in Chile did constitute control but in a very different way than Beer imagined. The military created the Department of National Intelligence (DINA), an organization that used the information it gleaned from torture and surveillance to detain and "disappear" those the military government viewed as subversive.

An Instrument of Revolution

When Beer returned to Chile on 16 April, what he found distressed him. On 19 April, the factory modeler Tomás Kohn wrote the cybernetician a lengthy letter. "The cybernetic adventure is apparently coming to an end, or is it not?" Kohn asked. "The original objective of this project was to present new tools for management, but primarily to bring about a substantial change in the traditional practice of management." In contrast, Kohn found that "management accepts your tools, but just them. . . . The final objective, 'the revolution in management' is not accepted, not even understood. . . . Ultimately your work is accepted as long as it provides *tools* to achieve a more effective *traditional* management."[80]

Beer responded to Kohn's letter on 27 April in a report which he titled "On Decybernation," a reference to the technological components of Cybersyn that were being used independent of the cybernetic commitment to changing government organization. Beer wrote, "If we want a new system of government, we have to change the established order," yet to change the established order required changing the very organization of the Chilean government. Beer reminded team members that they had created Cybersyn to support such organizational changes. Reduced to its component technologies,

Cybersyn was "no longer a viable *system* but a collection of parts." These parts could be assimilated into the current government system, but then "we do not get a new system of government, but an old system of government with some new tools. . . . These tools are not the tools we invented," Beer wrote.[81]

"On Decybernation" was influenced by the ideas of the Chilean biologists Humberto Maturana and Francisco Varela. Understanding the import of Beer's insistence on organizational change requires a brief explanation of how Maturana and Varela differentiated between organization and structure. According to the biologists, the "structure of a system" refers to its specific components and the relationships among these components. The "organization of the system" refers to the relationships that make the system what it is, regardless of its specific component parts. The structure of the system can change without changing the identity of the system, but if the organization of the system changes, the system becomes something else. In their 1987 book *The Tree of Knowledge*, Maturana and Varela use the example of a toilet to explain the difference between organization and structure: "In a toilet the organization of the system of water regulation consists in the relations between an apparatus capable of detecting the water level and another apparatus capable of stopping the inflow of water." One toilet could have a float and a bypass valve made of plastic and metal and another of wood and metal, but both would have the organization of a toilet.[82] To cite an example from business, a company can change the names of its individual departments and yet remain in essence the same company. For the company to become something else, more profound changes would have to take place. Beer extended these ideas to government and argued that structural change was not enough to ensure the revolution would succeed; revolutionary change required a more fundamental transformation in the organization of government.

Therefore, Beer challenged team members to reconsider their expectations for the project and push for meeting goals that were more ambitious than the project's technical objectives. Beer felt the team was on its way to meeting such a "technocratic objective" but that it had failed to help the people or to create a new system of government. "Members of our team are extremely confused, and there is no agreement on the extent to which our work can be called successful," Beer wrote. He attributed this confusion to the diverse composition of the project team, which had created different mixings of "technical, technocratic, social and political objectives," resulting in disagreements about how the project should continue.[83] His observation echoes a finding of the history and sociology of technology, which has shown that technological success is not an objective metric but rather one that is socially negotiated and tied to a specific context and set of goals. Cybersyn could be viewed as a success or a failure in many different ways. Privately, Beer saw the composition of the Cybersyn team as a key problem; in his account of the project, he noted, "Cybersyn had by now a professional and politically uncommitted staff of some seventy people."[84] Beer felt that this lack of unity in cybernetic and political purpose, combined with the absence of political leadership, was transforming the project into the type of technocratic endeavor he abhorred.[85]

In his April report Beer pushed those involved in the project to view Cybersyn as "an instrument of revolution," a point he emphasized with reference to Marx. "'The Way of Production' is still a necessary feature of the Chilean revolution," Beer argued, but "'the Way of Regulation' is an extra requirement of a complex world not experienced by Marx or Lenin."[86] Bringing about this type of organizational and regulatory revolution required profound changes in the organization of the government, including institutions such as CORFO, and this was a Herculean task.[87] Beer wondered, "Does it take more courage to be a cybernetician than to be a gunman?"[88] For Beer, revolution was not only about the nationalization of industry or increasing the public welfare; it was also about changing the very organization of society, beginning with the government institutions themselves. Cybernetics, the science of effective organization, could therefore be as powerful as a gun in effecting revolutionary change.

But Espejo had a different view from inside CORFO, and he knew the difficulties of what Beer was proposing. Espejo felt the team should put the ideological aspects of the system aside and focus more on technical goals such as improving the government's abilities to regulate the economy. "Within the government in the short term, I think the ideological problems are in a second place," Espejo wrote to Beer in May. "We can do models for effective problems of the economy. . . . Through them we can dismantle the bureaucracy."[89] Espejo regarded economic regulation as a more reasonable goal and one he might have a better chance of selling to his colleagues in CORFO. He also felt that this more technical approach did not necessarily abandon Beer's cybernetic goal of dismantling the Chilean bureaucracy.

These diverging views caused friction between Beer and Espejo, and Beer became increasingly frustrated with Espejo as 1973 progressed. "Raúl was supposed to make things work according to my plans," Beer said in a 2001 interview, but "he gradually stopped doing that and started doing what he wanted to do." At one point Beer even drafted a resignation letter, but did not submit it. He explained later that he felt that "since Raúl is taking over everything, I'm no longer any use."[90] Although Beer reduced these conflicting approaches to Project Cybersyn to the issue of technocracy, it would be overly simplistic to say that Espejo was a technocrat and Beer was more politically committed. The two men had very different ideas of what was possible and how the system could make the best contribution in an extremely complex and politically fraught situation.[91] Moreover, Espejo's desire to emphasize the technical aspects of Cybersyn did not mean he wanted to abandon the social and political dimensions of the project. His effort to adopt a more technocentric approach could also be viewed as a last-ditch effort to make Cybersyn useful to the government as it struggled to remain in power.

Yet from a different angle it may seem strange that Beer and Espejo were even having this debate, considering that the country was unraveling around them. In May, the opposition aggravated the economic crisis by supporting a labor strike in the nation's largest copper mine, El Teniente. The strike became the most serious labor conflict Allende had faced thus far. It disrupted the production of the nation's most important export and gave extremists an excuse to foment public disorder and violence. On 5 May the violent actions of the ultraright paramilitary group Fatherland and Liberty pushed the government to declare Santiago an emergency zone. Placing the city under martial law, Allende accused the opposition of "consciously and sinisterly creating the conditions to drag the country toward civil war."[92] The escalating conflict between the government and the opposition did not bode well for the future of Chilean socialism.

On 21 May the government reported that 26.7 percent of the nationalized enterprises responsible for half of the revenue from the Mixed and Social Property Areas had been connected to Project Cybersyn to some degree. This was a significant accomplishment for the Cybersyn project team, but in a way it was useless: by this point the government could not win the battle of production. Neither Cybersyn's technology nor its cybernetic philosophy could help the government make its socialist experiment successful.[93] In this context of crisis, however, the people involved with the project were willing to try anything.

Fernando Henrique Cardoso, one of the originators of dependency theory and later president of Brazil, argues that initiatives such as Project Cybersyn are evidence of Chile's inexperience with revolution. He writes in his memoir, "In a strange way, Chile's stable past became its biggest curse. With no experience of political upheaval, the country reacted a bit like a confused child, lashing out in a much more bizarre and severe fashion than any of its Latin American neighbors, which were more seasoned in the ways of political and economic chaos, would have responded under similar circumstances. Everyday life became ever more surreal."[94] Cardoso cites Project Cybersyn as an example of this surrealism. One night in 1973, when Cardoso was visiting Chile, he joined Flores and Beer for dinner at the home of a mutual acquaintance. Flores left the dinner early to arrest a right-wing terrorist. "The finance minister making an arrest! It was preposterous," Cardoso writes. Meanwhile, Beer told Cardoso about his work on Project Cybersyn, which left quite an impression on the future president. As Cardoso interpreted it, Beer "was building a Cold War–style 'situation room,' of all things, in the finance ministry, presumably so the economists could watch in safety while their country was going to hell."[95] Cardoso viewed Cybersyn as a fanciful, surreal effort that was divorced from the reality of political and economic crisis. To Beer, Cybersyn was a means to bring about organizational change and therefore an instrument of revolution. Yet to Cardoso it reflected Chilean inexperience with drastic political change. But both men used the system as a way to read Chile's revolutionary project and understand Allende's downfall.

Las Cruces

In June the National Computer Corporation hosted a conference on government electronic data-processing. Project Cybersyn appeared on the conference program, but it was presented as a technocentric endeavor. As figure 6.3 shows, the computer, not the worker, was at the heart of Cybersyn's operation. In his April report, Beer had called the dismantling of the system into its component technologies "utterly disastrous." But such an interpretation of the system better suited the interests of a room full of computer specialists than Beer, grounded as he was in his cybernetic view of revolution.

Beer returned to Chile on 20 June 1973, the beginning of winter in the Southern Hemisphere, and he stayed for six weeks. This time he opted to stay in the tiny coastal town of Las Cruces instead of his usual room at the Santiago Sheraton. This change in venue allowed Beer to stay out of the public eye and avoid attention from the opposition. Members of the project team also expressed concerns about Beer's personal safety and wanted to reduce his visibility.[96]

And considering how violence was escalating throughout the country, such concerns were warranted. On 29 June, nine days after Beer arrived in Chile, members of the

Figure 6.3
The computer, not the worker, appears at the heart of Project Cybersyn. This image originally appeared in the ECOM paper "Proyecto Synco Sistema Cyberstride" (June 1973) and is used with permission from CORFO.

military attempted to overthrow the government by force, attacking the presidential palace with tanks. Members of the military still loyal to the constitutional government quickly put down the coup attempt. However, the attempt made visible the divisions within the military and signaled that the president was losing the support of the armed forces. In response to these events, members of the Cybersyn team were understandably concerned about Beer's safety and their ability to protect him. Despite their efforts, Beer remained conspicuous in Las Cruces: he was a six-foot-tall Englishman living in a small Chilean town—and he accidentally set fire to the mayor's house shortly after he arrived.[97]

Las Cruces was useful to Beer for purposes other than reducing his visibility. The town appealed to Beer's growing rejection of his bourgeois lifestyle, while also providing him a quiet place where he could reflect on his time in Chile, process the new ideas inspired by this experience, and get a large amount of work done. The Canadian Broadcasting Corporation had asked him to give the prestigious Massey Lectures for 1973, a series of radio lectures to the Canadian public by a noted scholar in philosophy, politics, or culture. Beer felt pressure to produce something worthwhile. Previous Massey lecturers included Martin Luther King Jr., R. D. Laing, and John Kenneth Galbraith. Las Cruces allowed Beer a period of quiet time in which to work without interruption and draft his remarks in peace. (These lectures presented many of his insights from the Chile experience and were published in 1974 under the title *Designing Freedom*.)

Beer also used the time in Las Cruces for intellectual exploration. He pondered the various problems Cybersyn was encountering, including the greater attention that members of the Cybersyn team were paying to technology than to organizational change, and the failure of Chilean workers to use Cybersyn to assist their organization and management of production. He was frustrated that his Chilean colleagues viewed his ideas as unrealistic, that the political experiment he believed in was quickly falling apart, and that he could do little to fix the situation. He thought cybernetics could help him understand better what was taking place around him and perhaps help the team identify new ways to help the government.[98]

While thinking through these problems, Beer spent a substantial portion of his time in Las Cruces trying to map his cybernetic approach onto Marx's critique of capital. He expressed his ideas on cybernetics and Marxism in his 1973 essay "Status Quo," written in Las Cruces and never published but nonetheless included in his personal bibliography. Although he does not describe the essay in *Brain of the Firm*, his account of the Cybersyn Project, he did reference the essay years later in his 1994 book *Beyond Dispute*. There, Beer says that he continued throughout the 1970s and 1980s to tinker with the ideas presented in the essay.

Beer was not a Marxist, and though he claimed he read "all the Marxist literature" in preparation for his first Chile trip in 1971, he had not devoted the same level of attention to reading and discussing Marx as some of his Chilean colleagues.[99] "Status Quo" is only about fifty handwritten pages and offers a rather simple presentation of Marxist philosophy that many would find lacking.

Nor was Beer the first person to relate cybernetics to Marxism. For example, in 1961 the Soviet mathematician and philosopher Ernest Kolman used passages from Marx to show that Marx had anticipated the arrival of cybernetics and electronic computers and approved of such developments.[100] In fact, Kolman's project bore some similarity to Beer's: both men wanted to update Marx's philosophy to include recent technological developments. But unlike Kolman, Beer tried to translate ideas from Marx's philosophy into the language of his cybernetics.

"Status Quo" shows how ideas from biology and electronics shaped Beer's understanding of social and economic systems and how the Chilean revolution advanced Beer's cybernetic thinking. It also explains how Beer came to view organizational change as central to the Chilean revolution and why he saw cybernetics, the science of effective organization, as a useful approach for understanding the challenges the revolution faced. In the preface to "Status Quo," Beer writes, "Marx taught us to face facts, and to use scientific analysis rather than ideologies to investigate them. Here I use the science of cybernetics, which was not available to Marx." Beer even compliments Marx for his cybernetic intuition; his selection of the title "Status Quo" also paid homage to Marx. Beer writes, "For Marx, capital was evil and the enemy. For us, capital remains evil, but the enemy is STATUS QUO. . . . I consider that if Marx were alive today, he would have found the new enemy that I recognize in *my* title."[101] In "Status Quo" Beer used cybernetics to explore some of Marx's more famous ideas and to update them for the modern world, taking into account new technological advances in communication and computing. According to Beer, the class struggle described by Marx was out of date and "represent[ed] the situation generated by the industrial revolution itself, and [was] '100 years old.'"[102] Beer felt that capitalism had since created new forms of work and new exploitative relations.[103]

Beer approached this project much as one might expect a cybernetician would. To understand how capitalism functioned in the 1970s, he drew from social theory as well as from such fields as electronics and biology. Beer begins "Status Quo" by literally redrawing the capitalist system described in Marx. Starting with a cybernetic representation of class struggle, he substitutes the cybernetic idea of homeostasis for the dialectic relationship of labor and capital (figure 6.4). In the first section of "Status Quo" he expands on this diagram so that it incorporates production, politics, law, and those who are above the law—those whom he considers the true ruling class. Along the way he critiques the media, conspicuous consumption, and the public obsession with sports and glamour. The resulting system diagram bears the hallmarks of cybernetic thinking, with Beer using electronic components such as capacitors, amplifiers, and resistors to describe social, economic, and political relationships. For example, he

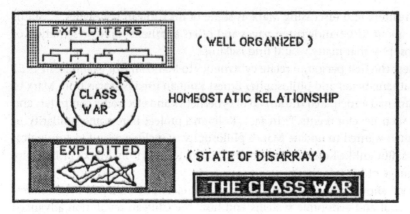

Figure 6.4
Labor and capital expressed in "Status Quo" as a homeostatic relationship. Image redrawn from the original and used with permission from Constantin Malik.

connects sports and glamour directly to ground, demonstrating his belief that such obsessions drain society.

As a circuit diagram, Beer's cybernetic model of capitalism makes no sense. At first glance it appears to be an extreme example of how cybernetics mixed concepts from electrical engineering with studies of social organizations. However, these diagrams also reveal how Beer saw and understood the world. I propose that their resistors, capacitors, and amplifiers, to borrow a phrase from psychologist Sherry Turkle, acted as Beer's "objects-to-think-with."[104] Historians such as Paul Edwards have shown that electrical technologies, including feedback circuits or electronic computers, provided models that scientists used to describe biological organisms and understand cognitive function in humans and animals.[105] In contrast, "Status Quo" shows that resistors, amplifiers, and circuit diagrams can also provide a means for understanding social theory, describing economic relations, and delivering a message for political change. As Turkle might put it, they are objects that bring "philosophy into everyday life."[106] In Beer's case, computers and other electronic machines provided a way to theorize revolution and imagine other possibilities for the future. Technologies such as computers not only offered a way for the cybernetician to diagram social and political change; they also gave Beer a means to represent social relationships and conceptualize the behavior of exceedingly complex systems.

"Status Quo" was also influenced by the contemporaneous work of Maturana and Varela, who were developing one of their best-known ideas—the theory of autopoiesis—which they published in their 1973 book *De máquinas y seres vivos* (On machines and living beings).[107] Beer was involved in the early discussion of the idea, and he later wrote the introduction to the English version of the book, which appeared in 1980 as *Autopoiesis and Cognition.*[108] Simply put, autopoiesis means that an organization survives by reproducing itself. While Maturana and Varela used autopoiesis to describe the survival of biological systems, such as a cell or an organism, Beer extended this idea in "Status Quo" to the survival of social systems, including the government bureaucracy. "Bureaucracy always favors the status quo," he argues, "because its own viability is at stake as an integral system." In order to survive, bureaucracy must reproduce itself, Beer claimed. This process constrains freedom in the short term and prevents change in the long term.[109] "This situation is a social evil," Beer asserts. "It means that bureaucracy is a growing parasite on the body politic, that personal freedoms are usurped in the service demands the parasitic monster makes, and above all that half the national effort is deflected from worthwhile activities." Beer concludes that since bureaucracy locks us into the status quo, "dismantling the bureaucracy can only be a *revolutionary* aim."[110] Beer had long railed against bureaucracy, but the idea of autopoiesis finally gave him a conceptual language for understanding and describing the enemy.[111] It also explained why organizations such as CORFO wanted to dismantle Project Cybersyn as a holistic system and instead integrate components of the system such as the telex network to support current practices.

Beer's use of the biological concept of autopoiesis is an example of how cybernetics used concepts from one discipline and applied them to another. It also shows the exchange of scientific knowledge that took place through Beer's work in Chile. Although Beer had been hired to import his expertise, he also drew from the ideas of Chilean scientists and used them to advance his own thinking. Latin American nations such as Chile are often relegated to the periphery of the scientific community, and it is often assumed that they receive their scientific knowledge from elsewhere. Yet "Status Quo" reveals that Beer did not simply share his knowledge; he also drew from the knowledge that Chilean scientists were producing.

Nevertheless, Beer's cybernetic analysis failed to tell him how to advise his Chilean friends and help them save Chile's political project. In fact, it led him to the opposite conclusion: that it was impossible for a small socialist country to survive within a capitalist world system. "If the final level of societary recursion is capitalistic, in what sense can a lower level of recursion become socialist?" he asks. "It makes little difference if capital in that socialist country is owned by capitalists whose subject is state controls, or by the state itself in the name of the people, since the power of capital to oppress is effectively wielded by the metasystem."[112] Or, to put it another way, Beer did not see how the Allende government could survive, given the magnitude of the economic pressure that a superpower like the United States was putting on the small country. But Beer continued to work for the Allende government even after he reached this conclusion, because his personal and professional investment in Chilean socialism outweighed the pessimistic judgment of cybernetics.[113]

Beer reports in *Brain of the Firm* that while in Las Cruces he received correspondence from members of the opposition who wanted to use Project Cybersyn after Allende was removed from power.[114] According to Beer, these members of the opposition wanted to continue work on Project Cybersyn but without its emphasis on worker participation. I did not find these letters in the archive of Beer's papers and cannot confirm this claim. But if it is true, it provides another example of how political actors separated the technology of Project Cybersyn from the political values Beer and the team tried to embed in its design. It would also reveal a public-private dichotomy in how members of the opposition viewed the project. In public, the opposition criticized the system as a form of totalitarian abuse, yet Beer's claim suggests that, privately, members of the opposition embraced the system and wanted to improve its ability to centralize government control.

Before returning to London, Beer met with President Allende. The meeting, which took place on 26 July, would be their last. While waiting to talk with Allende, Beer spoke at length with the navy captain Arturo Araya, an Allende aide-de-camp who was negotiating support in the navy for the constitutionally elected government. Members of a right-wing military group assassinated Araya that very night.

After Beer returned to England, he sent Allende a letter on 2 August. In it he expressed his regret that Chilean workers were not using Project Cybersyn. "We took every possible step to develop an approach to model-building which the workers could understand after a brief explanation," Beer wrote. But the workers in the industrial belts were still "inventing their own approach [to management] as they go along. They are doing all this without benefit of the general cybernetic approach which was prepared for them," Beer lamented. He continued, "I do not think, as do critics in the capitalist countries, that this [having technocrats control the system] makes the work a danger to freedom," but it "would be a grievous loss of opportunity for the Chilean process."[115] Beer's letter was never answered.

The End of the Democratic Road

In August the opposition staged a second truck drivers' strike to block distribution, sabotage the economy, and bring down the government. Once again the government used the telex network built for Project Cybersyn to implement a form of real-time adaptive management. As the director of informatics in the State Development Corporation, Espejo collected data on the national distribution of food, fuel, and raw materials and the number of trucks the government had at its disposal throughout the strike. According to Espejo, only 10 percent of trucks were in operation at the beginning of the strike, a figure that rose to 30 percent by the strike's end. By coordinating these limited transportation resources, the government kept food supplies between 50 and 70 percent of the normal supply. It also distributed normal levels of raw materials to 95 percent of the enterprises that had a strategic role in the economy. Moreover, the government maintained 90 percent of normal fuel distribution levels with only 65 percent of the tanker trucks in operation.[116] The strike managed to disrupt national distribution, but once again the government was able to adapt to these drastic conditions and survive. It is also worth noting that it would have been hard for the government to compile the statistics given here without the data transfer capabilities of the telex network. Beer, Espejo, and the other members of the team had, in effect, built the means to measure one aspect of their success.

During that second truck drivers' strike, "we felt that we were winning the battle of industrial control and distribution," Espejo writes. "But the political forces were too strong."[117] Although the network helped the government determine which trucks were available, where resources were located, and which roads were open, it could not stop the opposition from physically attacking the trucks, buses, and trains that continued to operate. By mid-August twenty people had been killed, and terrorists had blown up two major oil pipelines and a number of high-voltage electricity towers. In the factories, increasing numbers of Chilean workers affiliated themselves with the Movement of the Radical Left (MIR) and began preparing for armed conflict. As acts of violence increased, the military began searching Chileans for possession of arms, although the vast majority of searches were carried out in the places Popular Unity supporters worked, studied, or lived. In the midst of these developments, Allende named Flores the general secretary of the government, the post responsible for the government's internal and external communications. Flores now occupied one of the highest positions in a government that was under attack. He was thirty years old.

On 3 September the rightist Chilean magazine *Qué Pasa* used this prominent tease on its cover to tout its story about Project Cybersyn: "Exclusive: Secret Plan Cyberstride of the UP" (figure 6.5). Its article claimed that the project was advancing at an "accelerated rate," that the telex network was helping the government take control of factories, and that the system had given the government "a terrible weapon of control" that could lead to "the complete determination" of Chilean private life.[118] In reality, source materials show that the telex network did permit the government to collapse the data sent from all over the country into a single report, written daily at CORFO and delivered to the sector committees and the presidential palace. The detailed charts and graphs in the report used data generated three days earlier—a significant improvement over the six months it previously took the government to compile national economic data. This new form of reporting gave the government an overview of production and transportation activity and identified sites of crisis (figure 6.6).[119] The use of the telex network allowed the Allende government to see national economic activity in a way no other Chilean government had previously. Yet the claims that appeared in *Qué Pasa* must have seemed ludicrous to Espejo and to the others who had tried, and failed, to make the project more than a marginal endeavor. Instead, the *Qué Pasa* article once again demonstrated the opposition's reading of Project Cybersyn in ways that were consistent with its larger criticisms of the Allende government. Its aim was to promote

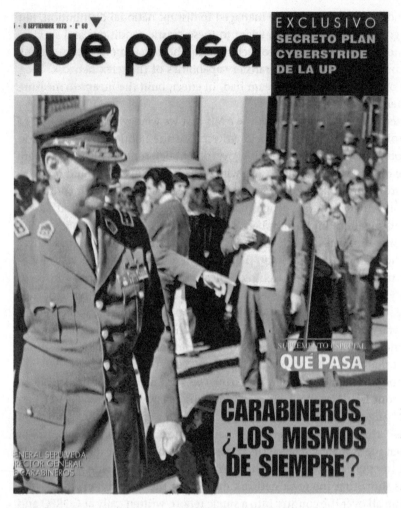

Figure 6.5
Reprint of the cover of the 6 September 1973 edition of *Qué Pasa*. The magazine was reissued in 2003 to commemorate the thirty-year anniversary of the death of Salvador Allende. Image used with permission from COPESA.

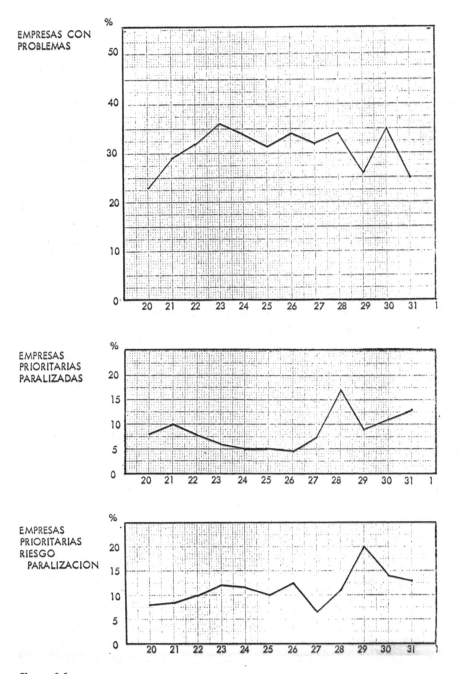

Figure 6.6

This graph shows national economic activity using data collected 20–31 August 1973, by the telex network. The network did not provide the government with a real-time representation of the economy, but it allowed the government to generate daily representations of economic activity using data that were only three days old. Reprinted from the Chilean government report Comando Operativo Central, "Situación general del país," 3 September 1973, 7.

fear and distrust of the constitutionally elected government and stir public support for a military coup.

Several days before the military brought Chile's socialist project to a violent end, Flores contacted the industrial designer Gui Bonsiepe and told him that Allende wanted to move the Cybersyn operations room from its current location to the presidential palace. Bonsiepe worried that installing the room there might harm the palace's historic architecture, and he began to brainstorm solutions. However, the president canceled their meeting at the last minute.[120]

Why Allende wanted the operations room in La Moneda is not clear. In a 2003 interview Flores warned that I should not interpret this invitation as a serious gesture of presidential support for the project; he observed that if the president had really wanted the room, he could have asked Flores to move it to the presidential palace at any point during 1973, which the president did not do.[121] Nevertheless, the president must have seen some value in the project if he contacted Bonsiepe in the final days of his presidency. Perhaps Allende was willing to try anything to regain control of his country, even something as fanciful as installing a cybernetic war room.

Technology and Politics

Throughout 1973 journalists, scientists, and members of the government interpreted Cybersyn in many ways and linked it to many different political projects. These myriad interpretations could lead to the conclusion that Cybersyn was in fact a neutral technology that was being read in different ways—much in the same way that one person might view a rock as a paperweight and another person might view it as a weapon. Yet if *neutral* is defined as something that exists outside political controversy, it is clear that Project Cybersyn was never neutral. Cybersyn was created to advance a particular political project and to achieve a set of political goals, among them helping to win the battle of production and creating a more horizontal distribution of power in Chilean society. More importantly, Cybersyn helped Popular Unity remain in power. Although the system did not help the government raise production levels, it did assist the government in its management of two dangerous national strikes.

The multiple readings of Cybersyn also reflect a shared recognition that technologies can influence how power is exerted at a time when shifts in global power had serious, even disastrous, consequences. These multiple readings of Cybersyn therefore show how historical actors navigated, influenced, worried about, and made sense of the cold war landscape. They also illustrate how Project Cybersyn was viewed through a range of political beliefs and entered into the larger ideological struggle of the cold war. Tracing the different interpretations of a technology such as Cybersyn thus enhances our understanding of the cold war and how it affected nations as different as Chile and England.

Why Project Cybersyn, a technological project that outwardly tried to decentralize Chilean power structures and support the revolution from below, was frequently read as a tool for centralized government control is a more complicated question. In some cases this interpretation was the result of misinformation, as was the case with the secrecy charges. In other instances it was the result of a willful attempt to cast the Allende government in a negative light. The Soviet embrace of cybernetics in the late 1950s and 1960s might also have influenced some to see Cybersyn as a centralizing technology. Terms such as *state, government,* and *the people* also were being constructed and demarcated in different ways by Beer, his colleagues, and his critics. Beer viewed Cybersyn as preserving the autonomy of the enterprise within a centralized state apparatus. But nationalization brought factories under the control of the state and made top factory management positions state appointments. If Beer's tools gave state-appointed managers greater control of their factories, did this create a form of decentralized control or did it increase the reach of the state and its centralizing power? This ambiguity might have prompted some to read Cybersyn as implementing a form of centralized control.

But it is also important to keep in mind that oftentimes these different interpretations of Cybersyn were not referring to the same system. Although it is tempting to reduce a technological system to its hardware, historians of technology have shown that technological systems are more than machinery. For example, Thomas Hughes, a historian of technology, has argued that technological systems are a "seamless web" of social, institutional, and technological relationships.[122] Many of the different interpretations of Project Cybersyn presented in this chapter resulted from Cybersyn's being treated as different sociotechnical systems.

To make Cybersyn function in the way that Beer desired, he needed to engineer each of the system's component technologies. He also needed to engineer the social and organizational relations that surrounded the technology. While Beer and his team consciously tried to design Cybersyn to uphold political values associated with Chilean socialism, they mainly did so by specifying certain social and organizational relationships instead of trying to engineer political values into the design of the technology itself.

For example, Beer wanted to change shop floor power dynamics by altering the relationship between workers and technologists. He wanted to institutionalize a decentralized approach to control by changing how hierarchies of command functioned within an organization. And he wanted to change decision-making practices by giving managers access to real-time information, recognizing that the collection and transmission of this information depended mostly on human labor. Altering any of these social and organizational relations would result in a very different sociotechnical system from the one Beer proposed. Thus reconfigured, the system could support different configurations of power and different political goals.

And it was easy for people to imagine other sociotechnical configurations for Project Cybersyn, especially since the configurations Beer imagined were nearly impossible to implement, given the polarized politics and the war economy. These alternative possibilities proved stronger than Beer's own sociotechnical description of Cybersyn. The requests Beer received from other governments to build systems similar to Cybersyn are evidence of this point. For example, the Brazilian and South African governments contacted Beer because they imagined that Cybersyn could be integrated with their social and political configurations for centralized control. The British Society for Social Responsibility in Science linked its understanding of the technology to the social and political configurations of Stalinism—and thus questioned the ethical implications of the system. Chilean industrial managers saw a partially finished set of tools that they could either incorporate in their existing practices or ignore. This separation of the social from the technical allowed historical actors to associate Project Cybersyn with many different political values, including those that ran counter to Chilean socialism. Project Cybersyn thus illustrates how difficult it is to embed political values in the design of sociotechnical systems. It also highlights the importance of viewing technology as a sociotechnical system when discussing its political or ethical ramifications.

Politics played a central role in Project Cybersyn. The Chilean political experiment had led to this technological innovation, but, conversely, the fate of the system also depended on the fate of Chilean socialism. And by September 1973 it was clear that Chilean socialism would not last much longer.

* * *

The military coup began at dawn on 11 September 1973. Shortly after 9 a.m. the president delivered his final radio broadcast. By noon Hawker Hunter jet fighters were firing rockets at the presidential palace. The impact shattered a long-standing symbol of Chilean democracy and enveloped its white facade in clouds of billowing smoke.

Flores, now one of Allende's closest aides, was with him during the bombing. Flores maintained almost constant telephone communication with the military, telling Allende of the military's demand for an immediate, unconditional surrender, which the president rejected. Allende sent Flores from the presidential palace to negotiate with the military. Flores never saw the president again. Flores was arrested as soon as he left the building, and by 2 p.m. Allende was dead.[123]

News of the coup sent Espejo into action. Early the next morning he went to his office at CORFO and put the project's documentation in order. He wrapped some of the most important documents from the project in four packages. He and his project coordinator, Guillermo Toro, planned to take these documents out of CORFO so they would not fall into the hands of the military.[124]

Espejo and Toro assessed the situation. Outside they heard low-flying planes and the firing of guns and tanks. Inside they saw people gathering what limited weapons they had in preparation for a last stand. The two men decided to take their chances outside and leave before the military arrived. As Toro told me in 2004, the documentation "needed to be saved to tell the story."[125] The military would violently cut short Chile's dreams of socialist change and cybernetic management. But the story of Project Cybersyn survived.

7 Conclusion: Technology, Politics, History

The military stopped work on Project Cybersyn after the coup and either abandoned or destroyed the work the team had completed. In some instances Cybersyn's destruction was brutal and complete. One member of the military took a knife and stabbed each slide the graphic designers had made to project in the operations room. Other military officials adopted a more inquisitional approach. They summoned members of the project team, as well as other Chilean computer experts who had not been involved in the project, and questioned them about the system. According to Isaquino Benadof, the ECOM computer scientist, the military failed to grasp the nuances of Beer's decentralized, adaptive approach to control, which ran counter to the idea of top-down control in the armed forces.[1] Or perhaps they did understand Beer's approach to control but saw little use in it. Military interest in the project soon waned.

And in the context of the new military government, Project Cybersyn no longer made sense. It was a system designed to help the state regulate the nationalized economy and raise production without unemployment. By 1975, the military had decided to back the neoliberal "shock treatments" proposed by the "Chicago Boys," a group of economists who had studied either with Milton Friedman at the University of Chicago or with professors at the Catholic University in Santiago who were well versed in Friedman's monetarist economic theories. The plan for the economy called for continuing cuts to public spending; freezing wages; privatizing the majority of the firms nationalized by CORFO, the state development agency; reversing the agrarian reform carried out during the Allende and Frei administrations (or reshaping it by selling Chilean farmlands to agribusiness); and laying off eighty thousand government employees.[2]

I began by framing this history as the intersection of two utopian visions, one political (Chilean socialism) and one technological (Project Cybersyn), that were linked by the science of cybernetics. In the pages that followed, I traced how members of the Chilean government along with foreign consultants such as Stafford Beer attempted to make these political and technological visions a reality and the events that made neither possible but nonetheless significant.

This history is a case study for better understanding the multifaceted relationship of technology and politics. In particular, I have used this history to address (1) how governments have envisioned using computer and communications technologies to bring about structural change in society; (2) the ways technologists have tried to embed political values in the design of technical systems; (3) the challenges associated with such efforts; and (4) how studying the relationship of technology and politics can reveal the important but often hidden role of technology in history and enhance our understanding of historical processes. Forty years later, this little-known story also has much to say about the importance of transnational collaboration, technological innovation, and the ways in which geopolitics influences technology.

Computer and communications technologies have often been linked to processes of political, economic, and social transformation. But claims that these technologies can bring about structural change in society—like the frequent assertion that computers will bring democracy or greater social equality—are often made in the absence of historical analysis. The history of Project Cybersyn documents how a government tried to use these technologies as a way to remake society by changing its economic, social, and political structures. Project Cybersyn began as a management system to help the government improve its oversight of the growing state-run industrial sector. Its creators aimed to improve communication between the state development agency and the nationalized enterprises and to help the government support the interventors, the government-appointed enterprise managers who often lacked the experience the job required. In addition, Cybersyn technologists saw the system as helping the government make rapid, informed decisions; predict future economic behavior; and head off crises. These capabilities, they argued, would help the government control the "commanding heights" of the economy and ultimately win the battle of production.

As the project progressed, members of the project team came to see Cybersyn not only as a way to improve economic management but also as a way to implement a form of management consistent with the ideals of Chilean socialism. For example, Cybersyn technologists tried to incorporate mechanisms for worker participation and ways to preserve factory autonomy within a context of top-down government control.

At the same time, there was no single view of how this technological system could best contribute to Chilean socialism or even consensus on whether it could contribute at all. These diverging views continued to proliferate as Allende's presidency progressed. For example, some saw the project as a way to improve economic management, collect recent data on industrial activity, or increase worker participation in government. That Project Cybersyn was never integrated fully into Chilean political or economic life caused others to view it as a whim with no connection to Chilean reality or as evidence of Chilean inexperience with political change. Still others focused merely on the advance in technology that the system represented. And these were only some of the views expressed.

Moreover, many people held very different ideas about the consequences Cybersyn would have once implemented. Beer, Flores, and the early members of the Cybersyn team tried to design the system to reflect and uphold the values of Chilean democratic socialism as they understood them. Even so, international onlookers and members of the Chilean opposition frequently viewed the system as a tool for totalitarian control. Such views reflected international cold war anxieties as well as opposition propaganda in the interest of removing Allende from office. The history of Project Cybersyn thus shows that there were many, sometimes conflicting, views of the system's design and operation; how the system would be used in the context of Chilean socialism; and even what constituted Chilean socialism.

This study has used the complexities of Chilean politics to reveal the social negotiations involved in the creation of this technological system, but it has also used the making of a technology to illustrate the complexities and multiple interpretations of Chilean politics. As we have seen, while some members of the Allende government and their international interlocutors viewed computers as tools for peaceful revolutionary change, others saw computers as a way for the government to limit Chilean freedom. This study also shows that no clear consensus existed about how to make Chile socialist or the role that Project Cybersyn should play in that process.

The history of Project Cybersyn provides a detailed case study of how technologists attempted to build political values into the design of technological artifacts, thereby illuminating the relationship of technology and human action. Time and again, Beer and his Chilean colleagues tried to embed values consistent with Chilean democratic socialism in the design of a technology. Limiting the number of production indicators collected by Project Cybersyn prevented information overload, but the decision also served as a safeguard against state micromanagement and abuse. Putting the control mechanism for the operations room slide projectors in the armrest of each chair, instead of placing only one control mechanism in the center of the room, gave all occupants an equal opportunity to select the data displayed in the room, thus allowing them to participate in conversations about the state-run economy. These two examples emphasize how technologists in this story engineered technologies to create social relationships that were congruent with the ideals of Chilean democratic socialism. However, as this book has suggested, technology alone could not enforce these relationships.

More often, Cybersyn team members attempted to embed political values in Cybersyn through sociotechnical engineering, meaning that they tried to build values not only into the function of the technology itself but also into the social and organizational relations of its construction and use. This attention to sociotechnical engineering is another innovative feature of Project Cybersyn, and it distinguishes the project from other efforts by the Allende government to make technology political, such as building low-cost consumer goods for mass consumption. Examples of this sociotechnical engineering include having Chilean technologists collaborate with Chilean workers in building factory models or having those in the CORFO telex room alert factory managers to potential production problems before alerting officials at higher levels of the Chilean government. In some instances, team members resorted to sociotechnical engineering because Chile's limited technical resources prevented them from building these values into the technology itself. For example, if Chile had had the financial and technical resources, the team might have been able to automate the algedonic notification process and thus embed the idea of decentralized control directly in the software and hardware of the Cybersyn system. However, in other instances this social and organizational engineering was necessary because socialist transformation demanded that social and organizational relations change, especially in Chilean factories.

Project Cybersyn was innovative in part because it connected the technological to the political and reflected the goals and values of an innovative political project. Chilean socialism broke from the political models of both the United States and the Soviet Union. It also stood in contrast to other socialist models, such as that of Cuba. This new political approach to socialist change led to the identification of new economic needs and new technological possibilities. In this context, Cybersyn technologists had a reason to work with new materials, learn new approaches to software development, and think differently about how to visually display information; they were able to develop a new perspective on computing and view information as a way to drive action. In addition, the new model of socialism enabled the technologists to reflect on how politics can shape design and how design can further political aims. Yet Chile was not the only socialist nation to view technology as part of socialist change: Nasser's Egypt, Tito's Yugoslavia, and Nehru's India each emphasized technology with greater or lesser success and may offer interesting points of comparison with the Chilean experience.

Political innovation also spurred technological innovation in Chile in other ways. For instance, the design of Project Cybersyn reflected a distinguishing feature of the Allende government. The tension inherent in Project Cybersyn between factory autonomy and the welfare of the national economy mirrored the struggle between centralized and decentralized control that plagued Allende's dream of Chilean socialism. Both Cybersyn and Allende's government emphasized the importance of individual freedoms while recognizing that some situations require the sacrifice of the needs of one group for the benefit of the whole. The history of the Cybersyn system shows that political ideologies not only articulate a worldview but can contribute to the design and application of new technologies to reconfigure state power. Its history also highlights the conceptual similarities in veins of scientific and political thought in the early 1970s and how this shared intellectual terrain brought together cybernetic principles and socialist principles.

Chile was not the first or even the latest country to view computer technology as a tool for becoming a socialist nation. Mid-twentieth-century Soviet efforts in the area of economic cybernetics predated Chile's attempt to use computers to help regulate the national economy. And, in 2010, the Chinese government made headlines for censoring web content, restricting web searches, monitoring web activity, and preventing access in China to certain web sites. Like Allende's Chile, the Chinese government wants to make its technological systems conform to a set of political beliefs, but it faces a different set of challenges. The ability of the Chilean government to develop Cybersyn, a national network, was limited in part by the dynamics of international geopolitics. In contrast, the Internet is an international network that the Chinese government is attempting to regulate and control by means of national laws and state policies. In the Chilean case, members of the government tried to use computer and communications technologies to change existing political, economic, and social structures. In the Chinese case, members of the government are trying to use these technologies to maintain the status quo. However, both cases draw our attention to the ways governments have attempted to embed political values in the operation of technological systems. How these values change in different national contexts and how technological and political environments interact and reinforce one another over time are questions worthy of further analysis.

Project Cybersyn is an example of the difficulty of creating a sociotechnical system designed to change existing social relationships and power configurations and then enforce the new patterns over time. Scientific techniques may conceal biases with a veneer of neutrality and thus lead to undesirable results. For example, Allende charged the Project Cybersyn team with building a system that supported worker participation. Yet the scientific techniques Chilean engineers used to model the state-controlled factories resembled Taylorism, a rationalized approach to factory production that disempowered workers and gave management greater control over labor. Time analysis, for example, emerged in the context of capitalist production, prioritizing efficiency and productivity over other values, such as the quality of shop floor life. By using time-analysis techniques, Cybersyn engineers could have inadvertently created production relationships that were counter to the Popular Unity platform and then solidified them in the form of a computer model.

Sociotechnical relationships must also remain intact for the system to maintain the desired configuration of power. Changing these technical, social, and organizational relationships may also change the distribution of power within the system. As I have shown, in some cases it is much easier to change a sociotechnical system than to hold it static. The history of Project Cybersyn suggests that the interpretation of sociotechnical relationships is especially malleable when a system is new, forms part of a controversial political project, or requires existing social, technical, and organizational relationships to change in substantial ways.

This malleability makes it extremely difficult to marry a sociotechnical system to a specific set of political values, especially if the goal is to create dramatic changes in the status quo. In the case of Cybersyn, journalists, scientists, and government officials all interpreted the system in different ways because they envisioned it functioning in different sociotechnical configurations. Once separated from the social and organizational relations that Beer imagined, the technology of Project Cybersyn could support many different forms of government, including totalitarianism. If Project Cybersyn had been implemented as Beer imagined, it might have become a system that supported such values as democracy, participation, and autonomy. But as its critics perceived, it would have been easy to circumvent the technological and organizational safeguards the team designed; therefore, it would have been easy for the system to support a different set of political values, especially in different social, organizational, and geographic settings.

Value-centered design is a complicated and challenging endeavor. Even if technologists attempt to build certain relationships into the design of a technological system, which itself is a fraught and socially negotiated process, they have no guarantee that others will adopt the system in the desired way—or that they will adopt the system at all. It is important to keep in mind that Project Cybersyn never reached completion, nor was it integrated into shop floor management or government economic policies in a substantial way. In that sense, it might be seen as a marginal experiment that did not succeed in changing factory management practices. It could even be seen as quixotic. But the reasons for Cybersyn's marginal status help us to better understand the history of Chilean politics as well as the history of this technological system. They also explain why Cybersyn technologists could not build the value-centered, holistic system that Beer imagined.

In the climate of political and economic collapse in which the Cybersyn technologists were working, it was impossible to make the organizational changes Beer wanted or convince factory managers to give serious attention to a high-risk technological prototype. These difficulties were further exacerbated by Cybersyn's sociotechnical shortcomings. Lengthy delays in transmitting data to and from the central telex room made Cybersyn's warning signals irrelevant to factory managers. It is highly probable that the amount of human labor required to update the displays of information in the operations room would have also created substantial obstacles to its full implementation.

But perhaps the most important shortcoming of the project, and why it was not adopted more broadly, was that it did not connect to the political, economic, and social processes that consumed the country. Even if the technological components of Project Cybersyn had reached completion, the system could not have addressed such problems as runaway inflation, lack of foreign credit, falling copper prices, and black-market hoarding. The system also did not connect to the changes that were taking place on the factory floor. Beer did not define worker participation in a way that overlapped with concurrent government, union, and worker initiatives, and yet to make Cybersyn participative in the way he desired would require a massive training program. Such a program would have diverted attention from the daily crises taking place in the factories as workers and managers struggled to maintain operations. Technologies do have politics in the sense that they are the product of a political moment, can be used to achieve stated political goals, and can form part of political strategies. Moreover, technologies can shape political history by making certain actions possible. However, the history of Project Cybersyn shows that it is very difficult to make technologies that are capable of creating and enforcing desired configurations of power and authority, especially if those configurations are radically different from those that preceded them.

Although it is commonly accepted that society shapes technology and that technology does not drive history, the history of Project Cybersyn underlines the ways that technologies do influence human action. It makes a case for why technologies matter as part of the historical record and is a reminder that technology plays an important, if often overlooked, role in understanding historical processes.

Technology can shape political history by making certain actions possible. As we've seen, the network of telex machines originally conceived as part of Project Cybersyn helped the Allende government survive two national strikes. This network allowed the government to send and receive messages from one end of the country to the other and connected the presidential palace to the events unfolding in Chilean factories and distribution centers.

Technologies can also help us understand history. The design of Project Cybersyn helps clarify Chile's revolutionary project and its limitations and thus illuminates assumptions about power in the context of political change. For example, the design of the operations room chair encouraged masculine forms of expression and did not incorporate a keyboard because it was associated with female clerical labor. This design decision demonstrates an assumption that state power would remain largely in the hands of Chile's male population, and that *worker* would refer to those employed in factories and not those performing clerical tasks. Similarly, disagreements about the level of worker involvement in Project Cybersyn were not only about technological feasibility; they demonstrate how class resistance to economic and social change shaped the dynamics between technical experts and members of the rank-and-file in Chilean factories.

Technological design thus reveals how dominant historical actors conceptualized the redistribution of power in the Chilean revolution by showing how ideas about gender and class entered into and shaped Chile's revolutionary process, defined who the government considered a revolutionary subject, and limited the ways historical actors envisioned the future and articulated new forms of modernity. Such observations encourage us to consider what assumptions underlie the design of technological systems today and how such assumptions might circumscribe our own social, political, and technological imagination.

Similarly, history can help us understand technology. Project Cybersyn was the result of a specific confluence of people, political goals, scientific ideas, and technological capabilities. As a result it highlights the contingency of historical events and technological development. This confluence also explains why a technology like Project Cybersyn was built in Chile in the early 1970s and not in more technologically advanced nations such as Britain, the United States, or the Soviet Union. If Flores had not read Beer's book *Decision and Control*, if Beer had ignored Flores's letter, if Allende had not made nationalization a central plank in his platform for socialist change, or if Chile had not already invested in the acquisition of computer and telex technology, it is unlikely that the Chilean government would have wanted or been able to build a technology like Project Cybersyn. Moreover, socialist revolution created a climate that embraced change and encouraged people to think in new ways. It made it possible for Flores, a young engineer with new ideas about technology, to occupy a high-level government position. It also gave him enough power to get an unorthodox project like Cybersyn off the ground.

This history further reveals that different nations have very different experiences with computer technology and that these experiences are connected to the political, economic, and geographic contexts of these nations. Chilean democratic socialism prompted the creation of a computer technology that furthered the specific aims of the Chilean revolution and would not have made sense in the United States. The Chilean context also differed from that of the Soviet Union in fundamental ways. Because Chile was significantly smaller than the Soviet Union in its geography, population, and industrial output, building a computer system to help regulate the Chilean economy was a more manageable affair. In addition, the Soviet solution used computers for centralized top-down control and collected a wealth of data about industrial production activities with the goal of improving state planning. In contrast, the Cybersyn team used Beer's view of management cybernetics to create a system that emphasized action as well as planning; and the system sent limited quantities of information up the government hierarchy, and tried to maximize factory self-management without sacrificing the health of the entire economy. As this contrast shows, technologies are the product of the people involved in their creation and the political and economic moments in which they are built.

While investigating the relationship of technology and politics in this case study, I also detailed a history of cybernetics set in Latin America. Although cybernetics was promoted as a unifying discipline, the ideas and applications that fell under the heading of cybernetics were not the same everywhere. Chilean cybernetics differed significantly from the better studied U.S., Soviet, and British cases. In the United States, cybernetics grew out of academia and was connected primarily to university research, whereas in Chile cybernetics had the greatest influence in government and, rather than being applied to research, it inspired the creation of a computer system that addressed one of the most pressing problems of the day and operated on a national scale. Chilean cybernetics also differed from Soviet cybernetics. In the Soviet Union, cybernetics was initially associated with U.S. political ideology, but by the end of the 1950s it had emerged as a universal language for the Soviet science program. In Chile cybernetics exerted the greatest influence within the small community of individuals involved in Project Cybersyn.

The Chilean history of cybernetics also differs from that of Britain, even though the Chilean experience draws heavily on the work of Beer. British cyberneticians such as Ross Ashby, Gordon Pask, Gregory Bateson, and Grey Walter were never able to build a system in their country anywhere near the scale of what Beer tried to accomplish in Chile. Project Cybersyn was short-lived, but it was one of the most ambitious applications of cybernetic ideas in history because of its national scope and because it formed part of a larger project for economic, social, and political transformation.

Project Cybersyn further frames cybernetic history as necessarily transnational. This is most evident in Beer's collaboration with the team of Chilean technologists who worked on Project Cybersyn and later formed part of the Group of 14, the small group of Chileans who studied cybernetics outside of their work on Project Cybersyn. However, Beer's cybernetic thinking was also shaped by what he saw and learned in Chile and by his interactions with Chilean scientists such as Humberto Maturana and Francisco Varela. For example, Maturana and Varela's idea of autopoiesis gave Beer a conceptual vocabulary for understanding and critiquing government bureaucracy. Heinz von Foerster, the Austrian émigré who edited the proceedings of the Macy conferences and directed the Biological Computer Laboratory at the University of Illinois, also figures in this story. Von Foerster collaborated intellectually with Maturana and Varela, was a friend to Stafford Beer, and was a teacher to the Group of 14. Like Beer, von Foerster was also influenced by Maturana and Varela's work. While the story of this connection lies outside the scope of this book, it warrants further analysis. Intellectually, Beer built on the work of others in the U.S. and British cybernetics communities, including Wiener and Ashby. He also repeatedly positioned his work in opposition to Soviet economic cybernetics. Thus, cybernetic history is not only a collection of national stories, for these ideas crossed national borders and shaped cybernetic thinking elsewhere. Moreover, these ideas did not flow only from Britain and the United States to Chile; they also flowed from Chile to Britain and, as I show in the epilogue, to the United States and to other nations in Europe, North America, and South America.

This particular transnational collaboration sheds light on processes of technological innovation in differently situated world contexts. Project Cybersyn, a case study of technological innovation, was a cutting-edge system using technologies that were far from the most technologically sophisticated. A network of telex machines transformed a middle-of-the-road mainframe computer into a new form of economic communication. Slide projectors presented new visual representations of economic data. Hand-drawn graphs showing data collected on a daily basis gave the government a macroscopic view of economic activity and identified the areas of the economy most in need of attention. Project Cybersyn thus challenges the assumption that advanced technologies need to be complex. Sophisticated systems can be built using simple technologies, provided that particular attention is paid to how humans interact and the ways that technology can change the dynamics of these interactions. Project Cybersyn may be a useful example for thinking about sustainable design or the creation of technologies for regions of the world with limited resources.[3]

This story of technological innovation also challenges the assumption that innovation results from private-sector competition in an open marketplace. Disconnection from the global marketplace, as occurred in Chile, can also lead to technological innovation and even make it a necessity. This history has shown that the state, as well as the private sector, can support innovation. The history of technology also backs this finding; for example, in the United States the state played a central role in funding high-risk research in important areas such as computing and aviation. However, this lesson is often forgotten. As we recover from the effects of a financial crisis, brought on in large part by our extraordinary faith in the logic of the free market, it is a lesson that is worth remembering.

The history of Project Cybersyn is, moreover, a reminder that technologies and technological ideas do not have a single point of origin. Ideas and artifacts travel and can come together in different ways depending on the political, economic, and geographical context. These unique unions can result in different starting points for similar technological ideas. For example, this history has suggested an alternative starting point for the use of computers in national communication and data-sharing networks. However, not all these technological starting points lead somewhere. What leads to the success of one technology and the demise of another cannot always be reduced to technological superiority. Ultimately, Cybersyn could not survive because it was tied to a political project that, in the context of the cold war, was not allowed to survive. As Project Cybersyn illustrates, geopolitics can affect which technologies fall by the wayside. Simply put, international geopolitics is an important part of the explanation of technological change, especially in nations that served as ideological battlegrounds during the cold war.

Given the progress made on Project Cybersyn before the military coup, there is reason to believe that the system was, for the most part, technically feasible and that many, if not most, of its technological components could have reached completion if given more time. But Project Cybersyn was also tied to Chile's peaceful socialist revolution, a political development that clashed with U.S. foreign policy in Latin America during the cold war. The United States funded government opposition parties and helped opposition-owned media outlets run a scare campaign against Allende and his government. It also established an invisible blockade to hurt the Chilean economy and decrease the value of U.S. exports, the levels of U.S. corporate investment in Chile, and the levels of available foreign credit. These actions fomented political discord and economic collapse, and pushed the county toward the violent military coup that ended

Chilean socialism and resulted in Allende's death. It is impossible to say what would have happened had Project Cybersyn reached completion or if it had been built during a period of greater economic and political stability. Maybe it would have helped the government regulate the economy, maybe not. However, international geopolitics clearly played a decisive role in halting work on the project. When Chile's dream of peaceful socialism died, its particular dream of cybernetic socialism died, too.

Geopolitics also shapes our understandings of technological development and technological change. If historians, technologists, designers, educators, and policy makers continue to give substantial and disproportionate attention to the technologies that triumph, a disproportionate number of which were built in the industrial centers of the world, they miss seeing the richness of the transnational cross-fertilization that occurs outside the industrial centers and the complex ways that people, ideas, and artifacts move and evolve in the course of their travels. Technological innovation is the result of complex social, political, and economic relationships that span nations and cultures. To understand the dynamics of technological development—and perhaps thereby do a better job of encouraging it—we must broaden our view of where technological innovation occurs and give greater attention to the areas of the world marginalized by these studies in the past.

Although Chile was never able to bring to fruition the political or technological utopias described in this book, we should not discount these efforts. Attempts to combine the political and the technological with the goal of creating a more just society can open new possibilities, technological, intellectual, political, and otherwise. These endeavors can have important legacies, even if they are never fully realized.

Epilogue: The Legacy of Cybersyn

The story of me-in-Chile
      please God
is by no means over.
—Stafford Beer, *Platform for Change* (1975)

The experience of working on Project Cybersyn transformed Stafford Beer and shaped the subsequent careers of core project participants. Documenting where the people and ideas of Project Cybersyn went after 1973 makes a fitting epilogue to this study of technology and politics. Chile's shift from democracy to dictatorship forced core members of the project team into exile, and they took Beer's ideas with them. These ideas were both mobile and mutable, and influenced the creation of management practices and technological systems in different national and political settings.

I met Stafford Beer only once. It was 2001, and I was a third-year doctoral student hoping to learn more about the history of Project Cybersyn. I had stumbled on the Cybersyn story by chance several months earlier while searching for information on the history of computing in Latin America. It felt like a good story.

Beer generously invited me to his home in Toronto to conduct a two-day interview. By then he had a number of health problems. Beer had written his books and most of his correspondence by hand in a distinctive cursive, but a stroke had taken away his elegant penmanship. At times it also prevented him from finding the precise word he wanted during our interview. But he nonetheless struck me as a highly articulate and charismatic man.

Beer's long beard was now completely white. Throughout our interview he drank a mixture of half water, half white wine from a goblet he referred to as his "wizard cup." He explained that he had tried to give up alcohol and had even succeeded for more than two years. But he eventually settled on a strategy of moderation rather than abstinence and thereafter diluted all his alcoholic drinks with water (figure 8.1).

His house in Toronto had some eccentricities reminiscent of his earlier home in the Surrey stockbroker belt. Mirrors surrounded the bathtub, and a small portable waterfall

Figure 8.1
Stafford Beer with his wizard cup in 2001. Photo by the author.

burbled in the sitting room. He gave private yoga lessons in a small studio in his home but only to students who did not ask him how much he charged. "Money gets in the way of everything, in my opinion," Beer said. He much preferred students who offered him incense, candles, or flowers as a gesture of thanks. "How do you charge for the channels of grace?" he wondered aloud. "It's absurd."[1]

The Chile project had been a turning point in Beer's life, and it had changed him in profound and lasting ways. As the Chilean biologist Humberto Maturana put it, Beer came to Chile a businessman and left a hippie.[2] After the Chile project came to an abrupt end, Beer took a hard look at the material demands of his bourgeois lifestyle and decided to change. In 1974 he embarked on a journey of spiritual and material reinvention, first by taking extended trips to the Welsh countryside. By 1976 he had relocated permanently to a small cottage in Wales that lacked running water. He and his wife separated but did not divorce until 1996, after all their children were fully grown. In 1981 Beer met Allenna Leonard at a cybernetics conference in Toronto and the two fell in love. Leonard, who remained his partner for the rest of his life, is an accomplished cybernetician in her own right. She later served as president of the American Society for Cybernetics (2002–2004) and president of the International Society for the Systems Sciences (2009–2010).

After working on Project Cybersyn, Beer published six books on cybernetics that mention his time in Chile. In addition, he published a second edition of *Brain of the Firm* (1981), which he extended to include his account of the Chilean project. Beer had always been interested in using cybernetic thinking for social good, but after 1973 the social dimensions of his work became more pronounced. His 1974 essay "Cybernetics of National Development" used Project Cybersyn as a case study to encourage developing nations to change their approach to economic planning and to use technology for goals other than economic growth and consumerism. Beer also remained critical of top-down, centralized control. His 1993 essay "World in Torment" connected atrocities such as starvation, war, and the exploitation of nature and indigenous peoples to attempts to overcentralize the control of global complex systems, as seen in Soviet centralized planning or the growing power of a small oligarchy in the Western capitalist world.

Beer's connection to Chile did not end on 11 September 1973. During the repressive dictatorship of General Augusto Pinochet (1973–1990), more than three thousand Chileans were "disappeared" or murdered at the hands of their own government.[3] Some estimates put the number of people tortured by the military government at 100,000, roughly 1 percent of the Chilean population at the time.[4] After the coup, Beer worked tirelessly to get his friends out of Chile and used his vast web of professional connections to help them establish new lives in other parts of the world. By the end of 1973, Beer had relocated two Cybersyn project managers, Jorge Barrientos and Tomás Kohn, to England with their families. Cybersyn project director Raúl Espejo also left Chile with Beer's help and even lived for a time in his home. In addition, Beer helped Roberto Cañete and his family relocate to Canada and secured employment for Cañete through his network of friends. In a letter to Heinz von Foerster dated 5 December 1973, Beer wrote, "God knows how I am earning my living—this business [of helping Chilean friends relocate] is all consuming."[5] Beer kept up these efforts until 1976, when the Pinochet government finally released Fernando Flores into exile.

Beer continued to work in Latin America after the collapse of the Allende government and received consulting invitations from governments in Uruguay, Mexico, and Venezuela. In 1982 Beer spent a year working for the government of Mexican president Miguel de la Madrid (1982–1988).[6] The government charged Beer with studying the Mexican bureaucracy and developing recommendations to improve government organization and end government corruption. But Beer found the Mexican bureaucracy to be a formidable adversary. After a year of work, the government institutions he was trying to improve ignored, stopped funding, or rejected his proposals outright. In December 1983 the Mexican newspaper *El Norte* ran the headline "He [Beer] Came to Mexico to Combat the Bureaucracy; He Left Mexico Fleeing from the Bureaucracy." In the article Beer described the Mexican bureaucracy as a pathologically autopoietic system that "does not have a function other than generating its own growth." He also suggested that the Mexican public administration could be run effectively with one-fourth of its current workforce.[7]

In 1985 Beer received an invitation from the office of Uruguayan president Julio María Sanguinetti to build a new version of Project Cybersyn for the Uruguayan government. It became known as Proyecto Urucib (short for "Uruguay-Cibernética"). Given that Proyecto Urucib consisted of a communications network, computer programs for the statistical filtration of economic data, an economic simulator based on systems dynamics, and a "new environment for decision making," it is no wonder that Beer referred to the Uruguay project as his "second Chile." According to Leonard, who worked with Beer in Uruguay, Proyecto Urucib did not get as far as the Chile project. It ran into financial difficulties, and most important, it lacked someone like Flores: a person Leonard described as "a real champion with enough clout and focus" to push the project through. Leonard also noted that Beer's work for the government of President Carlos Andrés Pérez in Venezuela did not get far because of political unrest in that country.[8]

Beer died in 2002 at the age of seventy-five. After his death the Operational Research Society established the Stafford Beer Medal, awarded annually for "the most outstanding contribution to the philosophy, theory or practice of Information Systems and/or Knowledge Management" as published in the *European Journal of Information Systems* or *Knowledge Management Research and Practice*.[9] Beer's ideas continue to be used by the international consulting firm Malik Management, a three-hundred-person organization that specializes in holistic management and mastering complexity.

Raúl Espejo continued to study management cybernetics after moving to England. In 1977 he joined the Aston Business School in Birmingham, England, as a senior lecturer. In 1985 he formed the consulting company Syncho Ltd., a name inspired in part by Synco, the Spanish name for Project Cybersyn.[10] In 1988 Espejo earned his doctoral degree from the Aston Business School. His dissertation credits Beer, von Foerster, Maturana, and Varela for the methodology Espejo used in his research.

Espejo's experience working on Project Cybersyn played a central role in his intellectual formation and in his professional career after 1973. He coedited the textbook *The Viable System Model: Interpretations and Applications of Stafford Beer's VSM* (1989) with Roger Harnden, one of his students at Aston.[11] Espejo remained at the Aston Business School until 1994, then left to join the faculty at the University of Lincoln in Lincoln, England. Of the Chile group, Espejo is clearly Beer's closest disciple, although the two did not always see eye to eye.

Espejo continues to teach and apply the principles of Beer's management cybernetics. Syncho Ltd. secured contracts with government agencies in Britain, Germany, Colombia, and Sweden, among others, but Espejo cites Colombia as the country most influenced by the ideas of management cybernetics. With Espejo's assistance the National Audit Office of Colombia used the Viable System Model to study and improve the organization of Colombian state enterprises. This effort included training hundreds of Colombians in organizational cybernetics to eventually serve as organizational "auditors" for the government.[12]

Herman Schwember had a more difficult time leaving Chile. The military sent Schwember to the Ritoque prison camp near Valparaíso, and he could not leave Chile until 1975. In 1976 Beer helped him secure a research fellowship in technology and management at Imperial College, London. In 1977 Schwember wrote a chapter for *Concepts and Tools of Computer-Assisted Policy Analysis*, edited by Hartmut Bossel, in which he recounted his experience with Project Cybersyn.[13] Schwember's chapter explores the relationship of technology and politics, and portrays Project Cybersyn as advancing the political aims of the Allende government. Two system diagrams drawn by Schwember illustrate the centrality of worker participation to Cybersyn's operation. In the first image (figure 8.2), Schwember depicts the nation, the central government, industry, and the individual companies as nested viable systems, each located recursively inside the other. The figure of a worker appears at the heart of these systems, reinforcing the perceived importance of workers to the Chilean nation. The second diagram (figure 8.3) shows a modified rendering of Beer's five-tier Viable System Model

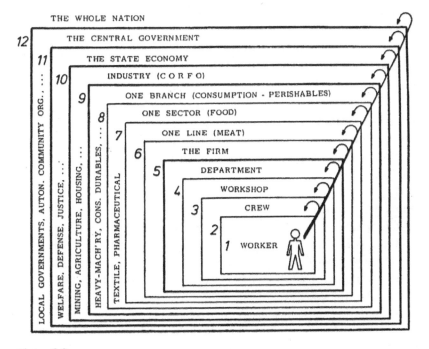

Figure 8.2
The worker is at the heart of all viable systems. Image taken from Herman Schwember, "Cybernetics in Government: Experience with New Tools for Management in Chile, 1971–1973," in Hartmut Bossel, ed., *Concepts and Tools of Computer-Assisted Policy Analysis* (Basel: Birkhäuser, 1977). Image used with kind permission of Springer Science+Business Media, Birkhäuser Verlag.

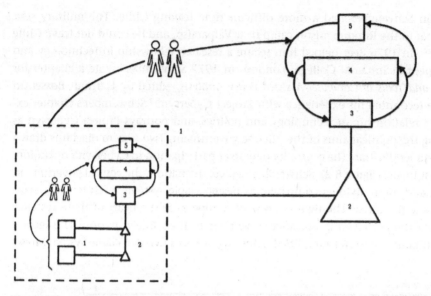

Figure 8.3
The Viable System Model drawn to show worker participation. Image taken from Schwember, "Cybernetics in Government." Image used with kind permission of Springer Science+Business Media, Birkhäuser Verlag.

with workers inserted into the structure of both System One and System Five. Here, workers contribute both physically and mentally to the production process, a graphic response to Marx's critique of alienated labor in capitalist societies.

The journal *Policy Sciences* credited *Concepts and Tools of Computer-Assisted Policy Analysis* with showing how computers could contribute to policy making in ways other than running long-term simulations or automating decision-making processes to take human beings out of the decision loop. But the journal also criticized Schwember's chapter, saying that his account of Project Cybersyn displayed a "high level of naivety about processes of social change, political institutions, and organizational behaviour on the part of the Cybersyn . . . team."[14] When I interviewed Schwember in 2001, it was obvious that he had spent a good deal of time reflecting on the Allende period, what had been done wrong, what could have been done differently, and what had been beyond government control. I suspect that, looking back, he would have agreed with the assessment in *Policy Sciences* that Cybersyn was, to a certain extent, politically naive.[15]

Schwember eventually returned to Chile and worked as an independent consultant. He advised Latin American and European nations on topics ranging from energy to the environment to higher education. Later in life he became an essayist, a prize-winning novelist, and a human rights advocate.[16] He died unexpectedly in 2008 at the age of sixty-nine.

Fernando Flores spent three years as a political prisoner. After the new military government arrested him on the day of the coup, it sent him to a prison camp on Dawson Island in Tierra del Fuego. He was held there for nine months with other top officials from the Allende government. The military later relocated Flores to the Ritoque prison camp near Valparaíso, where he crossed paths with Schwember.

While on Dawson Island, Flores and the other prisoners reflected on their experiences during the previous three years and, as a group, tried to understand the complexities of Chilean socialism and what had gone wrong. Flores offered the group a cybernetic interpretation of events, which resonated with Allende's former minister of mining, Sergio Bitar. When Bitar published a detailed history of the Allende government in 1986, he used cybernetics to explain in part what happened during Allende's presidency. Bitar writes, "In the present case [the Allende government], systemic variety grew because of structural alterations and disturbance of the existing self-regulatory mechanisms (principally those of the market). But the directing center (the government) did not expand its variety controls with the necessary speed; nor could it replace the existing self-regulatory mechanism with new ones." Bitar concludes that "when a complex system [the Chilean nation] is subject to transformation it is essential to master systemic variety at every moment."[17] This choice of language, seemingly out of place in a study of political history, shows that Chile's encounter with cybernetics not only led to the creation of Project Cybersyn but also shaped how some members of the Allende government made sense of the history they had lived.

Flores also used his time in prison to expand his intellectual horizons. After he was moved from Dawson Island, security was not as tight. He read broadly and asked his friends to send him reading material, which his wife, Gloria, smuggled into the prison. In addition, Flores told Schwember that he was interested in getting a degree in cybernetics, a message Schwember conveyed to Beer in England.[18] Beer tried to broker an arrangement with the Open University in Britain for Flores to work toward a doctoral degree while incarcerated, and Beer made human rights organizations outside Chile aware of Flores's imprisonment.[19]

But the more Flores read, the more he began to see the limitations of cybernetic thinking. While Flores still felt that the Law of Requisite Variety and the Viable System Model were useful concepts, he believed they were insufficient for the situations he had encountered while in Allende's cabinet. "My problem [in Allende's cabinet] was not variety; my problem was the configuration of reality, persuading other people," Flores said.[20] Understanding the configuration of reality became a driving intellectual pursuit for Flores, and he found the work of the Chilean biologists Maturana and Varela especially useful toward this end. In addition to developing the theory of autopoiesis with Varela, Maturana had conducted extensive work on optics. His 1959 work with Jerry Lettvin, Warren McCulloch, and Walter Pitts analyzed the frog's optical system and concluded that what a frog sees is not reality per se but rather a construction assembled by the frog's visual system. What the frog sees is therefore a product of its biological structure. This distinction formed the foundation for much of Maturana and Varela's later work in biology and cognition during the 1960s and 1970s, and later inspired the two biologists to break with traditional claims of scientific objectivity and emphasize the role of the observer. One of Maturana's best-known claims—"Anything said is said by an observer"—illustrates this point.[21]

Flores's dissatisfaction with cybernetics paralleled a similar dissatisfaction within the cybernetics community. Heinz von Foerster, who had worked with Maturana, Varela, and the Group of 14 in Chile, found it problematic that cybernetics claimed to create objective representations of real-world phenomena that were independent of an observer.[22] Von Foerster described this approach as "first-order cybernetics," which he defined as "the cybernetics of observed systems." However, von Foerster was influenced by Maturana's work and, like Maturana, became convinced that the observer plays a central role in the construction of cybernetic models. In the fall of 1973 von Foerester taught a yearlong course at the University of Illinois on the "cybernetics of cybernetics," or what became known as second-order cybernetics, "the cybernetics of observing systems."[23] Although von Foerster was not the only person involved in the development of second-order cybernetics, studies of this intellectual transition have credited von Foerster for bridging the gap between first-order and second-order cybernetic thinking.[24] Not surprisingly, Flores also took to the idea of second-order cybernetics, and in his later writing he would cite von Foerster's edited volume *Cybernetics of Cybernetics*.[25]

In 1976 the San Francisco chapter of Amnesty International succeeded in negotiating Flores's release from prison, and arranged for Flores to take a one-year research position in the computer science department at Stanford University. There he met Stanford computer scientist Terry Winograd, who would become his close collaborator in the late 1970s and the 1980s. Shortly after Flores's release, Beer traveled to Flores's new home in Palo Alto, California, and spent several days with him and his family.[26] But the two men went in different directions and gradually grew apart.

Flores pursued a doctorate at the University of California–Berkeley under the supervision of philosophers John Searle and Hubert Dreyfus and economist Ann Markusen. His 1982 dissertation explored how computers could improve management and communication in an "office of the future."[27] Flores said in a 2003 interview that "the concern for communication and organization I learned from Stafford, no doubt."[28] But despite the early influence of Beer on Flores's thinking, by the time Flores finished his dissertation, he had moved away from management cybernetics and toward speech act theory and Heideggerian philosophy, the areas of expertise of his doctoral committee.

Flores credits Maturana for leading him to the work of Martin Heidegger. Like Maturana, Heidegger rejected the existence of an objective external world and saw objects/texts as coexisting with their observers/interpreters. Heidegger's idea of "thrownness" also resonated with Flores—the idea that in everyday life we are thrown into the world and forced to act without the benefit of reflection, rational planning, or objective assessment. Looking back, Flores saw his time in the Allende cabinet as an example of thrownness rather than rational decision making. "My job was so demanding that I did not have the time to perfect [what I was doing]. I only had time to feel it. It was something I felt."[29] In the context of emergency, he had no time to study the laws of control laid down by cybernetics in order to determine how best to resolve government crises. Flores often had to lead with his gut, and his previous experiences and the traditions of Chilean society implicitly shaped his decisions. Flores also realized that "when you are minister and you say something, no matter what you say, it has consequences."[30] It was therefore important to use words deliberately. Flores found that management through variety control did not allow intuitive forms of decision making, nor did it account for the previous experiences and cultural situation of decision makers or accommodate the importance of communicating effectively and with intention.

In 1986 Flores published his first book, which he coauthored with Winograd. *Understanding Computers and Cognition* (1986) married questions about computers to "theories about the nature of biological existence, about language, and about the nature of human action."[31] It was chiefly concerned with understanding what computers could and could not do in the context of human practice.

Understanding Computers and Cognition begins by critiquing the rationalist assumption that an objective, external world exists. The critique builds on the ideas of Heidegger, Searle, Maturana, J. L. Austin, and Hans-Georg Gadamer to show that knowledge is the result of interpretation and depends on the past experiences of the interpreter and his or her situatedness in tradition. Winograd and Flores then argue that because computers lack such experiences and traditions, they cannot replace human beings as knowledge makers. "The ideal of an objectively knowledgeable expert must be replaced with a recognition of the importance of background," Winograd and Flores write. "This can lead to the design of tools that facilitate a dialog of evolving understanding among a knowledgeable community."[32] Building on this observation, the authors propose that computers should not make decisions for us but rather should assist human actions, especially human "communicative acts that create requests and commitments that serve to link us to others."[33] Moreover, computer designers should not focus on creating an artifact but should view their labors as a form of "ontological design." Computers should reflect who we are and how we interact in the world, as well as shape what we can do and who we will become. The American Society for Information Science named *Understanding Computers and Cognition* the Best Information Science Book of 1987. It is now considered a key text in the field of human-computer interaction.[34]

Understanding Computers and Cognition barely references Beer, although it does cite Project Cybersyn as an early example of a computer-based decision-support system. However, the ideas of the British cybernetician are present throughout the text. For example, the book repeats Beer's approach to problem solving, which is "not so much to solve them [problems] as to *dissolve* them."[35] Like Beer, the authors view computers as tools that can support decision making and drive action. They call for a holistic view of complexity that positions computer technology as one part of a complex system consisting of organizational, social, and technological practices.[36] And they do not shy away from synthesizing literature and findings from computing, philosophy, biology, and neurophysiology. I point to these parallels not to say that Beer was the sole originator of these ideas, for he clearly was not. Nor am I suggesting that Winograd and Flores usurped Beer's ideas without proper credit. Rather, I point to these commonalities to show that Beer and cybernetics had more of a lasting effect on Flores's thinking than is apparent from the citations and bibliography of *Understanding Computers and Cognition*.

Flores also spent the 1980s reinventing himself as a Silicon Valley entrepreneur. He started Logonet, an educational consulting firm, to teach ontological design to the business community. With Winograd he formed a start-up company, Action Technologies, and developed a software package called the Coordinator Workgroup Productivity System, which they billed as the first work-group system for computer networks. Consisting of a conversation manager and calendar, the system connected users through modems, local area networks, and time-sharing networks. It marked messages with labels such as "request" or "promise" to clarify employee intentions and responsibilities within a company and linked employee calendars through the network. One journalist later described the Coordinator as "one of the world's first social-networking software applications."[37] However, scholars of computer-supported cooperative work criticized the software for imposing a system of linguistic categories on organizations. Such categories, they argued, could not account for the full complexity and heterogeneity of communications within an organization and might even force these rich exchanges to adhere to new forms of order and institutional control.[38]

In 1989 Flores formed the consulting company Business Design Associates, or BDA. BDA sought to transform businesses in crisis by teaching the principles of speech act theory, such as making explicit requests and explicit promises. Such teachings, Flores claimed, improved company coordination, encouraged honesty, and helped employees become powerful by using words forcefully. At its peak BDA had 150 employees on three continents and annual billings of $50 million.[39] According to the magazine *Fast Company*, BDA charged $1 million for Flores's services. By 2007 Flores's net worth was an estimated $40 million.[40] As his wealth grew, so did his reputation. To some he was brusque, intimidating, direct to the point of rudeness, and off-putting. Yet his message and his success in both the academic and business communities transformed him into a cult figure for others.

In 1997 Flores coauthored a second book, *Disclosing New Worlds*, with his former mentor Hubert Dreyfus and fellow Berkeley Ph.D. and BDA executive Charles Spinosa. In this book, Flores returned to central themes in his writings, such as the configuration of reality and the relationship of knowledge and praxis. The book centers on the idea of "history making," or how human practices can change the world we live in. The authors argue that history making represents life at its best, and they give three examples of history makers: the entrepreneur, the virtuous citizen, and the culture figure. In the case of the entrepreneur, the authors explore how entrepreneurs develop a concrete vision of a new invention that can change society, and they use a composite biography largely based on Flores as an example. The example begins with Flores as the technical director of the Chilean State Development Corporation and ends with him creating a company to implement his ideas on computer-supported collaborative work. What the book views as history making is the later entrepreneurial work, not Flores's earlier role in helping to lead Allende's nationalization program. "A civil democracy with a market economy is the best political construction so far because it allows people to be history makers," the authors declare.[41] Flores's transformation from socialist minister was now complete: he had wholly remade himself in the image of neoliberalism.

Thus, by the end of the 1990s, Flores and Beer had switched places. Flores had morphed into a wealthy international consultant driven by the conviction that organization, communication, and action all were central to making businesses successful. Meanwhile, Beer had become increasingly interested in societal problems and changing the world for the better. His last book, *Beyond Dispute* (1994), proposed a new method for problem solving based on the geometric configurations of the icosahedron, a polygon with twenty equilateral triangle faces. He called this new method "syntegrity" and argued that it could serve as a new approach to conflict resolution in areas of the world such as the Middle East.

In 2002 Flores returned to Chile as a multimillionaire businessman and was elected to the Chilean Senate to represent the northernmost region of the country. Thus began a new phase of his career, that of politician. In 2008 he broke from the center-left coalition that supported his senatorial election and started his own political party, Chile First. In 2009 he switched sides completely and publicly backed the rightist candidate for the Chilean presidency, billionaire businessman Sebastián Piñera, who went on to win the election.[42]

Flores ranks Project Cybersyn as one of the four most important projects of his life; the others are Logonet, the Coordinator, and (when I interviewed him in 2003) trying to insert northern Chile into the nation's new economy.[43] But he views cybernetics as a product of the 1940s and 1950s and does not find it appropriate for the world of today. "How can a theory not have changed since the 1950s?" he mused.[44] Nevertheless, Flores recognized that Project Cybersyn played a formative role in his intellectual development and subsequent accomplishments. The project "was not the cause of what I did after [1973]," Flores told me. "But on the other hand, without [Project Cybersyn], I probably never would have done what I did."[45]

Flores's observation is not unique. Many of the project participants whom I interviewed saw Project Cybersyn as a life-changing experience. Most have gone on to have highly successful careers in academia, business, and government.[46] For example,

Isaquino Benadof, the director of the Cyberstride software project, credited Cybersyn for teaching him such practices as how to document code and test software. The project also taught him the value of cultivating team relationships and even prioritizing relationship skills over technical skills when building a project team. He viewed this insight as one of the most important lessons he learned from the project and one he continued to use throughout his career.[47] Other members of the Cybersyn project team have credited the project with teaching them how to visually display information, that information can drive action, and how politics can shape technological design.

   As a technological system, Project Cybersyn ended on the day of the military coup, but the project lived on in the subsequent careers of the people who were involved in its creation—the cybernetic revolutionaries. The wealth of knowledge, competence, and expertise that they acquired on this short-lived project is an example of how high-risk technological projects, and attempts to combine the technological and the political, can produce positive outcomes, even if they never reach completion and even if the central players themselves today have changed views about what they tried to do. The military coup created a rupture in Chile's technological and political landscape. But through the lives of the people in this story we can see the continuity of history, the significance of Chile's brief experiment with cybernetic socialism, how politics shapes the way that ideas and technologies travel, and the importance of a more inclusive geography in historical studies of science and technology.

Appendix 1: The Structure of the State-Run Economy

The State Development Corporation (CORFO) divided the state-run areas of the economy into four main *branches*: consumer goods, light industry, building materials, and heavy industry. They then divided each branch into different industrial *sectors*, each directed by its own sector committee. Each sector contained *enterprises* that were either in the Social Property Area (government-owned) or the Mixed Property Area (of which the government owned the majority share). An enterprise might consist of several *plants*.

Industries in the consumer goods branch manufactured goods for popular consumption, such as food, textiles, furniture, and pharmaceutical products. The light industry branch consisted of assembling industries such as the automotive industry, electric-electronics industry, makers of rubber and plastics, and copper manufacturing (not mining). The building materials branch included industries such as forestry and cement. The heavy industry branch included steel, energy, petrochemicals, and nitrates.

Industries in mining and agriculture reported directly to the Ministry of Mining and the Ministry of Agriculture, not to CORFO. The Chilean National Copper Corporation (CODELCO) directed the production, planning, and marketing for large-scale copper mining. The Agrarian Reform Corporation directed agrarian reform. Since Project Cybersyn was housed institutionally within CORFO, the system, for the most part, did not collect data from Chile's copper mines or from its agricultural production.

Appendix 2: Timeline on Computing and the Chilean State (1927–1964)

1927   Carlos Ibáñez del Campo is elected president with 96% of the vote.

         Chile imports 29 card-punching, sorting, and other tabulating machines from the United States.

1929   IBM opens its first Chilean branch office in downtown Santiago with 2 employees.

         Wall Street crashes and the Great Depression begins.

         Chile's central public administration has 30,147 employees.

1930   First national population census using Hollerith tabulating machines.

1931   Ibáñez resigns. Chile slides into political disarray.

1932   Six different governments come to power, including Chile's first "Socialist Republic."

         Arturo Alessandri elected president. His victory is a win for the center-right Liberal Alliance, a coalition of Radicals, Democrats, and Liberals. Once in office he introduces policies that spur local production to pull Chile out of the Depression. To do this, he increases the level of state intervention in the economy. He raises tariffs, introduces import licenses, and rations foreign exchange, among other measures. The number of Chilean factories doubles during his presidency and the size of the workforce in the manufacturing sector nearly doubles. The heightened role of the state in the national economy will provide another reason for the expansion of Chilean public administration.

1933   IBM has 20 employees in Chile.

1935   Chile's public administration has 41,266 employees.

         Chile imports 30 card-punching, sorting, and other tabulating machines from the United States.

1938   Pedro Aguirre Cerda elected president from the center-left Popular Front coalition. He and his supporters believe the state should play an even larger role in stimulating economic growth.

1939   A massive earthquake hits the southern cities of Concepción and Chillán.

         The government proposes the creation of two new agencies to assist with earthquake relief: the Relief and Reconstruction Corporation, which would rebuild areas most affected by the earthquake, and the State Development Corporation (CORFO), charged with directing national economic activities. CORFO becomes an instrument for the state to intervene in the Chilean economy.

IBM has 70 employees in Chile.

1940   The U.S. Export-Import Bank gives CORFO $17 million in credits for the purchase of machinery, materials, and technical assistance from the United States. The government decision to use external financing for CORFO, rather than internal financing through taxation, increases U.S. influence in the Chilean economy.

1941   Chile's public administration has 49,538 employees, with 17,355 in social and educational administration and 2,812 in economic and financial administration.

1942   Juan Antonio Ríos is elected president. He dies during his fourth year in office.

1945   Chile imports 82 card-punching, sorting, or other tabulating machines from the United States.

1946   Gabriel González Videla is elected president. Although he is elected by a coalition of Radicals, Communists, and Liberals, he is eventually pushed by the United States to move against the Communist Party and pass economic policies that favor Chilean private investors and U.S. business interests.

1948   González Videla passes the Law for the Permanent Defense of Democracy, which outlaws the Communist Party and eliminates 30,000 voters from Chilean voter registries. The law will remain in effect until 1958.

1949   IBM makes IBM Chile part of its IBM World Trade subsidiary. Thomas Watson Sr., president of IBM, visits Chile and lunches with President González Videla.

Chile's central public administration has 68,225 employees, with 25,483 in social and educational administration and 8,415 in economic and financial administration.

1951   Chile's public administration has 70,882 employees, with 27,536 in social and educational administration and 8,797 in economic and financial administration.

1952   Carlos Ibáñez del Campo elected to the presidency for a second time. He runs as an independent, promising to end corruption, clean house, and create a technocratic state that values expertise over political affiliation. Political affiliation is not a consideration in his appointments to government posts.

Chile's central public administration has 75,542 employees, with 28,899 in social and educational administration and 11,302 in economic and financial administration.

1956   The annual rate of inflation hits 86%. The U.S. consulting firm of Klein-Saks implements an economic stabilization program that cuts government expenditures, including subsidies for public services, implements wage controls, and removes price controls. These policies cut Chilean purchasing power and make life more difficult for Chilean workers and salaried white-collar employees.

IBM Chile has more than 100 employees.

1957   The National Petroleum Company (ENAP) installs IBM Unit Record Machines in Patagonia.

1958   Jorge Alessandri is elected president. He does not affiliate himself with a political party but appeals to a conservative base. He believes that the state should intervene less in the national economy, and his government takes initial steps to study the bureaucracy and make it more efficient.

1959   University of Chile acquires a Standard Electric Lorenz, a German electronic computer that reads data on yellow tape.

Chile's central public administration has 91,236 employees, with 36,103 in social and educational administration and 17,778 in economic and financial administration.

1960   The Budget Office of the Ministry of Finance forms OCOM to introduce organization and methods techniques and improve the functioning of Chilean public administration. OCOM is to oversee the importation and government use of tabulating machinery.

The strongest earthquake on record, 9.5 on the Richter scale, hits the southern city of Valdivia.

IBM Chile moves to a high rise in downtown Santiago.

1962   Chile begins to acquire electronic computers. The Customs Office, treasury, and air force all acquire IBM 1401 machines. The private sector will not acquire any IBM 1401s until 1963.

1963   Chile's central public administration has 103,151 employees, with 44,459 in social and educational administration and 15,850 in economic and financial administration.

The State Railroad Company (Ferrocarriles del Estado) and the Pacific Steel Company (CAP) acquire IBM 1401 machines. The Catholic University purchases an IBM 1620 for teaching and research.

1964   IBM announces its new System/360.

Eduardo Frei Montalva is elected president on a platform of a "revolution in liberty."

Sources: U.S. Department of Commerce, *Foreign Commerce and Navigation of the United States* (Washington, D.C.: U.S. Government Printing Office, 1923–1946); "Hablan los precursores," *IBM Diálogo* (1987): 4–5; Germán Urzúa Valenzuela and Ana María García Barzelatto, *Diagnóstico de la burocracia chilena (1818–1969)* (Santiago, Chile: Editorial Jurídica de Chile, 1971). Central public administration statistics do not include the number of Chileans in the armed forces or in semiautonomous national enterprises such as the National Electric Corporation, the Pacific Steel Corporation, and the National Oil Corporation.

Notes

Preface

1. The book was Armand Mattelart and Hector Schmucler, *Communication and Information Technologies: Freedom of Choice for Latin America* (Norwood, N.J.: Ablex, 1985); see pages 85–86.

2. In the U.S. context we have a good understanding of how computers shaped and were shaped by the business, defense, and academic communities. Two of the commonly cited overviews of U.S. computer history are Martin Campbell-Kelly and William Aspray, *Computer: A History of the Information Machine*, 2nd ed. (Boulder, Colo.: Westview, 2004), and Paul E. Ceruzzi, *A History of Modern Computing*, 2nd ed. (Cambridge, Mass.: MIT Press, 2003). More recent work has studied computer history in European nations, as well as in other regions of the industrialized world, such as Canada, Britain, and the Soviet Union. Experts on the history of computing and the history of technology communities have recognized the need to broaden the geography of computer history. In 2008 the *IEEE Annals of the History of Computing* published an entire issue dedicated to computer history outside the United States. Scholarly communities such as the Tensions of Europe have also produced studies of computing in the different nations of eastern and western Europe. Yet, we still do not know much about the experiences that nations in the global south have had with a technology that is now a ubiquitous part of life around the world. This gap severely limits our understanding of how distinctive cultural, economic, and political histories have both shaped the diffusion of computer technology worldwide and led to the creation of technological alternatives.

3. The literature on the history of technology in Latin America is small. However, a new wave of historical scholarship by such individuals as Lina del Castillo, Julia Rodriguez, Joel Wolfe, Margaret Power, Eve Buckley, Rubén Gallo, and Hugo Palmarola has positioned technology as a lens for understanding broader themes in Latin American history and suggests that this area of research is growing. Outside history, international relations scholar Emmanuel Adler, sociologist Peter Evans, and political scientist Paulo Bastos Tigre have all addressed computer development in Latin America. Ramón Barquín also wrote extensively on computing in Latin America while at MIT's Sloan School of Management in the 1970s. In addition, the anthropologists Anita Chan, Diane Nelson, and Yuri Takhteyev have studied the interaction of computer technology and the state in Peru, Guatemala, and Brazil. In Latin America the scholarship on the history of computing is extremely

limited, but a small yet vibrant community of scholars is forming. In 2008 a group of Latin American computer scientists and historians began a project to document the history of computing in Chile, Brazil, and Argentina. This group continues to grow and now includes scholars throughout Latin America. See Jorge Vidart, "Latin American Conference of the History of Computer Science," *IEEE Annals of the History of Computing* 33, no. 1 (2011): 80–81. And, in the history of technology, scholars such as Michael Adas, Daniel Headrick, Gabrielle Hecht, Clapperton Mavhunga, and Suzanne Moon have conducted pathbreaking work on the history of technology in Africa and Asia.

4. Ramón C. Barquín, "Computation in Latin America," *Datamation* 20, no. 3 (1974): 74; Martin Campbell-Kelly, *From Airline Reservations to Sonic the Hedgehog: A History of the Software Industry* (Cambridge, Mass.: MIT Press, 2003), 90.

5. Chile's commemoration of the thirtieth anniversary of the military coup invited a national process of remembrance and reexamination. The series of events tied to the anniversary spurred Chileans to embrace a new willingness to talk about the past and deeply affected the scope and depth of my research. This public reevaluation of the Allende period changed the scope of Chilean history, allowing for a greater number of voices to be heard and the documentation of new objects of study, among them, studies of Chilean science and Chilean technology. Some of my findings appeared in the Chilean and international press, and brought Project Cybersyn back into the public eye for the first time in decades. See Juan Andrés Guzmán, "Proyecto Synco: El sueño cibernético de Allende," *Clinic*, 10 July 2003, 5–8.

Introduction

1. The Christian Democratic government of Eduardo Frei Montalva (1964–1970) did have some noteworthy successes. It resulted in significant improvements to education and welfare, the aggressive pursuit of a program of agrarian reform, majority ownership of the nation's copper mines (a process known as Chileanization), and major strides in creating local self-help organizations for women and the poor (*promoción popular*). During Frei's tenure, the state housing corporation, CORVI, built about 87,000 new houses. The government established three thousand new schools, and 95 percent of Chilean children received a primary school education by 1970, Frei's last year in office. See Simon Collier and William F. Sater, *A History of Chile, 1808–1994*, 2nd ed. (New York: Cambridge University Press, 2004), 312. Political scientist Arturo Valenzuela has written that during Frei's presidency public expenditures on health increased by 136 percent, on housing by 130 percent, and on education by 167 percent. See Arturo Valenzuela, *The Breakdown of Democratic Regimes: Chile* (Baltimore: Johns Hopkins University Press, 1978), 25. However, Frei's presidency also oversaw an increase in foreign investment, particularly from U.S. multinationals. By 1970 foreign interests controlled forty of the top one hundred Chilean companies. Twenty-four of the thirty leading U.S. multinationals had branches in Chile. As Chilean private investment declined, foreign firms came to control one-quarter of all Chilean industrial capital. Government attempts to increase foreign investment deepened Chile's economic dependence, failed to alleviate unemployment, and gave priority to the needs of foreign companies and international lending agencies over domestic policies. For this reason Brian Loveman opines that the Frei government was a "dismal failure" in its attempts to modernize by increasing the flow of foreign capital into Chile. Brian Loveman, *Chile: The Legacy of Hispanic Capitalism*, 3rd ed. (New York: Oxford University Press, 2001), 238.

2. On Allende's economic program, see J. Ann Zammit, *The Chilean Road to Socialism: Proceedings of an ODEPLAN—IDS Round Table, March 1972* (Austin: University of Texas Press, 1973); Sergio Bitar, *Chile: Experiment in Democracy*, translated by Sam Sherman, vol. 6 (Philadelphia: Institute for the Study of Human Issues, 1986); Barbara Stallings, *Class Conflict and Economic Development in Chile, 1958–1973* (Stanford, Calif.: Stanford University Press, 1978); Valenzuela, *The Breakdown of Democratic Regimes*; Peter Winn, *Weavers of Revolution: The Yarur Workers and Chile's Road to Socialism* (New York: Oxford University Press, 1986). On worker participation, see Juan G. Espinosa and Andrew S. Zimbalist, *Economic Democracy: Workers' Participation in Chilean Industry, 1970–1973* (New York: Academic Press, 1978), and Peter Winn, "Workers into Managers: Worker Participation in the Chilean Textile Industry," in June Nash, Jorge Dandler, and Nicholas Hopkins, eds., *Popular Participation in Social Change: Cooperatives, Collectives, and Nationalized Industry* (Chicago: Mouton, 1976), 577–601.

3. From 1932 to 1973 Chilean presidents were elected by popular vote to serve single six-year terms (their immediate reelection was barred by law), and the transition from one administration to the next was peaceful. Chile also had a competitive and contentious tradition of party politics spanning the ideological spectrum. Parties often formed coalitions to win elections, a necessity given the number of active parties—ten in 1970, down from more than thirty in 1930. This fraught political environment posed a substantial challenge to the governing abilities of both the executive branch and the legislature, especially when internal disagreements within coalitions prevented consensus.

Although Chile's political parties have changed their names over time, several main players were influential by 1970. The National Party was formed in 1966 through the fusion of the traditional conservative and liberal parties and became the largest party of the Chilean right. The anticlerical Radical Party held the political center, as well as the presidential office, from 1938 to 1952. The Radicals were later removed as the dominant centrist party by the Christian Democratic Party (PDC), formed in 1957. The Communist and Socialist parties are the mainstays of the Chilean left. The Chilean Communist Party formed in 1922 and remained active in Chilean democratic politics until a 1948 law made the party illegal for ten years. The Socialist Party began in 1933, bringing together several small leftist movements that had long been active in Chile. Party leaders operated within the constitutional framework and respected democratic institutions. Many Socialist leaders were members of the middle class, and some were affluent. Among the founding members of the Socialist Party was a medical doctor from Valparaíso named Salvador Allende.

4. This figure includes grants and loans. See U.S. Senate, *Covert Action in Chile, 1964–1973: Staff Report of the Select Committee to Study Governmental Operation with Respect to Intelligence Activities* (Washington, D.C.: U.S. Government Printing Office, 1975), 151.

5. Peter Kornbluh, director of the National Security Archive's Chile Documentation Project, meticulously follows the paper trail left by the Nixon administration on U.S. intervention in Chile. See Peter Kornbluh, *The Pinochet File: A Declassified Dossier on Atrocity and Accountability* (New York: New Press, 2003).

6. By the end of Allende's presidency the manufacturing enterprises in the state-run sector constituted approximately 40 percent of Chile's total industrial production in terms of sales. Espinosa and Zimbalist, *Economic Democracy*, 50.

7. For example, see Donald Mackenzie, *Inventing Accuracy: A Historical Sociology of Nuclear Missile Guidance* (Cambridge, Mass.: MIT Press, 1990).

8. Langdon Winner engages with this debate in his classic article "Do Artifacts Have Politics?" in Winner, *The Whale and the Reactor: A Search for Limits in an Age of High Technology* (Chicago: University of Chicago Press, 1986), 19–39.

9. For example, see Andrew Feenberg, *Questioning Technology* (New York: Routledge, 1999).

10. For an extended discussion of technocracy in Chilean history, see Patricio Silva, *In the Name of Reason: Technocrats and Politics in Chile* (University Park: Pennsylvania State University Press, 2008). Theodore Roszak argues that negative views of technocracy helped give rise to the U.S. counterculture during the sixties, a period he contextualizes by looking at the years 1942 to 1972. Theodore Roszak, *The Making of a Counterculture* (Berkeley: University of California Press, 1995). Fred Turner offers a different reading of the story of technocracy and the counterculture by showing how counterculture and computer expertise came together from the 1960s to the 1990s to produce the high-tech cyberculture exemplified by *Wired* magazine. Fred Turner, *From Counterculture to Cyberculture: Stewart Brand, the Whole Earth Network, and the Rise of Digital Utopianism* (Chicago: University of Chicago Press, 2006).

11. See Gabrielle Hecht, *The Radiance of France: Nuclear Power and National Identity after World War II* (Cambridge, Mass.: MIT Press, 1998); Paul N. Edwards, *The Closed World: Computers and the Politics of Discourse in Cold War America* (Cambridge, Mass.: MIT Press, 1996); and Ken Alder, *Engineering the Revolution: Arms and Enlightenment in France, 1763–1815* (Princeton: Princeton University Press, 1997).

12. I am not the first to use the term *sociotechnical engineering*. For example, John Law and Michel Callon used the term in a 1988 article to describe how people, organizations, machines, and scientific findings are mobilized in engineering practice. Law also used the term in a 1987 review article, but he does not provide a definition of the term in that text. More recently the term has been used to refer to the practice of having systems designers work with stakeholders in designing computer systems that take into account the social context in which they will be used. See John Law and Michel Callon, "Engineering and Sociology in a Military Aircraft Project: A Network Analysis of Technological Change," *Social Problems* 35, no. 3 (1988): 284–297; John Law, "The Structure of Sociotechnical Engineering: A Review of the New Sociology of Technology," *Sociological Review* 35, no. 1–2 (1987): 404–425; Alexis Morris, "Socio-Technical Systems in ICT: A Comprehensive Survey," Technical Report #DISI-090-054, University of Trento, Italy, September 2009.

In contrast, I use the term to refer to the practice of engineering a technological artifact and to the social and organizational relationships that surround its construction and use. This type of sociotechnical engineering aims to produce a sociotechnical system capable of upholding a configuration of power that is consistent with the goals and values of a political project. My use of the term *sociotechnical engineering* is related to the idea of technopolitics proposed by Gabrielle Hecht, which she defines as "the strategic practice of designing or using technology to constitute, embody, or enact political goals." Hecht, *The Radiance of France*, 15. It would be accurate to view parts of this book as a case study of Chilean technopolitics. However, *sociotechnical engineering* provides a more appropriate framework for this study because it conceptually emphasizes the role of social and organizational design in the coproduction of technology and politics.

13. Previous works in the history of technology have also equated technologies and texts. For example, Larry Owens remarks that "machines could be read as weighty 'texts' embodying a variety of idioms—technical, intellectual, and ethical" (66). Owens uses the history of the analyzer to show how machines can embody the language of engineering and become "a catalog of [an engineer's] technical universe, lessons on the nature of mathematics and its instruments, and even expressions of the ethos which pervaded engineering education" (95). See Larry Owens, "Vannevar Bush and the Differential Analyzer: The Text and Context of an Early Computer," *Technology and Culture* 27, no. 1 (1986): 63–95. In contrast, I compare machines with texts to show how both are source materials for understanding processes of historical change.

14. Norbert Wiener, *Cybernetics: Or Control and Communication in the Animal and the Machine*, 2nd ed. (Cambridge, Mass.: MIT Press, 1965).

15. On cybernetics in the United States, see Flo Conway and Jim Siegelman, *Dark Hero of the Information Age: In Search of Norbert Wiener, the Father of Cybernetics* (New York: Basic Books, 2005); Peter Galison, "The Ontology of the Enemy: Norbert Wiener and the Cybernetic Vision," *Critical Inquiry* 21, no. 1 (1994): 228–266; Geoffrey C. Bowker, "How to Be Universal: Some Cybernetic Strategies, 1943–70," *Social Studies of Science* 23 (1993): 107–127; Steve J. Heims, *John von Neumann and Norbert Wiener: From Mathematics to the Technologies of Life and Death* (Cambridge, Mass.: MIT Press, 1982); Steve J. Heims, *The Cybernetics Group* (Cambridge, Mass: MIT Press, 1991); Lily E. Kay, "Cybernetics, Information, Life: The Emergence of Scriptural Representations of Heredity," *Configurations* 5, no. 1 (1997): 23–91; and Paul N. Edwards, *The Closed World*. On cybernetics in the Soviet Union, see Slava Gerovitch, *From Newspeak to Cyberspeak: A History of Soviet Cybernetics* (Cambridge, Mass.: MIT Press, 2002). On cybernetics in Britain, see Andrew Pickering, "Cybernetics and the Mangle: Ashby, Beer, and Pask," *Social Studies of Science* 32, no. 3 (2002): 413–437; Andrew Pickering, "The Science of the Unknowable: Stafford Beer's Cybernetic Informatics," *Kybernetes* 33, no. 3–4 (2004): 499–521; Andrew Pickering, *The Cybernetic Brain: Sketches of Another Future* (Chicago: University of Chicago Press, 2010). On cybernetics in France, see David A. Mindell, Jérôme Segal, and Slava Gerovitch, "Cybernetics and Information Theory in the United States, France, and the Soviet Union," in Mark Walker, ed., *Science and Ideology: A Comparative History* (New York: Routledge, 2003). On cybernetics in East Germany, see Jérôme Segal, "L'introduction de la cybernétique en R.D.A. rencontres avec l'idéologie marxiste," *Science, Technology and Political Change: Proceedings of the XXth International Congress of History of Science (Liège, 20–26 July 1997)* (Brepols: Turnhout, 1999), 1:67–80. On cybernetics in China, see Susan Greenhalgh, "Missile Science, Population Science: The Origins of China's One-Child Policy," *China Quarterly* 182 (2005): 253–276.

16. Ronald Kline, "The Disunity of Cybernetics," paper prepared for the Annual Meeting of the Society for the History of Technology, Lisbon, 11–14 October 2008.

17. Raimundo Toledo described his own calculating machine to Wiener as simple, lightweight, and inexpensive. He boasted that the mathematical principles he worked out while building the device might improve the construction of electronic computers such as the ENIAC (Electronic

Numerical Integrator and Computer), the massive machine engineers at the University of Pennsylvania's Moore School of Electrical Engineering unveiled in 1946. Toledo hoped Wiener might help him bring his device from Chile to Western markets so that it might contribute to these computing efforts. In asking for a copy of *Cybernetics*, Toledo explained that he did not have much money and said that it was impossible for him to acquire technical literature on computing in Chile. Wiener's reply was short and condescending: "I do not think it is impossible that you may have made some progress in the direction of a computing machine." He refused to send Toledo a copy of *Cybernetics* because "I cannot afford to dispose of them freely to unknown strangers, no matter how deserving their cases may be." Yet Wiener promised Toledo that he would forward his letter to "an important designer of computing machines." And he did. He sent the letter on to Princeton mathematician John von Neumann, arguably the most important designer of computer architecture at that time. Having access to such a distinguished audience would have been a boon to Toledo if Wiener had not opened his cover letter to von Neumann by saying, "Here is an amusing letter I got from Chile." Raimundo Toledo Toledo, letter to Norbert Wiener, 14 January 1949, MC 22, box 6, Norbert Wiener Papers, Institute Archives and Special Collections, MIT Libraries, Cambridge, Massachusetts; Wiener to Toledo, 21 January 1949, MC 22, box 7, Wiener Papers; Wiener to John von Neumann, 21 January 1949, MC 22, box 7, Wiener Papers. I thank Bernard Geoghegan for bringing this correspondence to my attention.

18. See my earlier work for a historical perspective: Eden Medina, "Designing Freedom, Regulating a Nation: Socialist Cybernetics in Allende's Chile," *Journal of Latin American Studies* 38, no. 3 (2006): 571–606; Eden Medina, "Democratic Socialism, Cybernetic Socialism: Making the Chilean Economy Public," in Bruno Latour and Peter Weibel, eds., *Making Things Public: Atmospheres of Democracy* (Cambridge, Mass.: MIT Press, 2005), 708–721; Eden Medina, "Secret Plan Cybersyn," in Stephen Kovats and Thomas Munz, eds., *Conspire: Transmediale Parcours 1* (Frankfurt, Germany: Revolver Press, 2008), 65–80. A brief discussion of Project Cybersyn appears in Andrew Pickering's book *The Cybernetic Brain,* but he uses the system to explain a central concept in Stafford Beer's work, namely, the Viable System Model, and does not interpret the system's significance in the context of Chile's socialist project.

19. In 2006 the Brainworks Gallery based in Santiago, Chile, put together a series of events in connection with a show called "Utopias in Process: Space, Technology, and Representation" and invited me to talk about the history of Project Cybersyn as a form of technological utopia. Chilean artist Mario Navarro assumed a more critical perspective in his 2006 work *Whiskey in Opsroom.* Navarro's project put a bottle of whiskey in an image of the Cybersyn operations room to portray the project as a drunken fancy of Stafford Beer. In 2007 the media artist group Or-Am created an installation about Project Cybersyn at the Cultural Center La Moneda, located below the Chilean presidential palace. It put Chilean technology history on display next to exhibits about Gabriela Mistral and the Selk'nam Indians, a now-extinct tribe indigenous to Tierra del Fuego. This juxtaposition linked Project Cybersyn to these exemplars of Chilean culture and implicitly made the point that technological prowess is as much a part of Chilean history as its poet laureates or indigenous peoples.

20. Jorge Bardit, *Synco* (Santiago: Ediciones B, 2008).

21. As one person who saw Beer lecture on Project Cybersyn put it: "There was this very large, rather voluble person [Beer] whose mannerisms gave the impression that he was sort of boasting about something, but one wasn't quite sure what the substance was behind it. . . . It seemed to me a bit like the machinations of a very clever, maybe self-important, even eccentric person." Ann Zammit, telephone interview by author, 27 January 2010.

22. Ronald Kline, "The Fate of Cybernetics in the United States: Decline, Revival, and Transformation in the 1960s and 1970s," unpublished manuscript, June 21, 2010, in the personal files of Ronald Kline.

23. Stafford Beer, *Cybernetics and Management*, 2nd ed. (London: English Universities Press, 1967), viii.

24. I thank Phillip Guddemi, vice president for membership of the American Society for Cybernetics, for supplying me with this information.

25. Readers interested in learning more about the technical aspects of Project Cybersyn should consult the accounts published by project participants. For example, see Raúl Espejo, "Cybernetic Praxis in Government: The Management of Industry in Chile, 1970–1973," *Cybernetics and Systems: An International Journal* 11 (1980): 325–338; Raúl Espejo, "Performance Management, the Nature of Regulation and the Cybersyn Project," *Kybernetes* 38, no. 1–2 (2009): 65–82; Raúl Espejo, "Complexity and Change: Reflections upon the Cybernetic Intervention in Chile, 1970–1973," *Cybernetics and Systems* 22, no. 4 (1991): 443–457; Herman Schwember, "Cybernetics in Government: Experience with New Tools for Management in Chile, 1971–1973," in Hartmut Bossel, ed., *Concepts and Tools of Computer-Assisted Policy Analysis* (Basel: Birkhäuser, 1977), 79–138; Roberto Cañete, "The Brain of the Government: An Application of Cybernetic Principles to the Management of a National Industrial Economy," paper presented at the 22nd Annual North American Meeting on Avoiding Social Catastrophes and Maximizing Social Opportunities: The General Systems Challenge, Washington, D.C., 13–15 February 1978; Stafford Beer, *Brain of the Firm: The Managerial Cybernetics of Organization*, 2nd ed. (New York: J. Wiley, 1981); Gui Bonsiepe, *Entwurfskultur und Gesellschaft: Gestaltung zwischen Zentrum und Peripherie* (Basel: Birkhäuser-Verlag, 2009); Stafford Beer, Raúl Espejo, Mario Grandi, and Herman Schwember, *Il Progetto Cybersyn: Cibernetica per la democrazia* (Milan: CLUP-CLUED, 1980).

Chapter 1

1. Fernando Flores, letter to Stafford Beer, 13 July 1971, box 55, Stafford Beer Collection.

2. Salvador Allende, quoted in Régis Debray, *Conversations with Allende: Socialism in Chile* (London: N.L.B., 1971), 85.

3. Salvador Allende, "The Purpose of Our Victory: Inaugural Address in the National Stadium, 5 November 1970," in Allende, *Chile's Road to Socialism*, ed. Joan E. Garcés, trans. J. Darling (Baltimore: Penguin, 1973), 59.

4. Sergio Bitar, *Chile: Experiment in Democracy* (Philadelphia: Institute for the Study of Human Issues, 1986).

5. Beer to Flores, 29 July 1971, box 55, Beer Collection.

6. According to Beer's partner, Allenna Leonard, Beer "finally in the last couple of years got running water [in the cottage] and, after being stuck with a malfunctioning car, agreed to his daughter's and my request [that] he get a phone installed. Of course, it didn't work when needed because the electricity had gone out and he had opted for a fax/phone instead of a no features land line." Allenna Leonard, e-mail to author, 30 March 2011.

7. Jonathan Rosenhead, telephone interview by author, 8 October 2009; Michael Becket, "Beer: The Hope of Chile," *Daily Telegraph*, 10 August 1973, 7.

8. Beer had eight children in all, Vanilla, Simon, Mark, Stephen, Matthew, Polly, Kate, and Harry. Kate was from his second wife's previous marriage.

9. He housed his department in a building he called Cybor House, a word he formed by combining *cybernetics* and *operations research* (OR). There he managed more than seventy employees.

10. Beer supervised Keith Douglas "Toch" Tocher, who developed the General Steelplant Program, which later evolved into the General Simulation Program. For more on these computer simulations, see B. W. Hollocks, "Intelligence, Innovation, and Integrity: K. D. Tocher and the Dawn of Simulation," *Journal of Simulation* 2 (2008): 128–137. According to Hollocks, Beer asked Tocher to model the steel plants of United Steel. Hollocks writes, "This was not a pioneering challenge in itself as steel plant simulation had already been carried out. . . . However, Tocher knew that United Steel had a number of steel plants across the north of England. The plants in Scunthorpe, Rotherham, Sheffield and Workington covered three different technologies: open-hearth, electric arc and Bessemer converter. . . . So, Tocher saw the challenge as in producing a comprehensive model that could be used for any of these sites—a General Steelplant Program, GSP" (132).

11. Beer helped build SIGMA from the ground up with financial backing from Metra International Group. Metra International consisted of the French company Société d'Economie et de Mathématiques Appliquées (SEMA) as well as companies in Belgium, Italy, West Germany, Britain, and Spain. Freed from the restrictions of United Steel, Beer began applying his cybernetics more broadly. At SIGMA "we did my stuff," Beer said. "We took on difficult jobs and solved them using my version of OR, which [was] quite different from what it is these days." Beer also started growing his famous beard during this period. Stafford Beer, interview by author, 15–16 March 2001, Toronto. More about the history of SEMA and Metra International appears in an article by Jacques Lesourne and Richard Armand, "A Brief History of the First Decade of SEMA," *IEEE Annals of the History of Computing* 13, no. 4 (1991): 341–349.

12. Jonathan Rosenhead, "Obituary: Stafford Beer," *Journal of the Operational Research Society* 54, no. 12 (2003): 1231.

13. Beer interview. In 2001 Beer said, "I would love you to have seen that I had some very big and preposterous houses. That study had cork walls, except for one which was fur."

14. Dick Martin and Jonathan Rosenhead, "Obituary: Stafford Beer," *Guardian*, 4 September 2002, 20.

15. I would like to thank the late Stafford Beer for providing me with a complete bibliography of his work up to the year 2000.

16. However, Beer had a faculty position at Manchester Business School and held visiting faculty appointments in Europe and the United States.

17. Beer writes that he arrived at Wiener's office unannounced while visiting Warren McCulloch at MIT but easily secured an audience with the mathematician. Wiener had reportedly read Beer's first book, *Cybernetics and Management,* and was so excited to meet Beer that he "almost vaulted his desk to embrace me." See Stafford Beer, "Retrospect: American Diary, 1960," in *How Many Grapes Went into the Wine: Stafford Beer on the Art and Science of Holistic Management,* ed. Roger Harnden and Allenna Leonard (New York: Wiley, 1994), 283.

18. Beer interview.

19. The Royal Army sent Beer to India, where he developed an interest in Eastern philosophy that influenced his subsequent work and stayed with him throughout his life.

20. When I interviewed Beer in 2001, he remarked, "I've always divided the world in two. People either think I'm terrific or they think I'm a charlatan. I've never had too much time to worry about it. I'm too busy."

21. Becket, "Beer: The Hope of Chile."

22. Beer interview. Beer later described Wiener's *Cybernetics* as "difficult, quixotic, immensely stimulating (then and now). . . . Think of it like this: a great man (he really was) holds forth to his friends after dinner, ruins the tablecloth by scribbling mathematics all over it, sings a little song in German, and changes your life. It is tough going: you have to stay the night." See Beer, "General Introduction to Cybernetics Itself," n.d., box 88, Stafford Beer Collection, Liverpool John Moores University, Liverpool, England.

23. Norbert Wiener, *Cybernetics: Or Control and Communication in the Animal and the Machine,* 2nd ed. (Cambridge, Mass.: MIT Press, 1965), 11. This is the definition that Wiener uses in his book. However, he was not the lone inventor of the term. In the text he describes being part of a group of scientists who expressed frustration with existing terminology to describe the new field and its central areas of concern and were thus "forced to coin at least one artificial neo-Greek expression to fill the gap" (11).

24. In *The Human Use of Human Beings: Cybernetics and Society* (New York: Da Capo, 1954), Wiener writes that Ampère used the term in the early part of the nineteenth century in the area of political science (15).

25. Wiener, *Cybernetics,* 12.

26. Wiener explicitly refers to a 1942 paper he co-wrote with MIT electrical engineer Julian Bigelow and Arturo Rosenblueth, a Mexican physiologist who was then teaching at Harvard Medical School, on the problems of central inhibition in the nervous system. The historian David Mindell includes in this origin story earlier work at such institutions as Bell Labs, the Sperry Company, the MIT Servomechanisms Laboratory, and the MIT Radiation Laboratory, as well as by such people

as Elmer Sperry, Harold Black, Harry Nyquist, and Hendrik Bode. See David A. Mindell, *Between Human and Machine: Feedback, Control and Computing before Cybernetics* (Baltimore: Johns Hopkins University Press, 2002).

27. For more detailed information about cybernetics and its origins, see, among other works, Paul N. Edwards, *The Closed World: Computers and the Politics of Discourse in Cold War America* (Cambridge, Mass.: MIT Press, 1996); Peter Galison, "The Ontology of the Enemy: Norbert Wiener and the Cybernetic Vision," *Critical Inquiry* 21, no. 1 (1994): 228–266; Slava Gerovitch, *From Newspeak to Cyberspeak: A History of Soviet Cybernetics* (Cambridge, Mass.: MIT Press, 2002); N. Katherine Hayles, *How We Became Posthuman: Virtual Bodies in Cybernetics, Literature, and Informatics* (Chicago: University of Chicago Press, 1999); Steve J. Heims, *The Cybernetics Group* (Cambridge, Mass.: MIT Press, 1991); Steve J. Heims, *John von Neumann and Norbert Wiener: From Mathematics to the Technologies of Life and Death* (Cambridge, Mass.: MIT Press, 1982); L. E. Kay, "Cybernetics, Information, Life: The Emergence of Scriptural Representations of Heredity," *Configurations* 5, no. 1 (1997): 23–91; and Mindell, *Between Human and Machine*. Andrew Pickering has written specifically on the history of British cybernetics and the work of Stafford Beer. See Andrew Pickering, "Cybernetics and the Mangle: Ashby, Beer, and Pask," *Social Studies of Science* 32, no. 3 (2002): 413–437, and *The Cybernetic Brain: Sketches of Another Future* (Chicago: University of Chicago Press, 2010).

28. Flo Conway and Jim Siegelman, *Dark Hero of the Information Age: In Search of Norbert Wiener, the Father of Cybernetics* (New York: Basic, 2005), 184. The lifting of wartime secrecy restrictions also allowed Wiener to publish a book in 1949 based on a paper he wrote in 1942 but could not publish because the government classified it as secret. See Norbert Wiener, *Extrapolation, Interpolation and Smoothing of Stationary Time Series, with Engineering Applications* (Cambridge, Mass: MIT Press, 1949; republished 1964 as *Time Series*).

29. Geoffrey C. Bowker, "How to Be Universal: Some Cybernetic Strategies, 1943–70," *Social Studies of Science* 23 (1993): 107–127.

30. Ronald Kline, for example, studies such criticisms of cybernetics and documents how the field changed from a universal science into a series of subdisciplines. See Ronald Kline, "The Fate of Cybernetics in the United States: Decline, Revival, and Transformation in the 1960s and 1970s," unpublished manuscript, 21 June 2010, in the personal files of Ronald Kline.

31. Conway and Siegelman, *Dark Hero*, 184.

32. Ibid., 185.

33. "Science: In Man's Image," *Time*, 27 December 1948, available at www.time.com/time/magazine/article/0,9171,886484,00.html.

34. See Heims, *Cybernetics Group*, 285. Attendees at subsequent meetings included Claude Shannon, often heralded as the founder of information theory; J. C. R. Licklider, who would direct the Information Processing Techniques Office at the U.S. Advanced Research Projects Agency (the agency better known as ARPA) in the early 1960s; and the psychiatrist W. Ross Ashby, whose 1952 book *Design for a Brain* combined concepts from psychology and computation.

35. W. Ross Ashby, *Introduction to Cybernetics* (London: Chapman and Hall, 1956), 4.

36. David Hounshell, "The Medium Is the Message, or How Context Matters: The RAND Corporation Builds an Economics of Innovation, 1946–1962," in Agatha C. Hughes and Thomas Parke Hughes, eds., *Systems, Experts, and Computers: The Systems Approach in Management and Engineering, World War II and After* (Cambridge, Mass.: MIT Press, 2000).

37. Paul N. Edwards, "The World in a Machine: Origins and Impacts of Early Computerized Global Systems Models," in Hughes and Hughes, *Systems, Experts, and Computers*, 229.

38. Their objectivity remains a matter of debate, and they certainly were not infallible. In 1962 McNamara noted, "Every quantitative measurement we have shows we are winning this war," and projected that the United States would be out of Vietnam in three or four years. But ten years later the United States was still in Vietnam, fighting an unwinnable war that, by one estimate, cost $111 billion and had 58,193 U.S. casualties. See Tim Weiner, "Robert S. McNamara, Architect of a Futile War, Dies at 93," *New York Times*, 6 July 2009, A1; Stephen Daggett, "Costs of Major U.S. Wars," *Congressional Research Service Report for Congress* (RS22926), Navy Department Library, available at www.history.navy.mil/library/online/costs_of_major_us_wars.htm; National Archives, "Statistical Information about Casualties of the Vietnam War," www.archives.gov/research/military/vietnam-war/casualty-statistics.html.

39. For more on the influence of cybernetics, operations research, and systems analysis in public policy and urban planning, see Jennifer S. Light, *From Warfare to Welfare: Defense Intellectuals and Urban Problems in Cold War America* (Baltimore: Johns Hopkins University Press, 2003). David R. Jardini shows how systems analysis shaped welfare policy in his "Out of the Blue Yonder: The Transfer of Systems Thinking from the Pentagon to the Great Society, 1961–1965," in Hughes and Hughes, *Systems, Experts, and Computers*, 311–358.

40. Light, *From Warfare to Welfare*, chapter 3.

41. "Chile: Futurism Now," *Latin America*, 12 January 1973, 10–12.

42. For example, Jardini writes, "The giving and taking of orders, deference to authority, and the centralization of command are intrinsic to the [U.S. Department of Defense's] operation. In this sense the DOD is a poor model for the democratic ideal many Americans hold for their government institutions." Jardini, "Out of the Blue Yonder," 341.

43. Edwards's 1996 book is entitled *The Closed World*.

44. Evelyn Fox Keller, *Refiguring Life: Metaphors of Twentieth-Century Biology* (New York: Columbia University Press, 1995), 86.

45. Psychiatry and military engineering were not separate domains in the postwar era, and work in cybernetics spanned both fields in the U.S. and British contexts. For example, the British cybernetician Gordon Pask received fifteen years of funding for his work on decision making and adaptive training systems from the U.S. Office of Navy Research. Military funding also supported the work of psychologists such as George Miller, who promoted the use of cybernetic ideas and information theory in psychology. See Edwards, *The Closed World*, chapter 7. In *The Cybernetic*

Brain, Pickering classifies Beer as a second-generation British cybernetician because he entered the field in the 1950s, after the conclusion of World War II and events such as the Macy conferences. He classifies Walter and Ashby as first-generation British cyberneticians.

46. Pickering, *Cybernetic Brain*, 6. Again, this boundary work of separating U.S. and British cybernetics as separate branches is not entirely accurate, as Pickering acknowledges. As Kline notes, Frank George, the first head of the Department of Cybernetics at Brunel University near London, made representational models of psychological and biological systems. Ronald Kline, "Cybernetics as a Usable Past," *Metascience* (2011): 1–6, available at www.springerlink.com/content/l27p28556438p101/.

47. Pickering, *Cybernetic Brain*, 6.

48. For example, Beer felt that management scientists spent too much time looking for the one "correct" solution when they should be looking for any member of a family of solutions that would allow the entity to maintain its stability. Such an approach would take a fraction of the time and would increase the company's ability to survive in the long term. Throughout his life Beer advocated the position that cybernetics and operations research should be used to do things in the world. He griped that in academia operations research scientists were not "solving problems, they are writing bloody Ph.D. theses about solving problems" (Beer interview). Beer viewed cybernetics and operations research as complementary fields. He saw operations research not as a science in its own right but rather as the practice of "doing science in the management sphere." Cybernetics, in turn, gave OR professionals a scientific foundation for their work, a set of mathematical theories, biological ideas, and approaches to complexity that they could use in systems analyses. Stafford Beer, *Decision and Control: The Meaning of Operational Research and Management Cybernetics* (New York: J. Wiley, 1966), 239.

49. When I interviewed him in 2001, Beer compared the problem-oriented applications of OR that came about during World War II with the later academic versions of OR, which he described as "mathematical masturbation" because they were too theoretical, overly quantified, and not focused on solving real-world problems. However, in his "Retrospect: American Diary, 1960," Beer expressed a more positive view of OR research in the United States. He was particularly impressed by Russell Ackoff, the former president of the Operations Research Society of America and the editor of the foundational text *Introduction to Operations Research*, and Charles Hitch, then president of the Operations Research Society of America, who would later serve as assistant secretary of defense under Robert McNamara. Beer wrote that Ackoff's 1960 talk at Case Institute of Technology "was most notable for advocating the complete integration of management sciences on a problem-orientated basis. Most of the symposiats (including myself) disagreed with him strongly on only one point: the idea that the organization of a system (in terms of both control and desired outcome) 'ought' to be expressed in the form of an equation. However, as he admits that this is rarely possible, perhaps there is little with which to disagree." With respect to Hitch, Beer wrote, "I was continually amazed to the extent to which Mr. Hitch was preaching the same gospel of Cybor House. He was also very interesting on the issue of whether to solve a problem in a particular system one had to study it within the higher systems in the hierarchy." Beer had a less positive view of the OR work taking place at MIT and wrote that the MIT Operational Research Group did "not appear to be doing anything unique." Beer, "Retrospect," 233–234, 282.

50. Wiener writes, "For a good statistic of society, we need long runs *under essentially constant conditions*. . . . Thus the human sciences are very poor testing-grounds for a new mathematical technique"; see Wiener, *Cybernetics*, 25, emphasis in the original. In contrast, Beer was not dissuaded by imperfect data sets. Nor was he convinced that all models needed to be mathematical. He reasoned that an engineer might look at a problem and see servomechanisms, a biologist might see cells, and an economist might see markets. Others might see the world through concepts in physics, neurology, psychology, mathematics, or sociology. Unlike those who pushed for scientific objectivity, Beer viewed these multiple disciplinary subjectivities as beneficial to the scientific process, especially when practitioners from different fields worked together in teams. Such collaboration would push the group to consider a range of models before selecting the most beneficial for understanding the behavior of the complex system under study. Stafford Beer, "The World, the Flesh and the Metal: The Prerogatives of Systems," *Nature* 205, no. 4968 (1965): 224.

51. Stafford Beer, *Cybernetics and Management*, 2nd ed. (London: English Universities Press, 1967), 17.

52. Ibid., 30.

53. According to Beer, the complexity of a system is not an innate property of the system but rather is conditioned by the outside observer. A window catch might be a simple system from the perspective of household use, but at the level of its molecular interaction the same latch could easily become an exceedingly complex system. The trick, then, is to select the correct level of complexity for the system so that it can be studied or controlled by an outside observer. This requires black-boxing the interactions of component parts at the lower levels. Even the study of simple systems requires a degree of black-boxing, and this process of simplification reflects the capabilities of the scientist-observer.

54. Stafford Beer, *Heart of the Enterprise* (New York: Wiley, 1979), 40.

55. Ashby, *Introduction to Cybernetics*, 25.

56. Beer, *Cybernetics and Management*, 50.

57. Beer often said that the Law of Requisite Variety was to management what the law of gravity was to physics. See, for example, Stafford Beer, "The Viable System Model: Its Provenance, Development, Methodology and Pathology," in David Whittaker, ed., *Think before You Think: Social Complexity and Knowledge of Knowing* (Oxford, U.K.: Wavestone Press, 2009), 134–157.

58. In *The Cybernetic Brain*, Pickering links this narrative of domination to the ethos found in modernist science and engineering projects. Recent advances in science and technology have given us better control of our bodies, but technologies such as birth control pills are still not 100 percent effective, and germs continue to resist advances in pharmacology. Large-scale engineering projects allow us to bend rivers, and advances in architecture allow us to create structures of greater creativity, ambition, and resilience. Yet hurricanes cause levees to overflow; earthquakes, mudslides, and forest fires destroy homes; and bridges collapse from atypical weather events or unforeseen structural failures. Pickering argues that Ashby and Beer offer an important counternarrative of adaptation instead of domination. On the failure of modernist applications of science and engineering, see James C. Scott, *Seeing Like a State: How Certain Schemes to Improve the Human*

Condition Have Failed (New Haven, Conn.: Yale University Press, 1998). Cybernetic critiques of domination also carried over to the domain of politics. For example, in *Introduction to Cybernetics*, Ross Ashby asks: "By how much can a dictator control a country? It is commonly said that Hitler's control over Germany was total. So far as his power of regulation was concerned, the law says that his control amounted to just 1 man-power, and no more" (213). One could counter that Hitler's power extended beyond that of a single man because it extended throughout the Third Reich as well as the political and military structures of Germany and the other Axis nations. However, Ashby's point still has merit. If Hitler truly wished to have total control of Germany, he would have needed the variety to control the actions of every single German, which of course he could not do.

59. Beer, *Cybernetics and Management*, 21.

60. Or, as Beer would put it, so that the variety in one subsystem could absorb the variety in another.

61. In *Introduction to Cybernetics*, Ashby observes that "the whole is at a state of equilibrium if and only if each part is at a state of equilibrium in the conditions provided by the other parts" (83). This focus on equilibrium, or homeostasis, required a different approach to the design of control systems and the building of models that simulated the behavior of complex systems. Instead of building a system from its component parts up, Beer advocated dividing the system up into a manageable number of interacting subsystems. The scientist would then concentrate on studying the behavior among the subsystems, rather than identifying the even smaller parts that constituted their makeup. The exact composition of the subsystems did not matter—they could be black-boxed from a practical standpoint.

62. Beer, *Cybernetics and Management*, 28.

63. Stafford Beer, "Management in Cybernetic Terms," in Beer, *Platform for Change: A Message from Stafford Beer* (New York: J. Wiley, 1975), 106; emphasis in the original.

64. Beer was not the only person writing on how computers could contribute to management decision making or how to create centralized or decentralized power configurations in management. These were ongoing themes in the work of the U.S. economist and Nobel laureate Herbert Simon, for one example. See Herbert Simon, *Administrative Behavior: A Study of Decision-Making Processes in Administrative Organizations*, 4th ed. (New York: Simon and Schuster, 1997); Herbert A. Simon, Harold Guetzkow, George Kozmetsky, and Gordon Tyndall, *Centralization vs. Decentralization in Organizing the Controller's Department* (New York: Controllership Foundation, 1954); Herbert Simon, "The Future of Information-Processing Technology," *Management Science* 14, no. 9 (1968): 619–624; Herbert Simon, "Applying Information Technology to Organization Design," *Public Administration Review* 33, no. 3 (1973): 268–278; and Herbert Simon, "The Consequences of Computers for Centralization and Decentralization," in M. L. Dertouzos and J. Moses, eds., *The Computer Age: A Twenty-year View* (Cambridge, Mass.: MIT Press, 1979): 212–228. See also Hunter Heyck, "Defining the Computer: Herbert Simon and the Bureaucratic Mind—Part I," *IEEE Annals of the History of Computing* 30, no. 2 (2008): 42–51; and Hunter Heyck, "Defining the Computer: Herbert Simon and the Bureaucratic Mind—Part II," *IEEE Annals of the History of Computing* 30, no. 2 (2008): 52–63.

65. Fernando Flores, interview by author, Santiago, Chile, 18 August 2003.

66. Fernando Flores, interview by author, Viña del Mar, Chile, 30 July 2003.

67. Ibid.; Oscar Guillermo Garretón, interview by author, Santiago, Chile, 4 August 2003.

68. Flores interview, 30 July 2003.

69. Gustavo Silva, interview by the author, Santiago, Chile, 5 September 2003.

70. Although *Platform for Change* was not published until 1975, Beer had prepared most of the manuscript by 1971.

71. Stafford Beer, "The Liberty Machine: Can Cybernetics Help Rescue the Environment?" *Futures* 3, no. 4 (1971): 343.

72. Organization gave structure to government planning processes and embedded the limitations of the organization in future government actions. "Planning is homologous to organization," Beer observed. "How can you have plans that are not couched in terms of the organization which must implement them? But if the organization is no longer well-adapted to the environment, how then can the plans possibly be relevant to existing threats?" Beer, "The Liberty Machine."

73. Ibid., 347.

74. Stafford Beer, *Management Science: The Business Use of Operations Research* (New York: Doubleday, 1968), 23.

75. Stafford Beer, "Operational Research as Revelation," in Beer, *Platform for Change*, 66.

76. Beer, "The Liberty Machine," 348.

77. Stafford Beer, "The Viable System Model," 134.

78. Stafford Beer, *Brain of the Firm: The Managerial Cybernetics of Organization*, 2nd ed. (New York: J. Wiley, 1981), 239.

79. Beer, "The Viable System Model,"134.

80. For example, Beer later introduced a new level in the model that he called System Three*. However, Beer hinted at this level in *Brain of the Firm* with his description of the parasympathetic nervous system. The Viable System Model can be difficult to understand at first, especially in its biological form. Beer wrote a trilogy of books to explain the model: *Brain of the Firm* (1972), *Heart of the Enterprise* (1979), and *Diagnosing the System for Organizations* (1985). Readers who want to learn more about the Viable System Model should start with the third book, *Diagnosing the System for Organizations* (New York: J. Wiley, 1985). In my opinion, it offers the clearest and most concise description of the model in the context of organizational management.

81. This caused some critics to dismiss the model as more analogy than science. Beer countered that analogy gave way to the scientific method when scientists moved from identifying conceptually similar behaviors in managerial and biological systems and toward the creation of a rigorous model of invariant behavior that could apply to both. He writes: "The generalized system that

comes out of this process, which applies to all systems of a particular class, is a scientific model. . . . The generalization of some behavior invariably and invariantly exhibited by the system as interpreted through this systemic model we usually call law." Beer conceded that this model could not be proved, it could only be falsified. However, it could be refined through its repeated application to new viable systems. Beer, "The Viable System Model," 137.

82. Ibid., 136.

83. Beer, *Brain of the Firm*, 156.

84. I thank Allenna Leonard for checking the accuracy of my description of the Viable System Model and for adding her own clarifications. At her suggestion I refrained from describing the model as consisting of five *hierarchical* tiers. Leonard noted that the model is hierarchical, "but it is a hierarchy of comprehensiveness not authority." Allenna Leonard, e-mail to author, 22 September 2010.

85. Beer, *Brain of the Firm*, 129.

86. Beer put it thus: "The notion of hierarchy cannot be altogether escaped in discussing the viable system, although all our enquiries reveal the equivalent importance of the five major subsystems. It really is not survival-worthy to have a brain that would support an Aristotle or a Newton or a you, if any of the major organs or physiological systems (such as the endocrine) closes down." Beer, *Diagnosing the System*, 91.

87. Ibid., 86.

88. Beer, *Brain of the Firm*, 176.

89. Beer later labeled this auditing capability as System Three*.

90. Beer writes, "All the sensory nerves report to the thalamus; everything that the cortex gets is sorted and switched through the diencephalon and basal ganglia (our fourth level)." Beer, *Brain of the Firm*, 98.

91. Karl Marx, "The Possibility of Non-Violent Revolution," in *The Marx-Engels Reader*, ed. Robert C. Tucker (New York: W. W. Norton, 1978), 522–524.

92. Allende, *Chile's Road to Socialism*, 150; Peter Winn, *Weavers of Revolution: The Yarur Workers and Chile's Road to Socialism* (New York: Oxford University Press, 1986), 185.

93. Beer, *Brain of the Firm*, 160–161.

94. Stafford Beer, "Homo Gubernator," in Beer, *Platform for Change*, 35.

95. Ibid., 36.

96. For example, see Mark Walker, ed., *Science and Ideology: A Comparative History* (New York: Routledge, 2003).

97. According to Leonard, Beer "basically charted his own course politically [and] eventually became disillusioned with the Labour party leading up to and including Blair and voted for Plaid

Cymru (Welsh party) the last couple of elections. . . . He never actually 'joined' a party." Allenna Leonard, e-mail to author, 30 March 2011.

Chapter 2

1. See chapter 1 for a more complete description of the Viable System Model and the Liberty Machine.

2. Stafford Beer, interview by author, Toronto, Canada, 15–16 March 2001.

3. In Chilean politics, members of the center have tended to portray Allende as a conflicted and contradictory figure whose love of women and bourgeois luxuries paralleled his political dreams for socialist transformation. Members of the left have transformed Allende into a martyr who refused to compromise his ideals and died gripping a gun given to him by Fidel Castro. Those on the right blamed Allende for dismantling the economy and creating an era of political chaos. More recently, members of the right, center, and center left have adopted a new line of argument that urges Chileans to move beyond the past and focus on the future. This strategic move undermines the importance of the UP, Allende, and current efforts to document the acts of violence and repression that occurred during the Pinochet dictatorship.

4. Salvador Allende, "Popular Unity Program," in *Salvador Allende Reader*, ed. James D. Cockcroft (Hoboken, N.J.: Ocean Press, 2000), 257–285.

5. See, for example, Paul E. Sigmund, *The Overthrow of Allende and the Politics of Chile, 1964–1976* (Pittsburgh: University of Pittsburgh Press, 1977), 131.

6. Chile had been a focus of the U.S. government before Allende's election. From 1962 to 1969, Chile received more than a billion dollars in U.S. aid, including grants and loans, through the U.S. Alliance for Progress, which hoped, in part, to prevent the spread of communism in Chile and in Latin America. See U.S. Senate, *Covert Action in Chile, 1964–1973: Staff Report of the Select Committee to Study Governmental Operation with Respect to Intelligence Activities*, 94th Cong., 1st sess., 1975, S. Rep. 63-372, 151.

7. Nathaniel Davis, *The Last Two Years of Salvador Allende* (Ithaca, N.Y.: Cornell University Press, 1985), 6.

8. U.S. Senate, Select Committee to Study Governmental Operations with Respect to Intelligence Activities, *Alleged Assassination Plots Involving Foreign Leaders: An Interim Report of the Select Committee to Study Governmental Operations with Respect to Intelligence Activities*, 94th Cong., 1st sess., 1975, S. Rep. 94-465, 227; U.S. Senate, *Covert Action in Chile, 1964–1973*, 170.

9. U.S. Senate, *Covert Action in Chile, 1964–1973*, 148.

10. Salvador Allende, *Salvador Allende: Obras escogidas, 1908–1973* (Santiago, Chile: Editorial Antártica S.A., 1992), 355.

11. Economic nationalization did not begin with Popular Unity; it goes back to Chile's attempts to recover from the Great Depression. In the aftermath of the Depression, early attempts to develop

national industries and increase the volume of exports became more urgent as Chilean leaders recognized the dangers of economic integration (that is, the danger of closely tying the Chilean economy to the economies of other nations) and the need for greater independence. Therefore the Chilean government turned to policies of import substitution industrialization and channeled its attentions toward spurring local production and domestic industrial growth. Import substitution policies, which had characterized Chilean economic policy before 1970, used the state to build national industry and infrastructure and to protect domestic industries through trade barriers. Allende's predecessor, Eduardo Frei Montalva, had heightened the role of the state in the national economy. For example, his government acquired the majority share in most of the nation's copper mines, a process he called "Chileanization." Popular Unity wanted to push these earlier initiatives to a new level.

12. Salvador Allende, "First Anniversary of the Popular Unity Government," in Cockcroft, *Salvador Allende Reader*, 116–125.

13. "The World: Prize for a Chilean Poet," *Time*, 1 November 1971, available at www.time.com/time/magazine/article/0,9171,905475,00.html.

14. Salvador Allende, "Letter about Pablo Neruda," in Cockcroft, *Salvador Allende Reader*, 64–65.

15. "¡El despelote! La más grandiosa recepción de la historia. ¡Todo Chile salió a la calle para aplaudir a Fidel y a Salvador!," *Clarín*, 11 November 1971, reprinted in Miguel González Pino and Arturo Fontaine Talavera, eds., *Los mil días de Allende*, 2 vols. (Santiago, Chile: Centro de Estudios Públicos, 1997), 2:1325; Manuel Rojas, "Señor don Fidel Castro," *Clarín*, 10 November 1971, reprinted in González Pino and Fontaine Talavera, *Los mil días de Allende*, 1:219–220.

16. Fernando Flores, interview by author, Viña del Mar, 30 July 2003.

17. Unless otherwise noted, all conversions in dollar values over time were made using the Consumer Price Index and the calculator at Samuel H. Williamson, "Six Ways to Compute the Relative Value of a U.S. Dollar Amount, 1790 to Present," *MeasuringWorth*, 2010, www.measuringworth.com/uscompare/ (accessed 6 January 2011).

18. José Valenzuela, letter to Stafford Beer, 22 October 1971, box 55, Stafford Beer Collection, Liverpool John Moores University, Liverpool, England. The first-class airfare was easily arranged because LAN was government-owned and Beer was employed as a government contractor. Beer said, "Now I traveled first class because this was a government operation [and LAN Chile was a state-run airline]. What else would you do? They weren't paying for me" (Beer interview).

19. Flores interview.

20. This list is not complete and I apologize for any omissions. It is understandable that those interviewed about these meetings could not remember the names of all who attended more than thirty years after the event. The individuals named here appeared in archival documents and were confirmed by Raúl Espejo.

21. Espejo remembered that he went to work with Beer even though he did not know much about Beer's work beyond what he had read in *Decision and Control*. "We felt that he was an important

man, that he was a man who had much to offer; that it was valuable that he had arrived; that it was good that he had accepted the invitation." Raúl Espejo, interview by author, 9 September 2006, Lincoln, U.K.

22. Stafford Beer, *Brain of the Firm: The Managerial Cybernetics of Organization*, 2nd ed. (New York: J. Wiley, 1981), 249.

23. Espejo interview.

24. After Schwember earned his Ph.D. in 1969 at the University of California–Berkeley, he returned to Chile to teach and met Flores. Both men became active in the university reform movement that was taking place on Chilean university campuses in the late 1960s, and both subsequently joined the MAPU. According to Schwember, the Chilean university reform (*reforma universitaria*) was inspired by the events that were taking place on campuses such as Berkeley in the United States and in France in the late 1960s. Schwember states, "In Chile [the university reform] took a very special form because the whole university system was reformed both from the top down and from the bottom up. They [the reforms] were very effective, and the Catholic University became a very socially aware institution. Ours was the university where the reformation was the most drastic, and we had a very charismatic leader, who was the president [rector] of the university. Somehow, for various reasons, I got involved in the process of transforming the university, and there I met Fernando Flores, who for a short while had been my student, and I also got more involved in politics." Herman Schwember, interview by author, Santiago, Chile, June 22, 2002.

25. Ibid.

26. Ibid.

27. Garretón also reported Beer's fascination with whiskey, cigars, and chocolate. It seems that these particular habits left quite an impression on people. Oscar Guillermo Garretón, interview by author, Santiago, Chile, 4 August 2003.

28. Beer interview.

29. Peter Winn, *Weavers of Revolution: The Yarur Workers and Chile's Road to Socialism* (New York: Oxford University Press, 1986), 142. Beer's notes do not show the increased value in real wages.

30. Sergio Bitar, *Chile: Experiment in Democracy*, trans. Sam Sherman (Philadelphia: Institute for the Study of Human Issues, 1986), 52.

31. Ibid., 45.

32. For example, Allende told Chilean workers on 1 May 1971: "to strengthen, broaden and consolidate the people's power means *winning the battle of production*." Allende, "International Workers Day Rally," in Cockcroft, *Salvador Allende Reader*, 78; emphasis in the original.

33. The history of CORFO has been well documented. See Luis Ortega Martínez, *Corporación de Fomento de la Producción: 50 años de realizaciones, 1939–1989* (Santiago, Chile: Universidad de Santiago Facultad de Humanidades Departamento de Historia, 1989).

34. Barbara Stallings, *Class Conflict and Economic Development in Chile, 1958–1973* (Stanford, Calif.: Stanford University Press, 1978), 131.

35. Stafford Beer, "Chile: First Visit Initial Notes," n.d., box 55, Beer Collection.

36. Stallings, *Class Conflict*, 132.

37. Winn, *Weavers of Revolution*, 228. According to Beer's notes, the government identified two hundred enterprises that it wanted to incorporate into the public sector. See Beer, "Chile: First Visit Initial Notes."

38. Stafford Beer, "Raul 10:XI:71" (Beer's handwritten notes), 11 November 1971, box 55, Beer Collection.

39. Juan Espinosa and Andrew Zimbalist define *co-management* as "a situation where joint decision-making authority is shared by worker and state representatives but either the former prevail or decision making is not conflictual." Juan Espinosa and Andrew Zimbalist, *Economic Democracy: Workers' Participation in Chilean Industry, 1970–1973* (New York: Academic Press, 1978), 6.

40. The government charged union leaders with implementing the measures outlined in the basic norms of participation, including setting up the new management structures and educating workers about their rights and responsibilities under the new system. However, the basic norms of participation also forbade union leaders from serving as worker representatives in the new system. As a result, some union leaders viewed the new management scheme as something that curbed union power and did not press for its implementation.

41. Julio Faúndez, *Marxism and Democracy in Chile: From 1932 to the Fall of Allende* (New Haven, Conn.: Yale University Press, 1998), 227.

42. Arturo Valenzuela, *The Breakdown of Democratic Regimes: Chile* (Baltimore: Johns Hopkins University Press, 1978), 66.

43. Ibid., 62.

44. Stafford Beer, consultants' presentation, 10 November 1971, box 55, Beer Collection.

45. Stafford Beer, "FF Exposition for Ministers," November 1971, box 65, Beer Collection.

46. This is what the government did in the textile sector, independent of Beer's advice.

47. Davis, *Last Two Years of Salvador Allende*, 23–26, 67–71.

48. Beer's shorthand notes state, "Signif[icant] enterprises have well-def[ined] hierarchies . . . metala[nguage] is in the banks, US Go [*sic*], US Govt!" (A metalanguage is a language that is used to describe the functioning of other languages.) Beer's notes recognize that the enterprises listed for expropriation by the Allende government were controlled by entities other than the Chilean government, in particular by lending organizations and the U.S. government. Beer, "FF Exposition for Ministers."

49. Flores argued that CORFO also needed to change its mentality from one of administration to one of control, shifting its primary focus from planning to implementation. This new stance

required CORFO to direct the path of Chilean socialism and move from advising to acting. Flores and Beer discussed whether Chilean government organizations suffered from overstability and whether not changing their manner of operation, including their organizational structure, would prevent Popular Unity from succeeding. Echoing the criticism that the Communists Party leveled against the interventors, Flores and Beer felt that the government had simply changed the names and party affiliations of those working in traditional organizational structures. Struggles among the political parties for choice positions further shifted attention away from national goals and blocked the government's ability to make social and economic changes. Beer, "Chile: First Visit Initial Notes"; Beer, "FF Exposition for Ministers."

50. Beer, "Chile: First Visit Initial Notes."

51. Notes on available ECOM computing resources, author unknown, 11 November 1971, box 55, Beer Collection.

52. IBM Chile, "Edición Especial de Aniversario, IBM 70 años en Chile," IBM Chile, Santiago, 1999. Buchanan, Jones, & Company acted as the agent for CTR machines in Chile from 1921 to 1929. In addition to tabulating machines, Chileans could purchase scales, time clocks, mechanical punches, reproducing punches, and vertical sorters; see "Hablan los precursores," *IBM Diálogo*, July 1987.

53. The "Frequently Asked Questions" document in the IBM Archives in New York says that the company opened its Santiago office in 1924. This date does not agree with the documentation provided by IBM Chile, which gives the date for the opening of the Santiago branch office as 1929; furthermore, IBM Chile celebrated its eightieth anniversary in April 2009.

54. "Hay una maquina Burroughs para cualquier negocio," *El Mercurio*, 12 October 1930.

55. U.S. Department of Commerce, *Foreign Commerce and Navigation of the United States* (Washington, D.C.: U.S. Government Printing Office, 1923–1946). German companies also tried to penetrate the Chilean office machinery market, building on their previous successes in exporting telegraph machines and other technological goods. However, World War I had dramatically changed the landscape of Chile's international relationships and frustrated these efforts. The outbreak of the war interrupted Chile's long-standing ties with Germany and Britain and enabled the United States to dominate Chilean trade markets. In 1918 U.S. trade composed more than 50 percent of all Chilean foreign commerce. By 1930 the United States accounted for 70 percent of all Chilean foreign investment and dominated the largest copper mines, which produced Chile's biggest export. Historians of Latin America have referred to this shift from European to U.S. economic dominance in the region as a process of "Americanization" that opened the door to U.S. technical expertise, capital, machinery, and cultural influence. In this context German office machine companies could not build the same client base as their U.S. counterparts. By the 1950s Chilean companies had incorporated IBM into their culture, as evidenced by the regular creation of "Hollerith departments," named after the Hollerith tabulating machines IBM sold. James Cortada reports that German companies eventually abandoned the office machine industry in favor of developing their expertise in areas such as automobile manufacture. James Cortada, *Before the Computer: IBM, NCR, Burroughs, and Remington Rand and the Industry They Created, 1865–1956* (Princeton, N.J.: Princeton University Press, 2000).

56. This argument is made in greater depth in my dissertation. See Jessica Eden Miller Medina, "The State Machine: Politics, Ideology, and Computation in Chile, 1964–1973" (Ph.D. diss., Massachusetts Institute of Technology, 2005). See also Eden Medina, "Big Blue in the Bottomless Pit: The Early Years of IBM Chile," *IEEE Annals of the History of Computing* 30, no. 4 (2008): 26–41.

57. On state expansion and the rise of the middle class in twentieth-century Chile, see Patrick Barr-Melej, *Reforming Chile: Cultural Politics, Nationalism, and the Rise of the Middle Class* (Chapel Hill: University of North Carolina Press, 2001); Karin Alejandra Rosemblatt, *Gendered Compromises: Political Cultures and the State in Chile, 1920–1950* (Chapel Hill: University of North Carolina Press, 2000); Patricio Silva, *In the Name of Reason: Technocrats and Politics in Chile* (University Park: Pennsylvania State University Press, 2008); and Adolfo Ibañez Santa María, "Los 'ismos' y la redefinición del Estado: Tecnicismo, planificación y estatismo en Chile, 1920–1940," *Atenea* no. 474 (1996): 23–50.

58. "Hablan los precursores."

59. The transition from tabulating machinery to computing machinery is actually more gradual than this sentence implies. During the 1950s IBM began introducing electronics and electronic programmability into its electromechanical tabulating equipment. For this reason Steven Usselman notes that "computers . . . called for many of the same qualities as the older technology." Steven Usselman, "IBM and Its Imitators: Organizational Capabilities and the Emergence of the International Computer Industry," *Business and Economic History* 22 (1993): 8–9. IBM unveiled the 1401 model in 1959, but it did not arrive in Chile for three more years.

60. "System/360 Announcement," 7 April 1964, IBM Archives, www-03.ibm.com/ibm/history/exhibits/mainframe/mainframe_PR360.html.

61. IBM helped prepare the voter registration lists.

62. President John F. Kennedy started the Alliance for Progress in 1962 with the ostensibly foremost goal of improving economic and social conditions for Latin Americans and the secondary, but more important, goal of curbing the spread of communism in the region. See Albert L. Michaels, "The Alliance for Progress and Chile's 'Revolution in Liberty,' 1964–1970," *Journal of Interamerican Studies and World Affairs* 18, no. 1 (1976): 74–99.

63. Organization and methods, or O&M, was a British administrative science that applied scientific techniques to improve the efficiency of clerical work. See Jon Agar, *The Government Machine: A Revolutionary History of the Computer* (Cambridge, Mass.: MIT Press, 2003).

64. For example, Frei's finance minister, Sergio Molina, theorized that "the science of informatics with its technological element, the electronic computer, has come to revolutionize administrative techniques." Sergio Molina Silva, *El proceso de cambio en Chile: La experiencia 1965–1970*, Textos del Instituto Latinoamericano de Planificación Económica y Social (Santiago, Chile: Editorial Universitaria, 1972), 177.

65. The System/360 was a new family of computers with compatible software and peripheral components.

66. "System/360 Announcement."

67. Tom Wise, "IBM's $5 Billion Gamble," *Fortune,* September 1966, 118–123.

68. Despite IBM's dominant position in the Chilean market, the first electronic computer at the University of Chile was not an IBM machine. The Department of Mathematics purchased a German-made Standard Electric ER-Lorenz in 1959.

69. EMCO, "Reseña Empresa de Servicio de Computación Ltda.," 1970, 1, in the personal files of Italo Bozzi, Santiago, Chile.

70. This was logical since France provided technical support and foreign aid to modernize Chilean public administration. France was also the center for IBM World Trade operations outside New York.

71. Eduardo Frei Montalva, "Discurso del Presidente Frei en inauguración computador electrónico," 1969, Oficina de Difusión y Cultura de la Presidencia de la República, Santiago, Chile.

72. EMCO, *Seminario sobre sistemas de información en el gobierno* (Santiago, Chile: EMCO with the collaboration of the United Nations Development Program, 1969), 6.

73. Ibid.

74. United Nations Department of Economic and Social Affairs, *The Application of Computer Technology for Development* (New York: United Nations, 1971), 15. A subsequent U.N. publication in 1973 asserted that Chile had a total of thirty-six computers in 1969; see United Nations Department of Economic and Social Affairs, *The Application of Computer Technology for Development: Second Report of the Secretary General* (New York: United Nations, 1973).

75. Ramón C. Barquín, "Computation in Latin America," *Datamation* 20, no. 3 (1974).

76. The name change largely stemmed from a trademark dispute: the Enterprise for Mechanical Construction Equipment claimed it had long owned the EMCO acronym. However, the official newspaper of the Chilean government, *La Nación,* wrote that the name change represented "the fact that the activities of this enterprise, and those that it will undertake in the future, go beyond the traditional limits of a computer service enterprise . . . this is an enterprise whose objectives are clearly national . . . and that will operate throughout the country." Although the original motivation for the name change was clearly practical, it was presented publicly as part of the increased scope and national importance of the enterprise. Italo Bozzi, "Cambio de Razón Social," 1970, in the personal files of Italo Bozzi; "ECOM: Nuevo nombre para una empresa que surge," *La Nacion,* 7 January 1971.

77. CINTEFOR-INACAP, "Empresa de Servicio de Computación," in *Curso de capacitación en documentación sobre formación profesional* (Santiago, Chile, 1970).

78. Molina Silva, *El proceso de cambio en Chile,* 177.

79. *Sexto mensaje del Presidente de la República de Chile don Eduardo Frei Montalva al inaugurar el periodo de sesiones ordinarias del Congreso Nacional, 21 May 1970* (Santiago, Chile: Departamento

de Publicaciones de la Presidencia de la Republica, 1970). Computer use in the Finance Ministry increased from 700 hours per month in 1964 to 1,260 hours per month in 1970.

80. Military cyberneticians encountered strong resistance from the Soviet state bureaucracy—the bureaucrats feared that the introduction of computer technology would leave them unemployed. The proposed computer system also left no room for the ideological leadership of the Communist Party and motivated at least one official within the Chief Political Directorate of the Army to ask, "Where is the leading role of the Party in your [computing] machine?" Slava Gerovitch, *From Newspeak to Cyberspeak: A History of Soviet Cybernetics* (Cambridge, Mass.: MIT Press, 2002), 267.

81. Slava Gerovitch, "Internyet: Why the Soviet Union Did Not Build a Nationwide Computer Network," *History and Technology* 24, no. 4 (2008).

82. Janet Abbate, *Inventing the Internet* (Cambridge, Mass.: MIT Press, 1999), 111.

83. See Margaret Power, "Modernity and Technology in Chile: The First National Congress of Scientists," *Latin American Studies Association*, Las Vegas, 7–9 October 2004.

84. Nigel Hawkes, "Chile: Planning for Science Faces Obstacles Old and New," *Science* 174, no. 4015 (1971): 1217.

85. For more on university reform, see Carlos Huneeus, *La reforma universitaria en la Universidad de Chile* (Santiago, Chile: CPU, 1973); Carlos Huneeus, *La reforma universitaria: Veinte años después*, 1st ed. (Santiago, Chile: CPU, 1988); Manuel Antonio Garretón, "Universidad política en los procesos de transformación y reservación en Chile, 1967–1977," *Estudios Sociales*, no. 26 (1980).

86. See Fernando Henrique Cardoso and Enzo Faletto, *Dependencia y desarrollo en América Latina* (Lima: Instituto de Estudios Peruanos, 1967).

87. José Valenzuela, "Apuntes sobre la política de acción del INTEC," *INTEC* 1 (1971): 11.

88. INTEC, "Introducción a una nueva revista," *INTEC*, December 1971.

89. Hawkes, "Chile: Planning for Science," 1217.

90. CONICYT, *Indicadores científicos y tecnológicos 1993* (Santiago, Chile: CONICYT, 1994).

91. Augusto Salinas Araya, *Ciencia, estado y revolución* (Santiago, Chile: Ediciones Universidad Finis Terrae, 1994), 264–265.

92. Flores interview.

Chapter 3

1. Stafford Beer, "Cybernetic Notes on the Effective Organization of the State with Particular Reference to Industrial Control," November 1971, box 64, Beer Collection, emphases in original.

2. Beer developed this idea further in his book *The Heart of the Enterprise* (New York: Wiley, 1979), published after the Chilean experience.

3. Stafford Beer, "Project Cyberstride," November 1971, box 56, Beer Collection. Raúl Espejo explains, "This deadline, as many others, was related to Stafford's visits to Chile. He wanted to have results at the time of each of these visits" (e-mail to author, 16 July 2008).

4. Fernando Flores, interview by author, Viña del Mar, 30 July 2003. The emphasis Beer placed on action and adaptation also caused him to emphasize real-time communication over large-scale information processing. Espejo shared the following anecdote: "For [Beer's] first visit, I prepared a document that described a process for developing an information system for industrial management. Its central part was a flow diagram that described a process that was more systematic than systemic with different points of decision. If the decision was affirmative it went to this side, if it was negative it went to the other side, with logical steps to complete the process. I passed it to Stafford. He read it without suggesting changes, but he commented that there were more powerful ways to do the same thing. From this moment on, he tried to make me think in terms of communications rather than in terms of information. More than [building] a system of information, it was necessary to develop communication channels. For me, this was an important part of the learning process during [Beer's] first visit." Raúl Espejo, interview by author, 9 September 2006, Lincoln, U.K.

5. Notes on Chilean computer resources, author unknown, 11 November 1971, box 55, Beer Collection.

6. Telex machines transmitted messages quickly (by the standards of the time), but the response time depended on when the recipient received the message and decided to answer. Ann Zammit, a British economist who worked in Chile with many high-ranking members of the Allende government, recalled: "When I was living in Chile, apart from telephone, which most people didn't have (nor did I), telex was the other form of rapid communication, nationally and internationally. But it was only available in a few places and mighty inefficient: you would sit there and tap something out and then you'd have to wait for hours to get some kind of response, if you were lucky." Ann Zammit, telephone interview by author, 27 January 2010.

Readers should note that Beer was not the first to propose creating a telex network for close to real-time control. For example, in 1961 the U.S. space program created a global communications network consisting of telex machines and radio voice links. This network allowed those on the ground to track the space capsule flying overhead and communicate with mission control. A description of this system appears in Gene Kranz's memoir, *Failure Is Not an Option: Mission Control to Apollo 13 and Beyond* (New York: Simon and Schuster, 2000).

7. Beer, "Project Cyberstride."

8. Ibid.

9. Stafford Beer, "Cyberstride: Preparations," January 1972, box 57, Beer Collection

10. John Law, "Technology and Heterogeneous Engineering: The Case of Portuguese Expansion," in Wiebe Bijker, Thomas Hughes, and Trevor Pinch, eds., *The Social Construction of Technological Systems: New Directions in the Sociology and History of Technology* (Cambridge, Mass: MIT Press, 1989).

11. Beer, "Project Cyberstride."

12. Stafford Beer, *Brain of the Firm: The Managerial Cybernetics of Organization*, 2nd ed. (New York: J. Wiley, 1981), 257.

13. Beer calculated that he had about four weeks to devote to the project between November and March.

14. Beer, *Brain of the Firm*, 257.

15. Stafford Beer, interview by author, 15–16 March 2001, Toronto, Canada.

16. Quoted in Beer, *Brain of the Firm*, 257.

17. Ibid., 258. This account draws on Beer's account in *Brain of the Firm*, my 2001 interview with Beer, and my interview with Roberto Cañete, Viña del Mar, Chile, 16 January 2003.

18. In his 1979 book *Heart of the Enterprise*, Beer used his conversation with Allende, and Allende's reference to "el pueblo," to show that "System Five includes many people. . . . In many firms, this group includes representatives of management, of shareholders, of investors. Maybe, in the future, it will include trade unionists—or better still, simply workers" (264).

19. Herman Schwember, interview by author, 22 June 2002, Santiago, Chile.

20. Described in Margaret Power, *Right-Wing Women in Chile: Feminine Power and the Struggle against Allende* (University Park: Pennsylvania State University Press, 2002), 153. According to Stefan de Vylder, the marchers overstated the shortage of food. Only the supply of beef could not meet demand. De Vylder notes that "food became short not because there was less available than before but because it was so cheap that the great majority of the Chilean people could now afford to eat much better than ever before, a circumstance which disturbed many upper-class Chileans, who were used to eating beef seven days a week." Stefan de Vylder, *Allende's Chile: The Political Economy of the Rise and Fall of the Unidad Popular* (New York: Cambridge University Press, 1976), 94.

21. Power, *Right-Wing Women*, 158.

22. Quoted in Nathaniel Davis, *The Last Two Years of Salvador Allende* (Ithaca, N.Y.: Cornell University Press, 1985), 44.

23. Unless otherwise noted, all conversions in dollar values over time were made using the Consumer Price Index and the calculator at Samuel H. Williamson, "Six Ways to Compute the Relative Value of a U.S. Dollar Amount, 1790 to Present," *MeasuringWorth*, 2010, www.measuringworth. com/uscompare/. All conversions between U.K. pounds and U.S. dollars were made using the Consumer Price Index and the calculator at Lawrence H. Officer and Samuel H. Williamson, "Computing 'Real Value' over Time with a Conversion Between U.K. Pounds and U.S. Dollars, 1830 to Present," *MeasuringWorth*, 2009, www.measuringworth.com/exchange/.

24. Fernando Flores, telex to Stafford Beer, 21 December 1971, box 66, Beer Collection.

25. Arthur Andersen and Company received £640 from the Chilean government to put together a proposal ($10,400 in 2009 dollars). Beer, "Cyberstride: Preparations."

26. Computer code is robust if it continues to function regardless of abnormalities in the input data. When all errors have been removed from a piece of software code, and it functions as intended, it is considered bug free.

27. Stafford Beer, telex to Fernando Flores, 13 January 1972, box 66, Beer Collection.

28. Ibid.

29. Beer telexed Flores, "Please reply urgently [about the contract with Arthur Andersen], since work has been going on since 10 January at my risk." Stafford Beer, telex to Fernando Flores, 18 January 1972, box 66, Beer Collection.

30. Of the £19,000, £17,500 went to pay consultant fees and the remaining £1,500 was paid for computer time. Beer, "Cyberstride: Preparations."

31. Fernando Flores, telex to Stafford Beer, 20 January 1972, box 66, Beer Collection.

32. Beer wanted the software to be sufficiently general that it could operate at any level of recursion specified by the model, from the factory floor to the Ministry of Economics.

33. According to its authors, the approach could "recognize, and respond appropriately to, transient errors and sudden changes of trend and slope." P. J. Harrison and C. R. Stevens, "A Bayesian Approach to Short-Term Forecasting," *Operational Research Quarterly* 22, no. 4 (1971): 341.

34. Beer, "Cyberstride: Preparations." Later this same feature would help the team respond to charges that it was building an overly centralized system to control Chilean workers.

35. The simulator would also identify the "trapped states" of the economy, the factors outside Chile that could stall the revolution and prevent change. Such factors, such as foreign exchange rates, could limit the efficacy of land reform programs and nationalization strategies. The simulator could also identify new ways for achieving the changes outlined in the UP platform. Beer wrote: "Cybernetic considerations certainly suggest that a new structure, involving new information pathways and the harnessing of motivational factors, will be needed to achieve Chile's radical political goals. The simulator will be the government's experimental laboratory." "Cyberstride: Preparations."

36. Ibid.

37. The Semi-Automatic Ground Environment (SAGE) was a computerized national air defense system developed at MIT with the assistance of IBM. The system networked twenty-three Direction Centers across the United States, each with an IBM AN/FSQ-7 computer that collected data from about one hundred sources such as ground-, sea-, and air-based radar systems. Air force personnel used the system to watch for bomber aircraft in the area of their Direction Center. The system, which went online in 1963, cost the U.S. government an estimated $8 billion. However, the development of intercontinental ballistic missiles quickly made the system less useful than the government hoped. According to Campbell-Kelly and Aspray, "The real contribution of SAGE was thus not to military defense, but through technological spin-off to civilian computing," including work by firms such as IBM, Burroughs, and Bell Laboratories. Martin Campbell-Kelly and

William Aspray, *Computer: A History of the Information Machine*, 2nd ed. (Boulder, Colo.: Westview, 2004), 150–151.

38. For more on Forrester and his work on system dynamics, see Fernando Elichirigoity, *Planet Management: Limits to Growth, Computer Simulation, and the Emergence of Global Spaces* (Evanston, Ill.: Northwestern University Press, 1999).

39. Jay Forrester, *Urban Dynamics* (Cambridge, Mass.: MIT Press, 1969), 115.

40. Jay Forrester's approach to World Dynamics formed the methodological backbone for the popular 1972 book *Limits to Growth*, ten million copies of which were sold around the world. It argued that "if the present growth trends in world population, industrialization, pollution, food production, and resource depletion continue unchallenged, the limits to growth on this planet will be reached sometime in the next one hundred years." Donella H. Meadows and Club of Rome, *The Limits to Growth: A Report for the Club of Rome's Project on the Predicament of Mankind* (New York: Universe Books, 1972), 24. The book was published with much fanfare but also generated substantial criticism. Critics pointed to a lack of evidence that the data used in the *Limits to Growth* study represented reality.

41. Elichirigoity, *Planet Management*, 97.

42. Stafford Beer, "Fanfare for Effective Freedom: Cybernetic Praxis in Government," Third Richard Goodman Memorial Lecture, Brighton Polytechnic, Brighton, U.K., 14 February 1973.

43. Anderton and Gilligan could secure computer time only at night, which further limited the amount of work they could accomplish by March. Beer, "Cyberstride: Preparations."

44. Ibid.

45. Roberto Cañete, letters to Stafford Beer, 13 and 28 January 1972, box 66, Beer Collection.

46. Roberto Cañete, letter to Stafford Beer, 19 January 1972, box 66, Beer Collection.

47. Members of the Christian Democratic Party charged the minister of the interior with "serious legal and constitutional infractions," such as arbitrary detentions and permitting the formation of illegal armed groups. See "Por graves infracciones constitucionales y legales DC acusa a ministro Toha," *El Mercurio*, 22 December 1971, reprinted in Miguel González Pino and Arturo Fontaine Talavera, eds., *Los mil días de Allende*, 2 vols. (Santiago, Chile: Centro de Estudios Públicos, 1997), 1:260–261.

48. "Declaración de la UP pide fin de prácticas sectarias," *El Mercurio*, 8 February 1972, reprinted in González Pino and Fontaine Talavera, *Los mil días de Allende*, 1:283–284.

49. Julio Faúndez, *Marxism and Democracy in Chile: From 1932 to the Fall of Allende* (New Haven, Conn.: Yale University Press, 1988), 224–225.

50. "Allende debe ponerse guantes de boxeo," *La Tercera de la Hora*, 3 February 1972, in González Pino and Fontaine Talavera, *Los mil días de Allende*, 1:282–283.

51. Faúndez, *Marxism and Democracy in Chile*, 225–226.

52. De Vylder, *Allende's Chile*, 89.

53. This logic of printing money to cover expenses, characteristic of structuralist economics, stressed the importance of winning the battle of production and supported initiatives to improve industrial management such as Cyberstride.

54. Among the most visible of these new additions were Tomás Kohn, Fernando Améstica, and Mario Grandi.

55. Cañete to Beer, 28 January 1972.

56. Cañete reports that they "were working on some kind of device that will allow us to make full use of their installations by producing a direct line to the National Post Office. This little gimmick has made things easier and a considerable number of enterprises have integrated the network without much effort and almost without cost." Cañete to Beer, 28 January 1972.

57. Ibid.

58. Stafford Beer, telex to Ron Anderton, 21 March 1972, box 66, Beer Collection.

59. These six individuals included three programmers, one systems analyst, one teleprocessor, and Benadof. At this point, all six worked under Hernán Santa María, who was in charge of all data processing for the project.

60. Ron Anderton, "CHECO1: A Preliminary Account of Principles and Operation," March 1972, box 58, Beer Collection.

61. Stafford Beer, "CHECO 1," 20 March 1972, box 62, Beer Collection.

62. Anderton, "CHECO1."

63. That said, the model did gloss over levels of complexity that could have significant political ramifications to the UP economic program. In his March report Anderton suggested changing the category of "consumer goods" to "luxury consumer goods" and "necessary consumer goods." However, deciding what constituted a luxury or a necessity varied significantly across the social strata. In a September 1972 survey, the magazine *Ercilla* asked upper-, middle-, and lower-class Chileans whether it was easy or difficult to buy essential products for their home. Only 1 percent of upper-class Chileans responded that it was easy, whereas 75 percent of lower-class Chileans said that it was. There are two main reasons for this difference. In some cases, factories deliberately made certain consumer goods, such as sheets, available to those who had never had them previously. However, members of different classes also had radically different perceptions about what they considered essential and had had different abilities to access these goods in the past. This must account for a significant part of the disparity noted in the survey. Survey cited in Arturo Valenzuela, *The Breakdown of Democratic Regimes: Chile* (Baltimore: Johns Hopkins University Press, 1978), 59.

64. Beer to Anderton, 21 March 1972.

65. Beer's cybernetics emphasized holism rather than reductionism. The use of synergy is a logical extension of this idea. However, it was not until the team met its first deadline in March that Beer

felt compelled to describe the system as such. "Following the success of the first plan," Beer wrote, "we could now think in terms of putting together the basic tools thereby created in the cause of cybernetic synergy." Beer, *Brain of the Firm*, 260.

66. It consisted of Raúl Espejo, Roberto Cañete, Humberto Gabella, and Hernán Santa María.

67. Stafford Beer, "Project Cybersyn," March 1972, box 60, Beer Collection.

68. Ibid.

69. Ibid.

70. In fact, radio receivers were three times more common than television sets. According to the Economic Commission for Latin America, Chile had 500,000 functioning television sets in 1972 and 1.5 million radios. Economic Commission for Latin America, *Statistical Yearbook for Latin America* (New York: United Nations, 1978).

71. Stafford Beer, "Project Cyberfolk," March 1972, box 61, Beer Collection.

72. From the outset of Allende's campaign, Popular Unity debated dissolving Congress to form a "People's Assembly." Beer wondered how cybernetic thinking and modern technology might make such a governing body more effective. These musings grew into Project Cyberfolk.

73. Beer, "Project Cyberfolk."

74. Stafford Beer, notes in green folder, n.d., box 65, Beer Collection. Beer also proposed using children for some of these experiments, although he did not elaborate why.

75. Lawrence Lessig, *Code: And Other Laws of Cyberspace* (New York: Basic Books, 1999); Langdon Winner, "Do Artifacts Have Politics?" in *The Whale and the Reactor: A Search for Limits in an Age of High Technology* (Chicago: University of Chicago Press, 1986); and Batya Friedman, ed., *Human Values and the Design of Computer Technology* (New York: Cambridge University Press and CSLI, Stanford University, 1997).

76. By giving everyone access to the same information at the same time, algedonic meters differed from the computerized "instant response" technique that focus groups use to monitor voter reactions to political speeches, debates, or advertisements second-by-second in real time.

77. Beer, *Brain of the Firm*, 285.

78. At CEREN Beer presented Cyberfolk to the sociologists Manuel Garretón (the brother of Oscar Guillermo Garretón), Franz Hinkelammert, and perhaps others. Stafford Beer, "Meeting at CEREN," 22 March 1972, box 62, Beer Collection.

79. Ibid.

80. Arguably this is a good thing. The parallel between Project Cyberfolk and the CNN meters suggests an interesting pitfall of the Cyberfolk technology: if politicians had access to viewer feedback in real time, they could adapt their message—but this would not mean that politicians would actually change their actions or beliefs in ways that better served the people.

81. Stafford Beer, "The Next Phase," 23 March 1972, box 60, Beer Collection.

82. E. J. Gerrity, memo to H. S. Geenan, 29 September 1970, cited in International Telephone and Telegraph Corporation and Bertrand Russell Peace Foundation, *Subversion in Chile: A Case Study in U.S. Corporate Intrigue in the Third World* (Nottingham, U.K.: Bertrand Russell Peace Foundation, 1972), 39–41.

Chapter 4

1. The rightist newspaper *El Mercurio* noted that these were "practically all of the most serious economic problems that a country can face, with the exception of unemployment," thus trivializing the success of Allende's programs to lower unemployment through labor-intensive projects and increased hiring in state-owned factories. Chilean unemployment rates had dropped from 6.3 percent in 1970 to 3.5 percent in 1972 and would continue to fall in 1973 to the lowest levels ever recorded. This drop in unemployment in part stemmed from the tremendous growth in the number of employees in Chilean government agencies, state-owned factories, and the universities. For example, the State Development Corporation swelled from six hundred to eight thousand employees during the Allende period. See "No puede ser peor el estado económico del país," *El Mercurio*, 1 April 1972, reprinted in Miguel González Pino and Arturo Fontaine Talavera, eds., *Los mil días de Allende*, 2 vols. (Santiago, Chile: Centro de Estudios Públicos, 1997), 1:329–331; Barbara Stallings, *Class Conflict and Economic Development in Chile, 1958–1973* (Stanford, Calif.: Stanford University Press, 1978), 173; and Augusto Salinas Araya, *Ciencia, estado y revolución* (Santiago, Chile: Ediciones Universidad Finis Terrae, 1994), 265. Chile began compiling unemployment statistics in 1956.

2. Julio Faúndez, *Marxism and Democracy in Chile: From 1932 to the Fall of Allende* (New Haven, Conn.: Yale University Press, 1988), 229.

3. Roberto Cañete, letter to Stafford Beer, 15 June 1972, box 66, Stafford Beer Collection, Liverpool John Moores University, Liverpool, U.K.

4. He attended the conference from 5 to 8 May 1972. "NASA brought up two of everybody. Two astronauts . . . two science fiction writers . . . and two cyberneticians. I was one, the other was Marv Minsky," Beer said. He believed that the U.S. government stopped his collaboration with NASA because of his involvement in Chile. Stafford Beer, interview by author, 15–16 March 2001, Toronto.

5. Stafford Beer, telex to Fernando Flores, n.d., box 66, Beer Collection. Beer added that "there are some [commitments] which I must maintain to preserve continuity—otherwise I shall have no income from the moment my engagement in Chile ends."

6. Beer to Flores.

7. In early May the cybernetician sent Cañete a telex that reads, "Experiencing great embarrassment re cancellations made to effect Chilean visits. Disappointed that no letter to show" (Stafford Beer, telex to Roberto Cañete, 4 May 1972, box 66, Beer Collection). Beer's increased involvement pleased Allende and Pedro Vuskovic, the minister of the economy, or at least this is what Beer

was told. A telex to Beer from Flores, Espejo, and Cañete reads, "Allende and Vuskovic are under notice of your possible coming and they are very happy about it." Fernando Flores, Raúl Espejo, and Roberto Cañete, telex to Stafford Beer, n.d., box 66, Beer Collection. Flores later acknowledged that he had drafted the letter from Allende to Beer. Although Allende and Vuskovic both knew about Project Cybersyn, they were also struggling to manage a growing number of political and economic upheavals that threatened the administration's ability to lead and even survive. Project Cybersyn was a marginal endeavor by comparison, and Beer's increased involvement was probably not a priority for either leader in light of other pressing issues. Flores was and continued to be the central political force behind the project. His connections secured a greater role for Beer, and Beer's involvement helped the Chilean team make rapid progress on Cybersyn.

8. Isaquino Benadof, interview by author, 10 April 2002, Santiago, Chile.

9. Ibid.

10. Fernando Flores, interview by author, 30 July 2003, Viña del Mar, Chile.

11. Magic realism is "a literary genre or style associated esp. with Latin America that incorporates fantastic or mythical elements into otherwise realistic fiction." *Merriam-Webster's Collegiate Dictionary*, 11th ed. (Springfield, Mass.: Merriam-Webster, 2003).

12. Stafford Beer, "Cybersyn: The New Version," 22 May 1972, personal files of Roberto Cañete.

13. Sonia Mordojovich, interview by author, 16 July 2002, Santiago, Chile. Mordojovich said she was one of two women who graduated her year in business administration in a class of more than eighty men. She was also the only woman on the core Cybersyn team.

14. Beer, "Cybersyn: The New Version."

15. Salvador Allende, "Discurso pronunciado por el presidente de la República de Chile, Salvador Allende Gossens, en la Ceremonia inaugural de la UNCTAD III," in González Pino and Fontaine Talavera, *Los mil días de Allende*, 2:1108–1120.

16. G. E. Hemmings, "Memorandum of Status of the Cyberstride System," n.d. (7–12 May 1972), box 59, Beer Collection.

17. Ibid.

18. Benadof interview.

19. David Kaye, letter to Stafford Beer, 1 August 1972, box 59, Beer Collection.

20. Stafford Beer, letter to David Kaye, 3 August 1972, box 59, Beer Collection.

21. Ibid.

22. In a telex dated 14 April 1972, Espejo tells Beer that the Chileans want a copy of the DYNAMO II compiler and a user's manual because "we are interested in developing our own simulation language for the Chilean economic characteristics." Raúl Espejo, telex to Stafford Beer, 14 April 1972, box 66, Beer Collection.

23. Ron Anderton, letter to Stafford Beer, 26 June 1972, box 58, Beer Collection.

24. Mario Grandi, "CHECO Progress Report," June 1972, box 56, Beer Collection.

25. CHECO team, "Background on the Chilean Economic Structure," n.d., box 63, Beer Collection. Although this document is not dated, references to this document found in other archival documents suggest that it was written in August 1972.

26. Checo Team, "Simulation Model of the Chilean Economy," September 1972, box 58, Beer Collection.

27. Ron Anderton, letter to the CHECO team, 24 August 1972, box 58, Beer Collection.

28. Arturo Valenzuela, *The Breakdown of Democratic Regimes: Chile* (Baltimore: Johns Hopkins University Press, 1978), 57.

29. U.S. Senate, *Covert Action in Chile, 1964–1973: Staff Report of the Select Committee to Study Governmental Operation with Respect to Intelligence Activities*, 94th Cong., 1st sess., 1975, S. Rep. 63-372, 182; Valenzuela, *The Breakdown of Democratic Regimes: Chile*, 57.

30. Checo Team, "Simulation Model of the Chilean Economy."

31. Mario Grandi contrasted CHECO with the World Dynamics models built by Jay Forrester in the 1970s: "The World Dynamics model that was developed for the Club of Rome . . . had a long-term horizon and dealt with macro-variables that were dynamically slow. It was possible to make a reasonable hypothesis on the laws of control . . . the parameters external to the model, the value of the constants, and the characteristics of the delays." In contrast, with CHECO, "Our time horizon was short-term (3-5 years), the variables were extraordinarily dynamic, and many of the parameters and laws of regulation were unknown or excessively dynamic." He concluded that "as a mathematical model, CHECO was a failure." Mario Grandi, e-mail to author, 30 July 2010.

32. Stafford Beer, *Brain of the Firm: The Managerial Cybernetics of Organization*, 2nd ed. (New York: J. Wiley, 1981), 267.

33. Luis Ortega Martínez, *Corporación de Fomento de la Producción: 50 años de realizaciones, 1939–1989* (Santiago, Chile: Universidad de Santiago Facultad de Humanidades Departamento de Historia, 1989), 233–234; Hugo Palmarola Sagredo, "Productos y socialismo: Diseño industrial estatal en Chile," in Claudio Rolle, ed., *1973: La vida cotidiana de un año crucial* (Santiago, Chile: Editorial Planeta, 2003), 225–296. The University of Chile similarly supported the application of technological resources to the creation of goods for mass consumption; see *Hacia una política de desarrollo científico y tecnológico para Chile* (Santiago, Chile: Universidad de Chile Rectoría, 1972), 15.

34. In 1971 Minister of the Economy Pedro Vuskovic ordered the manufacture of a utility vehicle akin to the jeep that would cost less than $250 to produce. The Yagán was Citroën's response. Automobiles were among the most highly politicized technologies of the UP era. Although the Popular Unity program banned government workers from using automobiles for private use, government workers received priority in the distribution of new cars produced by Chilean factories, which sparked charges of favoritism. In 1971 CORFO created the Automotive Commission in an effort to coordinate the distribution of Chile's limited automobile supply in the face of rising

demand and to bring Chilean automobile production in line with the goals of the UP. Among the core objectives was the production of utility vehicles and automobiles for mass consumption. *Primer mensaje del Presidente Allende ante el Congreso Pleno, 21 de Mayo de 1971* (Santiago, Chile: Departamento de Publicaciones de la Presidencia de la República, 1971), 119.

35. Interview of Cristián Lyon, "Creando El Yagán," 2003, formerly available at the Web site of Corporación de Televisión de la Pontificia Universidad Católica de Chile, now defunct.

36. CORFO controlled 51 percent of the company, while RCA maintained the minority share of 49 percent. CORFO, "Comité de las Industrias Eléctricas y Electrónicas," *CORFO en el gobierno de la Unidad Popular*, 4 November 1971, Santiago, Chile.

37. CORFO Relaciones Públicas, "Rol de CORFO en los propósitos de cambios," *CORFO en el gobierno de la Unidad Popular*, 4 November 1971.

38. Nigel Hawkes, "Chile: Trying to Cultivate a Small Base of Technical Excellence," *Science* 174, no. 4016 (1971): 174.

39. Silvia Fernández, "The Origins of Design Education in Latin America: From the Hfg in Ulm to Globalization," *Design Issues* 22, no. 1 (2005): 10.

40. Max Bill made this statement on 5 July 1954 to commemorate the first phase of construction of the Ulm School. "History: From the Coffee Cup to the Housing Estate," *Hfg Archiv Ulm*, www.hfg-archiv.ulm.de/english/the_hfg_ulm/history_4.html.

41. Bonsiepe said, "Under the direction of Tomás Maldonado, I designed a complete pictogram system in analogy with language, differentiating pictograms for 'verbs,' 'adjectives,' and 'nouns' that could be combined for the large control panel. In 1960 we didn't have the technical term *interface,* much less *human-user interface.*" Gui Bonsiepe, interview by author, 21 May 2008, La Plata, Argentina.

42. Although Bonsiepe completed the curriculum, it was never implemented.

43. Bonsiepe interview.

44. Bonsiepe signed a one-year contract initially, which he subsequently extended until 1970.

45. There are multiple readings of why the Ulm School closed. Some historical analyses cite internal conflicts and financial difficulties as the main reasons. Bonsiepe also credits political conflicts between the school and "conservative government circles" as leading to the closure of the institution: "For the conservative environment the school was too irritating because it did not maintain the silence of the cemetery that is so highly cherished by the forces of the status quo. The fact that members of the school organized a protest march against the war in Vietnam did not fare well with the population in Ulm." Gui Bonsiepe, e-mail to author, 19 August 2010.

46. Chilean universities began offering courses in design as early as 1966, the first at the University of Chile in Valparaíso. Fernando Shultz said that he did not know about the course offerings in Valparaíso when he was deciding where to study. Fernando Shultz, interview by author, 9–10 September 2008, Mexico City, Mexico.

47. Ibid.

48. The Department of Design was an interdisciplinary endeavor from the outset. Most professors were from the Faculty of Fine Arts and the Faculty of Architecture, two campuses located in different parts of the city. Moreover, the department depended administratively on the Faculty of Engineering, located in yet another part of the city. Since the university couldn't find a way to bring the department under the control of a single faculty, "they put us there like an island," Shultz said. "This gave us a certain internal autonomy." Shultz interview.

49. Carmen (Pepa) Foncea, interview by author, 25 July 2006, Santiago, Chile. However, this is not the whole story. Although Foncea remembered that the graphic design students at the Catholic University were predominately female, the students in graphic design at the University of Chile were predominately male. Understanding the gender dynamics present in Chilean design education in the late 1960s and early 1970s is beyond the scope of this book and warrants greater analysis.

50. Bonsiepe interview.

51. Ibid.

52. Foncea interview.

53. Bonsiepe interview.

54. Gui Bonsiepe, memo to Stafford Beer, "Sketches for the Op-Room," 21 April 1972, box 62, Beer Collection; INTEC, "Sala de operaciones anteproyecto," April 1972, box 62, Beer Collection.

55. Shultz interview.

56. Stafford Beer, telex to Gui Bonsiepe, 27 June 1972, box 66, Beer Collection.

57. Roberto Cañete, letter to Stafford Beer, 14 August 1972, box 66, Beer Collection.

58. George A. Miller, "The Magical Number Seven, Plus or Minus Two: Some Limits on Our Capacity for Processing Information," *Psychological Review* 63 (1956): 81–97.

59. Bonsiepe interview.

60. For a detailed description of the operations room design, see Grupo de Proyecto de Diseño Industrial, "Diseño de una sala de operaciones," *INTEC* 4 (1973): 19–28.

61. Rodrigo Walker, interview by author, 24 July 2006, Santiago, Chile.

62. Cañete to Beer, 14 August 1972.

63. Roberto Cañete, telex to Stafford Beer, 16 August 1972, box 66, Beer Collection.

64. Walker interview.

65. Ibid.

66. Stories differ on where the chairs were constructed. Roberto Cañete remembers driving to the countryside to pick up the fiberglass chairs from a workshop and, upon arriving, finding a chicken perched on top of one of the futuristic seats. Cañete interview.

67. Shultz interview.

68. Gui Bonsiepe, memo to Stafford Beer, 28 August 1972, box 56, Beer Collection.

69. Beer, *Brain of the Firm*, 270.

70. Beer said the occupants of the operations room would view a keyboard as "calling for a typing skill, and [would] want to insinuate a girl between themselves and the machinery. . . . It is vital that the occupants interact directly with the machine, and with each other." Stafford Beer, *Platform for Change: A Message from Stafford Beer* (New York: J. Wiley, 1975), 449.

71. Bonsiepe interview.

72. The design of the room supports a common criticism of the Popular Unity government, namely, that it held an ambivalent attitude toward women and that the Chilean left focused on the largely male groups of industrial workers and, to a lesser extent, rural peasants. For example, during the Popular Unity period, Chilean social scientist Lucía Ribeiro criticized existing bodies of social theory for failing to address the experiences of Chilean women and privileging production outside the home over reproduction and related domestic activities. Years later historian Sandra McGee Deutsch concluded, "Existing studies have stressed the left's inability—of which there are numerous examples—to conceive of female participation in the struggle for socialism." In a similar vein, the historian of Chile Thomas Miller Klubock writes, "The popular fronts, with the support of labor and the Left, built their political hegemony on the foundation of a gendered political ideology that defined the rights and benefits of national citizenship in terms of the male worker and head of household and the female housewife." See Lucía Ribeiro, "La mujer obrera chilena: Una aproximación a su estudio," *Cuadernos de la realidad nacional*, no. 16 (1973); Sandra McGee Deutsch, "Gender and Sociopolitical Change in Twentieth-Century Latin America," *Hispanic American Historical Review* 71, no. 2 (1991): 297–298; and Thomas Miller Klubock, "Writing the History of Women and Gender in Twentieth-Century Chile," *Hispanic American Historical Review* 81, no. 3–4 (2001): 507.

73. This is a tally that I was able to create from the documents in the Beer archive. However, Beer also writes that, by October 1972, 60 percent of the enterprises in the "socio-industrial" economy were included in the Cybersyn system. This figure seems high. Stallings writes that 150 enterprises were placed under state control by the end of 1971 and another 61 were requisitioned or intervened by October 1972 (*Class Conflict*, 131–132). The 1972 numbers do not include the enterprises that the government purchased or expropriated. Sixty percent of this total is 126 enterprises, which well exceeds the number of enterprises connected to the system, according to archival sources.

74. Tomás Kohn, interview by author, 5 September 2003, Santiago, Chile.

75. Institute modeler Tomás Kohn speculated that these flow charts must have been useful to the interventor, regardless of whether he planned to use Project Cybersyn in his decision making. Kohn interview.

76. Beer writes that in practice most plants could be adequately monitored using ten to twelve production indicators from the enterprises; see Beer, *Brain of the Firm*, 253.

77. Ibid.

78. Humberto Gabella, Eugenio Balmaceda, Luis Berger, and Julio González, "Análisis empresarial para la determinación de indicadores de Muebles Easton," July 1972, Library, Beer Collection.

79. Humberto Gabella, memorandum to Stafford Beer, 7 July 1972, box 56, Beer Collection.

80. Operational Research Service, "Progress Report on the Development of Indices to be Transferred to CORFO," 10 July 1972, box 56, Beer Collection.

81. Consumer Goods Branch Report, September 1972, box 56, Beer Collection.

82. Kohn interview.

83. Ibid.

84. Beer, *Brain of the Firm*, 276. Allende had created the Social Property Area in part to increase worker participation in decision making; see Juan G. Espinosa and Andrew S. Zimbalist, *Economic Democracy: Workers' Participation in Chilean Industry, 1970–1973* (New York: Academic Press, 1978), 46.

85. Eugenio Balmaceda, interview by author, 28 January 2003, Santiago, Chile.

86. Granted, I have not been able to speak with individuals in all the enterprises the modelers visited. In fact, from 2003 to 2005, when I was conducting the bulk of my interviews, it was very difficult to locate individuals who remembered the system if they were not members of the project team. Because of the quantity of documents from the Allende period that were destroyed by the Pinochet government, I found it difficult to locate the names of interventors. I thank Peter Winn for giving me the names of individuals he interviewed in his study of the Yarur Textile Mill and for accompanying me on two of the interviews. I also attended meetings of the National Labor Federation, met with workers at the factory MADECO, and placed a newspaper ad in a leftist newspaper hoping to find workers who remembered hearing of a cybernetic system for economic management, but to no avail. Since the time of my initial research, Project Cybersyn has received substantial media attention in Chile. Now that the topic is better known, future scholars may have more luck putting together a more complete picture of the factory experience.

87. Balmaceda interview.

88. The Yarur Textile Mill provides a telling example. In his classic study of the mill, Peter Winn notes that Yarur was the first enterprise seized by its workers and the first to set up a system of worker participation, and it went well beyond the norms established by the government. Yarur was a flagship enterprise for the government nationalization process; its transition to a state-controlled enterprise was closely watched, and it received the best of everything. Understandably, Yarur was one of the first factories connected to the Cybersyn system and, given its strong history of worker involvement, would have been an ideal candidate for bringing workers into the modeling process. Yet Yarur interventor Patricio Taulis maintained the workers did not know anything about the system. Patricio Taulis, interview by Eden Medina and Peter Winn, 28 July

2003, Santiago, Chile. In addition to Taulis, I spoke with two other interventors from the Yarur Textile Mill, Juan Francisco Sánchez and Vicente Poblete.

89. Peter Winn describes the introduction of Taylorism in the Yarur Textile Mill as "a capitalist's dream" and a "worker's nightmare." Workers, especially those who were older, could not keep up with the accelerated pace demanded by Taylorism, and yet the factory environment was redesigned to maximize cost-efficiency regardless of the working conditions it produced. Workers who failed to keep up with the new production levels were fired. See Peter Winn, *Weavers of Revolution: The Yarur Workers and Chile's Road to Socialism* (New York: Oxford University Press, 1986), 45.

90. For a history of numerical control technology and labor, see David F. Noble, *Forces of Production: A Social History of Industrial Automation*, 1st ed. (New York: Alfred A. Knopf, 1984).

91. Angel Parra, interview by author, 31 January 2008, Berlin.

92. Ibid.

93. According to Angel Parra, José Miguel Insulza was also a "great singer of boleros." Parra interview.

94. Ibid.

95. [Angel Parra], "Letanía para una computadora y para un niño que va a nacer," song lyrics, box 64, Beer Collection.

96. Beer did not specify whether these individuals were apolitical, sympathetic to the opposition, or UP supporters who wanted the system to be politically neutral.

97. Beer, *Brain of the Firm*, 312.

98. An original copy of the booklet is stored in the Beer Collection. It was reprinted in Beer, *Brain of the Firm*, 291–305.

99. Fourteen more telex machines were in the process of being installed. Memorandum, 7 July 1972, box 56, Beer Collection.

100. Fernando Améstica and Isaquino Benadof, "Project Teledata Working Plan," August 1972, box 56, Beer Collection.

101. Cañete to Beer, 14 August 1972.

102. In June 1972 the president even replaced his minister of economics, Pedro Vuskovic, with a moderate technocrat from the Socialist Party. Allende moved Vuskovic to head the State Development Corporation, a demotion many believed was triggered by Vuskovic's position on nationalization, which was more aggressive than Allende's.

103. Stafford Beer, telex to Roberto Cañete, 28 September 1972, box 66, Beer Collection.

104. Roberto Cañete, telex to Stafford Beer, 28 September 1972, box 66, Beer Collection.

Chapter 5

1. Enrique Farné, interview by author, 16 October 2008, Denia, Spain.

2. Espejo responded, "I will not deny [these charges of technocracy]. I think that technology dazzles me. . . . I accept it as a criticism, but I was not the only one with this bias." Raúl Espejo, interview by author, 9 September 2006, Lincoln, U.K.

3. Stafford Beer, "The Extension of Cybernetic Management Systems to the Enterprises: A Reconsideration of the Political Context," 14 October 1972, box 57, Stafford Beer Collection, Liverpool John Moores University, Liverpool, U.K. Beer says the meeting the project team had in Los Andes in September 1972 provided the motivation for the report. He does not mention the strike in the text.

4. Beer, "Extension of Cybernetic Management Systems."

5. "Llamo a la cordura y a la reflexión . . . ," *Las Noticias de Última Hora*, 13 October 1972, reprinted in Miguel González Pino and Arturo Fontaine Talavera, eds., *Los mil días de Allende*, 2 vols. (Santiago, Chile: Centro de Estudios Públicos, 1997), 1:479–480.

6. Beer writes, "I suggest that this approach, full of panache, is *both* the most effective way to amplify the variety of 'the project,' and *also* a powerful political instrument." Beer, "Extension of Cybernetic Management Systems," 3.

7. Herman Schwember, "Commentaries to 'The Extension of Cybernetic Management Systems to the Enterprises,'" n.d., box 57, Beer Collection.

8. The historical record supports such concerns. For example, the Soviets had tried but failed to build a system for automated economic management, in part because such a system would have undermined the authority of the Central Statistical Administration and the State Planning Committee. Slava Gerovitch, "Internyet: Why the Soviet Union Did Not Build a Nationwide Computer Network," *History and Technology* 24, no. 4 (2008): 335–350.

9. Herman Schwember, interview by author, 22 June 2002, Santiago, Chile.

10. "Doce mil dueños de camiones inician un paro indefinido en apoyo a transportistas," *La Prensa*, 10 October 1972, reprinted in González Pino and Fontaine Talavera, *Los mil días de Allende*, 1:474–475.

11. "Valparaíso: 80%, Viña del Mar: 90%," *La Estrella*, 13 October 1972, reprinted in González Pino and Fontaine Talavera, *Los mil días de Allende*, 1:481–482.

12. People are shown clinging to the outside of buses in the film *La Batalla de Chile: La lucha de un pueblo sin armas—tercera parte: El poder popular*, directed by Patricio Guzmán (Chile: Unifilms, 1979), 100 minutes.

13. Barbara Stallings, *Class Conflict and Economic Development in Chile, 1958–1973* (Stanford, Calif.: Stanford University Press, 1978), 141–142; Guzmán, *La Batalla de Chile*.

14. Stallings, *Class Conflict*, 142.

15. "Llamo a la cordura y a la reflexión," 479–480.

16. Ibid.

17. Stallings, *Class Conflict*, 143, 281. In some cases it was not that the government did not want to return a factory, but that its workers prohibited the government from doing so.

18. Arturo Valenzuela, *The Breakdown of Democratic Regimes: Chile* (Baltimore: Johns Hopkins University Press, 1978), 79.

19. Stallings, *Class Conflict*, 141.

20. Mario Grandi, e-mail to author, 30 July 2010.

21. Fernando Flores, interview by author, Viña del Mar, 30 July 2003.

22. These command centers were not all in the same location; some were established in the State Development Corporation and the Ministry of Economics, in addition to the presidential palace. However, the State Development Corporation had the greatest capacity for sending and receiving messages, because of the telex network created for Project Cybersyn.

23. Grandi e-mail.

24. Espejo interview.

25. Ibid.

26. Gustavo Silva, interview by author, Santiago, Chile, 5 September 2003.

27. Stafford Beer, interview by author, 15–16 March 2001, Toronto. Espejo provided the figure of twenty telex machines when I interviewed him in 2006.

28. Espejo interview.

29. Stafford Beer, *Brain of the Firm: The Managerial Cybernetics of Organization*, 2nd ed. (New York: J. Wiley, 1981), 314.

30. Beer interview.

31. Espejo interview. Grandi also opined that while the telex network played an important role in helping the government withstand the strike, it was not nearly as important as "the spirit of the people who worked to prevent the collapse of the country and the fall of the government" (Grandi e-mail).

32. See Peter Winn, *Weavers of Revolution: The Yarur Workers and Chile's Road to Socialism* (New York: Oxford University Press, 1986), 239; Stallings, *Class Conflict*, 143–144; Valenzuela, *The Breakdown of Democratic Regimes*, 82; Brian Loveman, *Chile: The Legacy of Hispanic Capitalism*, 3rd ed. (New York: Oxford University Press, 2001), 254–255.

33. Herman Schwember, letter to Stafford Beer, 6 November 1972, box 66, Beer Collection.

34. Herman Schwember, letter to Stafford Beer, 12 November 1972, box 64, Beer Collection.

35. Schwember to Beer, 6 November 1972.

36. Flores interview.

37. Beer, *Brain of the Firm*, 322.

38. Schwember interview.

39. Beer, *Brain of the Firm*, 322.

40. He sent Flores a personalized copy of the diagram that he addressed to Aureliano from Melquíades, a reference to the names the two had drawn from García Márquez's *One Hundred Years of Solitude*.

41. Herman Schwember, telex to Stafford Beer, 27 October 1972, box 66, Beer Collection.

42. Stafford Beer, telex to Raúl Espejo, 6 November 1972, box 66, Beer Collection.

43. Ibid.

44. Stafford Beer, letter to Herman Schwember, 13 November 1972, box 66, Beer Collection.

45. Beer interview.

46. Beer to Schwember, 13 November 1972.

47. Stafford Beer, telex to Raúl Espejo, 1 March 1973, box 66, Beer Collection.

48. Beer writes, "Fernando is now the Minister. That has to change everything. What is included in the economy? That is to say what are the Systems One? 1. The economy is fed by production— then *Industry* 2. The economy consumes; it feeds and clothes the people; it conditions their way of life—then *Communities* 3. These two have to be connected—the *Distribution*." Stafford Beer, "One Year of (Relative) Solitude: The Second Level of Recursion," December 1972, box 60, Beer Collection.

49. Beer, *Brain of the Firm*, 323.

50. Beer's heightened interest in worker participation came at the exact moment the government had decided to focus its attentions elsewhere. In July 1972 representatives from the worker participation bodies in each of the nationalized firms in the textile sector came together at a meeting known as the *encuentro textil*, which was meant to be the first of a series of sector meetings on participation. The goal was to take the successful lessons from worker participation at the enterprise level and apply them to the sector level, the next level up, and eventually integrate worker participation in the whole economy. Pedro Vuskovic, the former minister of the economy and now the head of CORFO, strongly supported these efforts and viewed the social property area as his chance to demonstrate the success of Chilean socialism with worker participation. However, the October Strike cut these efforts short, as simply staying in power became the government's main priority. That Beer viewed the October Strike as a reason to increase government emphasis on worker participation shows the disconnect between his understanding of the political situation and that of high-ranking members of the Chilean government.

51. Beer, "One Year of (Relative) Solitude."

52. Ibid.

53. Harry Braverman, *Labor and Monopoly Capital: The Degradation of Work in the Twentieth Century* (New York: Monthly Review Press, 1974), 193; emphasis in the original. Although Beer was not a Marxist, he did use some of the concepts from Marx's writings when studying Chilean industrial production and, like David Noble and Braverman, was also interested in how computer technology could change social relations on the shop floor. Yet he conceptualized the dynamics of this relationship in a very different way and saw other possibilities for how technology could change the power relationships among types of labor.

54. David F. Noble, *Forces of Production: A Social History of Industrial Automation*, 1st ed. (New York: Alfred A. Knopf, 1984), 351.

55. Shoshana Zuboff, *In the Age of the Smart Machine: The Future of Work and Power* (New York: Basic Books, 1988), 271.

56. Norbert Wiener, *The Human Use of Human Beings: Cybernetics and Society* (1954; repr., New York: Da Capo 1988), 162.

57. Braverman, *Labor and Monopoly Capital*, 39.

58. For a more detailed discussion of the history of participatory design, see Gro Bjerknes and Tone Bratteteig, "User Participation and Democracy: A Discussion of Scandinavian Research on System Development," *Scandinavian Journal of Information Systems* 7, no. 1 (1995): 73–95, and Andrew Clement and Peter Van den Besselaar, "A Retrospective Look at PD Projects," *Communications of the ACM* 36, no. 4 (1993): 29–37.

59. Had Beer written his report ten years later, he might have drawn from this body of Scandinavian research to further his position. He also might have used the findings from this body of scholarship to refine his proposal. For example, work in participatory design has shown that having workers participate in the design of a technology does not guarantee that management practices will change or that workers will have a greater voice in workplace decision making. Moreover, Beer's proposal does not resolve the question of who would participate, whose knowledge would be incorporated in the system, or what ramifications would result from embedding worker knowledge in a management technology. As studies of automation have shown, the incorporation of worker knowledge in a computer system often disempowers workers and gives them less control over production processes.

60. See James W. Wilson, "Freedom and Control: Workers' Participation in Management in Chile, 1967–1975" (Ph.D. diss., Cornell University, 1979).

61. Beer was of the moment in thinking about how giving people tools to participate in the world around them might produce a more just society. For example, at this time, liberation theology was calling for lay practitioners to participate in developing their own interpretations of the Bible rather than simply following the interpretations handed down by church hierarchy. Liberation theology urged lay practitioners to use their own interpretations of religious texts as a guide

in taking action against social injustice and poverty. Beer was also writing four years after the Brazilian educator Paulo Freire published *Pedagogy of the Oppressed* in Portuguese (published in English in 1970), a book that rejected an education imposed from above by teachers-colonizers and instead called for students to participate in discussions with teachers to co-produce meaning. Brazilian director Augusto Boal demonstrated that such forms of participation could also operate in the realm of theater. He presented the audience with a narrative of oppression and encouraged it to stop the actors and change the storyline at any time during the performance. Arguing that this type of audience participation created "spect-actors," not spectators, Boal encouraged the audience to imagine new alternatives that could lead to political action. In 1974 he published these ideas in the book *Teatro del oprimido* (later published in English as *Theater of the Oppressed*). In the United States the United Farm Workers of America also used theater as a form of participation. Productions by El Teatro Campesino provided a vehicle for farm workers to tell their own stories and participate in raising public awareness and money to support political change. While there is no indication of whether Beer was familiar with any of these contemporaneous efforts, these examples show that his ideas about participation were part of a larger intellectual context.

62. See the analysis of worker participation in Juan G. Espinosa and Andrew S. Zimbalist, *Economic Democracy: Worker's Participation in Chilean Industry, 1970–1973* (New York: DaCapo, 1978).

63. Ibid., 114.

64. Winn, *Weavers of Revolution*, 238.

65. Beer, "One Year of (Relative) Solitude."

66. Stafford Beer, *Decision and Control* (New York: J. Wiley, 1966), 346.

67. Nor was Beer the only individual in Chile to notice the value of worker involvement in technological design; members of the INTEC Industrial Design Group were also inviting workers to contribute to the design of their projects and viewed these contributions as beneficial. However, these instances of participatory design in INTEC were not viewed as formal mechanisms for increasing worker participation in factory management.

68. Beer, *Brain of the Firm*, 329.

69. Farné interview.

70. Flores interview.

71. "Operations Room Monthly Report: October," October 1972, box 56, Beer Collection.

72. Raúl Espejo, "Activities Report," December 1972, box 64, Beer Collection.

73. Espejo interview.

74. Ibid.

75. Ibid.

76. J. Y. Lettvin, H. R. Maturana, W. S. McCulloch, and W. H. Pitts, "What the Frog's Eye Tells the Frog's Brain," *Proceedings of the Institute of Radio Engineers* 47, no. 11 (1959): 1940–1951.

77. According to one of von Foerster's former students, von Foerster did not share Beer's interest in the management applications of cybernetics and often equated management with "manacles." Although von Foerster and Beer traveled in the same circles and enjoyed each other's company, von Foerster did not contribute to Project Cybersyn. Stuart Umpleby, telephone interview by author, 23 July 2009.

78. Schwember to Beer, 12 November 1972.

79. Espejo, "Activities Report."

80. CHECO Team, "Progress Report No. 5," November 1972, box 64, Beer Collection. The current version included, among other things, a subroutine that recognized the government was printing money to underwrite its budget. Other parameters included levels of foreign currency, production, price, demand, supply, savings, and inflation. The team planned to validate these models with data from 1960 and 1970 and predicted that they could soon be used to assist policy making.

81. Isaquino Benadof, "Status," 22 November 1972, box 64, Beer Collection.

82. Beer, "Extension of Cybernetic Management Systems." Training sixty people at a time meant that it would be possible to train teams from twelve enterprises (each team consisting of two senior managers, two workers, and the leader of the work on defining production indicators). To do so would require a space large enough for sixty people and twelve smaller working rooms, a space requirement that could be met by a hotel.

83. Schwember proposed that the project move forward with simpler media, such as slide projectors and audiotapes, but Beer still wanted to pursue the idea of training films; he began investigating other options, such as making a generic set of films that used Chile as a case example and thus could be sold internationally, or having the Chilean government finance filming in London for £25,000 to £50,000 (roughly $380,000 to $759,000 in 2009). Herman Schwember, "Re: Training Programme and Training Center," 2 November 1972, box 66, Beer Collection; Stafford Beer, telex to Herman Schwember, 8 November 1972, box 66, Beer Collection.

84. The first setback was that the team could not locate film for making slides and asked Beer to bring rolls with him during his next visit. Then the government balked at the construction budget for the room, which halted construction until the team could reduce the budget by a third. Finally, after the first site fell through, Espejo located a new space, but the owners of the building were members of the right and opposed the Allende government. Given the dire circumstance, Espejo visited the family personally and used every argument in his arsenal to convince the owners to rent the space to the government. In particular he stressed that the project "was legitimate and for the benefit of the whole country, not just Popular Unity." This line of argument proved effective. After the family gave its permission, construction began immediately. The final plans for the space included the main operations room plus three offices, two bathrooms, and one kitchenette. Even while under construction, the room made an impression. One day a curious woman wandered in off the street and entered the room through an open door, her arms laden with shopping bags. She looked at what the team was building and surmised aloud, "Ah, they are building another discotheque here." "We all laughed," Fernando Shultz recalled, because "there was a certain irony here regarding the design of the room. To other people it looked like a crazy thing, a frivolous

thing," yet it represented the cutting edge of Chilean industrial design and had taken considerable human and material resources to build. Espejo interview; Fernando Shultz, interview by author, 9–10 September 2008, Mexico City, Mexico.

85. Stafford Beer, "Welcome to the Operations Room," n.d., box 63, Beer Collection. There is no date on the speech Beer composed for Allende, although it was most likely written in December 1972 or January 1973. In *Brain of the Firm* Beer states that he wrote the speech in January 1973. However, other archival documents dated from December 1972 record Beer's suggesting that the president should deliver a speech to inaugurate the operations room. For this reason I decided to use the speech in this chapter, which covers December 1972, rather than chapter 6, which covers January 1973.

86. As mentioned in the prologue, the summer heat had raised the temperature of the electronics in the room beyond their tolerance and caused the slide projectors to malfunction. Rodrigo Walker described the president's visit as follows: "A group of people arrived [including Allende, Flores, and Prats] and started using [the room] and the projectors went crazy; you would push [the armrest button] for one thing and something else would appear." Rodrigo Walker, interview by author, Santiago, Chile, 24 July 2006. Roberto Cañete similarly telexed Beer that the room's electronics "behaved awfully" during the president's visit. Roberto Cañete, telex to Stafford Beer, 3 January 1973, box 66, Beer Collection. Nevertheless, Allende and Prats were still taken with the space. According to Flores, Allende said, "Shoot, it would be good to have it working. Keep going [Pucha que sería bueno tenerla andando, sigan trabajando]." Prats was also impressed with the room and its potential applications for military command and control. Juan Andrés Guzmán, "Fernando Flores habla sobre el Proyecto Synco," *Clinic*, July 24, 2003, 9. (The *Clinic* is a newspaper published in Santiago de Chile.)

Chapter 6

1. Sergio Bitar, *Chile: Experiment in Democracy*, trans. Sam Sherman (Philadelphia: Institute for the Study of Human Issues, 1986), 125; Arturo Valenzuela, *The Breakdown of Democratic Regimes: Chile* (Baltimore: Johns Hopkins University Press, 1978), 55.

2. Throughout 1973 the government developed plans to promote Chilean scientific and technological accomplishments, including a plan to distribute the publication *Science and Technology Week* to all Chilean embassies beginning in August 1973. The magazine would serve as a vehicle for the international dissemination of Chile's science and engineering achievements. *Mensaje Presidente Allende ante Congreso Pleno, 21/Mayo '73* (Santiago, Chile: Departamento de Publicaciones de la Presidencia de la República, 1973), 263.

3. Stafford Beer, interview by author, Toronto, Canada, 15–16 March 2001. News of the project first appeared in the underground science newsletter *Eddies*, but this publication had a substantially more limited audience than the *Observer*. Nigel Hawkes, "Chile Run by Computer," *Observer*, 7 January 1973.

4. Ibid.

5. Stafford Beer, telex to Doreen Morril, 9 January 1973, box 66, Stafford Beer Collection, Liverpool John Moores University, Liverpool, U.K.

6. Stafford Beer, letter to Ron Anderton, 7 February 1973, box 58, Beer Collection.

7. "En aumento acciones ilegales de las JAP," *El Mercurio*, 21 January 1973, reprinted in Miguel González Pino and Arturo Fontaine Talavera, eds., *Los mil días de Allende*, 2 vols. (Santiago, Chile: Centro de Estudios Públicos, 1997).

8. Bitar, *Chile: Experiment in Democracy*, 146.

9. "Chile: Futurism Now," *Latin America*, 12 January 1973, 10–12.

10. Nigel Hawkes, "The Age of Computers Operating Chilean Economy," *St. Petersburg Times*, 17 January 1973.

11. "El 'Hermano Mayor' de Mr. Beer," *Ercilla*, 23–30 January 1973.

12. Ibid.

13. Ibid. The phrase "the poor eat bread and the rich eat shit, shit" comes from the song "Que la tortilla se vuelva" by the Chilean folk music group Quilapayún, whose music formed part of the Nueva Canción movement and was linked to the politics of the Chilean road to socialism.

14. Stafford Beer, telex to Raúl Espejo, 29 January 1973, box 66, Beer Collection.

15. Stafford Beer, *Brain of the Firm: The Managerial Cybernetics of Organization*, 2nd ed. (New York: J. Wiley, 1981), 336.

16. Bruno Latour, *Science in Action* (Cambridge, Mass.: Harvard University Press, 1987), 104.

17. Ibid.

18. Here Beer is actually quoting himself in *Brain of the Firm*.

19. Beer's lecture was published as Stafford Beer, "Fanfare for Effective Freedom: Cybernetic Praxis in Government," *Platform for Change: A Message from Stafford Beer* (New York: J. Wiley, 1975), 450–451.

20. Andy Beckett, *Pinochet in Picadilly* (London: Faber and Faber, 2002), 116.

21. Beer, "Fanfare for Effective Freedom," 428.

22. Ibid.

23. Ibid., 423; emphasis in the original.

24. Ibid., 448.

25. Ibid., 425.

26. Ibid., 429.

27. Raúl Espejo, telex to Stafford Beer, 2 February 1973, box 66, Beer Collection.

28. Ibid.

29. Stafford Beer, telex to Raúl Espejo, 6 February 1973, box 66, Beer Collection.

30. Espejo to Beer, 2 February 1973; Beer to Espejo, 6 February 1973.

31. Beer, "Fanfare for Effective Freedom," 428.

32. Ibid., 442.

33. Beer's use of the word *autonomy* might also have confused listeners. He argued that Cybersyn preserved autonomy for each level of recursion—sector committees, enterprises, plants, workers—but he cited the ability of factory managers to add new production indexes to the Cyberstride software as an example of their autonomy. However, the Cyberstride software monitored factory activities and reported anomalous behavior to higher management. Giving factory managers the ability to increase these monitoring capabilities or change how they were being monitored therefore presented a questionable form of manager autonomy. Beer argued that Cyberstride gave factory managers greater autonomy than state micromanagement, but since he did not mention whether such micromanagement was common in the Chilean public sector in the 1970s, it was difficult for his British audience to determine whether the Cyberstride software did, in fact, increase autonomy.

34. Stafford Beer, telex to Sonia Mordojovich, 16 February 1973, box 66, Beer Collection.

35. Stafford Beer, letter to Fernando Flores, 17 February 1973, box 66, BS Collection.

36. Joseph Hanlon, who was British, would later become an authority on development policy and financial lending, especially in Mozambique.

37. Beer to Mordojovich, 16 February 1972. The *New Scientist* article highlights that there were positive accounts of Beer and Project Cybersyn published in trade journals. For example, in April and May 1973, the trade publication *Data Systems* ran articles that depicted the system in a positive light. See Rex Malik, "Chile Steals a March," *Data Systems*, April 1973, 14–15, and Rex Malik, "Inside Allende's Economic Powerhouse," *Data Systems*, May 1973, 14–16.

38. Joseph Hanlon, "Comment: The Technological Power Broker," *New Scientist*, 15 Februrary 1973, 347.

39. Ibid.

40. Stafford Beer, letter to the editor, *New Scientist*, 22 February 1973, 449.

41. Beer to Flores, 17 February 1973.

42. See chap. 5 of Slava Gerovitch, *From Newspeak to Cyberspeak: A History of Soviet Cybernetics* (Cambridge, Mass.: MIT Press, 2002).

43. While working on a biography of Norbert Wiener, Flo Conway and Jim Siegelman acquired the CIA reports on Soviet cybernetic activity through the Freedom of Information Act in 2000. See Flo Conway and Jim Siegelman, *Dark Hero of the Information Age: In Search of Norbert Wiener, the Father of Cybernetics* (New York: Basic Books, 2005).

44. On John J. Ford, see Conway and Siegelman, *Dark Hero*, and Ronald Kline, "The Fate of Cybernetics in the United States: Decline, Revival, and Transformation in the 1960s and 1970s," unpublished manuscript, 2010, in the personal files of Ronald Kline.

45. Harry Braverman, *Labor and Monopoly Capital: The Degradation of Work in the Twentieth Century* (New York: Monthly Review Press, 1974), 37–38.

46. Stafford Beer, telex to Raúl Espejo, 1 March 1973, box 66, Beer Collection.

47. ECOM, telex to Raúl Espejo, 4–6 April 1973, box 64, Beer Collection.

48. Espejo offered two concrete examples of workers' participation in the creation of Cybersyn factory models—the Easton Furniture company, discussed at length in chap. 4, and the tire factory INSA. However, these examples further illustrate how little had been done to make Cybersyn a participative technology. At Easton, worker participation consisted of Chilean technical experts' talking to workers and managers but did not involve workers in the actual model-building process. Even though Espejo credited this type of worker participation with improving the "organization of the activities in the enterprise," it was a far cry from the type of worker participation Beer imagined in his December report. Espejo wrote that workers assumed a greater role in creating the flow diagrams for the INSA tire factory and that the INSA experience "allows us to conclude that the workers are perfectly able to understand and execute all of the conceptual development we have proposed." Unfortunately, archived source materials do not document the modeling process at the INSA factory in any detail. See CORFO [Corporación de Fomento de la Producción], ed., *Proyecto Synco conceptos y práctica del control; Una experiencia concreta: La dirección industrial en Chile* (Santiago, Chile, 1973), 46–47.

49. Raúl Espejo, interview by author, 9 September 2006, Lincoln, U.K. Espejo's statement that the participatory aspect of Project Cybersyn never got much beyond the level of discussion does confirm that little headway was made on worker participation.

50. Humberto Gabella, "Técnica de la flujogramación cuantificada para efectos del control en tiempo real," CORFO, March 1973, Beer Collection.

51. Roberto Cañete, letter to Stafford Beer, 6 March 1973, box 66, Beer Collection.

52. "Plan Secreto 'Cyberstride': La UP nos controla por computación," *Qué Pasa*, 15 March 1973.

53. Espejo interview.

54. In 1973 at least one leftist journal, *Chile, Hoy*, adopted a critical stance toward science and technology, calling them bourgeois, elitist, imperialist, and thus counterrevolutionary. For example, *Chile, Hoy* criticized a 1973 symposium of the American Association for the Advancement of Science that took place in Mexico City as a form of "cultural imperialism," a way to further capitalist interests, and an attempt "to program on a continental scale total [Latin American] dependence on North American technology and to orchestrate the exploitation of Latin America." See Augusto Salinas Araya, *Ciencia, estado y revolución: Un análisis del caso chileno: 1964–1973* (Santiago, Chile: Ediciones Universidad Finis Terrae, 1994), 297–298. However, such criticisms were not written by Chileans nor were they affiliated with the Popular Unity coalition. In general,

the Popular Unity coalition viewed science and technology as important parts of socialist change and wanted to take science out of the university and apply it to solving national problems. Project Cybersyn supports this stance. See also Margaret Power, "Modernity and Technology in Chile: The First National Congress of Scientists," Latin American Studies Association, Las Vegas, 7–9 October 2004.

55. Herb Grosch, letter to the editor, *New Scientist*, 15 March 1973. Grosch is a rather interesting character in the history of computing, known first for his self-coined "Grosch's Law," which governed the mainframe computing industry during the 1960s and 1970s, and also for his notoriously cantankerous personality. (The harshness of his commentary in *New Scientist* may be attributed in part to the latter.) Grosch had traveled to Santiago during the late 1960s to advise the government of Eduardo Frei Montalva on ways to improve Chile's computer capabilities. He was thus well informed of Chile's computer capabilities and understandably skeptical that the system Beer described in Brighton had been built in such a short period of time. Beer, in turn, charged that Grosch was working under the mistaken assumption that Project Cybersyn followed in the footsteps of U.S. computing, something Beer said he repudiated, "as my writings have shown [for] over twenty years." Responding to Grosch in the pages of *New Scientist* (letter to the editor, 22 March 1973), Beer wrote, "Perhaps that room in Santiago is an optical illusion, and the photographs of it are faked. Or perhaps it is intolerable to sit in Washington, D.C., and to realize that someone else got there first—in a Marxist country, on a shoestring." In private correspondence to Grosch, Beer added that his Chilean colleagues believed Grosch's comments were part of a U.S. campaign to discredit the Allende government: "My friends there [in Chile] will find it very naïve of me not to believe that you are working for the CIA, but somehow I don't." Stafford Beer, letter to Herb Grosch, 5 April 1973, box 63, Beer Collection.

56. Grosch, letter to editor.

57. Ibid. Grosch claimed that the BASF project illustrated that "modelling *does* work, has worked—with or without matrix inversion" and that this project predated Project Cybersyn; see Herb Grosch, letter to Stafford Beer, 2 April 1973, box 63, Beer Collection.

58. According to the World Bank, in 1973 the GDP of the United States was $14.2 trillion, the German GDP was $3.6 trillion, and the Chilean GDP was $169 billion in 2008 dollars. The German data refer to the Federal Republic of Germany before unification. I obtained this information from the World Bank's Data Finder Web site, http://datafinder.worldbank.org, which no longer posts data earlier than 1980.

59. Raúl Espejo, telex to Stafford Beer, 1 March 1973, box 66, Beer Collection. Two of these reports are cited in notes 49 and 51.

60. Herman Schwember, letter to Stafford Beer, 22 March 1973, box 63, Beer Collection.

61. Stafford Beer, telex to Raúl Espejo, 28 March 1973, box 66, Beer Collection.

62. Espejo had tried to promote cybernetics on the shop floor; for example, he had contacted the painter Francisco Ariztía in 1972 and asked him to paint cybernetic murals in the state-controlled factories. Ariztía visited a factory with Espejo but relocated to the mining city of Chuquicamata

before he could bring the idea to fruition. Francisco Ariztía, interview by author, 13 October 2008, Lisbon, Portugal.

63. Raúl Espejo, telex to Stafford Beer, 29 March 1973, box 66, Beer Collection.

64. Raúl Espejo, telex to Stafford Beer, 5 April 1973, box 66, Beer Collection.

65. Raúl Espejo, "Memorandum January–March Activities," 16 April 1973, box 64, Beer Collection.

66. Ibid.

67. There might have been a few exceptions. Raimundo Beca was both director of the National Computer Corporation (ECOM) and interventor to the domestic appliance factory MADEMSA during the Popular Unity government. He claimed that mapping the vital indexes of production motivated workers because it was used to calculate workers' rewards and promoted collective production instead of individual output. However, Beca noted that the use of the Cybersyn models in factories depended strongly on the interventors' support. For example, MADEMSA discontinued all work on Cybersyn's implementation after Beca left the factory. Raimundo Beca, interview by author, 9 September 2003, Santiago, Chile.

68. Espejo wrote that the Cyberstride temporary suite never operated with less than a fifteen-day delay for the enterprises in the textile sector and for the tire factory INSA, which were among the first factories modeled for Project Cybersyn. Espejo to Beer, 29 March 1973.

69. Story told by Hernán Durán, the interventor from Cemento Polpaico, and related in Andrés Varela G., "Gestión de los trabajadores en las empresas del Área de Propiedad Social: un análisis testimonial," in Miguel Lawner, Hernán Soto, and Jacobo Schatan, eds., *Salvador Allende: Presencia en la ausencia* (Santiago, Chile: LOM, 2008), 239–240.

70. Isaquino Benadof, interview by author, 10 April 2002, Santiago, Chile.

71. Alberto Martínez, the director of planning at CORFO, said in a 2003 interview that he was in favor of building mechanisms to help centralize the economy but that Chile's factories could not account for their activities in real time or even daily. He also felt that the system had nothing to do with worker participation. Martínez's comments are consistent with archived source materials, which show him as being openly opposed to the CHECO economic models. Martínez reports that Pedro Vuskovic, the vice director of CORFO, did support Cybersyn, as demonstrated by Vuskovic's willingness to fund the project. However, judging from the frustration Espejo expressed in his correspondence with Beer, it does not seem that Vuskovic pushed the agency to adopt Cybersyn and cybernetic management. Alberto Martínez, telephone interview by author, 7 October 2003.

72. These numbers come from Beer's own financial records in Stafford Beer, accounts, n.d., box 67, Beer Collection.

73. Rosenhead declined Beer's offer to work on the project because he felt Beer wanted "true believers" who followed his approach to management, whereas Rosenhead wanted a chance to implement his own ideas. Rosenhead would become president of the Operational Research Society in 1986, a position Beer had held in 1970. Jonathan Rosenhead, telephone interview by author, 8 October 2009.

74. Ibid.

75. Ibid.

76. John Adams, "Chile: Everything under Control," *Science for People*, April–May 1973.

77. Beer drafted his response immediately after the *Science for People* article appeared in print. His response ran in the next issue of the publication. See Stafford Beer, letter to the editor, *Science for People*, June–July 1973, 5.

78. Rosenhead interview.

79. Beer, letter to editor, *Science for People*, 5.

80. Tomás Kohn, letter to Stafford Beer, 19 April 1973, box 63, Beer Collection.

81. Stafford Beer, "On Decybernation: A Contribution to Current Debates," 27 April 1973, box 64, Beer Collection.

82. Humberto Maturana and Francisco Varela, *The Tree of Knowledge: The Biological Roots of Human Understanding* (Boston: Shambhala, 1998), 47.

83. Beer, "On Decybernation."

84. Beer, *Brain of the Firm*, 343.

85. Beer, "On Decybernation."

86. Ibid.

87. The state bureaucracy grew by leaps and bounds under Allende. According to Salinas Araya, the size of CORFO grew from 600 to 8,000 employees. Such growth made it even more difficult to change the organization of the state apparatus. Salinas Araya, *Ciencia, estado y revolución*, 265.

88. Beer, "On Decybernation."

89. Raúl Espejo, letter to Stafford Beer, 22 May 1973, box 66, Beer Collection.

90. Beer interview.

91. Bitar writes that the opposition used political-legal obstructionism against the Allende government that included bringing constitutional indictments against members of Allende's cabinet, contesting the March election results, setting the judiciary and the comptroller against the executive, supporting a propaganda campaign against popular organizations such as the *cordones industriales* [industrial belts], and achieving a majority vote in the Chamber of Deputies that condemned the government for violating both Chilean law and the constitution. According to Bitar, "This vote provided the legal cover for the overthrow of the government." Such tactics were designed to prevent the government from making organizational changes. Moreover, patronage appointments within the government and the rising number of government employees (a product of Allende's policies to reduce unemployment) would have made it extremely difficult to change the state apparatus even within a stable political environment. The combination of patronage and

the opposition's desire to end Chilean socialism made the organizational changes Beer wanted impossible. See chap. 9 of Bitar, *Chile: Experiment in Democracy*.

92. "Declaración UP sobre un presunto golpe de estado," *La Prensa*, 9 May 1973, reprinted in González Pino and Fontaine Talavera, *Los mil días de Allende*, 630.

93. *Mensaje Presidente Allende ante Congreso Pleno, 21/Mayo '73*, 412–413.

94. Fernando Henrique Cardoso, *The Accidental President of Brazil: A Memoir* (New York: PublicAffairs, 2006), 120.

95. Ibid.

96. During this final visit, members of the project team traveled to Las Cruces to meet with Beer, and Beer did most of his traveling at night.

97. Espejo had arranged for Beer to stay in a vacant house belonging to the mayor. One day Beer made a fire in the fireplace and walked down to the coast to do some thinking. "I was sitting out there, and I looked back at my cottage as I always did . . . and there were a large number of people on the roof," Beer recalled. They were firefighters. Beer had forgotten to remove the straw stuffed in the chimney and had accidentally set the house on fire. Beer interview.

98. Beer, *Brain of the Firm*, 345.

99. Beer claimed Groucho was his favorite Marx. Given the extensive bibliography generated by Karl Marx and his interlocutors, Beer's claim to have read it all must be an exaggeration. However, since Beer was an avid reader, it is highly probable that he did read some of Marx's writings in preparation for Chile. Beer also read Trotsky and found inspiration in Trotsky's critique of the Soviet bureaucracy. Herman Schwember remembered Beer's reading Trotsky during his time in Las Cruces and remarked that Beer was doing the wrong reading. Schwember said that Beer spent a lot of time studying political theory at Las Cruces: "One day I went there and I saw that all of his political background was works by Trotsky and Trotskyites. Now you don't need to be very expert in politics to realize that . . . Trotsky's approach . . . is bound to fail. You try to stress the contradictions to make them as acute as possible. And that usually means total failure. . . . And so it seems to me that Stafford, no matter how clever he is, or how knowledgeable of people he was, could not have a full understanding of all the political elements in Chile." Herman Schwember, interview by author, 22 June 2002, Santiago, Chile.

100. In *From Newspeak to Cyberspeak*, Gerovitch shows that in 1953 Kolman made the opposite argument, using passages from Marx to critique cybernetics. Gerovitch uses Kolman to illustrate how the Soviet stance toward cybernetics changed from the early 1950s to the early 1960s.

101. Stafford Beer, "Status Quo," in the personal files of Allenna Leonard and Raúl Espejo. I thank both for sharing this unpublished document with me.

102. Beer, "Status Quo."

103. When I interviewed Beer in 2001, he recalled, "I said to Allende with a lot of vehemence, the proletariat as conceived by Marx was the great mass of people who were toiling in looms. . . . So I was going to interpret [Marx] for him. That's why I wrote 'Status Quo.'"

104. See Sherry Turkle, *The Second Self: Computers and the Human Spirit*, twentieth anniversary ed. (Cambridge, Mass: MIT Press, 2005), 27.

105. See Paul N. Edwards, *The Closed World: Computers and the Politics of Discourse in Cold War America* (Cambridge, Mass.: MIT Press, 1996).

106. Turkle, *Second Self*, 27.

107. Humberto Maturana and Francisco Varela, *De máquinas y seres vivos: Una caracterización de la organización biológica* (Santiago, Chile: Editorial Universitaria, 1973).

108. Humberto Maturana and Francisco Varela, *Autopoiesis and Cognition: The Realization of the Living* (Boston: D. Reidel, 1980).

109. For this reason, Beer argues in "Status Quo," bureaucracy supports rightist governments and resists those with a leftist agenda. Moreover, technologists drawn to civil service work tend to favor stability and the status quo, so they use technology to strengthen the existing organization rather than to bring about drastic change.

110. Beer, "Status Quo," emphasis in original. Beer believed that capitalism was also autopoietic. Referring to his cybernetic diagram of capitalism, Beer argues that the structure of society has changed—old parts have taken on new forms and new parts have arisen—but the organization of society has not changed. "Every new development has been assimilated into the pre-existing structure to enhance its effectiveness and power," Beer argues in "Status Quo."

111. In this vein, Beer's work parallels how Norbert Wiener used concepts such as feedback and control to understand the behavior of an Axis fighter pilot and to create an antiaircraft servo-mechanism. See Peter Galison, "The Ontology of the Enemy: Norbert Wiener and the Cybernetic Vision," *Critical Inquiry* 21, no. 1 (1994).

112. Beer, "Status Quo."

113. During June and July, Beer and the team discussed what could be done "with the insights and tools of cybernetics" to assist the government. Beer, *Brain of the Firm*, 345.

114. Ibid.

115. Stafford Beer, letter to Salvador Allende, 2 August 1973, box 55, Beer Collection.

116. Raúl Espejo, "Cybernetic Praxis in Government: The Role of the Communication Network," November 1973, in the personal files of Raúl Espejo.

117. Ibid.

118. "Avanza 'Cyberstride': Plan UP de control por computación," *Qué Pasa*, 6 September 1973, 8–10.

119. Comando Operativo Central, "Situación general del país," 3 September 1973, in the personal files of Roberto Cañete.

120. Gui Bonsiepe, interview by author, 21 May 2008, La Plata, Argentina.

121. Flores was quite adamant that he did not push Project Cybersyn in the final months of the Allende government. By mid-1973 he felt that giving more attention to Project Cybersyn and moving the room to the presidential palace would be akin to a crime because it would have diverted government attention from more pressing matters. "If I put that [the room] more in the center I would be an accessory [to such a crime]," Flores told me. "I am very happy with myself that I didn't do that. Clear?" However, it is also important to bear in mind that Flores made these comments with thirty years of hindsight and at a moment when Chile was commemorating the thirty-year anniversary of Popular Unity and reexamining the events of this period in detail. Fernando Flores, interview by author, 30 July 2003, Viña del Mar, Chile.

122. See Thomas P. Hughes, "The Seamless Web: Technology, Science, Etcetera, Etcetera," *Social Studies of Science* 16, no. 2 (1986): 281–292; and Thomas P. Hughes, "The Evolution of Large Technological Systems," in *The Social Construction of Technological Systems: New Directions in the Sociology and History of Technology* (Cambridge, Mass: MIT Press, 1987), 51–82.

123. See Óscar Soto, *El ultimo día de Salvador Allende* (Santiago, Chile: Aguilar, 1998), 90–91, 129. See also *Salvador Allende*, directed by Patricio Guzmán (Chile: Icarus Films, 2004), 100 minutes.

124. Guillermo Toro, e-mail to author, 5 June 2004. Guillermo Toro had replaced Sonia Mordojovich as project coordinator in June 1973 when she left to have a baby.

125. Toro, e-mail to author.

Chapter 7

1. Isaquino Benadof, interview by author, 10 April 2002, Santiago, Chile.

2. Chapter 2 of Peter Winn, ed., *Victims of the Chilean Miracle: Workers and Neoliberalism in the Pinochet Era, 1973–2002* (Durham: Duke University Press, 2004), 14–70. An analysis of the neoliberal economic policies put in place by the Pinochet dictatorship is outside the scope of this book. See Patricio Meller, *Un siglo de economía política chilena (1890–1990)* (Santiago, Chile: Editorial Andrés Bello, 1996); Ricardo Ffrench-Davis, *Entre el neoliberalismo y el crecimiento con equidad: tres décadas de política económica en Chile* (Santiago, Chile: Dolmen Ediciones, 1999); Juan Gabriel Valdés, *Pinochet's Economists: The Chicago School of Economics in Chile* (New York: Cambridge University Press, 1995); and Eduardo Silva, *The State and Capital in Chile: Business Elites, Technocrats, and Market Economics* (Boulder, Colo.: Westview, 1996). The neoliberal program promoted by the "Chicago Boys" appears in Centro de Estudios Públicos, *"El ladrillo": bases de la política económica del gobierno militar chileno* (Santiago, Chile: Centro de Estudios Públicos, 1992). Joaquín Lavin, *Chile: A Quiet Revolution*, trans. Clara Iriberry and Elena Soloduchim (Santiago, Chile: Zig-Zag, 1988), contains pro-government propaganda about the neoliberal "economic miracle."

3. For example, in 2009 the Nicaraguan NGO SIMAS (Mesoamerican Information Service about Sustainable Agriculture) began building a computer system for the Nicaraguan Ministry of Agriculture to transmit the prices of agricultural goods across the nation. Its creators cited Project Cybersyn as an inspiration for the new system and even christened it ALBAstryde, a

combination of the free-trade agreement ALBA (Boliviarian Alternative for the Americas) and the Cyberstride software suite built for Project Cybersyn. The system will track the fluctuating prices of different agricultural products and make the information available to Nicaraguan farmers through a network of radio stations and computers running open-source software. It aims to make price information widely available and improve the bargaining position of Nicaraguan farmers. Like Project Cybersyn, ALBAstryde is comparatively low-tech—it uses radio instead of a high-speed Internet connection to make information broadly available. It also aims to distribute decision making and increase the visibility of national production activities. See Johannes Wilm, "Nicaragua Builds an Innovative Agricultural Information System Using Open Source," *Linux Journal*, 12 November 2009, www.linuxjournal.com/content/nicaragua-builds-innovative-agricultural-information-system-using-open-source-software.

Epilogue

1. Stafford Beer, interview by author, 15–16 March 2001, Toronto, Canada.

2. Humberto Maturana, interview by author, 8 September 2003, Santiago, Chile.

3. According to the Truth and Reconciliation Commission of 1990–1991, state agents were responsible for 2,905 deaths or disappearances under the Pinochet dictatorship, and an additional 139 deaths were the result of political violence. However, historian Steve Stern puts the number of deaths and disappearances at 3,500 to 4,500 and argues the numbers might be even higher. See Steve J. Stern, *Remembering Pinochet's Chile: On the Eve of London, 1998* (Durham, N.C.: Duke University Press, 2004), 158–160.

4. Steve J. Stern, *Battling for Hearts and Minds: Memory Struggles in Pinochet's Chile, 1973–1988* (Durham, N.C.: Duke University Press, 2006), xxi.

5. Stafford Beer, letter to Heinz von Foerster, 5 December 1973, box 69, Stafford Beer Collection, Liverpool John Moores University, Liverpool, England.

6. Miguel de la Madrid favored the free market, and the number of state industries dramatically decreased during his presidency. In this sense his government was very different from that of Popular Unity in Chile. However, de la Madrid had won on a platform calling for a "moral renovation of society" and had declared a war against corruption. His desire to end corruption overlapped with Beer's desire to create more effective organizations and eliminate needless bureaucracy.

7. "Viene a México a combatir la burocracia: Sale de México huyendo de la burocracia," *El Norte*, 6 December 1983.

8. Allenna Leonard, e-mail to author, 10 December 2009. Beer was not the only veteran of the Chile project who tried to build a version of Project Cybersyn in another part of the world. After the coup, Roberto Cañete, Beer's translator, relocated to Canada and later worked for the Canadian firm Sorés, Inc. While there he drafted a proposal to build a version of Project Cybersyn for the Algerian government that included a reproduction of the Cybersyn operations room. The proposal never came to fruition.

9. For more information about the award, see OR [Operational Research] Society, "The OR Society and Its Activities: Stafford Beer Medal," www.theorsociety.com/orshop/%28aepw4wvq p4zdbkrden52hmmp%29/ORContent.aspx?inc=activity_awards_beer.htm&fp=/ors/activity/ activity_awards_beer.htm.

10. Espejo also named his company after the book *Order out of Chaos* by Ilya Prigogine and Isabelle Stengers. As he explained, "This book gave me the idea of a play on words: SYNergy out of CHaOs, or SYNCHO. But clearly I [also] wanted to return to the roots of Project Cybersyn." Raúl Espejo, interview by author, 9 September 2006, Lincoln, U.K.

11. In addition, Espejo coauthored the book *Organizational Transformation and Learning: A Cybernetic Approach to Management*. The book describes the application of the Viable System Model to the German company Hoechst AG in ways inspired by the Chile project. Raúl Espejo, Werner Schuhmann, Markus Schwaninger, and Ubaldo Bilello, *Organizational Transformation and Learning: A Cybernetic Approach to Management* (New York: Wiley, 1996).

12. Espejo interview.

13. Herman Schwember, "Cybernetics in Government: Experience with New Tools for Management in Chile, 1971–1973," in Hartmut Bossel, ed., *Concepts and Tools of Computer-Assisted Policy Analysis* (Basel, Germany: Birkhäuser, 1977).

14. Colin Eden, review of *Concepts and Tools of Computer-Assisted Policy Analysis*, in *Policy Sciences* 9, no. 3 (1978): 356.

15. In 1979 Schwember wrote Beer: "We were no less wrong than the other [political] factions. But good tools [Cybersyn] are no substitute to [sic] deep political consensus." Herman Schwember, letter to Stafford Beer, 27 August 1979, box 88, Beer Collection.

16. In 2005 Chilean president Ricardo Lagos gave Schwember the difficult task of helping to reintegrate the residents of Villa Baviera into Chilean society. Villa Baviera, formerly known as Dignity Colony, was founded by the ex-Nazi Paul Schäfer in the 1960s, and it had existed largely outside the Chilean state until 2005, when Schäfer was arrested. Subsequent investigations of the colony revealed child molestation, torture, and generally oppressive living conditions—what Schwember called the "most explicit violation of human rights that had happened in Chile since the time of the Pinochet government." Police searches of the colony also turned up caches of arms. It is now suspected that the colony harbored former Nazis and had connections with the Chilean military intelligence agency DINA during the Pinochet dictatorship. Although Schwember stepped down from his government appointment at the end of 2006, he continued to work with the residents of the colony until he died. Mariela Herrera Muzio, "Revelaciones de Villa Baviera post era Schäfer," *El Mercurio*, 31 May 2009; Patricio Tapia, "Falleció Herman Schwember, ex Delegado de Gobierno para Villa Baviera," *La Tercera*, 31 May 2008.

17. Sergio Bitar, *Chile: Experiment in Democracy*, trans. Sam Sherman (Philadelphia: Institute for the Study of Human Issues, 1986), 193. Bitar also references Ross Ashby and Stafford Beer, explains the Law of Requisite Variety, and asserts that "viability is control" (193–195).

18. These actions are described in a letter to "Mark Perry," a code name Herman Schwember used for Beer when sending correspondence from Chile to Britain in 1974. Schwember called himself Gerardo. Schwember writes: "[Flores] might be confined for quite a long time, but he can read and study. . . . As a matter of fact, he has been reading like hell. He—and I—feel that in spite of his limitations he could do very useful academic work. He is obsessed with getting a degree in Cybernetics (he even talks of a Ph.D. or equivalent). . . . In these conditions the sole hope is a British University. As I understand [it], only the English are wise enough—or crazy enough—to confer degrees on the basis of achievements rather than based on liturgy." Gerardo, letter to "Mark Perry," 8 July 1974, box 70, Beer Collection.

19. See the documents housed in the folder "Fernando's Defense," box 70, Beer Collection. Related documents also reside in the Heinz von Foerster Papers at the University of Illinois, Urbana–Champaign. These documents show that von Foerster put Beer in touch with Paul Drake, a prominent U.S. scholar of Chile who at the time was also teaching at the University of Illinois. Drake forwarded the dossier Beer had assembled on Flores to the Emergency Committee to Aid Latin American Scholars set up by the Latin American Studies Association. See Heinz von Foerster, letter to Stafford Beer, 16 November 1973, box 1, Heinz von Foerster Papers, University of Illinois, Urbana–Champaign; Paul Drake, letter to Stafford Beer, 27 November 1973, box 70, Beer Collection; Stafford Beer, letter to Paul Drake, 5 December 1973, box 70, Beer Collection. I thank Ronald Kline for pointing me to these documents in the Heinz von Foerster Papers.

20. Fernando Flores, interview by author, 18 August 2003, Santiago, Chile.

21. J. Y. Lettvin, H. R. Maturana, W. S. McCulloch, and W. H. Pitts, "What the Frog's Eye Tells the Frog's Brain," *Proceedings of the Institute of Radio Engineers* 47, no. 11 (1959): 1940–1951. Variations on the quotation "Anything said is said by an observer" have appeared in a number of Maturana's writings. For example, see Humberto Maturana, "Neurophysiology of Cognition," in Heinz von Foerster, ed., *The Cybernetics of Cybernetics: The Control of Control and the Communication of Communication* (Minneapolis: Future Systems, 1995), 113.

22. Von Foerster, *Cybernetics of Cybernetics*.

23. Ibid., 1.

24. N. Katherine Hayles, *How We Became Posthuman: Virtual Bodies in Cybernetics, Literature, and Informatics* (Chicago: University of Chicago Press, 1999), 132.

25. See Terry Winograd and Fernando Flores, *Understanding Computers and Cognition: A New Foundation for Design* (Norwood, N.J.: Ablex, 1986).

26. Stafford Beer, letter (no specified recipient), 6 December 1976, box 70, Beer collection.

27. Carlos F[ernando] Flores L., "Management and Communication in the Office of the Future" (Ph.D. diss., University of California–Berkeley, 1982). In the dissertation Flores acknowledges Schwember, Espejo, Beer, Maturana, and Varela for providing "important contributions to the intellectual space in which this work has been done." He also writes, "I owe a lasting debt to Stafford and my other friends of the Cybersyn project for their role in deepening my practical

understanding. I see this thesis as a continuation of that pioneering effort, exploring the related issues of language and understanding."

28. Flores interview.

29. Ibid.

30. Ibid.

31. Winograd and Flores, *Understanding Computers and Cognition*, xii.

32. Ibid., 76.

33. Ibid.

34. I thank Jeff Bardzell for explaining the significance of *Understanding Computers and Cognition* in the field of human-computer interaction.

35. Winograd and Flores, *Understanding Computers and Cognition*, xiii. In *Designing Freedom* (1974), Beer writes, "I urge this precept on you: it is better to *dissolve* problems than to solve them" (42–43). Variations of this phrase also appear in Beer's books *Decision and Control* (1966) and *Platform for Change* (1975). Stafford Beer, *Designing Freedom* (New York: J. Wiley, 1974).

36. Winograd and Flores, *Understanding Computers and Cognition*, 6.

37. Lawrence Fisher, "Fernando Flores Wants to Make You an Offer," *Strategy + Business*, 24 November 2009, www.strategy-business.com/article/09406?gko=ce081.

38. Lucy Suchman, "Do Categories Have Politics? The Language Perspective Reconsidered," *Computer-Supported Cooperative Work (CSCW)* 2 (1994): 177–190.

39. BDA reached its peak in 2000, according to Fisher in "Fernando Flores Wants."

40. Harriet Rubin, "The Power of Words," *Fast Company*, 31 December 2007, www.fastcompany .com/magazine/21/flores.html.

41. Charles Spinosa, Fernando Flores, and Hubert L. Dreyfus, *Disclosing New Worlds: Entrepreneurship, Democratic Action, and the Cultivation of Solidarity* (Cambridge, Mass.: MIT Press, 1997). The authors position *Disclosing New Worlds* in conversation with Francis Fukuyama's book *The End of History and the Last Man* (New York: Free Press, 1992). Fukuyama points to the triumph of liberal democracy over other forms of government and predicts the eventual triumph of capitalism over other forms of economy (such as socialism). Since he believes liberal democracy and capitalism will retain their position as the dominant political and economic frameworks in the future, he argues that these two developments represent an "end of history." However, liberal democracy provides less incentive for people to take risks in pursuit of higher ideals. Thus, Fukuyama acknowledges, there is a danger of becoming a detached, self-absorbed "last man." In contrast, Spinosa, Flores, and Dreyfus argue that capitalism and democracy allow people to be history makers and thus live life at its best.

42. When a journalist from CNN-Chile pressed Flores about how a former minister from the Allende government could back the candidate from the right, Flores became angry. At the end of

the interview he told the journalist, on air, that he would not grant him another interview for a year for asking such stupid questions. The interview Flores gave CNN is available at www.youtube .com/watch?v=zoInCYb_MMk.

43. Flores interview by author.

44. Flores also criticized Espejo for having stayed with management cybernetics and for not having changed his intellectual orientation over time.

45. Flores interview.

46. In addition to Flores, Beer, Schwember, and Espejo, whose careers I have already traced, Cybersyn team members went on to work for the United Nations, became top executives in the private sector, taught at universities in Latin America and Europe, and formed their own companies.

47. Isaquino Benadof, interview by author, 10 April 2002, Santiago, Chile.

Bibliography

This bibliography is a list of primary sources that I consulted, including government and institutional repositories, archival repositories, and interviews. It also contains a list of periodicals. Secondary sources appear in the notes.

Interviews

Interviews that were not conducted in person are marked as such here and in the endnotes. I list the original language of each interview to indicate when I translated interview excerpts. Not all these interviews are cited in the notes, but all of these individuals contributed to my understanding and interpretation of this history.

Cybersyn Participants

Eugenio Balmaceda (Spanish), 28 January 2003, Santiago, Chile.

Jorge Barrientos (Spanish), 26 July 2006, Santiago, Chile.

Raimundo Beca (Spanish), 9 September 2003, Santiago, Chile.

Stafford Beer (English), 15 and 16 March 2001, Toronto, Canada.

Isaquino Benadof (English), 10 April 2002, Santiago, Chile.

Gui Bonsiepe (Spanish), 21 May 2008, La Plata, Argentina.

Roberto Cañete (English), 16 January 2003, Viña del Mar, Chile.

Raúl Espejo (Spanish), 9 September 2006, Lincoln, U.K.

Enrique Farné (Spanish), 16 October 2008, Denia, Spain.

Fernando Flores (English), 30 July 2003, Viña del Mar, Chile, and 18 August 2003, Santiago, Chile.

Carmen (Pepa) Foncea (Spanish), 25 July 2006, Santiago, Chile.

Mario Grandi (Spanish), 30 July 2010, e-mail correspondence.

Tomás Kohn (English), 5 September 2003, Santiago, Chile.

Sonia Mordojovich (Spanish), 16 July 2002, Santiago, Chile.

Herman Schwember (Spanish), 22 June 2002, Santiago, Chile.

Fernando Shultz (Spanish), 9 and 10 September 2008, Mexico City, Mexico.

Guillermo Toro (Spanish), 5 June 2004, e-mail correspondence.

Eduardo Vidal (Spanish), 9 February 2004, Santiago, Chile.

Rodrigo Walker (Spanish), 24 July 2006, Santiago, Chile.

Others Consulted
In addition to members of the Project Cybersyn team, I consulted a number of people whose experiences speak to the historical context of this story. This list includes people who worked in or managed Chilean factories, worked with members of the Project Cybersyn team in various capacities, or encountered the project but were not part of the project team. It also includes members of the Chilean computer industry, the Frei and Allende governments, the international cybernetics and operations research communities, and the Chilean science and engineering community.

Alfredo Acle (Spanish), 18 and 23 December 2004, Santiago, Chile.

Francisco Ariztía (Spanish), 13 October 2008, Lisbon, Portugal.

Edgardo Boeninger (Spanish), 28 July 2006, Santiago, Chile.

Italo Bozzi (Spanish), 14 July 2006, Curacaví, Chile.

Juan Ignacio Cahís (Spanish), 2 January 2004, Santiago, Chile.

Marcelo Energici (Spanish), 17 December 2003, Santiago, Chile.

Enrique d'Etigny (Spanish), 23 June 2006, Santiago, Chile.

Osvaldo Garcia (Spanish), 25 September and 6 October 2003, Santiago, Chile.

Oscar Guillermo Garretón (Spanish), 4 August 2003, Santiago, Chile.

Patricio Léniz (Spanish), 23 December 2003, Santiago, Chile.

Carmen Gloria Leon (Spanish), 4 February 2004, Santiago, Chile.

Allenna Leonard (English), 10 December 2009 and other dates, e-mail correspondence.

Alberto Martínez (Spanish), 7 October 2003, telephone interview.

Humberto Maturana (Spanish), 8 September 2003, Santiago, Chile.

Pedro Medina (Spanish), 20 December 2004, Santiago, Chile.

Jaime Mendoza (Spanish), 26 August 2003, Santiago, Chile

Sergio Molina (Spanish), 15 January 2004, Santiago, Chile.

Jorge Morales (Spanish), 9 August 2002, Santiago, Chile.

Andrés Navarro Hauessler (Spanish), 15 January 2004, Santiago, Chile.

Virginia Olmos (Spanish), 4 February 2004, Santiago, Chile.

Angel Parra (Spanish), 31 January 2008, Berlin, Germany.

René Peralta (Spanish), 12 January 2004, Santiago, Chile.

Vicente Poblete (Spanish), 31 July 2003, Santiago, Chile.

Guillermo Ríos (Spanish), 6 October 2003, Santiago, Chile.

Jonathan Rosenhead (English), 8 October 2009, telephone interview.

Luis Salazar (Spanish), 19 August, 2003, Santiago, Chile.

Juan Francisco Sánchez (Spanish), 27 July 2003, Santiago, Chile.

Gustavo Silva (Spanish), 5 September 2003, Santiago, Chile.

Patricio Taulis (Spanish), 28 July 2003, Santiago, Chile.

Stuart Umpleby (English), 23 July 2009, telephone interview.

Fernando Villanueva (Spanish), 9 and 16 December 2003, Santiago, Chile.

Ann Zammit (English), 27 January 2010, telephone interview.

Archival Collections and Document Repositories

In addition to the sources listed here, I also consulted the institutional libraries and/or repositories at INTEC, IBM Chile, CONICYT, and CORFO, which were located at their respective offices in Santiago, Chile.

Archives of the Pontificia Universidad Católica de Chile, Santiago, Chile. This repository holds important documents on the history of computing at the Catholic University of Chile and publications from the Center for Studies on National Reality (CEREN).

Stafford Beer Collection, Liverpool John Moores University, Liverpool, U.K.

Nettie Benson Collection, University of Texas, Austin. Contains primary source material on the state of science and technology in Chile during the 1960s and 1970s and foreign assistance made available to Chile during that time period.

Biblioteca Nacional de Chile, Santiago. As Chile's National Library, this is a valuable repository for primary source materials, including government documents and publications on Chilean computing. The National Library also contains extensive newspaper and magazine holdings.

Heinz von Foerster Papers, University of Illinois Archives, Urbana-Champaign, Illinois.

Fundación Eduardo Frei, Santiago. This repository houses documents from the presidency of Eduardo Frei Montalva, including presidential speeches.

Library of the Dirección de Presupuestos, Ministerio de Hacienda, Santiago, Chile. Contains government documents on the early use of computers in public administration.

Library of the Economic Commission for Latin America and the Caribbean (ECLA), Santiago, Chile. This repository contains a wealth of papers on Chilean economic theory and policy during the Frei and Allende periods.

Library of the Facultad de Ciencias Físicas y Matemáticas, Universidad de Chile, Santiago. Contains documents on Project Cybersyn from the now-defunct National Computer Corporation (ECOM).

Library of the Instituto de Ingenieros de Chile, Santiago. This repository contains extensive primary source holdings that document the history of engineering in Chile.

Library of the Instituto Nacional de Estadística, Santiago, Chile. A valuable repository for statistics, census data, and primary source information on the history of Chilean computing.

Records of the U.S. Bureau of Foreign and Domestic Commerce, Government Documents Repository, Harvard University, Cambridge, Massachusetts. Contains records of U.S. exports to Chile.

Norbert Wiener Papers. Institute Archives and Special Collections, MIT Libraries, Cambridge, Massachusetts.

Periodicals Consulted

The following periodicals were all published in Chile.

Cuadernos de la Realidad Nacional

Ercilla

Estadística Chilena

IBM Diálogo

Informática

Ingenieros

INTEC

El Mercurio

Mundo NCR

La Nación

Qué Pasa

Revista Chilena de Ingeniería y Anales del Instituto de Ingenieros

Señal

Sondauta

The following volumes contain an extensive collection of Chilean press accounts from the Allende period that span the right, left, and center:

González Pino, Miguel, and Arturo Fontaine Talavera, eds. *Los mil días de Allende*. 2 vols. Santiago, Chile: Centro de Estudios Públicos, 1997.

Selected Bibliography

This list contains primary source materials (and a few secondary sources) that I consulted and that may be of interest to readers who want to learn more about cybernetics and Chilean socialism.

Allende

Allende, Salvador. *Chile's Road to Socialism*. Ed. Joan E. Garcés. Trans. J. Darling. Baltimore: Penguin, 1973.

Allende, Salvador. *Nuestro camino al socialismo: La vía chilena*. 2d ed. Buenos Aires: Ediciones Papiro, 1971.

Allende, Salvador. *La revolución chilena. 1*. Buenos Aires: Editorial Universitaria de Buenos Aires, 1973.

Allende, Salvador. *Salvador Allende: Obras escogidas, 1908–1973*. Colección Chile en el siglo XX. Santiago, Chile: Editorial Antártica S.A., 1992.

Cockcroft, James D., ed. *Salvador Allende Reader*. Hoboken, N.J.: Ocean Press, 2000.

Debray, Régis, and Salvador Allende. *Conversations with Allende: Socialism in Chile*. London: N.L.B., 1971.

International Telephone and Telegraph Corporation and Bertrand Russell Peace Foundation. 1972. *Subversion in Chile: A Case Study in U.S. Corporate Intrigue in the Third World*. Nottingham: Bertrand Russell Peace Foundation.

Kornbluh, Peter. 2003. *The Pinochet File: A Declassified Dossier on Atrocity and Accountability*. New York: New Press.

Miguel, Lawner, Hernán Soto, and Jacobo Schatan, eds. 2008. *Salvador Allende: Presencia en la ausencia*. Santiago, Chile: LOM.

Mensaje del Presidente Allende ante el Congreso Pleno, 21 de Mayo de 1972. Santiago, Chile: Departamento de Publicaciones de la Presidencia de la República, 1972.

Mensaje Presidente Allende ante Congreso Pleno, 21/Mayo '73. Santiago, Chile: Departamento de Publicaciones de la Presidencia de la República, 1973.

Primer mensaje del Presidente Allende ante el Congreso Pleno, 21 de Mayo de 1971. Santiago, Chile: Departamento de Publicaciones de la Presidencia de la República, 1971.

Soto, Óscar. *El último día de Salvador Allende*. Santiago, Chile: Aguilar Chilena de Ediciones, 1999.

U.S. Senate. *Covert Action in Chile, 1964–1973: Staff Report of the Select Committee to Study Governmental Operation with Respect to Intelligence Activities*. Washington, D.C.: U.S. Government Printing Office, 1975.

U.S. Senate. Select Committee to Study Governmental Operations with Respect to Intelligence Activities. *Alleged Assassination Plots Involving Foreign Leaders: An Interim Report of the Select Committee to Study Governmental Operations with Respect to Intelligence Activities*. Washington, D.C.: U.S. Government Printing Office, 1975.

Cybernetics and Stafford Beer
A complete bibliography of Stafford Beer's writings is available from the Cwarel Isaf Institute.

Ashby, W. Ross. *Introduction to Cybernetics*. London: Chapman and Hall, 1956.

Beer, Stafford. *Beyond Dispute: The Invention of Team Syntegrity, the Managerial Cybernetics of Organization*. New York: Wiley, 1994.

Beer, Stafford. *Brain of the Firm: The Managerial Cybernetics of Organization*. 2nd ed. New York: J.Wiley, 1981.

Beer, Stafford. *Cybernetics and Management*. 2nd ed. London: English Universities Press, 1967.

Beer, Stafford. *Decision and Control: The Meaning of Operational Research and Management Cybernetics*. New York: Wiley, 1966.

Beer, Stafford. *Designing Freedom*. New York: J. Wiley, 1974.

Beer, Stafford. *Diagnosing the System for Organizations*. New York: J. Wiley, 1985.

Beer, Stafford. *Heart of the Enterprise*. New York: Wiley, 1979.

Beer, Stafford. *Management Science: The Business Use of Operations Research*. New York: Doubleday, 1968.

Beer, Stafford. "On Heaping Our Science Together." *Progress in Cybernetics and Systems Research* 2 (1975): 3–11.

Beer, Stafford. "Operations Research and Cybernetics." Paper presented at the 1st International Congress on Cybernetics, Namur, 1956.

Beer, Stafford. *Platform for Change: A Message from Stafford Beer*. New York: Wiley, 1975.

Beer, Stafford. "A Technical Consideration of the Cybernetic Analogue for Planning and Programming." Paper presented at the 1st International Congress on Cybernetics, Namur, 1956.

Beer, Stafford. "Ten Pints of Beer: The Rationale of Stafford Beer's Cybernetic Books (1959–94)." *Kybernetes* 29, no. 5–6 (2000): 558–569.

Beer, Stafford. *Think Before You Think: Social Complexity and Knowledge of Knowing*. Ed. David Whittaker. Oxon, U.K.: Wavestone Press, 2009.

Beer, Stafford. *"Why Government Should Investigate OR" Automatic Data Processing.* London: Business Publications Ltd, 1962.

Beer, Stafford. "World in Torment: A Time Whose Idea Must Come." *Kybernetes* 22, no. 6 (1993): 15–43.

Beer, Stafford. "The World, the Flesh and the Metal: The Prerogatives of Systems." *Nature* 205, no. 4968 (1965): 223–231.

Harnden, Roger, and Allenna Leonard, eds. 1994. *How Many Grapes Went into the Wine: Stafford Beer on the Art and Science of Holistic Management.* New York: Wiley.

Lettvin, J. Y., H. R. Maturana, W. S. McCulloch, and W. H. Pitts. 1959. "What the Frog's Eye Tells the Frog's Brain." *Proceedings of the Institute of Radio Engineers* 47 (11):1940–1951.

Maturana, Humberto R., and Francisco J. Varela. *Autopoiesis and Cognition: The Realization of the Living.* Boston: D. Reidel, 1980.

Müller, Albert, and Karl Müller, eds. *An Unfinished Revolution? Heinz von Foerster and the Biological Computer Laboratory (BCL), 1958–1976.* Vienna: Edition Echoraum, 2007.

Von Foerster, Heinz, ed. *The Cybernetics of Cybernetics: The Control of Control and the Communication of Communication.* Minneapolis: Future Systems, 1995.

Whittaker, David. *Stafford Beer: A Personal Memoir.* Oxon: Wavestone Press, 2003.

Wiener, Norbert. *Cybernetics: Or Control and Communication in the Animal and the Machine.* 2nd ed. Cambridge, Mass.: MIT Press, 1965.

Wiener, Norbert, *The Human Use of Human Beings: Cybernetics and Society.* New York: Da Capo, 1988.

Science, Technology, and Design in Chile, 1969–1973

Bonsiepe, Gui. "Subdesarrollo, tecnología y universidad. Reflexiones metatecnológicas." *Cuadernos de la realidad nacional,* no. 11 (1972): 137–149.

Bonsiepe, Gui. "Trazado de una alternativa de diseño." *Revista Summa,* no. 48 (1972): 17–29.

Bonsiepe, Gui. "Vivisección del diseño." *Revista AULA,* no. 24–25 (1973): 7–12.

EMCO. *Seminario sobre sistemas de información en el gobierno.* Santiago, Chile: EMCO and United Nations Development Program, 1969.

Friedmann, Efraín. *La gestión y los computadores: Conferencias.* Santiago, Chile: Empresa de Servicio de Computación Ltda., 1969.

Friedmann, Efraín. "Management of Computer Resources in LDCs." Paper presented at the Jerusalem Conference on Information Technology, Jerusalem, August 1971.

Hacia una política de desarrollo científico y tecnológico para Chile. Santiago, Chile: Universidad de Chile Rectoría, 1972.

Maturana, Humberto R., and Francisco J. Varela. *De máquinas y seres vivos: Una caracterización de la organización biológica.* Santiago, Chile: Editorial Universitaria, 1973.

United Nations Department of Economic and Social Affairs. 1971. *The Application of Computer Technology for Development.* New York: United Nations.

United Nations Department of Economic and Social Affairs. 1973. *The Application of Computer Technology for Development: Second Report of the Secretary General.* New York: United Nations.

Yunis Ahués, Eugenio. *Asignación de recursos y política de investigación para la ciencia y la tecnología: El caso de la Universidad de Chile.* Santiago, Chile: Ediciones C.P.U, 1972.

Project Cybersyn
See the endnotes to the introduction for additional participant accounts of Project Cybersyn.

Barrientos, Jorge, and Raúl Espejo. 1973. "Un modelo cibernético para la dirección del sector industrial." *INTEC* 4:5–18.

Cañete, Roberto. "The Brain of the Government: An Application of Cybernetic Principles to the Management of a National Industrial Economy." Paper presented at the 22nd annual North American meeting of the Society for General Systems Research, Avoiding Social Catastrophes and Maximizing Social Opportunities: The General Systems Challenge, Washington, D.C., 13–15 February 1978.

CORFO [Corporación de Fomento de la Producción]. *Proyecto Synco conceptos y práctica del control; Una experiencia concreta: La dirección industrial en Chile.* Santiago, Chile, 1973.

Espejo, Raúl Espejo. "Complexity and Change: Reflections upon the Cybernetic Intervention in Chile, 1970–1973." *Cybernetics and Systems* 22 (4) (1991): 443–457.

Espejo, Raúl. "Cybernetic Praxis in Government: The Management of Industry in Chile, 1970–1973." *Cybernetics and Systems: An International Journal* 11 (1980): 325–338.

Espejo, Raúl. "Performance Management, the Nature of Regulation and the CyberSyn Project." *Kybernetes* 38, no. 1–2 (2009): 65–82.

Grupo de Proyecto de Diseño Industrial. 1973. "Diseño de una sala de operaciones." *INTEC* 4:19–28.

Guzmán, Juan Andrés. (July 24, 2003). "Fernando Flores habla sobre el Proyecto Synco." *Clinic*, 9.

Harrison, P. J., and C. R. Stevens. "A Bayesian Approach to Short-Term Forecasting." *Operational Research Quarterly* 22, no. 4 (1971): 341–362.

Schwember, Herman. "Cybernetics in Government: Experience with New Tools for Management in Chile, 1971–1973." In *Concepts and Tools of Computer-Assisted Policy Analysis*, ed. Hartmut Bossel, 79–138. Basel: Birkhäuser, 1977.

Index

Page numbers in italics indicate illustrations and those followed by "t" indicate tables.